IN THE
SHADOW OF
BOONE AND
CROCKETT

IN THE SHADOW OF BOONE AND CROCKETT

Race, Culture, and the Politics of Representation in the Upland South

IAN C. HARTMAN

The University of Tennessee Press / Knoxville

Chapter 1 originally appeared in a different form in *American Nineteenth Century History* 13(2), 2012. Reprinted by permission of Routledge, Taylor, & Francis Group. tandfonline.com

Chapter 4 originally appeared in a different form in *Journal of Southern History* 80(3), 2014. Reprinted by permission of the Southern Historical Association.

The paper in this book meets the requirements of American National Standards Institute / National Information Standards Organization specification Z39.48-1992 (Permanence of Paper). It contains 30 percent post-consumer waste and is certified by the Forest Stewardship Council.

Library of Congress Cataloging-in-Publication Data

Hartman, Ian C.
In the shadow of Boone and Crockett : race, culture, and the politics of representation in the upland South / Ian C. Hartman. — First edition.
   pages cm
 Includes bibliographical references and index.
 ISBN 978-1-62190-169-3 (hard cover : alkaline paper)
1. Appalachian Region, Southern—Race relations—History—20th century. 2. Appalachian Region, Southern—Social conditions—20th century. 3. Appalachian Region, Southern—Public opinion. 4. Appalachians (People)—Public opinion. 5. Poor whites—Appalachian Region, Southern—History—20th century. 6. Poor whites—Government policy—United States—History—20th century. 7. United States—Race relations—Political aspects—History—20th century. 8. United States—Politics and government—20th century. 9. Public opinion—United States—History—20th century. I. Title.
F217.A65H38 2015
305.008975'0904—dc23
2014043993

CONTENTS

ILLUSTRATIONS

ACKNOWLEDGMENTS

This book began as a seminar paper at the University of Illinois in 2006. I was first struck by how ubiquitous images of southern whites had become during the late 1950s and 1960s. Within the context of civil rights and the black freedom struggle, I wondered why some of the most visible liberals—the Kennedys, LBJ, Michael Harrington, writers for the *New York Times,* and many others—fixated so much on the spectacle of white poverty. It's taken the better part of ten years to come up with answers with which I'm almost satisfied. And although I had set rather modest goals for that seminar—to not embarrass myself in front of respected peers, maintain good standing in the graduate program, and continue to improve my writing—I had nonetheless stumbled onto a topic that has culminated with this book.

Like that seminar, and we might as well add graduate school and then the academic job market, I could not have completed this book without the assistance of many people. Nine years since completing the seminar and five years since finishing my dissertation, my interests in race and poverty have only increased. But since then, I've rewritten, reshaped, and reframed this study into something that I hope readers will find instructive. Still, this project would have never come to fruition without the productive (and some not so productive, but quite fun) discussions I've had with colleagues. I'd like to thank the following people: Dave Bates, Andy Bruno, Nathan Chio, Anna Claydon, Heidi Dodson, Andy Eisen, Sarah Frohardt-Lane, Janine Giordano-Drake, David Greenstein, Kwame Holmes, Ashley Howard, Kerry Pimblott, Emily Pope-Obeda, Zack Poppel, Stephanie Seawell, Emily Skidmore, Troy Smith, Martin Smith, T. J. Tallie, and Alonzo Ward. For the last three years that I lived in Urbana, Anna Kurhajec graciously took me in as a roommate; her kindness knows no bounds.

The GEO, our graduate employee's union, provided a space that at once protected my job, but also brought me into contact with wonderful people outside of the history department. Thanks to Peter Campbell, Ingbert Floyd, John Gergely, Natalie Havlin, Amy Livingston, Katie Walkiewicz, and the countless others who have worked diligently on behalf of public education in Illinois and beyond. These women and men created what may well have been one of the most vibrant spaces of community activism and old-fashioned fun found across the cornfields of central Illinois. My longtime friends Michael Brady, Matthew Delgado, and Dennis Gump also offered steady companionship throughout. Indeed, I am most privileged to have worked and played alongside such brilliant minds.

During my six years in Illinois, the department of history provided a welcoming academic home, and I'm grateful for the moral and intellectual support that I received. The department of history also extended the necessary financial backing to conduct research well beyond the excellent campus libraries. These trips included the National Archives in Washington DC and College Park, MD, the Lyndon B. Johnson Presidential Library in Austin, the Wilson Library and Southern Historical Collection at the University of North Carolina at Chapel Hill, the Albert and Shirley Small Special Collections Library at the University of Virginia in Charlottesville, the M. E. Grenander Department of Special Collections and Archives at the State University of New York at Albany, and the Indiana State Library in Indianapolis. Several historians at Illinois also played critical roles in this project, and none more so than Jim Barrett, Dave Roediger, Antoinette Burton, Augusto Espiritu, and Kathy Oberdeck. And while I came to Illinois to study the history of race and labor, each graciously tolerated and even welcomed the deviations that my intellectual path has taken. Jim's guidance as an advisor throughout my graduate career exemplifies the humanity that might still be found in some outposts of higher education, and for that, I thank him.

Since leaving Illinois, I have called Anchorage, Alaska home. Here, I like to think of myself as the northern-most historian of the US South. My colleagues in the Department of History at the University of Alaska Anchorage have been a delightful, close-knit group. Ray Ball, Mark Rice, Liz Dennison, Paul Dunscomb, Bill Meyers, Kelly Shannon, Jay Sylvestre, Songho Ha, Curtis Murphy, and Kathy Woodhead have greatly eased the transition to the 49th State. In addition, Will and Mina Jacobs and Chuck and Ayse Gilbert welcomed me in from the cold and have become dear friends.

In the process of finalizing the manuscript, I have lopped off chapters to publish as articles, all in a mad dash to build a career in the trying atmosphere of the post-Great Recession academy. Without the constructive feedback of the editorial teams and anonymous reviewers at *American Nineteenth Century History,* the *Journal of Southern History,* and the University of Tennessee Press, my research would be confined to the hard drive of an old laptop that's now collecting dust in storage. I'd like to thank Thomas Wells at the University of Tennessee Press for reaching out to me nearly three years ago to inquire about the project. I am forever grateful he did so. His patience and willingness to work with me has made this book a reality. Emily Huckabay's work preparing the manuscript for production exceeded my expectations, and Gene Adair, a tremendously skilled copyeditor, caught more embarrassing typos and oversights that I'd care to admit. The press has proven an ideal outlet, and its team has exemplified professionalism at every step of the way.

My family has provided the most inspiration of all. Without my partner, Eliza Salvo, I could not have kept mind, body, and soul together to complete this project. I have moved her across the country, only somewhat against her will, in pursuit of gainful employment, and she has been a terrific sport throughout. A gracious confidant, I can't imagine life without her. My grandparents, Marge and Warren Leonhardt, together for over seventy years, have graced this planet with a level of humility and acceptance that I greatly admire and seek to emulate. My father, Larry Hartman, has imposed a loving sense of discipline and duty that I believe has served me well and has been as loving of a father as I believe exists in this world.

In early 2012, my mother broke the news to me that she had been diagnosed with leukemia. Though devastated, I remained optimistic that she'd recover and continue to fill this world love and kindness. Unfortunately, the cruel illness took her life on April 2, 2013. Mom was a profoundly beautiful and kind-hearted woman. She taught elementary and special education at a public school just outside of Pittsburgh, Pennsylvania. A respected educator and a loving mother, daughter, sister, and friend, she has touched innumerable lives and dedicated her life to serving others. She is missed every day. While no amount of gratitude can adequately convey my appreciation for her life and its impact on so many, as but one small measure I dedicate these pages to Donna Anna Hartman (1950–2013).

Ian C. Hartman
Anchorage, AK
November 2014

IN THE SHADOW OF DANIEL BOONE AND DAVID CROCKETT

The Troubled Legacy of Race Histories

> The vast movement by which this continent was conquered and peopled cannot be rightly understood if considered solely by itself. It was the crowning and greatest achievement of a series of mighty movements. . . . Its true significance will be lost unless we grasp, however roughly, the past race-history of the nations who took part therein.
>
> —Theodore Roosevelt, 1889[1]

During the winter of 1887, Theodore Roosevelt returned to his opulent Manhattan home fresh from an extended sojourn in the Dakota Badlands. There, he had hunted big game, busted broncos, lived off of the land, and engaged in "manly outdoor sports."[2] What began as a trip to overcome the emotional anguish of having experienced the death of his wife and mother on the same day three years earlier ended as a spiritual journey that altered the New York aristocrat's outlook on politics, the environment, and, perhaps most of all, his conception of race and masculinity. On the expanse of the Great Plains, Roosevelt believed he had channeled the pioneer spirit of Daniel Boone and David Crockett. The adventure was so formative that the twenty-nine-year-old immediately convened a few of his closest friends to initiate a new organization. Days later, Roosevelt, with Massachusetts representative Henry Cabot Lodge and naturalist George Bird Grinnell, established the Boone and Crockett Club, named in honor of the "tutelary deities of American hunting lore."[3]

Over the next five years, the Boone and Crockett Club grew into an exclusive social gathering as much as a sporting and conservation organization, convening Ivy League men who counted themselves among the nation's elite. Politicians, academics, lawyers, and philanthropists joined Roosevelt's club. A smattering of the members included Henry L. Stimson, the future governor-general of the Philippines and then secretary of war; Carl Akeley, the noted explorer of sub-Saharan Africa; George Eastman, the eminent innovator of film and photography; and Frederic Remington, the nation's foremost artist of the American West. They fraternized in elegant New York City ballrooms and donned attire that one night consisted of the latest Fifth Avenue fashion and the next buckskins tanned for an evening under the stars; they lobbied to preserve the nation's once pristine environment, now bearing the scars of urbanization and industrial development. By protecting the land, forests, and animals, though notably not the indigenous population, these men sought to journey one day into a backcountry that resembled what Boone and Crockett encountered upon first crossing into the trans-Appalachian West.[4]

In 1893 Madison Grant, a twenty-eight-year-old graduate of Yale Law School, joined the Boone and Crockett Club. Interested in the environment and natural history, as well as New York's high society, Grant had participated in the burgeoning conservation movement since his days in New Haven. He advocated for declining species like the Rocky Mountain goats, American bison, and others that had been decimated by the acceleration of white settlement. Additionally, like his fellow club members, Grant asserted that his ancestors were not only among the continent's first European settlers but that some became revolutionary patriots and conceivably served alongside Daniel Boone himself. However, by the fin de siècle he and others who shared this prized heritage, Grant proclaimed, were as endangered as the bison languishing on the western plains or the ancient forests logged by a rapacious timber industry. Imperiled Anglo-Saxon pioneers, like the felled redwoods and endangered animals, also required preservation and restoration, according to Grant, Roosevelt, Lodge, and Grinnell. These vanishing Anglo-Saxons derived their value not only from their evocative presence in the natural world but also their "race-history" and supposed contributions to Western civilization.[5]

Yet, from the vantage point of some of the most luxurious neighborhoods in Manhattan and Boston, it appeared as though manly frontiersmen in the mold of Daniel Boone and David Crockett now stalked a chaotic nation only as mythological specters lurking amid the shadows of a new reality, one that hunting expeditions and forays into the woods failed to change. At the dawn of the twentieth century, many elite white men, like those in the Boone and Crockett Club, viewed the people who poured over North America's shores as a shrunken and frail, unskilled, and inferior horde. After all, these immigrants came from the unfamiliar reaches of eastern and southern Europe, and they seemed to have failed to grasp what it meant to be citizens of a republic. Rather than taming the wilderness, they hovered between the foreboding gates of industrial factories and toiled for wages, only to take respite in seething tenements located just blocks from the stately doorsteps of men who belonged to Roosevelt's club. The antithesis to the knife-wielding, virile Daniel Boone, it seemed, were the Italian and Slavic laborers who crowded the refuse-lined streets of the Lower East Side.[6]

Hence the club was more than a collective of East Coast patricians who enjoyed nature and the thrill of the hunt. The club revealed how uneasy its members had grown over the perception that deficient workers and deficient men had overwhelmed their northern European blood. The Boone and Crockett Club was one way for these native-born white men to express the bubbling anxieties that accompanied notions of race, gender, and economic disparity in the United States. While the club was certainly a novel idea, there were many others, and most were not as benign. In fact, responding to the apparent threats posed to self-fashioned Anglo-Saxons defined, at least in part, many reform movements throughout the late nineteenth and twentieth centuries.

The interplay among race, gender, and reform from the Gilded Age and Progressive Era forward has inspired considerable scholarship. Unlike much of that work, however, the focus here is not primarily on the industrial cities of the North, those urban spaces teeming with the immigrants whom Roosevelt and his colleagues directed their measured consternation; nor is it on the obliterated plantation society of the post–Civil War Deep South, that which was firmly in the repressive grip of Jim Crow by the early 1900s and would remain so for more than sixty years.[7] Instead, this book emphasizes the rural hills and hollows of the upland South. Here, outside observers believed they had discovered a sanctuary of strong men and virtuous women whose race and culture defied the seemingly endless stream of immigration or the influence of formerly enslaved people. Since the Revolutionary Era, the southern Appalachian and Ozark Mountains, along with the rolling hills and river valleys that connect them, have emerged in lore as the setting where not only Boone and Crockett but also such figures as Kit Carson, David Edward Jackson, John Colter, George Rogers Clark, and Andrew Jackson, among others, forged a modern nation and headed west. These men, according to theorists like Roosevelt, Grant, and Lodge, already held the biological advantages of the Anglo-Saxon, but they had grown even stronger as they overcame the challenges of the wilderness. The subjugation of Native lands and people contributed to the formation of an exceptional and pure US American identity, an evolutionary culmination of "sturdy Anglo-Saxon racial stock," constituted through the violent, manly culture of the frontier.[8] The upland South, leading academics, politicians, and writers agreed, was the laboratory where these environmental and genetic factors mingled and coalesced.[9]

Yet, the region stood out for another, ostensibly contradictory reason. Even as prominent figures celebrated the ancestry, frontier history, and natural beauty of the upland South, the region also assumed a place in the national imagination as a breeding ground for impoverished white people. Today, much of West Virginia, Kentucky, Tennessee, and the Ozarks conjure stereotypes of poverty and backwardness more than images of pioneer independence or rugged individualism.[10] This contradiction begs a few questions. How and when did the region synonymous with the settler masculinity of Boone and Crockett become equally associated with poor whites, exemplified by churlish if amiable "hillbillies" on the one hand, or deviant "white trash" on the other? In what ways did this conflicted perception affect the nation's political and popular culture? And perhaps most fundamentally: what happened when the allegedly strongest and most advanced race failed to live up to its expectations?

This book provides answers and documents the anxiety wrought by what I refer to as the collapse of Anglo-Saxonism. If whites from the upland South somehow lost or never possessed what was said to be innate to the vaunted Anglo-Saxon race—high intelligence, industriousness, manly independence, and feminine propriety— then one of the nation's foundational hierarchies appeared compromised. Poor Anglo-Saxons thus undermined many preconceived notions about race and gender, ones that for generations had informed US law, culture, and politics. In sum, the upland South presents a singular opportunity to explore the contradictions of a "pure" white identity where it received its clearest articulation. Likewise, among the southern hills, one finds some of the most tenacious efforts to restore the purported sanctity of this very identity and all that it represented.[11]

Through a series of thematic case studies, this book explores how and why academics, missionaries, politicians, journalists, and cultural workers have labored to rejuvenate the people they described as racially pure but who had seemingly devolved both biologically and culturally. The first chapter locates the national fascination with southern Appalachia at the turn of the century as a response to US imperialism and immigration. In these years, observers first proclaimed that a subregion of the US South was a bastion of undiluted blood, home to thousands of "unmixed" Anglo-Saxons.[12] With its unforgiving topography, the southern mountains were said to guard against the contamination of lowly immigrants within the nation and peoples encountered abroad as the United States expanded its nascent empire into the Pacific and Caribbean. But at about the same time, Christian missionaries and some skeptical travel journalists claimed to have witnessed dangerous moral lapses and behavioral deficiencies in the remote reaches of West Virginia, western Virginia, eastern Kentucky, and East Tennessee. The chapter concludes with an unsettling paradox between what was *supposed* to be an isolated population of superior individuals, the very descendants of stouthearted frontiersmen, and what *seemed* to be the menacing reality of racial decline and Anglo-Saxon collapse. Understanding and resolving this paradox is the focus of the rest of the book.

The second chapter positions the US eugenics movement as an early effort to resolve the paradox and address the threat posed by impoverished white southerners who had migrated to Indiana at the turn of the century. This chapter first narrates the life of a religious leader, Oscar McCulloch, who relocated to Indianapolis in the 1870s. McCulloch was a transitional figure in the development of what historian Alice O'Connor has called "poverty knowledge."[13] His career maps a model of private benevolence and charity that eventually gave way to modern, statist approaches to mitigating poverty. Indiana instituted bureaucratic solutions to problems such as vagrancy, idleness, and feeblemindedness, all of which were closely associated with the state's growing population of upland southern migrants. One Hoosier nebulously termed these solutions the "Indiana Plan."[14] Accordingly, state officials tried to "purge" the so-called Anglo-Saxon and Teutonic races of their apparent impurities: first, through confining those they deemed defective and then, through mandatory sterilization. No one illustrated the necessity for such drastic measures as starkly as did the large family known as the Tribe of Ishmael "discovered" by McCulloch. The Ishmaels were undoubtedly a motley crew, but their coveted ancestry, which evidently included courageous pioneers from Kentucky and Tennessee, made their poverty noteworthy and their condition troublesome.[15]

A breakdown of such monumental proportions led to a wave of state intervention. New institutions like the Committee on Mental Defectives (CMD) and the Board of State Charities (BSC) assumed roles formerly held by churches and private benevolent societies. Freshly hired state employees who had received their education in the fields of public health, medicine, evolutionary science, and eugenics targeted the very bodies of poor white southerners for further observation. With the prudent use of modern science and medicine, these workers believed they could repair a damaged race by pruning those whom they viewed as disgraced or fallen members, people like the Ishmaels. Consequently, in 1907 Indiana passed the world's first sterilization laws in an effort to stem the apparent failings of native-born whites. The chapter then proposes that an organized, state-sponsored eugenics movement coalesced around an effort to eliminate white poverty and stave off biological collapse. And the only way to accomplish this, reasoned Indiana's advocates of "racial hygiene," was to neutralize those aberrant Anglo-Saxons who threatened to corrode the race from the inside out.[16]

Like Indiana, Virginia loomed large in the annals of racial science and public policy. The third chapter investigates the contradictory representations of those who lived in and adjacent to the Blue Ridge and Cumberland Mountains. While some assumed these women and men were pure Anglo-Saxons and thus superior citizens, others reported to the contrary. To address this discrepancy and preserve an idealized form of whiteness, Virginia lawmakers passed the Racial Integrity Act of 1924; this criminalized intimate relationships of any kind between whites and nonwhites. Contamination from people with dark skin, the courts and state legislators concluded, weakened Virginia's Anglo-Saxon population. Meanwhile, the notorious Supreme Court ruling *Buck v. Bell* (1927) upheld Virginia's policy of mandatory sterilization and paved the way for other states to carry out the procedure, or to continue doing so under legal cover. As Virginians learned from the Ishmaels in Indiana, degeneracy *within* the race due to afflictions like feeblemindedness and defectiveness could be as hazardous as miscegenation. The Racial Integrity Act, with its punitive focus on racial mixing, tackled the latter threat; the *Buck* decision addressed the former. Virginia legislators acted urgently and believed that these measures might reverse the commonwealth's biological deterioration before it reached epidemic proportions.[17]

As in chapter 2 with Oscar McCulloch, this chapter also features a key figure: renowned musical composer and native Virginian John Powell. Among his endeavors, Powell founded the Anglo Saxon Clubs of America (ASCoA) to lobby the Virginia General Assembly to pass the Racial Integrity Act, and he later organized a folk festival that drew thousands to a remote Virginia mountaintop every summer for nearly ten years. These seemingly disparate pursuits convey how popular culture and public policy were interrelated. Indeed, culture and politics mutually constituted one another; studying one enables a better understanding of the other and offers a well-rounded sense of how and why many believed that the upland South was so distinct. The Indiana and Virginia case studies also present how two states responded to the fear of Anglo-Saxon collapse during the first half of the century.[18]

But the paradox of poverty that had long infused the region with its identity had national implications that persisted and came into clearer view after the Second World War. Two decades of steady economic growth, coupled with the proliferation of mass media and televised entertainment, rendered the upland South as anomalous as ever and augmented the public's fascination with the hills. The fourth chapter thus scrutinizes the "rediscovery" of poverty amid the relative affluence of the 1950s and 1960s. Here, the preceding arguments constitute the vital context from which to reinterpret the origins and outcomes of postwar liberalism. While the eugenics movement was largely discredited after World War II, a similar discourse, referencing racial and manly strength, permeated discussions about the upland South and marked the region's poverty as a troubling phenomenon.[19]

As a result, many liberals concluded that economic impoverishment, resulting from the mechanization of the coal and lumber industries, had disproportionately affected white southern men, and they emphasized their plight when proposing initiatives. Images of downtrodden mountaineers and emotional appeals to assist once-vital frontiersmen framed the era's domestic politics and left an enduring imprint on the postwar welfare state. John F. Kennedy relied heavily on the imagined legacy of race and the mythology of the frontier to win West Virginia's Democratic primary and, soon after, the 1960 presidential election. Around the same time, poverty warriors like Michael Harrington and Harry Caudill again propelled the upland South onto the national stage as they accentuated the faces of poor whites to garner political support. Throughout the late 1950s and early 1960s, news and popular programming were saturated with rural southerners; without these depictions and the rising awareness of economic hardship in the upland South, national leaders may well have failed to wage a war on poverty.[20]

Chapter 5 connects political events like Kennedy's victory in West Virginia and Lyndon Johnson's tour of eastern Kentucky to lobby for his Economic Opportunity Act to the surging popularity of situation comedies, notably the CBS primetime lineup. *The Real McCoys, The Andy Griffith Show, The Beverly Hillbillies, Green Acres, Petticoat Junction,* and a few other popular comic strips, books, and television shows deepened the fascination with white southerners. Although these portrayals were generally sympathetic if stereotypical, the programming at times conveyed a message of whiteness in decline, or at a minimum, comically absurd. Additionally, the depictions venerated the conservatism that many white southerners embraced at a moment when the nation underwent rapid social change and faced challenges to the status quo. Amid the civil rights movement, the escalation of the Vietnam War, and the crises brewing in the nation's cities, endearing, if stubborn, hillbillies materialized as particularly well-suited figures to critique a nation that some feared had come apart. To men like Al Capp, Andy Griffith, and Paul Henning, creator of *The Beverly Hillbillies,* people from the upland South stood for laudable family values and had commonsense wisdom born of their experiences in small-town and rural America.

The shows' protagonists also yielded a countervailing image of southern white identity, one that contrasted with the reactionary forces that violently opposed the civil rights movement. The ubiquity of these programs must be interpreted alongside the rediscovery of poverty, fixated as it was on these same men and women. Together, the fourth and fifth chapters blend political with cultural analysis to demonstrate some rather surprising continuities, as well as obvious differences, with earlier movements that privileged the upland South as an exceptional outpost of racial purity and cultural authenticity. Panning out from the local and state levels, these chapters showcase a more extensive discourse that was national in scope.[21]

Bridging the decades before and after World War II, *In the Shadow of Boone and Crockett* exhibits the persistence with which representations of the upland South shaped the nation's culture and politics, and it calls into question some common assumptions. For one, many historians have argued that postwar liberalism responded to the civil rights movement, juvenile crime, and urban disintegration. While these were essential, the ascent of liberalism and the War on Poverty, specifically, should also be considered in relation to—and in some ways as a continuation of—previous attempts to revitalize Anglo-Saxon whiteness from the precipice of collapse. These two chapters show how the apprehensions that surrounded race and gender during the Progressive and Depression Eras recurred through the postwar decades, even as they modified and took on new forms. Recognizing how this anterior discourse had animated many white liberals and cultural workers in the 1950s and 1960s hints at how and why politics changed so dramatically in the last quarter of the twentieth century.[22]

Interest in eccentric mountaineers and frontiersmen, and the region from whence they came, eventually waned as the tumult of civil rights and the rise of Black Power received greater coverage across the media and political landscape. Significantly, this undermined the optics of the War on Poverty and changed how the nation viewed economic inequality. Despite the intentions of some liberals, an institutionalized welfare state on par with other western democracies never materialized. Instead, the social disunity of the 1960s led the Johnson administration to emphasize law enforcement, even as he signed the transformative provisions of the Great Society. But while Johnson moved towards law-and-order policies, he and his congressional allies nevertheless lost favor with millions of white voters who increasingly believed that the War on Poverty had inadvertently supported and possibly facilitated urban unrest and black militancy.[23]

The final chapter then explains how the perception (if not the reality) of the War on Poverty shifted from a benefit program for rural, white, and mostly southern men to a catalyst for African American revolt in cities across the United States. Rather than restoring Anglo-Saxon masculinity, as some ardent poverty warriors had conceived of the program, the War on Poverty, its detractors argued, had instead unmasked the inherent criminality of black men and led urban communities to depend on the support of white taxpayers. Therefore, the years between 1964 and the early 1970s were a turning point in the nation's policy towards, and perceptions of, the poor. Until the middle of the 1960s the majority of state and federal efforts to address poverty, even at their most invasive and objectionable, were aimed explicitly at white people who had failed to achieve the wealth, status, and power that their race was *supposed* to confer upon them. Since these years, policies designed to alleviate poverty have declined in popularity, and politicians have increasingly stigmatized poor people as undeserving of public assistance.[24]

Both Republican and Democratic administrations, albeit at different paces, have steadily dismantled the modest social safety net stitched together by the New Deal and Great Society coalitions. As they have, economic inequality has increased and now exceeds previous record levels, and the poverty rate has once again risen.[25] But the response to these social maladies has taken yet another direction. Since the late 1960s and 1970s, as the perception of who is poor and why has changed, legislators have passed a series of policies that have greatly expanded the prison system and transferred responsibility to local police departments to regulate poor communities. And while few lament the end of legal segregation and other virulent forms of oppression that marred much of the nation's history, mass incarceration and the turn towards increased and often times aggressive law enforcement illustrates the endurance of institutional racism and the retrenchment of the welfare state. Scholars from across the humanities and social sciences have proposed that the prison is now the primary site where a new "racial caste system" has taken root. Legal historian Michelle Alexander has provocatively referred to the disproportional impact that mass incarceration has had on black communities as "the new Jim Crow."[26]

The last chapter and conclusion thus trace the rise of modern conservatism, law-and-order politics, and mass incarceration from the waning influence of postwar liberalism on the one hand and the changing rhetoric and imagery surrounding poverty on the other. This intervention, however, must be placed in conversation with what the first five chapters demonstrate. Those locate some of the most concerted efforts to address poverty embedded within long-running, deeply held concerns about genetic decline. Their numerous differences aside, Progressive Era reformers, pop culture icons, as well as postwar liberals and conservatives, fueled these concerns. These men and women fastened their celebration of settler colonialism, manly strength, feminine purity, and racial supremacy to the upland South and its people.

But there they also found poverty and a culture perplexingly at odds with their preconceived notions. On this basis, a peculiar American regional identity, informed by anxiety and myth, has had an outsized and perhaps surprising impact on the nation's politics and popular culture. Admittedly, the history of the upland South told here is mostly one of perceptions and impressions. As is often the case, though, perceptions and impressions have composed reality for an array of significant historical actors, and we must take them seriously. Furthermore, my interpretation of the upland South is thoroughly relational; the region has derived meaning in and through representations of race, gender, and poverty outside of it as much as within it. This was as true for the first half of the century when the representation of the upland South stood in juxtaposition to immigration and imperialism as it was for the second half when the southern mountains gained renewed prominence against the backdrop of civil rights and urban rebellion.

Readers may not accept all of the connections this book makes, but it will have succeeded if historians consider more fully the variegated ways in which the upland South has had an impact on the nation's history. And though the book presents a bold central argument, the individual chapters mostly echo or expand on the conclusions of others. Scholars have investigated the topics herein with skill and precision. And they have passed along insightful analyses, all of which have greatly contributed to this study. Since the centennial of Indiana's sterilization laws in 2007, for example, there have been no less than a dozen studies (including monographs, chapters, and articles) exploring the personalities and policies of the Hoosier State; researchers have also heaped attention on Virginia's vexed history.[27] Put in relation to one another, however, these case studies might be synthesized and recontextualized in a way that casts brighter light on the respective topics and brings them into fresh perspective.

It is also my good fortune to have this book published as the nation commemorates the fiftieth anniversary of the War on Poverty. *In the Shadow of Boone and Crockett* will join numerous other works that evaluate postwar liberalism and its commitment to civil rights and the social movements of the 1960s. Some of these studies will bolster the conclusions presented here; others will assuredly pose challenges that deserve reflective and thoughtful consideration. So as this book delves into well-trodden territory, it hopes to provoke spirited debate and bridge conversations that have taken place across disciplines.

Finally, to offer some methodological disclosure, *In the Shadow of Boone and Crockett* aspires to belong in a genre that historian Alan Trachtenberg has usefully labeled "critical cultural history."[28] By design, the narrative is not comprehensive, but it nonetheless discerns "significant figurative patterns . . . not as a unified homogenous field but as elements interrelated even where divergent and conflicted."[29] By exploring published and archival sources, the writings of travel journalists, the reports of missionaries, the diary of a displaced Midwestern reverend, the records of an Appalachian folk festival, eugenic family studies, the rhetoric of midcentury liberals, and the images and dialogue of situation comedies, *In the Shadow of Boone and Crockett* weaves a tapestry of cultural and political expression. Viewed holistically, these sources bring coherence to a set of ideas that has had remarkable traction throughout late-nineteenth and twentieth-century America. In sum, this study takes Theodore Roosevelt's audacious claim quite seriously. If Boone and Crockett had mightily contributed to the nation's "race-history," as Roosevelt believed they had, then it is in their shadow that we will test the endurance of his proposition.

CHAPTER 1

APPALACHIAN ANXIETY AND
THE PARADOX OF PURITY
IN AN AGE OF EMPIRE

> Actual societies, and with them their systems of control, have
> been so shattered, mutilated and deformed by war, famine, de-
> population, immigration, race degeneration, and class conflict,
> that no laws can be framed for them that shall hold true.
> —Edward A. Ross, 1901[1]

The fears expressed in the above passage informed Edward A. Ross's 1901 study on the rise and fall of societies, *Social Control: A Survey of the Foundations of Order*. As the Stanford sociologist completed his authoritative work, the United States fought wars of conquest and counterinsurgency in Cuba, the Philippines, Hawaii, Guam, and Puerto Rico. Meanwhile, millions of people whom Ross considered suspect arrived in the United States. The twelfth census documented that 37 percent of New York City residents were foreign born; more strikingly, 77 percent claimed foreign parentage. The majority of the city's population arrived from Ireland, Russia, Italy, or the Baltics. Only 5 percent filed their papers as "native born" English.[2] These statistics led Ross to ominously predict the implosion of American civilization, destroyed from within by those he believed were too inferior—the poor, the black, and the foreign—to handle its civic responsibilities.[3]

Ross was one of many Progressive Era intellectuals who interpreted these demographics and responded to the nation's newly acquired status as an imperial power. Others included Theodore Roosevelt and Stanford University's first president and early advocate of eugenics, David Starr Jordan. Echoing Ross in *Social Control* and Roosevelt in *The Winning of the West*, Jordan surmised: "The blood of a nation determines its history. . . . The history of a nation determines its blood."[4] These scholars argued that the Anglo-Saxon was superior, both as a citizen and as a race—innately equipped to administer the world's leading industrial societies. The three men also noticed that English-speaking Anglo-Saxons had colonized not only North America, but also Australia, the southern tip of Africa, and the Indian subcontinent, among other reaches of the planet, by the late nineteenth century. Roosevelt triumphantly described this advancement of white men as the "crowning and greatest achievement" to have occurred in human history.[5]

The "Teutonic origins thesis" explained how strong populations flourished.[6] Accordingly, the modern "Anglo-Saxon race" shared a genealogy with the Teutonic and Nordic races. Through thousands of years of brutal warfare, these Teutonic and Nordic men spread from Scandinavia to northern and western Europe in successive waves of territorial conquest. The subarctic climate cultivated hardiness within Teutonic people; they mastered the elements with austere discipline. Ross explained:

> In Scandinavia a prolonged struggle in the North Temperate
> Zone, with a harsh, though not depressing natural environment,
> endows the Teuton with unusual energy and initiative. Then
> centuries of wanderings in which the strong set forth and the
> weak and timid stay behind, brings the Teuton to the west of
> Europe, to the British Isles, and to, America, with a courage
> and enterprise, and self assertion rare in the history of man. The
> Teuton becomes the Anglo-Saxon. . . . Moreover, the constant
> fighting brought about by his migrations accentuates warlike
> traits in the Teuton and breeds in him violence and aggression,
> the propensities of predatory man.[7]

At the same time, however, highborn academics like Roosevelt, Ross, and Jordan increasingly feared that the arrival of Slavs, Irish, Italians, Jews, and Hungarians imperiled US American ascendency, itself the culmination of aggressive Anglo-Saxon expansion. These men also worried that Filipinos, Hawaiians, Cubans, Puerto Ricans, and other darker races might bring further devastation. Literary critic Amy Kaplan has captured this latter tension, noting that imperialism was the "nightmare of its own success, a nightmare in which movement outward into the world threatens to incorporate the foreign and dismantle the domestic sphere of the nation."[8] By 1900 the United States had reached a tipping point. Could a nation born of Teutonic wanderings and the manly conquests of Anglo-Saxons overcome the ruinous and sustained contact with "lesser races"? How could the United States, a nation that required the labor of millions of men whose fitness remained in serious doubt, as well as the natural resources where still other inferior populations dwelt, possibly retain its "racial character"?[9]

These questions confounded observers and initiated a surge of interest in the upland South.[10] It would not be the last. If "race degeneration," precipitated by the dual processes of immigration and empire, could shatter the United States, as Ross direly forecasted, then it became urgent to find people who might offer a counterweight. And nowhere more than the hills we now know as Appalachia did writers, social scientists, and journalists believe they had located such a bastion of biological purity and cultural authenticity. Free from the foreigners of the industrial city and the encounters that inevitably occurred as the United States established a foothold in foreign lands, the southern mountains represented an untapped reservoir of "original Anglo-Saxon stock."[11]

Unfortunately, others relayed a decidedly different story. In contrast to the works of fiction and the academic treatises written by Ross, Roosevelt, Jordan, and others, Christian missionaries recorded disturbing examples of turpitude among the Anglo-Saxon mountaineers. These missionaries also believed that the population *should* have been superior in blood and culture but were shocked to find that those who may have been distant relatives of Daniel Boone or David Crockett were among the poorest, most sexually promiscuous people they had ever come across. If true, these reports undermined some fundamental social hierarchies and presented quite the paradox: Anglo-Saxons who nonetheless exhibited unrivaled levels of economic impoverishment and cultural decline. To map the origins of this paradox, this chapter first details representations of the region in popular literature. Next it explores the fraught relationship between turn-of-the-century notions of biology and the people of the southern mountains. It concludes with the missionaries who questioned the superiority and culture of the white upland southerners.

Historians have long noted that the southern mountains emerged as a distinct American region during the last quarter of the nineteenth century.[12] They have expertly demonstrated how the idea of Appalachia—more than the lived experiences of the region's people—has shaped our collective understanding of it. However, these scholars have failed to consider how the suspicion of immigrants on the one hand and the intertwined ideologies that justified an empire and gave rise to racial pseudoscience on the other hand created the necessity for such an exceptional American region in the first place. If, as Frantz Fanon famously argued, "Europe is literally the creation of the third world," one might configure Appalachia as the creation of the era's imperial anxieties as well as the nation's racial and gender instabilities.[13] And over the next seventy years, these apprehensions repeatedly bubbled up as the region became a focal point for broader discussions about race, poverty, and culture.

Immigration, Panic, and the Origins of a Myth

By the end of the 1870s, the nation convulsed with newly arriving immigrants and reeled from economic volatility. In 1873 industrial capitalism collapsed under the weight of reckless speculation.[14] Jay Cooke, railroad financier turned public enemy, had become the personality most associated with an unyielding national depression. Impoverished tenements seized urban landscapes, unemployment reached new heights, and massive strikes shut down nearly every rail depot between Baltimore and St. Louis. Approaching its centennial, the United States was ripe for a dose of nostalgia. It was in this moment that William Wallace Harney believed he had discovered, in the midst of the economic panic and millions of immigrants, a "strange land and peculiar people" in the southern mountains.[15] Life there issued respite from the conflicts of industrial modernity and harkened back to what he reckoned was a simpler era. Safely tucked away from the urban upheaval, the southern highlander remained isolated from the corrosive effects of immigrants and other dangerous foreign subversives. While the depiction of southern Appalachia as an exceedingly isolated outpost appeared before the Civil War, Harney's piece received a wider readership in the popular middle-class periodical *Lippincott's* and helped initiate a national fascination with the rural white people who lived in this pocket of the upland South.[16]

Beyond Harney and his brief piece, perhaps no literary figure elevated the status of the southern mountains more than John Fox Jr., one of the most celebrated novelists and journalists of the 1890s and early 1900s.[17] To the Virginia-born writer, it was a preserve of unadulterated whiteness. Fox's female protagonist in his 1899 novel, *A Mountain Europa,* for example, displayed the qualities of virginal innocence and white femininity.[18] Like his other novels, *A Mountain Europa* featured a tortured romance between a beautiful woman from the southern backcountry and a worldly, handsome suitor from a northern city. Fox's literature expertly mobilized race and gender as pivotal narrative devices. The mysterious and nameless woman in *A Mountain Europa* was the object of desire for Easter Hicks, the cosmopolitan traveler who had arrived in East

Tennessee for business. Predictably, Hicks immediately grew enamored with the exotic female mountaineer. She had an "unusual grace about her. . . . Her features were regular, the nose straight and delicate, the mouth resolute, the brow broad, and the eyes intensely blue. . . . Her figure was erect, and her manner, despite its roughness, savored something high-born. Where could she have got that bearing? She belonged to a race whose descent, he had heard was unmixed English; whose lips lingered words and forms of speech that Shakespeare had heard and used."[19]

Fox's characters evoked a nostalgic if fictional sense of white feminine purity. In a nation increasingly populated by non-Anglo-Saxon immigrants, the southern mountains contained a "race" that remained "unmixed English." Though Fox's enigmatic mountain woman was uneducated, her Shakespearean phrasing distilled an innately lyrical quality to her speech, only possible through her isolation from the noxious forces of the modern age. These qualities could not be found among the impure women of the city, according to Easter Hicks.

A Mountain Europa, however, was only a prelude to Fox's best-known work, *The Trail of the Lonesome Pine* (1908). The bestselling novel wove a tale of mountain seclusion, violence, and romance into a drama that contributed to the nascent stereotypes of Appalachian lawlessness and feuding.[20] The novel's protagonist, another "furriner" named John Hale, traveled to the southern mountains to survey the land. He soon learned that the area "was a perfect example of an arrested civilization and they [the mountaineers] are our closest link we have with the old world." In *Lonesome Pine,* like *A Mountain Europa,* Fox's conception of frontier masculinity signified a regional as well as a racial identity. "They live like the pioneers," wrote Fox, "the axe and rifle are still their weapons and they have the same fight with nature." The author described June Tolliver, a mountain heroine pursued by Hale, as "beautiful . . . pure English descent" who "spoke the language of Shakespeare."[21] The success of Fox's novels hinged largely on their ability to affirm readers' expectations that they might find in Appalachia an exotic place that at once contained manly pioneers as well as pure and virginal women. In either case Fox's mountaineers, with their racial and sexual innocence, conveyed exceptional qualities.[22]

Beyond his career as a novelist, Fox moonlighted as a journalist for *Harper's Weekly,* where he covered Theodore Roosevelt's famed Rough Riders during the Spanish-American War. As a correspondent, he seldom missed an opportunity to praise the nation's imperial adventures and exalt "Anglo-Saxon mastery" over foreign lands. In one dispatch, Fox and his fellow journalists remarked that the invasions of Cuba, Hawaii, and the Philippines were necessary since "it remains true that there is no land in which Englishmen have founded colonies that are not better in every way for their coming."[23] He further proposed that the United States and Britain shared a common heritage and could most effectively steward the planet's valuable resources: "The roots of the two nations go deep into a rich and historic past. It is from the old Teutonic soil that we draw the innate instincts of self-government and our strong sense of individual liberty."[24] In language similar to his fiction, Fox argued that concepts such as republicanism and individualism were attributes found first within the Teutonic race and later in its genetic successor, the Anglo-Saxons.[25]

This provided the moral justification to seize territory and refashion societies in the image of English-speaking people. Only in the fertile "Teutonic soil" did enlightened civilization sprout and flourish, Fox argued. Analyzed alongside his coverage of the US conquest of Cuba, Fox's novels assume greater meaning. The gendered and racial signifiers Fox used in his writing transmitted an unmistakable imperial logic. Accordingly, self-identified Anglo-Saxons had a "civilizing mission" to elevate the world's allegedly less advanced, non-white people.[26] His account of Appalachia as a nostalgia-laden fantasyland, home to a prized population, contrasted with his depiction of dark-skinned peoples from the Pacific and Caribbean Islands. While the threat of contamination was one cost of building an overseas empire, according to many observers, Fox and his readers took solace in knowing that amid the isolation of the southern hollows there still predominated women with a "pure strain" of English blood.[27]

In fact, these bodies could replenish the nation's depleted stock and reproduce unmixed whiteness. This racial pre-ferment, safely ensconced in the southern mountains, counteracted the biological devaluation that resulted from colonial contact. The women of *A Mountain Europa* and *The Trail of the Lonesome Pine* thus offered valuable sexual nourishment for Teutonic and Anglo-Saxon men. Fox believed his "unmixed English" enclave might soon be needed to revitalize an increasingly contaminated population who—while collectively satiating their violent instincts on islands afar—had nevertheless compromised the precise genetic composition that originally led to their supremacy.[28]

Beside Fox's dispatches to *Harper's,* the weekly periodical published the work of others who shared his zeal for the upland South and its people; few were as prolific as Julian Ralph. His first entry, "Where Time has Slumbered," described West Virginia. He asserted that the Mountain State preserved both an endangered way of life and people. Ralph's slice of Americana was Spartan in its furnishings and hardy in its inhabitants. He compared West Virginia to the territory of New Mexico; the former was the more attractive and curious place. He explained:

> The mountain districts of West Virginia are as strange in their
> primitive population as in their tossed and tumbled surface. . . .
> The greater part of the State is made up of mountains, and it
> is there that we see how unique are her people and their ways.
> New Mexico, with its glare of sands and its half-Mexican pop-
> ulation, is more foreign, but it is not so picturesque nor nearly
> so peculiar as this abiding place of a genuine and pure Amer-
> ican population, whose civilization has stood for more than a
> century.[29]

Like Fox, Ralph never hid his sentimentality. Both men transferred their readers from the demographically changing, socially unstable northern city to what they believed were more primitive settings. Ralph achieved this by detailing the relative topographic and cultural foreignness of two places. The complexion of New Mexico's people matched the desiccated, brown desert flora on which they walked; they were "not so picturesque." But West Virginia's "toss and tumbled" interior, on the other hand, secured a "pure and genuine" population.

This portrayal of West Virginia also implicitly drew into relief its rugged terrain with the industrialized landscape of Ralph's Manhattan home. The latter, permanently altered by people and mutated into a routinized grid, reflected the managerial discipline, brutal efficiency, and strict order imposed on its working-class and immigrant population. The implied contrast to New York, as well as the explicit comparison to New Mexico, neatly framed Ralph's conclusions. Only in West Virginia, he inferred, could one find a natural landscape unmolested by the forces of industrial capitalism yet so thoroughly secluded as to maintain its racial and cultural homogeneity. Here, Ralph and Fox feminized the topography. With their impenetrable hollows and imposing peaks, the Appalachian Mountains stymied intensive economic development, even as they maintained an eroticized aesthetic. The perception of virginal purity and natural beauty fashioned the mountains, as well as the "unmixed English" women who lived among them, into targets of manly desire, exploration, and conquest. The isolation of the mountain South communicated by

Fox and Ralph aligned with regional immigration patterns. Of West Virginia, North Carolina, Tennessee, and Kentucky, only the last had a "foreign" population exceeding 3 percent, according to the 1890 census.[30] North Carolina received the lowest total immigration of any state in the nation at 0.27 percent between 1880 and 1900, and the state likely received even lower totals in its western highlands.[31]

Well before Fox and Ralph penned their respective pieces, Appalachia had already experienced seismic changes and would continue to do so for generations. This belied representations and portended a very different future for the region. In actuality, a market economy shaped by resource extraction and land speculation was manifest in southern Appalachia by the late eighteenth century.[32] Prior to the Civil War, railroads connected the upland South, including much of the Appalachian Mountains, to the urban centers on the East Coast and in the Midwest.[33] Industrialization and migration into the mountains continued almost as soon as the war concluded. By 1910, 15 percent of West Virginians claimed an identity other than "native white"; Kentucky had similar figures.[34] In the coal-mining counties of these states, native-born whites worked alongside African Americans, Italians, and Hungarians, often in equal numbers.[35] Ronald Lewis's data-driven study on the timber industry corrects Ralph's assertion that an arrested civilization persisted in southern West Virginia through the duration of the nineteenth century. During these years, the "torch of capital" had lit a flame of industrialization and environmental exploitation as timber companies cleared thousands of acres of virgin forests by century's end.[36]

Additionally, upholding the myth of Anglo-Saxon purity required these writers to ignore the sizable numbers of indigenous people, mostly Cherokee and some Muscogee (Creek), who had occupied the mountains long before European settlers laid a single claim. Furthermore, African Americans lived in the upland South as enslaved and free people for generations. Cultural exchange between blacks and Cherokees was ubiquitous, and some Cherokee had even owned slaves and plantations.[37] While North Carolina, for example, may have had limited immigration, it was not demographically homogenous. As John Inscoe has pointed out, between 15 and 25 percent of all heads of household in the state's western counties of Burke, Caldwell, Henderson, and McDowell owned slaves. And on the eve of the Civil War, these same counties reported the greatest increases of human chattel in all of North Carolina.[38] Beyond western North Carolina, Wilma Dunaway's exhaustive sociological investigations have revealed the widespread reach of slavery throughout two hundred Appalachian

John Fox Jr., Library of Congress.

counties, demonstrating how prevalent the institution had become throughout the mountain South. Despite variations, small and midsize plantations—defined as having nineteen slaves or fewer—were commonplace. So by any measure, whether enslaved or free, people of color were indispensible to the history of the region.[39] Overall, recent historiography has debunked the myth of Appalachian whiteness once advocated by the likes of Fox and Ralph.[40]

That these demographic and economic realities contradicted the literary representation of the southern mountains mattered little to those who propagated the specious narrative; indeed, depictions of Appalachia as a pocket of preindustrial frivolity, racial purity, feminine innocence, and frontier heroism continued in earnest. Meanwhile, the simultaneous processes of immigration within the nation and expansion beyond it created an angst-ridden backdrop from which the fiction of Ralph and Fox reached a mass audience. Both struck an optimistic tone; the nation could still find a population of white people who were not exposed to racial mixing or class antagonism. This renewed hope that the Jeffersonian dream of an agrarian republic was not completely laid to rest at the gates of the factory, the holding stations of Ellis Island, or atop the battlefield at San Juan Hill.[41]

From Literature to Science

While Fox and Ralph circulated their literary interpretations of the upland South, their counterparts in the sciences devised some of the most imaginative fictions of all. Scholars from various disciplines concocted theories of race and gender that relied on a mistaken or misleading understanding of history. Ross's "Teutonic thesis" was an iteration of an idea that received great currency throughout the US academy at the end of the nineteenth century and into the twentieth.[42] By the time he was forty, Ross held professorships at Cornell, Stanford, and finally Columbia. In 1914 he served as president of the American Sociological Society, the discipline's flagship professional organization, making him the de facto voice of American sociology.[43]

Ross's theories had permeated the academy long before he ascended to the top of his profession. By the 1880s and 1890s, he had influenced many aspiring academics; however, none would exceed the import of Theodore Roosevelt. Before his political career, Ross's student completed his multivolume history of North America, *The Winning of the West*. Methodologically indebted to the Teutonic thesis, the study exposed Roosevelt's belief that race and biology were history's prime movers. The books solidified Roosevelt's position as a premier public intellectual; they also anticipated the imperial policies that partly defined his presidency. The volumes meticulously explained how a small group of Anglo-Saxons in North America triumphed to become a global power.[44] Along the way, they evolved into a new race of men: "the Kentuckian." To Roosevelt, the upheaval of the American Revolution and the colonization of the trans-Appalachian frontier forged the Kentuckian into someone altogether different from his European forebears. Confronting the British Army and Native Americans, the Kentuckian at once violently suppressed indigenous peoples in the West and Redcoat provocateurs in the East, proving they were "stout hearted men . . . fruitful as they are hardy."[45]

After the revolution, the Kentuckians traveled further over the mountains and plains, and they proliferated their strong breed into the American West. They were, Roosevelt contended, "the distinctively and intensely American stock who were pioneers of our people in their march westward, the vanguard of the army of fighting settlers, who with axe and rifle won their way from the Alleghenies to the Rio Grande and the Pacific."[46] Those who courageously and violently settled the North American interior, according to Roosevelt, had become a new "Kentucky" or "backwoods race." Together, these men constituted an exceptional population Roosevelt referred to more generally as "American stock"; distinct from the European races, they represented the leading edge of human evolution.[47]

Roosevelt also claimed that religion contributed to the Kentuckian's disposition. According to the future president, the mountaineer's steadfast Protestantism bolstered his already strong makeup. He reminded his readers that the men who evolved into Kentuckians had fled the Old World to escape religious persecution; as a result, they were the "Protestants of the Protestants," reformers of a culture already built on reform and racial strength.[48] Teutonic people were characterized by their manly use of force and a principled belief in individualism, traits supposedly unique to Protestant Christians. By contrast, the Slavic, Baltic, and Irish races displayed such allegedly innate attributes as servility, communalism, and dependency, all of which were apparently, and not coincidentally, manifest in Catholicism.[49] Here, the biological determinism of many of the era's leading intellectuals affirmed their belief in Protestant religious supremacy as well.

Likewise, Roosevelt's trans-Appalachian pioneer was akin to those who occupied Ireland hundreds of years earlier. Its brutal subjugation, Roosevelt surmised, completed the Anglo-Saxon conquest of the British Isles and foreshadowed the events to come. Like their British-Anglo predecessors, the Kentuckian "detested and despised the Catholics."[50] Once in North America, Roosevelt claimed, this very population further mastered the art of colonial dominance. Waging perpetual war against indigenous people apparently honed their craft. This specific confluence of geographic, biological, and cultural arrangements—that which Roosevelt famously summarized as the "strenuous life" of the frontier—provided the basis for *Ubermenschen* like Boone and Crockett, but also Andrew Jackson, Sam Houston, Kit Carson, James Robertson, and other notable American frontiersmen.[51]

Daniel Boone captured Roosevelt's imagination more than the others. This legendary backwoodsman, Roosevelt believed, exemplified how the world's strongest race evolved through the trials and tribulations of the borderlands. According to Roosevelt, surviving in the hostile wilderness required men to cultivate and breed increasing levels of virile aggression. Roosevelt's description of "Boone and the Settlement of Kentucky" presented a Revolutionary War hero who had attained peak manliness and racial acumen. During the conflict Boone valiantly fought back the English, a population who shared his Anglo-Saxon blood. At the same time, he led white settlers west beyond the Cumberland Gap with campaigns directed against the Shawnee Indians. The fateful convergence of this isolated breeding, social conditioning, and persistent warfare explained how Boone and his ilk had "won the west."[52] The trying circumstances of the new continent, Roosevelt concluded, forced the "backwoods race" to progress beyond the original Anglo-Saxons and Teutons who waged wars of conquest in Europe.[53]

Nevertheless, in a subsequent installment of *The Winning of the West*, Roosevelt had slightly tweaked his analysis. Acknowledging the widespread economic deprivation in his celebrated region, the historian suggested that those who arrived in Kentucky, western Carolina, and Virginia after the revolution left much to be desired. "Many of these new-comers were 'poor whites,'" contended Roosevelt, "or crackers; lank, sallow, ragged creatures living in poverty, ignorance, and dirt. . . . With every chance to rise, these people remained squalid cumberers of the earth's surface, a rank, up-country growth, containing within itself the seeds of vicious, idle pauperism and semi-criminality."[54] Here, the historian spoke plainly, and his indignant tone suggested some personal distress over the depravity and poverty that gripped at least some reaches of the upland South.

But as vehemently as he denounced this parasitic growth on the landscape, Roosevelt quickly reminded his readers: "By far the largest number of the new-comers were of the true, hardy backwoods stock, fitted to grapple with the wilderness and to hew out of it a prosperous commonwealth."[55] The passage on poor whites, buried deeply in the multivolume study, was as candidly as Roosevelt spoke about the specter of racial collapse in the southern mountains. But notably, even before he fully elaborated upon the contradiction, "far larger numbers" exhibited manly, frontier instincts. These men, according to Roosevelt, were the true standard-bearers of the commonwealth. By immediately counterbalancing the rare though debased white pauper with the more numerous population of "backwoods stock," Roosevelt repositioned his thesis back onto solid ground. Still, this observation exposed potential cracks and alarming contradictions in an ideology that had so nicely served the interests of a self-identified Anglo-Saxon elite, men like Ross and Roosevelt.

While those two contributed to the academic disciplines of sociology and history, respectively, Ellen Churchill Semple echoed many of their findings within the new field of study known as anthropogeography. Semple and her colleagues proffered that geography could accurately determine the behavioral and physical characteristics of specific populations.[56] Her 1901 study,

The Anglo Saxons of the Kentucky Mountains: A Study in Anthropogeography, located heightened racial purity and manly rigor among those residing in the eastern half of the state. Semple's Kentuckians were the "purest Anglo-Saxon stock in the United States," and they spoke "the English of Shakespeare's time." Their customs suggested they may as well have "disembarked from an eighteenth-century vessel."[57] The Kentuckian, she continued, was "kept free from the tide of foreign immigrants" and contained not a "trace of admixture."[58] The region's ancestors, Semple claimed, fought in the Revolutionary War and remained "superb horsemen," gallant warriors with a pioneer spirit. She conceded that the nation's rapid economic development left some behind and curiously primitive, but Semple concluded, "Their stock is as good as any in the country." Notwithstanding their "bare feet and ragged clothes," the Kentuckians' "hearts bow anew with the inextinguishable excellence of the Anglo-Saxon race."[59] Like Roosevelt, Semple's Kentuckians were perplexing and sometimes menacing figures. Nevertheless, the "excellence" of their race ensured a privileged position atop the human hierarchy.[60]

The focus on white-settler manhood among these would-be scientists—all of whom aimed to uphold the dispassionate objectivity that their fledgling disciplines exuded—provided a fitting counterpoint to the novelists' preoccupation with Anglo-Saxon womanhood. Directing the reader's gaze upon sexually innocent and exotic women injected the literature with some of its dramatic fodder. The men of the southern mountains, on the other hand, apparently served a more "serious" function, worthy of academic inquiry at the highest levels.[61] But whether it was fiction or nonfiction, these writers framed the southern mountaineer in relationship to seemingly ancillary issues like immigration and imperial expansion. Novelists, journalists, and social scientists were not the first to couple biological notions of race with national conceptions of manhood and womanhood. But they were among the first professional, credentialed observers to write in the service of a US American imperial project that received much of its legitimacy through appeals to Anglo-Saxon supremacy.[62]

Illustrating the point, the preeminent transcendentalist Ralph Waldo Emerson had proposed a unified history of the United States a full generation before Ross, Roosevelt, or Semple. Anticipating the Teutonic thesis, as well as Roosevelt's *The Winning of the West,* Emerson's *English Traits* (1856) argued that the Anglo-Saxons of New England were, as historian Nell Irvin Painter has written, "the final product of a process of distillation that had earlier turned Norsemen into Englishmen over the course of the millennium."[63] From this extended period of racial breeding and cultural fine-tuning, New

Englanders were "even more English than the English." For Emerson, this was proof that the most able and fit Anglo-Saxons were the "double-distilled" men and women who settled Massachusetts.[64] But in contrast to that of later observers, Emerson's vision of superior Anglo-Saxon manliness emphasized measured discipline, cautious judgment, and intellectual curiosity over impetuous displays of aggression. The elite Boston Brahmin, that most genteel and enlightened of all New World men, was thus the pinnacle of human evolution to Emerson. To no one's surprise, such a formulation uncannily positioned Emerson himself firmly within these distinguished ranks.

However, much had changed between Emerson's mid-century formulation and the findings of the scientists who published a generation later. What Emerson believed was the height of perfection and Anglo-Saxon civilization these academics interpreted as waning masculinity and lame inadequacy. Among several turn-of-the-century concerns was what historian Gail Bederman has called a "masculinity crisis."[65] During these years, physicians diagnosed many educated, affluent white men with a new disease known as neurasthenia. The affliction revealed the predicament that had beset Anglo-American achievement. On the one hand, encouraging numbers of Anglo-Saxon men had attained unprecedented levels of material comfort and prospered in professions such as finance, trade, business, law, and management. On the other hand, none of these occupations required them to harness their masculinity in the ways of rugged frontiersmen or colonial conquerors. According to the era's medical orthodoxy, "The mental labors of advanced civilization drained [men] of their nervous energy necessary to build a strong, masculine body."[66]

The illness acutely affected those who rose through the ranks of corporate management and other professional bureaucracies; many moved into the streetcar suburbs of northern industrial cities. Far removed from the continental wilderness or the imperial battlefields, these "nervous men" shunned Theodore Roosevelt's strenuous life and effectively emasculated themselves in pursuit of the bourgeois life.[67] This new bureaucratic man, his affluence aside, wallowed impotently in downtown office buildings and suburban homes; meanwhile, men who lived among the southern mountains appeared to have subsisted in conditions reminiscent of the great American frontier.[68]

The fear of neurasthenia thus necessitated a thorough reconsideration of white manliness, locating its model practitioners farther to the south and west than someone like Emerson previously envisaged. To an ever more anxious intelligentsia that feared the unintended consequences of turn-of-the-century modernity, Appalachian women and men became objects of fantasy, hope, desire, and fascination. Industrialists had long exploited the southern mountains and the western frontier for their abundance of coal, timber, and ore. Might the region's people supply the most crucial resource of all? By century's end, "pure Anglo-Saxon" blood was every bit as coveted as highland hickory and bituminous coal. But to complicate matters, not any type of Anglo-Saxon blood would do, and certainly not that which was drawn from effete and stuffy New Englanders. As evidence, even though Emerson's stature grew throughout the nineteenth century and beyond, his investigations into race and biology never garnered the same accolades as his literature and philosophy, and *English Traits* remained at the margins of his oeuvre. For Roosevelt, Semple, Ross, and other theorists, the transcendentalist issued neither inspiration nor influence.

Rather, Nathaniel Southgate Shaler, a Harvard paleontologist best known for his research on ants and other insects, laid the foundation for Roosevelt's interpretation of US history and Semple's anthropogeography.[69] Shaler's *Kentucky: A Pioneer Commonwealth* (1884) portrayed the Kentuckian as the true exemplar of Anglo-Saxon manliness. In contrast to the New Englander, who was pious, communal, and rooted in the English merchant class, the Kentuckians, according to Shaler, arrived in North America resentful of their status as indentured servants and pent up with aggressive vengeance. As soon as they gained their freedom, they spread across the frontier, violently settling the Kentucky, Virginia, and Carolina backcountry. Apart from the stifling conformity of Puritan societies, the upland southerner crossed the mountains in pursuit of property and sought individual gain. Shaler believed such men had an "absorbing passion . . . for the possession of land . . . this appetite for land seems never to have been a part of New England desires but in Virginia and Kentucky it was the ruling passion."[70]

Beyond lust for private property, war equally shaped the Kentucky frontiersman, at once advancing his evolution and enhancing his masculinity. Shaler, himself a Civil War veteran who fought for the Union, believed the Kentuckian was integral to the nation's illustrious military history. "The offspring of the Revolution," Shaler wrote, they were "fed by tradition . . . and nearly continuous combat down to the time of rebellion." He continued, "They were a strength to Virginia in the revolution, and their children gave character to the army of Jackson in the Civil War."[71] This patriotic voluntarism further distinguished the Kentuckian (as well as similar breeds supposedly found across East Tennessee and western Virginia) from his fellow New Englander, who, Shaler commented, long ago lost the urge to fight and conquer. Shaler's reference to the enthusiasm that many upland southerners had for Confederate general Stonewall Jackson belied the myth of Union loyalty in the region during the Civil War even as he affirmed the role of violence as a means of racial and manly rejuvenation.[72] In any case, the acquisition of property and an abiding desire to engage in continuous struggle were hardwired into this new and desirable man: the Kentucky pioneer.[73]

These theorists claimed the southern mountaineer, along with the soldiers of imperial wars, were among the lucky few who managed to ward off the insidious effects of neurasthenia and biological devolution. Men who fought in the Atlantic and Pacific participated in an exercise similar to that of Daniel Boone and David Crockett: expansion, land appropriation, and resource extraction, all buttressed by manly aggression and innate racial tendencies. Just as assertive violence and the quest for land in the southern backcountry staged the rise of Boone and Crockett, many believed that conflicts in the Philippines, Hawaii, Cuba, Puerto Rico, and elsewhere offered fertile ground for the next phase of evolution and masculine revitalization. If the Teutonic and Nordic races gave rise to the Anglo-Saxon, and from here evolved Roosevelt's favored Kentucky and backwoods race, perhaps additional expansion could fashion even better men.[74]

Beyond the academy, others held this position, including Albert Beveridge, Indiana's outspoken senator and fierce advocate of an expansionist foreign policy. According to Beveridge, an overseas empire channeled the instincts that had served the nation so well to that point. Beveridge claimed, "Our race is distinctly the exploring, the colonizing, the administering force of the world. We are this, not from necessity, but from irresistible impulse, from instinct, from racial and unwritten laws inherited from our forefathers. Our pioneers reclaimed Kentucky."[75] While it is not clear how Beveridge's colonizers *reclaimed* something that never belonged to them in the first place, his statement nonetheless echoed Shaler, Roosevelt, Ross, Ralph, and Fox. And like those five, Beveridge confidently believed imperial expansion defined Anglo-Saxonism. The Anglo-Saxon, he continued, "could not help it. . . . wherever our race has gone, it has governed; wherever it has governed, law, order, justice and the rights of man have been established and defended."[76] His justifications for empire further revealed the importance of the upland South in these years. The forbidding hills and treacherous hollows were decisive stages on which the mythological trope of US exceptionalism, built on notions of frontier masculinity, white supremacy, and western expansion, first took place. In their racial origin story, Beveridge, Roosevelt, Ross, Semple, and Shaler believed that imperial dominance was the logical outcome, as well as the instinctual expression of this long, though inevitable, process. At the very same time, however, the Indiana senator's assertion that the Anglo-Saxon was sine qua non to order and civilization encountered a threatening contradiction. In fact, those who traveled to the southern mountains reported an outright lack of law and order, a subversion of civilized behavior and all that was supposed to be innate to these sturdy backwoodsmen.[77]

From Theory and Representation to Observation

By the early 1900s, despite the significantly more nuanced reality, the upland South represented a secluded reserve of purity and cultural authenticity. On the one hand, some argued, the mountains shielded its inhabitants from the unintended, emasculating side effects of Anglo-Saxon urban refinement; on the other hand, this same isolation protected the mountaineer from the dangerous contamination of the immigrant-filled cities and the people contacted through imperial conquest. In the interim, however, the southern mountaineers cultivated a reputation for vigilantism. Historian Altina Waller has noted that rapid economic modernization contributed to an environment already ripe with animosity that lingered since the Civil War.[78] This combustible combination introduced prodigious levels of conflict into the hills, and not surprisingly, such inexorable forces at times led to extralegal violence. The feud between the Hatfields and McCoys remains an infamous example of these tensions. This and other reports of family rivalries fed the perception of widespread lawlessness, medieval clannishness, behavioral deficiency, and lax morality among the white southerners.

These stories sensationalized life in the upland South and exploited the region and its people for financial gain. But in curious and unforeseen ways, the high-profile feuds also undermined the suppositions that leading figures had proposed about the pedigree of Appalachian people. Furthermore, first-hand accounts directly challenged those who espoused the supremacy of the upland Southerner. This countervailing reportage presented a clear danger to the era's hierarchies. What did it mean if descendants of Boone and Crockett were little more than truculent feudists? What if Roosevelt's "squalid cumberers" turned out to be the rule rather than the exception? Could these impetuously volatile men truly be the heirs to Daniel Boone and these churlish women the sole source of Anglo-Saxon fertility? Or would they be known simply as "feuding hillbillies" and "poor white trash?"[79] The troubling observations made by a group of missionaries expressed these fears and exposed the contradictions embedded in the constructed identity of the upland South.[80]

The American Missionary Association (AMA) was formed in the antebellum years, and many of its members were abolitionists. After the Civil War, the AMA assisted Reconstruction efforts in the Deep South. As Reconstruction unceremoniously ended in the 1880s, the AMA was shocked to find that poor African Americans had nonetheless come further than many poor whites by at least a few measures. The explosive implications challenged the very status of the southern mountaineer as the standard-bearer of a "pure and genuine" American race.[81] One missionary, Washington Gladden, arrived in the southern mountains in 1883 after having spent time in sub-Saharan Africa, Mexico, and East Asia. As Theodore Roosevelt launched his academic career, Gladden extensively surveyed the socioeconomic conditions of eastern Kentucky, East Tennessee, and northern Georgia. Particularly interested in literacy rates and civic participation, Gladden alarmingly reported, "The number of illiterate white voters increased during the last ten years, 24 percent—almost as fast as the population, while the illiterate Negro voters increased during the same period *less than five per cent.*"[82] He added, "The whites . . . are scarcely doing more than holding their own; but the Negroes are gaining splendidly; it is to them that the large increase in the percentage of intelligent voters is mainly due."[83] By suggesting that these white men and women were less intelligent or that they failed to keep pace with freed blacks, Gladden implicitly undermined the logic of Anglo-Saxon superiority.[84]

George Phillips, another veteran of the AMA damningly uncovered "an alarming drift toward barbarism" and shocking behavior in Kentucky's Cumberland Mountains.[85] The very term "barbarism" typically referenced colonized, non-Christian, and nonwhite people abroad or the newly arriving immigrants who crowded northern and western cities. Phillips further observed that the "white population in those parts are as destitute of the elements of education as are their colored neighbors," and he continued, "They lack the desire for improvement with which the coloreds and their lately acquired freedom has kindled in those once enslaved."[86] Those Kentuckians who greeted Phillips were overwhelmingly illiterate, poor, and socially and politically inept, and they did not seem to be aware—or did not care—that their descendants were courageous pioneers who settled the West. To Phillips and Gladden, these white southerners had achieved less than African Americans who were reared in slavery.

Reverend and educator Charles G. Fairchild believed that this was a crisis warranting urgent attention and a pivot from the AMA's historic mission. "Some hesitate," Fairchild proposed, "[to extend] the work of this Association beyond the blacks, but they (the whites), have little hope, for this section of the map of our country is black through illiteracy."[87] Like Phillips, Fairchild compared the Anglo-Saxon mountaineer with freed people. Cognizant of Kentucky's heralded history, the missionary quipped, "More than half of the adult white population is native born, of the same stock and lineage that furnished . . . the Clays and Breckenridges, that gave to this country Abraham Lincoln—more than half of this white population cannot read or write."[88] "Stock" had long signified race and ancestry, and its use reminded readers of the Kentuckian's distinguished heritage. Invested in spreading literacy, civic engagement, and Christianity, Fairchild took as his example not famous frontier heroes associated with Kentucky or Tennessee but rather the Bluegrass State's luminary political figures known for their oratory. Still, the sentiment was the same: upland southerners had a demonstrable record of improvement as well as Christian virtue; the AMA could not allow them to languish and their inherent talents dissipate.[89]

Over the next fifteen years, the AMA prioritized white people in the upland South, arguing that impoverishment in the mountains was unacceptable. One missionary and former commissioner of the Freedmen's Bureau, Oliver Otis Howard, addressed the problems faced by "mountain people—people who have our best blood in their veins, and yet have been overlooked and left behind in all our educational privileges."[90] After traveling over the Blue Ridge in 1898, W. E. Barton requested that the AMA shift its focus from African Americans in the Deep South and non-Christians around the world to white southerners. He also opposed military adventurism and believed that it was misguided to seize land abroad, especially if "our own race" required immediate assistance.[91] The missionary contended:

> An isolated people, living in a great inland empire composed
> of eastern Kentucky, east Tennessee, West Virginia and corners
> of adjacent states, and with a population of nearly 3,000,000
> destitute of navigable streams, and until recently of railroads,
> these people who are of the purest British blood which this
> continent affords have lived for a century almost unknown to
> the outer world. . . . They marry early and have large families
> of sturdy American children. They are worth more to us than
> any ten million Cubans or Filipinos, and are in every way worth
> annexing to our sympathy and affection.[92]

Like other writers, Barton's mountaineers assumed greater value in an imperial framework. He opposed US involvement in the Caribbean and the Pacific because he believed that the Spanish-American War unnecessarily diverted limited resources from "sturdy and pure" American children at a time when they most needed them.

Maybe Barton failed to notice, but as early as 1894 the AMA had already redirected significant funds to a region it identified as the "Mountain South," roughly coterminous to the southern Appalachians but extending into western portions of Kentucky and Tennessee as well as the Ozarks of northern Arkansas and southern Missouri. In 1895 the Mountain South received $24,323 of the AMA's budget, second only to the entire African continent.[93] The shift to poor whites marked a departure for a group historically focused on black uplift in the cotton belt. In response to this changing emphasis, Dr. Charles H. Richards, another high-ranking missionary and secretary of the AMA, believed, "The Southern mountaineer, the Indian, the African, the Chinese, together with the Anglo-Saxon, all are to have their part in the great work" of spreading the word of Christ.[94] Richards's taxonomy and the AMA's budget documented the organization's priorities after the Civil War. But more important, Richards made a distinction between "the Southern Mountaineer" and "the Anglo-Saxon." This belied the more common assertion that southern mountaineers were, to reiterate Ellen Churchill Semple, "the purest Anglo-Saxon stock" or "double-distilled" Englishmen and women. The missionaries seemed to have grasped the complexity of poverty in the upland South and what it potentially revealed about the contested issues of race, sexuality, culture, and biology in ways that the scientists had not, or that they had, perhaps, willingly overlooked.

The Lingering Paradox

Richards's distinction between the southern mountaineer and the Anglo-Saxon was more significant than he may have intended. Consciously or not, the missionary vanquished from the ranks of the latter those who never obtained its defining marks of strength and progress. Richards, along with the other missionaries who spent even minimal time in hills, challenged the suppositions of Fox, Roosevelt, Ross, Semple, and Shaler, among others. How could one group of theorists locate white supremacy precisely where others found rampant dysfunction? Such divergent interpretations could not coexist with any credibility. Then again, at no time in US history have conceptions of race and gender been inherent or stable. In retrospect, this instability exemplified the intellectual bankruptcy that accompanied artificial and hierarchical notions of biological difference.[95] That the AMA reached radically different conclusions than those of academic writers like Semple and Shaler or a novelist like John Fox Jr. thus might not be viewed as fully unexpected. But for our purposes, the AMA's newfound interest in the upland South, coinciding as it did with the end of Reconstruction, a generation of intensive immigration, and the rise of an empire, was no less remarkable.

Torn between competing claims, the region's identity came up for grabs, and the stakes could not have been higher. At the turn of the century, ideologues had launched wars for territorial gain and glory in the name of Anglo-Saxon superiority. Daniel Boone and David Crockett, embodiments of frontier masculinity and unadulterated whiteness, became exemplary national archetypes. Around the same time, Frederick Jackson Turner delivered his famous "frontier thesis" and proposed that white settlers' conquest of the West had resulted in an exceptionally independent and democratic US American character. According to Turner, this explained why the United States stood above and apart from the ossified, class-stratified nations of Europe, bearing as they did the legacy of aristocracy and monarchical rule.[96] In each instance, settler colonialism received high praise; its brutal practitioners were regarded as heroes deserving of adulation and even emulation.[97]

Amid the fanfare, however, a monumental collapse unfolded before all who cared to look. True, what the missionaries found throughout the southern mountains was not new, and for at least two centuries, coastal elites worried incessantly about the dangerous population they referred to as poor white trash, lubbers, and backcountry crackers.[98] Well before the AMA arrived, journalist Rebecca Harding Davis posited much that was objectionable, if strangely enticing, about the southern mountains. In an 1875 issue of *Lippincott's*, Davis described her travels through the Cumberlands. What struck the young reporter most about the people she met was not their pure English blood. Instead, she unnervingly relayed that they wore "incredibly dirty clothes . . . [and] were not encumbered with dishes, knives, forks, beds, or any other impediment of civilization: they slept in hollow logs or in a hole filled with straw under loose boards of the floor. But they were contented and good-natured: they took life, leaky roof, opossum and all, as a huge joke, and were honest gentlefolk despite their dirty and bedless condition."[99] She continued, "Money . . . throughout this region is one of the unknown luxuries of civilization; and it is startling (if anything could be startling up yonder) to find how easily and comfortably life resolves itself to its primitive conditions without it."[100] A bemused Davis never alluded to the race of the mountaineers, a notable omission in hindsight. Had she written the piece a decade or two later, she would have likely commented on the ancestry, blood, lineage, or stock of those she met throughout West Virginia and eastern Kentucky; her fellow journalists certainly did.[101]

Nevertheless, what in 1875 may have seemed like a harmless though "strange land and peculiar people" appeared far more ominous twenty-five years later, at least to some. The quaint though impoverished region that Harney and Davis nostalgically described became a site of racial failure at the most inopportune of times. Any decline among a "pure and genuine population" of "unmixed English" undermined many ingrained assumptions that self-identified Anglo-Saxons harbored about themselves. So while the regional identity of the upland South had sprung from the precise ideological impulses that sanctioned white supremacy at home and abroad, it did so with glaring and even awkward contradictions, as well as embarrassing inconsistencies. These stood out further over subsequent decades as observers from both inside the region and out continually gazed bewilderingly upon this confounding pocket of the US South that was supposed to be an enclave of frontier manhood and sexually pure womanhood.[102] Reconciling the gulf between these divergent interpretations has constituted this strange land and configured the stereotypes of its peculiar people.[103]

Still, an additional question remains: what if these lowly mountaineers, already a challenge to the nation's cherished myths solely by virtue of their impoverished existence, moved from the remote hills and hollers of Appalachia and the Ozarks to the heart of nation? Chapter 2 takes up this question and endeavors to resolve, or at least further understand, the paradox of purity. Someone or something would need to limit the damage wrought by a breakdown of the nation's prized stock. A trip across the Ohio River into the Midwest, where thousands of southerners made a similar trek over a century ago, reveals some potential answers.[104]

CHAPTER 2

THE STRANGE CAREER OF
OSCAR MCCULLOCH

The Problem with Upland Southerners and the Progressivism of the "Indiana Plan"

Eugenical sterilization purports to prevent the reproduction by certain definitely and legally described cacogenic persons. It claims that by so doing the race will be purged of some of its degenerate and defective stock. It is effective in so far as it is an insurance against reproduction by the individuals operated upon.
—Harry H. Laughlin, 1922[1]

In 1936 Harry Hamilton Laughlin, a soft-spoken scientist from Oscaloosa, Iowa, arrived as an academic celebrity at Germany's oldest and one of its most prestigious institutions of higher learning, the University of Heidelberg. He came to accept an honorary degree in the "science of racial cleansing."[2] Laughlin's crowning intellectual achievement, *Eugenical Sterilization in the United States* (1922), furnished the Nazi-controlled Reichstag with the template for its infamous Law for the Prevention of Hereditarily Diseased Offspring, enacted three years before his visit. By the time the young Iowan was the toast of Hitler's Germany, the Third Reich had already sterilized nearly a quarter of a million people.[3]

From afar, Adolf Hitler long admired the work of not only Laughlin but also the well-known eugenicist and Boone and Crockett Club alum Madison Grant. He even proclaimed Grant's landmark study, *The Passing of the Great Race* (1916), "my bible."[4] Apparently, the Nazi Fuehrer was a student of the eugenics movements, the leading scholars of whom established their careers in the United States and Great Britain. And he may have also known that over two decades before the Nazis assumed power, the State of Indiana debated and passed the world's first compulsory sterilization law.[5] Following Indiana, thirty other states passed sterilization laws, and the Supreme Court upheld the practice in its 1927 *Buck v. Bell* decision (a topic of later discussion).[6] Though Nazi Germany had earnestly implemented eugenic policies and carried out the world's most calculated, systematized, and brutal genocide, the fundamental ideology was largely conceived across the Atlantic.[7] US American eugenicists never initiated a holocaust, but they did permeate local, state, and federal government; they demanded and received the authority to tamper with the reproduction of tens of thousands of women and men; and they institutionalized those whom they classified as degenerate, sexually deviant, or simply unfit.[8]

At the turn of the century, perhaps no populations were more despised in the United States than African Americans and recent immigrants from southern and eastern Europe.[9] But surprisingly, neither were the first targets of the eugenics movement. Rather, southern mountaineers, those who seemed to have fallen from the heights of distinction reached by their pioneer forebears, presented clear and dangerous obstacles to the genetic health of the nation. In response, eugenicists, poverty workers, and politicians advocated an unprecedented effort to heal the damaged racial character and punish the alleged sexual improprieties of those who were said to have once been the strongest, most fit men and women.[10]

The story unfolds not in the nation's coastal cities but in the midwestern state where sterilization first gained legal status. An itinerant reverend named Oscar McCulloch located an extended family of white people languishing in Indianapolis's crime- and vice-ridden neighborhoods. He soon learned that these men and women had ancestors who blazed a trail through the unforgiving mountains of western Carolina and Virginia; they later fought in the American Revolution; more recently, they tamed the East Tennessee and eastern Kentucky wilderness as the nation plunged toward civil war. But in Indiana these same men and women had lost their way and exhibited the traits of hereditary degeneracy; according to McCulloch, they had become a deviant tribe of wanderers.[11] They also provided a contrast to those whom Theodore Roosevelt contemporaneously described as the pinnacle of human evolution, a uniquely US American breed, the "backwoodsmen," with origins deep in the southern backcountry.[12]

McCulloch's Indianapolis discovery culminated in the publication of *The Tribe of Ishmael: A Study in Social Degradation* (1888), a foundational work that influenced a generation of eugenicists like Laughlin and Grant.[13] And like the American Missionary Association's findings, McCulloch's study further linked economic impoverishment to tensions over race, gender, and sexuality. This claim bridges the social and cultural history of the upland South with the Midwest through the migration of millions of poor whites; it also contravenes scholars who have downplayed the role of race in the debates about poverty in Indiana. Historian Brent Ruswick, for example, has argued, "McCulloch announced that since pauperism knew no boundaries of religion or race, the COS [Charity Organization Societies] ought to work for all inhabitants of the city, regardless of race or ethnicity, and without proselytism or religious instruction."[14] But to qualify as a pauper, as McCulloch understood the term, implied a specific racialized and gendered identity; "pauperism," it turned out, named the perceived decline of Anglo-Saxon men and women.[15] That said, this chapter concurs with historian Jason Lantzer who has correctly noted, "Although there has been relatively little historical attention to Indiana's eugenic past, the state was on the cutting edge of Progressive reforms, including eugenics."[16] But Lantzer could go further and supplement the point: the Hoosier State, if unwittingly, was on the "cutting edge" of reforms precisely because of its proximity to the upland South and its frontline position in a battle to prevent racial collapse from spreading into the nation's heartland.

Hence, this chapter presents two interrelated arguments. First, Indiana's trailblazing sterilization laws, passed in 1907, reacted to the perceived hereditary devolution of a once-superior population of southern mountaineers. These men and women arrived in the state unprepared or unwilling to participate in the burgeoning industrial economy. Perversely, to address this problem and restore the race meant that some defective members, in the words of Laughlin, would need to be purged. Second, enacting this purge required bureaucratic organization and invasive technologies. New state agencies, staffed by public health workers, brought the latest scientific and medicinal knowledge to bear upon the crisis. These bureaucrats carried out the custodial labor of cleaning up and improving those who had displayed signs of decline.

Oscar McCulloch's career in Indiana provides a lens through which to view the state's changing demographics and turbulent economic rise. Ironically, McCulloch's "discovery" precipitated a wave of state involvement that rendered obsolete the model of private charity and benevolence that he himself exemplified and advanced throughout his life. After all, the problems associated with Indianapolis's poor whites necessitated professional intervention far beyond what any single layperson could administer. After surveying the arc of

McCulloch's career, I then analyze the discourse surrounding the mountain-eers who came to Indiana and the poverty workers who saw them as primal threats. This confluence of events, migration, and personalities led to the first attempt to resolve the paradox of purity and restore the once-robust character of a fallen race.[17]

The Strange Career of Oscar McCulloch

Reared in Ohio during the Second Great Awakening, Oscar McCulloch grew up in an avowedly Protestant family. After a disappointing stint as a salesman, McCulloch returned to his passion and dedicated his life to his faith. Upon completing his training at the Chicago Theological Seminary in 1870, the twenty-seven-year-old accepted his first position at a church in Sheboygan, Wisconsin, a fairly affluent town on Lake Michigan settled by German immigrants. There he established his ministry and detailed his experiences in a diary. Content with his new career and home, he proclaimed, "Oh Sheboygan! My heart is here."[18] Within a few months, McCulloch built a healthy congregation and volunteered the church as a community-gathering place. The modest church hosted concerts, a public reading room, and a bible study group for immigrant boys who he feared might otherwise spend their idle evenings drinking alcohol and getting into trouble.[19] McCulloch laid down his roots and made himself at home along the shores of a great lake, but controversy loomed.

McCulloch soon developed an interest in science and pondered secular explanations to life's questions, a pursuit that sometimes placed him at odds with the conservative Sheboygan religious community. In one instance, McCulloch invited a biologist to deliver several lectures on Darwin's theory of evolution. Intrigued by the notion of natural selection though still committed to a Christian worldview, McCulloch tried to reconcile the two in a series of sermons; he even theorized that the New Testament articulated a view of the evolution of species. His congregation was not impressed, and he reported in his diary that half had turned against him and rejected his unorthodox interpretations.[20]

Making matters worse, McCulloch reportedly suffered from hay fever, migraines, and asthma, all of which led him to cancel several church functions. He had also gained a reputation for some rather bizarre antics. The reverend would repeatedly burn the tip of his nose with a match; he smoked cubeb; and he administered low-grade electrical shocks to himself in an effort to keep his sundry afflictions at bay.[21] His inability to stay healthy, coupled with his odd behavior and controversial sermons, eventually led to a declining congregation. By 1876, five years after he had arrived, attendance at McCulloch's church slumped, and much to his dismay, community leaders pressured him to leave. Unfortunately, McCulloch's only offer came from the booming railroad town of Indianapolis: "The call to Ind., the increased salary, the prospect of the position have no fascination for me. I had rather be here [in Sheboygan] on a thousand dollars a year than anywhere else on five."[22] Circumstances dictated otherwise, and in July 1877 McCulloch and his family relocated to central Indiana after he accepted a position at the Plymouth Congregational Church in downtown Indianapolis.

McCulloch's Indiana arrival occurred four years into the nation's worst depression to date. Born into middle-class comfort, McCulloch had lived a rather sheltered existence, relatively unexposed to human deprivation. What awaited him in Indianapolis, then, was personally unprecedented and gravely disconcerting. The city had ballooned from forty-eight thousand people in 1870 to nearly eighty thousand by decade's end, a pace of growth eclipsed in the United States by only Chicago and San Francisco.[23] McCulloch observed that Indianapolis's infrastructure woefully failed to keep up with the city's expansion. Downtown streets remained unpaved and unlit, and the city did not provide basic sanitation services.[24] Nicknamed the Railroad City, Indianapolis served as a key junction between east-west and north-south rail lines. That some of the world's most fertile farmland lay just beyond downtown assisted in its ascent as well.

But even a fortuitous location and stunning population increase did not shield Indianapolis from the same depression that gripped the rest of the nation. In fact, as a rail hub reliant on the transportation industry, the city was particularly susceptible to the depression as well as the upheaval of the Great Railroad Strike of 1877. That year, thousands of railway workers from Martinsburg, West Virginia, to St. Louis, Missouri, protested wage cuts and work conditions in one of the largest labor uprisings in US history.[25] Workers in Indianapolis were arguably among the worst off since the railroad industry had a near stranglehold on the local economy. Like other junction towns, many rail operators fired their adult male workers and hired cheaper labor such as children and women. Wages declined each consecutive year after the 1873 crash, bottoming out at a paltry $391 yearly take-home pay for industrial workers in 1879, barely a dollar a day on which to live.[26] Sometimes these earnings were issued as company scrip and were useless if the operator folded, an increasingly common outcome as depression wore on. Aside from the falling wages among those who kept their jobs, another 23 percent of the city's population, many of whom were able-bodied men, remained unemployed altogether.[27]

Beyond Indianapolis's undiversified economy and rapid growth, McCulloch's adopted city stood out for another reason. While the metropolises of Chicago, New York, and San Francisco attributed their growth to overseas immigration, Indianapolis was a center of white migration from the South. According to the 1880 census, McCulloch was among 83 percent of the thirty thousand new Indianapolis residents who arrived as natural-born citizens.[28] In comparison, Chicago, New York, Philadelphia, Pittsburgh, and Cleveland all had a "foreign-born" or "foreign-born parentage" population between 60 and 80 percent during the years 1890–1910.[29] Indianapolis grew at a similar rate as these cities, but it enticed white people from Kentucky, Tennessee, West Virginia, and North Carolina at a far greater pace than it did Poles, Italians, Croatians, Russians, or Jews. Kentucky alone furnished over 14 percent of the city's migrants between 1890 and 1900 and continually supplied the most out-of-state migrants through 1940.[30] This pattern intensified beyond Indianapolis's city limits. Ninety-one percent of all newcomers to Indiana's southern counties trekked from just across the Ohio River in Kentucky.[31] The commonly uttered phrase, "Kentucky has taken Indiana without firing a single shot," referenced this migration as well as the longstanding rivalry between Indiana, a free state, and its southern neighbor, once a slave state.[32]

McCulloch experienced these jarring demographic and economic changes as he traveled to Indianapolis and across much of Indiana. The reverend had hesitatingly left a stable Wisconsin town bustling with affluent German immigrants and relocated to a city reeling from growing pains. And decisively, McCulloch witnessed deprivation not among immigrants from eastern and southern Europe or the grinding poverty that typified much of the Jim Crow South. Rather, he recorded widespread desperation among people who he believed shared his race and culture; they were also the same people whom many leading social scientists had held in high regard. In this context McCulloch located one particularly impoverished neighborhood filled with "wandering tribes" of poor whites who had traveled at most a few hundred miles northward.[33] They were "largely illegitimate and subject to fits . . . not monogamous, they [intermarry]."[34] He called the poorest of these families the "Tribe of Ishmael," a literary allusion to the biblical son of Abraham. In contrast to the Ishmaelites who, according to the Bible, settled Egypt and Assyria and later became the Arabs, McCulloch's tribe "came mostly from Kentucky, Tennessee, and North Carolina"; their "family stem" dated back to the Revolutionary War.[35]

Like the AMA, McCulloch made his observations around the time that Theodore Roosevelt, Ellen Churchill Semple, and Nathaniel Southgate Shaler had published their respective studies. Roosevelt, like his colleagues in the social sciences, argued that the Kentuckians were descended from a mobile race of men—those "stalwart sons of Odin" led by "kings of Teutonic or Scandinavian blood"—who had conquered Europe and then settled North America, where they held sway with equal prowess.[36] McCulloch concluded otherwise, and he enthusiastically presented his findings to all who listened. Aside from his religious services, he delivered public lectures about evolution, poverty, behavior, and race. In one talk, McCulloch argued, "The development of the present Englishman and American from the Angles and the Saxons" mirrored "the development of plants, fruits and animals from their original species."[37] In each case, these disparate species improved through natural selection, he proclaimed. However, interlopers could thwart the process. "Pauperism," McCulloch reasoned, derailed human evolution.[38]

McCulloch's pauper referred to people who had devolved; they represented a parasitic invasion of an otherwise strong race. Indeed, the pauper was a "Saxon or Teutonic" whose "self-help has given way to a parasitic life."[39] Unwilling to contribute to society, paupers depended on others for sustenance; they were little more than "a shapeless mass with only the stomach and reproductive organs left."[40] To reverse this decline, the reverend worked with the Indianapolis chapter of Charity Organization Societies (COS). According to McCulloch, the COS delivered "[relief to] the worthy poor without breaking down the sturdy, self-dependence which is characteristic of the Teutonic races."[41] "Indiscriminate giving," McCulloch feared, "[broke] down the Teutonic races."[42] To avoid this, he created a board of directors for the COS that would decide whether an applicant was "worthy"—"the temporarily poor, the sick, or the disabled . . . and widows who are struggling to keep together and bring up a family"—or whether they were "chronically poor paupers."[43] That McCulloch believed poverty demonstrated racial decay and hereditary weakness at once affirmed his belief in the otherwise biological supremacy of the so-called Teutonic and Anglo-Saxon races. But it also indicated how race itself was a mutable concept, susceptible to devolution as well as evolution. Indianapolis, with its atypical demographics, teeming with impoverished Anglo-Saxons and Teutonics, issued proof of the unsettling proposition.

The Ambiguous Transformation of an Indiana Reverend

Never a static thinker, McCulloch gradually and unevenly changed some of his views on race and poverty. As the economic depression continued, the reverend increasingly looked to the labor movement, as well as the church, as the two institutions capable of overcoming pauperism and restoring Teutonic and Anglo-Saxon virtue. This meant that he needed to reconcile his biologically determinist interpretation of poverty with his inchoate class-based critique of inequality, rooted in the structural forces of industrial capitalism. For the duration of his career, McCulloch wavered between the two positions. But at the time of his death, the man who authored one of the first eugenic family studies and whose name remains inextricably linked to the families he called the Ishmaels, McCulloch had recanted the positions he espoused in the famous study.

As early as 1878, McCulloch had sided with downtrodden workers. In one address to his Indianapolis congregation, he declared: "The most barbarous doctrine of the regnant political economy is that labor is a commodity in the market just like any other commodity. . . . The man who works, lives and feels; he has his hopes, his ambitions, his loves. . . . There will be unrest and storm and disaster till civilization is organized to meet living exigency; till it tries to do its best for man rather than money."[44]

By the middle of the 1880s, he wrote regular columns for the *Labor Enquirer* and the *Labor Signal,* two of the more radical publications in Indiana. Both reprinted some of his sermons days after he had delivered them. In one, McCulloch issued a "defense of labor and the endorsement of trade unions."[45] He claimed, "My sympathies are with those who live so close to the line of bare existence. . . . The cardinal doctrine of Christianity, self-sacrifice, finds its finest expression among the trade unions."[46] In another address, McCulloch urged the era's industrialists to afford a "fair wage and work day"; this fostered "a Christian life to treat men fairly—to do justice and love mercy."[47] These sermons, with references to the commodification of labor and working-class exploitation, sounded more conversant with Karl Marx's *Capital* than with Francis Galton's work on heredity.

As McCulloch cut his teeth in the labor movement, the Federation of Organized Trades and Labor Unions called on lawmakers to implement the eight-hour workday. Again McCulloch spoke on behalf of Indianapolis's poor and working class, though in quite gendered terms. He believed the attainment of Christian virtue was possible only if workingmen could provide for their families and fulfill their patriarchal duties. On December 20, 1885, at his congregation's annual Christmas service, McCulloch conveyed these ideals in a sermon melodramatically entitled, "The cold, passionless, and automatic life of the world's richest man, Cornelius Vanderbilt."[48] The reverend belittled Vanderbilt's manliness and deemed the robber baron an effete coward for taking up finance rather than earning his money through the sweat of his brow. To McCulloch, Vanderbilt was a "gambler . . . who had no love of humanity."[49] In his pursuit of wealth, an emasculated Vanderbilt had lost sight of what brought men honor: devotion to family and manual labor.[50] McCulloch's militant tone typified many of his speeches throughout the middle of the 1880s and diverged from his earlier preoccupation with pathological explanations for social and economic problems.

In the spring of 1886, workers across the nation went on strike for the eight-hour workday; some of the largest stoppages occurred in Chicago. To the disdain of Indianapolis's conservative press and many other religious leaders in the city, McCulloch supported the movement. One antagonistic reporter wrote to McCulloch, "A union meeting should be held in a hall and not in a church."[51] The city's largest newspapers, the *Indianapolis Journal* and the *Indianapolis Sentinel,* were both antilabor and quickly denounced the Haymarket rally in Chicago. As reports came in that violence had broken out on the third day of the rallies between workers and police, the papers called for a crackdown on the workers and believed that anyone found guilty of shooting at Chicago police must be swiftly hanged.[52] Initially, McCulloch was cautious about weighing in on the events; but he wrote in his diary that those accused of firing at the police "had suffered much," and he pondered their "upbringing and family life."[53]

By the time the alleged conspirators went to trial and were sentenced, however, McCulloch publicly opposed what he believed was a faulty verdict. In an editorial published by the *Indianapolis Journal,* McCulloch patronizingly suggested, "These men, they know not what they do," but then added: "They are in the midst of human sorrows and sufferings. They see hundreds of men out of work. They hear the cry of many thousand children who work in the mills, factories and foundries of Chicago. They see young girls who work without wages sufficient for life. They see women working for thirty cents a day. They see machinery displace men who go about vainly asking for work. They see all this and then denounce."[54] He implored his countrymen to offer forgiveness and acknowledge the "regnant political economy" that bred such radicalism. The *Journal's* editors attacked McCulloch's piece as "unmitigated hogwash" and denounced his defense of "imported scoundrels, naturally at war with civilized society; men who have never done an honest day's work in their lives, but who are parasites and leeches by nature and preference."[55] The irony was thick. As McCulloch defended the Haymarket martyrs, he too put forth the same parasite metaphor to describe the desperation that he found in his own city among the "unworthy paupers."

That McCulloch sometimes exhibited such awareness of the structural forces that led to class conflict and economic inequality, but willingly dismissed these same forces at other times, exposes an ambiguity of his character that seems difficult to reconcile in a modern context. That said, McCulloch's activism aligned with a contemporary strain of Progressive Era evangelical Protestantism. Reformers in this tradition called for a more humane capitalism, one that respected the rights of workers as Christian men who were entitled to basic levels of material comfort and access to spiritual growth. These reform-minded urban Progressives, men like McCulloch but also Henry George, John Dewey, Jacob Riis, Lewis Hine, and others, at once espoused the virtues of manly labor yet maintained suspicion towards more radical solutions to the problems of the industrial age. They were equally suspicious of migrants whose religion and culture appeared alien to the values of middle- and upper-middle-class Anglo-Saxon Protestants. Here, McCulloch's contradictory pronouncements might be interpreted as rather typical for a Protestant reformer of his time.[56]

Indeed, while McCulloch advocated for the labor movement, his analysis of poverty remained fraught with contradictions. He spoke with eloquence on behalf of workingmen, but he seemed fearful and distrustful of poor people, especially the southern whites who crowded Indianapolis. His advocacy rarely went beyond speeches, and he delivered most of them from the comfort of his church. Little evidence suggests that McCulloch organized with or among workers or poor people. Additionally, McCulloch's fiery speeches usually associated physical labor with manly rejuvenation and Christian redemption. He argued that fraternal organizations and unions protected work from corporate tyrants and the excesses of capital.

In this sense, he anticipated Progressives who supported labor reform as a means to strengthen the manliness, as well as the moral fabric of the nation. These same Progressives, however, steadfastly opposed radical changes to the political economy. They cautiously spoke for workers but kept them at a distance, casting a suspicious eye on the militants.[57] Moderate labor reform, far from undermining the ideological suppositions of Teutonic or Anglo-Saxon supremacy, could in fact be marshaled to bolster such ideologies; McCulloch exemplified this tendency. Consequently, his "discovery" of racial collapse, as he believed he had witnessed among the Ishmaels, might be reversed if fair pay, decent hours, and the protection of a labor union accompanied one's work.[58]

The legacy of McCulloch's life becomes legible through these tensions and contradictions. He delivered the speech that was eventually published as *The Tribe of Ishmael: A Study in Social Degradation* at the annual Conference of Charities and Corrections in Buffalo, New York, in 1887. Four years later he succumbed to Hodgkin's disease. During the intervening years, he had gained accolades for what many regarded as a major scientific intervention. His Buffalo speech and book on the Ishmaels provided insight to a generation of public health and welfare workers about poverty in the industrial age. But curiously, even as McCulloch's name became synonymous with the Ishmaels, he returned to the National Conference on Charity and Corrections to give one final speech that repudiated his earlier address. Whereas he had previously warned of the destabilizing implications of pauperism, he now lectured not on parasites, leeches, or a weakened Teutonic race. Instead, he proclaimed, "I see no terrible army of pauperism, but a sorrowful crowd of men, women and children."[59] In a striking turnaround, he then proposed to eliminate the classification of "pauper" from all national charities and with it any distinction between the worthy and unworthy poor. As Brent Ruswick has usefully noted, at the end of his life McCulloch believed that society should assist all poor people, regardless of whether or not they met his previous criteria of worthiness.[60]

However, McCulloch's final public address, delivered weeks before his death, never received as much publicity as did his speech on the Ishmaels four years earlier, and his advocacy for workingmen would be largely forgotten. Soon, another Indiana man eclipsed McCulloch's significance in the labor movement. Eugene V. Debs gained credibility in activist circles that McCulloch never approached nor deserved. As head of the American Railway Union (ARU), Debs led the famous 1894 Pullman Strike in Chicago, was investigated by federal authorities, and ultimately jailed for his activism. This only strengthened Debs's reputation within the labor movement and raised his profile nationally. The upstart Hoosier ran for president as a socialist in five elections; in the 1912 campaign, he won more than 6 percent of the popular vote. Debs had surpassed McCulloch in name recognition and political stature. But while the former may have secured a legacy as one of the foremost labor radicals in American history, the latter left a more troubling imprint on the nation's domestic policies, regardless of what he may have desired at the end of his life.[61]

What the Minister Wrought: Indiana and the Birth of the US Eugenics Movement

McCulloch's funeral was a somber though expected affair. His abbreviated life included notable accomplishments: he founded Indianapolis's Charity Organization Society; he initiated several community programs; and he defended the labor movement and believed that white able-bodied men should join a union. Most of all, his observations of poor people who had arrived en masse from the upland South raised additional questions and unsettling possibilities about the nature of economic inequality in the United States. Leaving behind a treasure trove of notes and reflections to accompany his study, the public grew ever more interested in the Ishmaels, as well as in the idiosyncrasies of those who came from the upland South and settled in the Midwest.

In the final decade of McCulloch's life, Indiana's correctional facilities doubled in size, confining over ten thousand people by 1900.[62] The state repurposed its prison and hospital, both built during the Civil War to house captured Confederate soldiers, to hold not only criminals but also those labeled as insane, feeble-minded, or imbecilic. While some of these inmates had acted violently, most were locked up for vagrancy and pauperism, terms McCulloch had affixed to race. Between 1897 and 1900, as Indiana's population rose at a record pace, the cost of maintaining the state's dilapidated facilities increased nearly fourfold from $93,555 to $360,162.[63] As money flowed into the correctional facilities, institutionalization took the place of material assistance and private benevolence for the state's poor. In 1896 Indiana disbursed aid, defined as clothing, food, and shelter, to 82,235 individuals; a decade later that number had plummeted to 37,724, despite the influx of migrants.[64]

Some questioned Indiana's ability to pay for the runaway costs associated with indefinite confinement and believed that pauperism might be addressed in other ways. The newly hired Indiana State Health Commissioner, John N. Hurty, and his colleague, Harry Sharp, proposed a more cost-effective method that they argued would remedy the pauper problem at its source. By sterilizing those who clogged the correctional facilities, such afflictions as insanity, feeblemindedness, and even compulsive masturbation would supposedly cease beyond the present generation of "mental defectives."[65] Hurty claimed the procedure was painless and could be "done in six minutes without general anesthesia."[66] It also circumvented an unwieldy legal bureaucracy and saved money by reducing the number of institutionalized Indianans: "The costly, ponderous courts [and prisons] only restrain crime, not in the least curing it."[67]

Furthermore, sterilization mitigated the racial breakdown that appeared at the center of the pauper problem. Hurty proclaimed, "We cannot rationally hope at present that extensive breeding from the best will improve human stock to any appreciable degree."[68] Known as negative eugenics or "cacogenics," this theory proposed that society had to purge its defective elements lest they overwhelm the so-called good stock.[69] In contrast, positive eugenics proposed that the strongest Teutonic and Anglo-Saxons could "outbreed" or procreate at higher rates than the so-called unfit. Hurty and Sharp preferred negative eugenic solutions. Hurty summarized his bold tactics this way: "We must sterilize all lily livered loons who would prate of an individual right to perpetrate defectiveness and spread horrible diseases which bring pain, sorrow, agony, torture, and anguish to the tender and innocent, and which destroy the race."[70]

Hurty did not require an adjective to specify which race he meant, given the ancestry of the typical poor white who had languished in Indiana and become his first targets. Without drastic action, Hurty and Sharp feared, Indiana would be overrun by thousands of paupers who would assuredly pass on their deficiencies to the next generation. And most ominously, as historian Nathaniel Deutsch has succinctly observed, "The danger posed by people like the Ishmaels lay in the very fact that they possessed the same names, physical appearances and, frequently, some of the same ancestors as the genetically superior members of their communities, including it should be noted, the eugenicists, themselves."[71] The state most affected by white migration from the upland South, or "people like the Ishmaels," was precisely where the eugenics movement achieved its first policy objective: a law that mandated sterilization for its troublesome residents. Harry Sharp referred to it as the "Indiana Plan."[72]

Locating the Problem: Hereditary Degeneracy and Hill Folks

How these ppl started to hunt those defective elements

Politicians in other parts of the country tried to prevent Anglo-Saxon collapse by segregating native-born whites from African-Americans and immigrants.[73] To do so, they passed antimiscegenation and immigration-restriction laws. But what happened if the biggest problem came from within the allegedly pure population itself? Indiana's demographics and McCulloch's "discovery" portended such a predicament. As a result, Governor James Frank Hanley, at Hurty's lobbying, introduced a bill to the state legislature to legalize sterilization.[74] In the spring of 1907, the legislature obliged and passed the world's first mandatory sterilization law; the sweepingly broad language singled out "confirmed criminals, idiots, rapists, and imbeciles" under the auspice that "heredity plays a most important part in the transmission of crime, idiocy and imbecility."[75] A "committee of experts and the board of managers" decided *who* qualified as an idiot or an imbecile, and they determined the "probability of improvement of [their] mental condition." If the committee determined that the likelihood for improvement was zero or low, "it shall be lawful for the surgeons to perform such operations for the prevention of procreation."[76]

Vesting a rather hastily assembled committee of experts with such nebulous and broad-based authority ensured high levels of capricious surveillance. And those most vulnerable to overreach were the thousands of poor families throughout the state. As such, the legislation also signaled a new direction in public policy and a turning point in how Indiana dealt with the growing problems of crime and destitution, along with their insidious accompaniments: racial deterioration and sexual deviancy. State-run bureaucracies rapidly assumed the role that McCulloch had designated for private charities and benevolent societies.[77] An ascendant class of educated public health and social workers monitored what Indiana University professor Thurman Rice called the state's "racial hygiene" and staffed these new agencies.[78]

The Indiana Board of State Charities and Corrections (BSC) was among the first organizations formed to locate pauperism and, as Hurty described, deal with it at its source. Enterprising medical professionals, some of whom had received training in academic departments such as anthropology and sociology as well as in institutes of medicine and public health, fanned out across Indiana to search for feebleminded paupers. In 1915 funding for the BSC was transferred to still another bureaucracy, the Committee on Mental Defectives (CMD). Much like the BSC, this group of researchers and medical practitioners conducted fieldwork throughout Indiana, and they recommended ways to address the widespread poverty.[79]

A generation after Oscar McCulloch's discovery of the Ishmaels, CMD fieldworker Helen Reeves teamed up with a young evolutionary biologist named Arthur H. Estabrook. Estabrook had obtained McCulloch's copious notes, and with the help of Reeves he located the surviving Ishmaels within the same Indianapolis neighborhoods. The biologist wondered whether they had become, as he defined it, productive members of society, or if they had devolved even further.[80] As Estabrook and Reeves investigated the Ishmaels, they came across dozens of other poor families. This seemed to affirm Hurty's fears of an extensive pauper problem rooted in the migration of Kentuckians and others from the upland South. Reeves claimed that "2200 pauper idiots" had arrived from the Bluegrass State and would undoubtedly breed thousands more. "Everything degenerate in Indiana," she asserted to Estabrook in a private correspondence, "hailed from . . . Kentucky."[81]

In another report CMD researchers surveyed several Indiana counties and rural towns. In each, the committee found "idiots, imbeciles, and morons" who displayed various levels of pauperism. In one locale, designated as "G county," the committee reported a "high rate of red eye sores, the result of venereal disease," likely syphilis. These reports were not surprising given the isolation and sexual promiscuity for which the Kentuckian was known, according to the committee.[82] Making matters worse, county inhabitants held no "progressive attitudes," nor did they "[demand] more of its citizens."[83] Aside from Kentucky, the "degenerate mountain folks from North Carolina have come into the county," and together they made up a "growing pauper problem."[84] Physician and CMD researcher Jane Griffiths carried out her fieldwork in Delaware County, northwest of Indianapolis. There she found several families who had signs of "feeble-mindedness": running eyes, shabby clothes, persistent illness, and ramshackle homes she described as "a horror."[85] Griffiths calculated that one family, the Milners, had spent a paltry $18.25 over the last several years on clothes and shelter. At age sixty-eight, Mrs. Milner's husband was "far too old" for her and displayed the reckless behavior of an "idiot." Griffiths predictably relayed, "This is another Kentucky family."[86]

Then there was the Holly family. The CMD declared, "It is almost impossible to describe . . . the miserable conditions under which they live." Here again the researchers were dismayed that a "perfectly happy and care free" family could live among "indescribably filthy" conditions with "absolutely no attempt at cleanliness." Stella Holly, with her tobacco-stained teeth, had four children with her husband, Jim, who "came from Kentucky." All four kids, according the committee, were defective and shiftless; the family "represents almost as deplorable conditions as one could find." Alarmingly, the CMD located similar "country slum children" across Indiana. Like the Hollys, these children "seem more like rats than human beings," another report concluded.[87]

The committee located several other candidates for sterilization or confinement. Aside from the Holly family, others included the Riley, Dye, and Curtis families; they also lived in "filth and squalor . . . utmost poverty."[88] "Irresponsible, happy go lucky [and] as pleased to be lame as whole," committeewoman Jane Griffiths recorded, these men and women failed the mental hygiene test. All arrived from East Tennessee or eastern Kentucky and now threatened to spread sexual impropriety, laziness, and, most of all, racial defection throughout the Hoosier State.[89] To a committeewoman like Griffiths, these families broke all of the rules: they chose unacceptable sexual partners; their clothes and shelter belied Griffith's middle-class expectations of comfort and sanitation; and they had arrived from the southern backcountry unequipped or unwilling to participate in the twentieth-century industrial economy.

Eventually, the CMD traveled to the rural southeastern corner of the state. There, researchers believed they had uncovered defectiveness beyond what they reported in County G or even had witnessed among the Ishmaels in Indianapolis. Switzerland County (also recorded as "County C") abutted the Ohio River and was an entry point for Kentuckians, Tennesseans, and North Carolinians. In fact, over 90 percent of the county's newcomers had arrived from the upland South, especially Kentucky.[90] The CMD reported, "In proportion to the population, the percentage of mental defectives from 'C' County now under care in state institutions is higher than any other county in the state."[91] The "low-grade mentality" of the "Lookout Ridge Population" and the "Kentucky Hill-Folk in Indiana" alarmed Arthur H. Estabrook and committeewoman Hazel Hansford. Pseudonymously referred to as the Beatty-Calverts, the Shannon Clan, and the Simpsons, these families ventured from the southern hills; their pauperism and moral turpitude were not only unrivaled but also expensive. The petty crime and poverty of these families, Estabrook estimated, cost Indiana over $4 million annually.[92]

But one could not so easily put a price tag on the damage that hereditary decline did to strong Anglo-Saxon and Teutonic stock. The CMD concluded their report with a damning allegation as well as an ominous prediction: "The defective members of the population seem to be recruited from the degenerate members of fine old families. 'C' county inhabitants are . . . from the present and steady influx of undesirable immigration from neighboring states. Further investigation might easily show these families of kindred strains. On account of unusual isolation of the county, these strains will certainly continue to multiply in the same or greater ratio of the past."[93]

Thus, Switzerland ("C") County's high rate of degeneracy suggested a wicked confluence of perfidy that turned the era's racial hierarchy on its head. "Fine old families" evoked the best of Roosevelt's favored Kentucky race, but they had evidently squandered their promising bloodlines over generations of idleness, deviancy, and poverty. That the committee used the adjectives "defective" and "degenerate" interchangeably indicated that these families had become Teutonic paupers. Most seriously, however, was the proposition that they shared "kindred strains," an allusion to incest. This transgression provided an explanation as to how the nation's most vaunted race could turn out so badly. The isolated, hilly geography, combined with the rural and agrarian ways of many southern migrants, had created an environment conducive to consanguinity, the CMD concluded. Incest epitomized depravity more than any other behavior, and it illustrated why sterilization had become a necessity. The CMD dealt not with just any population of poor people; they faced defectors from their own proud race who had abdicated in the worst way imaginable. In the words of one committeeman, they were little more than "poor white trash from the South."[94]

Accusations aside, the documents offer no conclusive evidence that consanguinity occurred at higher rates in rural Indiana among migrant Kentuckians or Tennesseans than among other communities, rural or urban. Instead, the reports convey the predictable effects of poverty with which the families had to contend. Indeed, what Estabrook, Reeves, Griffiths, and other researchers described as intrinsic traits were common among poor people regardless of where they lived or their ethnic identity. Social and economic dislocation occurred throughout the United States at the turn of the century, and the material conditions found among white southerners in Indiana were not markedly different from the immigrant slums of New York City or Chicago on the one hand, or the Jim Crow South where African Americans experienced debt peonage and political disenfranchisement on the other hand. The difference, of course, was that Indiana's poverty workers confronted a unique dilemma: in their state, the descendants of distinguished "fine old" families had become the detritus of their race, or more simply, "poor white trash." The confusion necessitated drastic action lest the racial collapse and mental defection spread further.[95]

Indiana and Beyond

When Oscar McCulloch arrived in Indianapolis during the turbulent summer of 1877, he brought with him an ebullient spirit of Christian benevolence. Vast inequality greeted him. In response, he built institutions and relationships to alleviate the despair that plagued his adopted city and state. At first, he understood poverty in Indiana as a genetic and, ultimately, a racial problem. McCulloch's pauper was either a fallen Teutonic man who lost his work ethic or a woman whose sexual proclivities clashed with normative middle-class standards of feminine propriety. As long as these poor families grew, so too did the pauper problem. But by the end of his life, McCulloch regarded the

Oscar McCulloch. Courtesy of the Rare Books and
Manuscript Collection, Indiana State Library.

unchecked power of the era's robber barons at least as dangerous to the wellbeing of Teutonic men and women as pauperism. Fortunately, the rough edges of
industrial capitalism could be smoothed over by dignified, well-compensated
work, preferably backed by a union. Class solidarity and manly labor were
central for a city like Indianapolis and a state like Indiana to stem the tide of
hereditary decline, according to McCulloch at his life's end.[96]

Still, with its indictment of the city's poor, *The Tribe of Ishmael* overshadowed McCulloch's personal evolution and shaped how a generation of reformers understood the causes and effects of poverty. And though few recognized
it at the time, the study also facilitated the transition of poverty work from the
private to the public; it contributed to the establishment of state bureaucracies
and revealed the limitations of private benevolence and charity.[97] Arthur H.
Estabrook, Jane Griffiths, Helen Reeves, and their colleagues on the Committee on Mental Defectives and the Board of State Charities carried out the
investigative work once done primarily through McCulloch's church or other
private benevolent societies. Others, such as Harry Sharp and John Hurty, be-

Arthur Estabrook. Courtesy of the Eugenics
Archive of the American Philosophical Society.

lieved they had blazed an exciting trail of medical advancement. But all these men and women were especially motivated to understand how and why their own superior breed of people had succumbed to such wretched behavior.[98] This same population, after all, had just received high praise from the likes of Theodore Roosevelt, Nathaniel Southgate Shaler, and Edward A. Ross.

Not all agreed with Sharp's Indiana Plan or the CMD findings, and some questioned the legal and moral implications of sterilization. The Indiana legislature briefly overturned the law in 1909; however, they reinstated the procedure during the next session. This time, the law remained in place for over sixty years until the Indiana Supreme Court overturned it in 1974.[99] But in the meantime, doctors performed over twenty-three hundred sterilizations at the request of the CMD and other state authorities. Women underwent the procedure at a rate double that of men.[100]

Finally, as evidenced by Laughlin's invitation to Nazi Germany, the Indiana Plan traveled well. Its proponents advocated similar laws elsewhere, and eugenicists brought early-century strategies of public health and social work to bear on what they perceived as destabilizing forces within the population. They believed that poverty was an embodied and pathological condition rather than an economic one and proposed solutions accordingly. The Indiana Plan, with its intent to cleanse Anglo-Saxon and Teutonic stock of its noxious impurities, also reflected broader Progressive Era concerns about widespread inequality. Of course, improving the race and addressing the so-called pauper problem were related undertakings and cannot be disentangled from one another. And while Indiana was a target-rich environment to take on the threats posed by racial collapse and rural impoverishment, the southern mountains remained the epicenter. There we shall return.

CHAPTER 3

A PIONEER DANCE

Virginia's Search for Purity
in the Interwar Years

Whether musician, writer or layman, the principle is the same;
for every human being has the creative instinct in some form;
perhaps never developed. And this development will be only
in proportion to the degree to which he has utilized his own
personal and racial inheritance.

—Annabel Morris Buchanan, c. 1935[1]

The tragic story of Carrie Buck is well known among historians of Virginia, the Supreme Court, and the US eugenics movement. She was born in a mountain hollow not far from Charlottesville in 1906. Her mother, Emma, after having been abandoned by her husband, put young Carrie up for adoption; within a year, the toddler found a home with foster parents, John and Alice Dobbs. Aside from spending her infancy in an orphanage, Buck experienced an uneventful childhood: she attended school, earned adequate grades, had a few friends, and was apparently courted by a few of her male classmates. Her youth seemed typical of many young girls and women who came of age in one of the many small towns that dotted southern Appalachia.[2]

All of that changed, however, in 1923 when a family member raped and impregnated seventeen year-old Carrie. Her adoptive father, John Dobbs, refused to accept the overwhelming evidence that his nephew committed the crime. Instead, he accused Carrie of lying and covering up what he believed was her shameful promiscuity. Days later, Dobbs committed his foster daughter to the Virginia Colony of Epileptics and Feebleminded. After a cursory assessment of the young woman, Virginia authorities agreed with Dobbs and proclaimed that Carrie Buck had engaged in incorrigible behavior. Months later, while still in custody, Buck gave birth to a child named Vivian, but because of what the state described as mental incompetence and sexual lasciviousness, she had to surrender the infant to the Dobbses. Vivian died seven years later from intestinal colitis. Virginia authorities, meanwhile, eventually paroled Buck and placed her under supervision. But they limited her contact with Vivian throughout the girl's brief, pain-stricken life. Following her daughter's death, estranged from her paternal and foster families, Carrie Buck began her life anew and married a man named William Eagle. She and Eagle had no additional children despite their desire to do so. As a condition of her release from State Corrections, Buck was sterilized. She outlived Eagle and died alone in a Virginia nursing home at the age of eighty-three.[3]

While harrowing, the details of Carrie Buck's life would have been likely forgotten had her sterilization not resulted in an ignominious Supreme Court decision. Buck challenged Virginia's sterilization policy on the grounds that the invasive procedure violated her equal protection to bear children. After nearly four years of litigation in which leading eugenicists testified against her, the Supreme Court heard the case in 1927. After a week of deliberations, the court sided with Virginia in a decisive eight-to-one ruling. Writing for the majority, Oliver Wendell Holmes famously quipped that "three generations of imbeciles are enough."[4] The matter was settled, and by 1979 when Virginia finally halted the procedure, authorities had sterilized between seventy-three hundred and eighty-three hundred supposedly defective and feebleminded citizens.[5]

Scholars from various disciplines have dissected Buck's life and the landmark Supreme Court decision that bears her name. This chapter builds on the plethora of scholarship regarding not only Buck but also eugenics in Virginia; it recognizes the familiarity with which many will approach the topic. However, the chapter situates Buck and Virginia's interwar policies more broadly amid the racialized and gendered anxieties that hung over the upland South. This more clearly exposes why state leaders used bodily regulation and coercion as a means to address poverty. Notably, Virginia authorities fought to enact and uphold sterilization and other race-based policies with the same zeal that Indiana's CMD searched Switzerland County for defective white families like the Ishmaels. And like their counterparts in the Midwest, Virginia eugenicists and lawmakers wanted to restore a downtrodden race, or at least prevent the spread of what they perceived as dangerous genetic deterioration.[6] Virginia is thus an ideal companion to Indiana; after all, the Supreme Court upheld in Virginia that which was first practiced in Indiana twenty years earlier. If the

Hoosier State had initiated use of the grim procedure and institutionalized the eugenics movement within key state bureaucracies, Virginians nevertheless sterilized more people per capita than did any other state by the end of World War II.[7]

With its sizable population of poor whites in the western counties and African Americans in the Piedmont and coastal regions, Virginia lawmakers perceived that their state was especially vulnerable to racial pollution. As we have seen, two serious threats to the native-born Anglo-Saxons and Teutonics were racial mixing, more commonly referred to as miscegenation, and the degeneracy that occurred *within* the race as a result of hereditary decline. In 1924 the Virginia legislature passed the Racial Integrity Act, making it illegal for white people to marry or have sexual contact with anyone who had "one-sixteenth Negro or Indian blood" or more.[8] This minimized, if not totally eliminated, the supposed damage brought about by miscegenation. Sterilization, by contrast, reversed the breakdown of those who had allegedly disgraced the race, people like Carrie Buck.[9]

Virginia also stood out for the lengths to which some of its citizens went to display what they believed were the cultural achievements of the Anglo-Saxon, or what writer Annabel Morris Buchanan called "racial inheritance." Like the local color writers, novelists, and theorists we encountered earlier, several high-profile Virginians claimed to have found a pure race among the state's isolated Appalachian hollows. John Powell, a renowned composer of classical music and native Virginian, fashioned his career to counter what he believed were the embarrassing and misleading narratives about poor whites such as Carrie Buck in his home state, or the Ishmaels in Indiana for that matter. If Buck and the Ishmaels represented the *worst* of the Anglo-Saxons, Powell endeavored to showcase the very *best* the race had to offer.

This chapter presents Powell's career, much like Oscar McCulloch's, as a way to frame the culture and politics of one specific state and then distill some broader trends. Hence, lawmakers and cultural workers in interwar Virginia, perhaps more than anywhere else, crafted a coherent set of policies that responded to the perception of Anglo-Saxon collapse. Powell played a lead role. He helped establish Virginia's Anglo-Saxon Clubs of America (ASCoA) into the one of the nation's largest organizations dedicated to propagating racial pride. It extolled the supposed inherent virtue of an esteemed though vulnerable population. Additionally, Powell and his colleagues, some of whom had worked for Indiana's Committee on Mental Defectives, promoted legislation to ban miscegenation and restrict immigration; they launched committees reminiscent of the CMD to study the Old Dominion's impoverished rural people; and they even created arts and music festivals to celebrate those Virginians who remained free from the contamination of "Negro or mongrel blood." These measures demonstrate the imaginative steps Powell and his colleagues took to curb a threat they feared could ruin Virginia and spoil a nation.[10]

A Musician's Case for Racial Integrity

Born in Richmond in 1882, John Powell displayed an unusual talent for music from a young age. Before he turned twenty, Powell had completed primary school and graduated with a degree in musical composition from the University of Virginia. He then spent his early twenties in Vienna, Austria, performing with European composers and classical musicians. By age thirty-five, he had written several highly acclaimed concertos, rhapsodies, and etudes; he shared the stage with some of the world's renowned orchestras. The highlight of his early career came when the thirty-eight-year-old Virginian toured Europe with the New York Symphony, performing classical standards alongside his own compositions.[11]

Notwithstanding such a prolific start to his career, Powell experienced a crisis of musical identity. As an American composer, he continually faced accusations that his native country lacked a musical tradition in the vein of Germany, France, or Russia. The United States offered no equivalent to Beethoven, Wagner, Ravel, or Tchaikovsky, and Powell's European rivals proposed that the genetics of the Anglo-Saxon were to blame. He recounted, "People who heard my music doubted that I was a Virginian. . . . Anglo Saxons they all declared were notoriously unmusical. And as proof they brought forth the staggering argument that Anglo Saxon people have no folk music."[12] Unsatisfied with such logic, Powell set out to overturn these impressions and worked tirelessly to promote what he felt was a rich tradition of American music, one that was inextricably connected to the precise genetic composition of Anglo-Saxons who had settled the continent three hundred years earlier.

The composer believed that the United States should "develop a national music," and he was quite clear about its source: "It must be founded upon the music of the Anglo-Saxon races which were the pioneers in America."[13] But unfortunately, according to Powell, each passing day brought about the further erosion of his beloved race, increasingly weakened because of miscegenation and degeneracy. Unless state and national leadership restricted immigration and aggressively protected the remaining vestiges of undiluted Anglo-Saxon heritage, the United States might lose its racial character and its accompanying culture. In light of such imminent danger, Powell mobilized his fame in Virginia to lobby for the nation's most stringent antimiscegenation laws. Only through such efforts, he believed, could Virginia preserve and eventually spread the cultural achievements of an unadulterated people who had proven to be the world's most fit.

In 1923, upon returning from a successful European tour where Powell played "his uniquely 'American' compositions, such as 'the Banjo Picker,' 'Pioneer Dance,' and 'In Old Virginia',' he began a new project stateside.[14] Not coincidentally, on Columbus Day, Powell, along with public health advocates and physicians Walter Plecker and Ernest Sevier Cox, adjourned a convention and founded the Anglo-Saxon Clubs of America (ASCoA). Held in Powell's hometown of Richmond, convention participants drafted the organization's constitution and pledged to expand the clubs nationwide. Their mission statement echoed Edward A. Ross's observations in *Social Control* and Madison Grant's more recent prognostications in *The Passing of the Great Race*. For the previous quarter century, the club's manifesto proclaimed, there "occurred a rapid submergence of the original American stock in many parts of the country" because of "alien groups; the intensification of racial animosities; the increase of foreign language and race newspapers."[15] The "Principal object" of the ASCoA was "the maintenance of Anglo-Saxon institutions and ideals, and in furtherance of the attainment of that object this organization stands for the support of the Constitution and Laws of the United States of America . . . for the preservation of racial integrity; for the supremacy of the white race in the United States of America."[16] The club's bold racism positioned it among a wider resurgence of nativist, anti-Catholic, and anti-Semitic organizations. One of these, the Ku Klux Klan, achieved its peak popularity in the 1920s by appealing not only to white supremacists but also to anti-immigration sentiment that rose precipitously after the First World War.[17] But perhaps more than the various hate groups that flourished in the decade, Powell's club accessed political power and secured some major policy objectives.

The Anglo Saxon Clubs of America sought three primary outcomes: "The strengthening of our Anglo-Saxon instincts, traditions and principles among representatives of our original American stock; second, by intelligent selection and exclusion of immigrants; and third, by fundamental and final solutions of our racial problems in general, most especially of the Negro problem."[18] Phrases such as "intelligent selection" and "final solution" not only presaged the horrific results of the eugenics movement abroad, but they also connected the club's goals to the work of men like Arthur H. Estabrook, Madison Grant, and Harry H. Laughlin. And like those three, the ASCoA diligently worked to ensure "the maintenance of the color line."[19] Powell collected over two hundred thousand signatures on a petition that urged Virginia legislatures to pass immigration restrictions and stronger penalties for miscegenation; he also advocated that Virginia sterilize its alleged defectives. Collectively, Powell referred to these objectives as racial integrity.

Powell had been an outspoken activist before he started the Anglo-Saxon Clubs, and he long feared that the United States might become a "negroid nation" subsumed by "Negro blood." With "over sixty centuries of history from which we can draw inferences," he argued, the results would be devastating.[20] In one editorial, Powell concluded that the "maintenance of racial purity, racial integrity and lofty racial ideals . . . depends on its social standards and on its morality not less on its laws."[21] If Virginia failed to act, the state would incur the high "price of pollution."[22] During the spring of 1923, just before the Virginia legislature held hearings on racial integrity, Powell wrote to Richmond's daily paper with instructions for lawmakers:

1. Institute immediately a system of registration and birth certificates showing the racial composition of every resident in the state.
2. No marriage license shall be granted save upon presentation and attestation under oath by both parties of said registration.
3. White persons marry only whites.
4. For the purposes of this legislation, the term "white persons" shall apply only to individuals who have no trace whatsoever of any blood other than Caucasian.[23]

Significantly, this language ended up in the final version of the Racial Integrity Act passed by the legislature during the 1924 session.[24]

To gain credibility as an academic theorist, Powell moonlighted as an anthropologist and reported from the field on the dangers of racial pollution. In a study of each congressional district in Virginia entitled *The Last Stand,* Powell argued that the "threat to the color line" had reached its apogee.[25] He first examined Hampton, Norfolk, and towns along the Chesapeake Bay and James River, the location, he explained, of "the oldest permanent English speaking settlement in America, Yorktown, where American liberty was brought forth."

He continued, "Here we should expect to find unbroken maintenance of the old ideals and traditions."[26] But instead he found at least "six cases" where Native Americans and African Americans had "collapsed the color line," and a "decadence of racial sense" prevailed.[27]

The case of a man Powell referred to as Bob Doe exemplified the confusion. Doe, an easily recognizable figure in his community, looked unsettlingly ambiguous to Powell. He relayed the below exchange between two people who knew Doe, one of whom addressed him by his informal first name and the other, by the more respectful surname:

> "Since when have you been on intimate terms as to call Bob Doe by his first name?" [Powell asked] to which Resident A replied, "I call him by his first name as I do every Negro to whom I speak." Resident B replied: "why Bob Doe is no Negro. I have known him all of my life." Resident A, "why so have I and I can tell you he is a Negro." The registrar attempted to find out but one half who were asked claimed he was white and another half claimed he was black. They could never know.[28]

Powell desperately wanted to solve this dilemma. Racial mixing made Doe illegible to those around him and called into question his position on a social hierarchy that disbursed benefits and privilege according to one's skin color. To many, Doe passed as white and thus attained a social status that belied his "negro blood." If others did the same, the Anglo-Saxon faced nothing short of extinction. A "homogenous America," by which Powell curiously meant homogeneously "miscegenated," meant that "a race of octaroons" could dominate the United States. This, he apocalyptically predicted, "would mean the death of all civilization in our country and in the world."[29]

Luckily for Powell and his followers, Virginia legislators heeded their calls and passed the Racial Integrity Act of 1924, written verbatim from the language on the ASCoA petition. It took effect at midnight on June 16. The *Richmond Times Dispatch* marked the occasion by loftily stating, "It may take rank in history with the half dozen major reforms which have contributed most to the advancement of civilization. This is the racial integrity law."[30] "Passage of the bill," the newspaper recorded, "was due entirely to the efforts of John Powell, world famous composer and pianist and organizer of the Anglo-Saxon Clubs of America, and Major Ernest Sevier Cox, nationally known ethnologist."[31] Other eugenicists heralded the musician's efforts. Madison Grant, a man whose writings Powell referenced, personally praised the Virginia composer. In a letter, Grant told Powell that his Racial Integrity Act lived up "to Virginia's great traditions"; it was a significant step towards "maintaining race purity."[32] Lothrop Stoddard, another leading eugenicist, wrote to Powell and credited him with "safe-guarding" the "purity of the white race . . . from possibility of contamination with non-white blood."[33] Already an accomplished musician, Powell's name became equally synonymous with scientific racism.

By the end of the 1920s, Powell and his associates had built support for racial integrity and instilled the fear of a "color-line collapse" within many of the state's prestigious universities. The University of Virginia, the Virginia Military Institute, the Virginia Polytechnic University (Virginia Tech), and Washington and Lee University had opened ASCoA chapters; many students and faculty embraced the pseudoscience of the eugenics movement with open arms.[34] Indeed, the popularity of the ASCoA, the passage of the Racial Integrity Act of 1924, and the decision of the Supreme Court to hear Carrie Buck's case suggest that the Old Dominion had supplanted Indiana as the front line in the battle to preserve and protect the supposed sanctity of the Anglo-Saxons. And perhaps not surprisingly, some of the very figures we first encountered in Indiana resurfaced in Virginia.

Hoosier Connections to the Old Dominion

In 1910, Arthur H. Estabrook, along with Charles Davenport and Harry H. Laughlin, founded the Eugenics Records Office (ERO) in Cold Spring Harbor, New York. The ERO quickly turned into a flagship institution for hereditary research in the United States. Meanwhile, Estabrook's research took him from the Berkshire Hills of western Massachusetts to Indiana and to upstate New York. He and Davenport first coauthored *The Nam Family: A Study in Cacogenics* with support from the ERO.[35] The Nams were descendants of the "Dutch or English" and belonged to the "Revolutionary generation." According to the two eugenics researchers, "[they] had intermarried little with immigrant stock, and were therefore strictly American." But by the middle of the nineteenth century, the Nam family settled in the hilly western half of the state and steadily declined. They participated in "unconventional" behavior, including nonprocreative sex, miscegenation, and, worst of all, incest.[36]

Estabrook's next study, *The Jukes in 1915,* reinforced the findings from *The Nam Family.* Estabrook traveled to rural New York to follow up on a well-known family first written about by amateur ethnographer Richard Dugdale nearly forty years earlier. Despite the passage of time, Estabrook concluded that nearly all "the girls and young women were very comely in appearance and loose in morals."[37] The Jukes still constituted a "community of criminal men, semi-industrious laborers, and licentious women."[38] The Nam and Juke family studies propelled Estabrook's career as a eugenicist. Following his time in Massachusetts and New York, he then went to Indiana to work with the CMD. He and fellow researchers reexamined McCulloch's work on the Ishmaels and surveyed the extensive damage done to the state by the so-called mental defectives who arrived from elsewhere. Estabrook's experience in the Midwest suggested that the path to understanding Anglo-Saxon collapse ultimately passed through the upland South.

He arrived in Virginia soon after the implementation of the Racial Integrity Act of 1924 and as the Carrie Buck case wove through the lower courts.[39] Estabrook and his assistant, Ivan E. McDougle, traveled to the state's hilly interior; there they found a "mongrelized area" that warranted close scrutiny. They first came across some racially mixed mountaineers they called "Isshies." The moniker evoked Indiana's Ishmaels as well as former slaves to whom Union troops "issued" freedom during the Civil War. These freedmen and women had moved to the countryside and "amalgamated" with Native Americans, Estabrook and McDougle hypothesized. Eventually the Isshies introduced "Indian and Negro blood" to the vulnerable Anglo-Saxon population.[40] These "White, Indian, Negro" families became the basis of Estabrook and McDougle's study, *Mongrel Virginians: The Win Tribe* (1926).

The two men scoured the area for more evidence of "mongrelization." They sent their findings to each other and left behind dozens of letters and notes. In one correspondence, they referred to a man named Silas Branham, "a typical coon although he has straight hair."[41] A woman named Emma Willis John looked "exactly like a mulatto . . . a mean white woman who had a little negro blood in her," according to Estabrook.[42] "Triple crosses," like the Willis and Branham family, lived in "one or two room shacks so often found in areas where there is low mental and social development."[43] An unnamed white woman who lived in "Guilder Hollow" had a reputation for "chastity and moderate intelligence" until she settled down with a "lazy and unambitious" Native American man who "would not pay his debts."[44] Though the couple never married, they had several "mongrelized children" who behaved erratically. A once-upstanding woman in the "Brown family . . . mixed with full-blooded Indians," and another woman named Belinda Jones "mated with a half negro." The children of these women, the two men agreed, were "very ignorant and amounted to nothing."[45] No matter what their ancestry may have been, they had now all joined the ranks of the triple-cross Win tribe and had set forth on a path of hereditary decline.

Estabrook thus largely blamed the mongrelization of Virginia on a relatively small but critical number of Anglo-Saxon women who had betrayed their race and amalgamated with African-American or Native American men.[46] This narrative rehearsed notions of fallen white womanhood and stoked the familiar flames of passion that arose on the topic of interracial sex, especially between white women and men of color. It also located the causes of deterioration externally, rooted in the proliferation of so-called mongrel blood. In other words, Estabrook believed that deviant and impoverished Virginians were not "pure" Anglo-Saxons or Teutonics at all. Instead, degraded triple-crosses, the progeny of prohibited unions, compromised the state's racial integrity and caused intractable problems. This at once upheld his preconceived belief in white supremacy, but it also made clear the high stakes of maintaining the color line.

Still, Estabrook's assessment of the region as one teetering on the brink of collapse, "mongrelized" by triple crosses on the one hand and a few licentious white women who coveted African-American and Native-American men on the other hand, contradicted other studies of western Virginia. Mandel Sherman and Cora B. Key, child development specialists who studied Virginia's Blue Ridge population, published their work at about the same time as Estabrook and McDougle. They too located the "ancestry of these people" and found that "mountain children" displayed many troubling characteristics such as low intelligence and laziness.[47] In contrast to the Win Tribe, the families who lived among the Blue Ridge, Sherman and Key proposed, "were settled in the pre-colonial period by English and Scotch-Irish immigrants. . . . They are descendants of the original settlers who married relatives and mixed very little with the people outside of the hollows."[48] Between 1929 and 1933, as Estabrook proposed dangerous levels of racial mixing, Sherman and Key concluded the opposite: "Since the ancestry of the children of all Hollows came from the same stock the claim cannot be made that some of the of these mountain people are 'degenerate' and therefore their children are expected to be retarded intellectually, a claim too often advanced for the supposed inferiority of isolated mountain children."[49]

Sherman coauthored his next study with Thomas Henry, a eugenicist and field researcher. Their book, *The Hollow Folk* (1933), detailed the "origins" of the Colvin, Needles, Oakton, and Rigby families from Virginia's Cumberland

Gap. These families were "almost pure Anglo-Saxon stock, sheltered in tiny, mud-plastered cabins and supported by primitive agriculture" and underwent "steady deterioration."[50] But while Sherman, Key, and Henry differed with Estabrook and McDougle over whether Virginia's rural mountaineers were mongrelized or pure, they all claimed to have witnessed troubling levels of degeneracy. In addition, none believed that the descendants of "original settlers" could have lived in such poverty without some intervening circumstances or scientific explanation. Estabrook traced the degeneracy to the introduction of inferior blood; Sherman blamed the low intelligence of the region's children on environmental factors such as social and economic isolation.

The region confounded others as well. Madison Grant believed that "poor whites of the Cumberland Mountains" were "men of Nordic breed," but some "hereditary forces [are] at work that are little understood."[51] Travel writers Horace Kephart and John C. Campbell, neither affiliated with the eugenics movement, gained some fame through their descriptions of the Appalachian mountaineer.[52] Campbell playfully critiqued how perfunctory it had become to claim the "Southland" as a bastion of the "purest Anglo-Saxon blood." "Few discourses on mountain questions," Campbell wrote, "are complete without this reference."[53] To correct the record, he instead proposed that the region "seems . . . saturated with the Anglo-Celt idiom to the exclusion of every other."[54] As overdetermined as these differences sound to the modern observer, Sherman, Key, Grant, Kephart, and Campbell, all believed that western Virginia's rugged terrain harbored an exceptional population, and they agreed that these men and women had descended from white settlers who came from the British Isles hundreds of years earlier. Precisely which British Isles, however, remained a matter of dispute. In any case, of the five, only Estabrook and his assistant recorded widespread mixing among African Americans, Native Americans, and whites.

Not surprisingly, Estabrook's tendentious findings perfectly suited his eugenics credentials and his advocacy for the Racial Integrity Act of 1924. He even included the text of the law in the appendix of *Mongrel Virginians* as a model for other state governments to adopt. His research in Virginia affirmed his hypothesis: "It is evident from this study that the intellectual level of the Negro and the Indian race as now found is below the white." In nearly all instances, Estabrook concluded, "The white stock . . . was at least of normal ability [before] amalgamation." Afterwards, Estabrook and McDougle wrote, "the general level of the white lowered in the mixing."[55] In sum, the two men believed they had uncovered indisputable evidence that the "white race" was at least "average." Frighteningly, however, "one drop" of inferior blood had irreversible consequences. This, the authors stridently resolved, was not a "theory or . . . a prejudiced point of view but a careful summary of the facts of history."[56]

Estabrook's self-assuredness apparently boosted his credibility as leading public officials called on him for counsel. As he and McDougle finalized *Mongrel Virginians,* the Supreme Court of Appeals in Virginia and shortly after, the Supreme Court of the United States, summoned the two men to testify against Carrie Buck.[57] One Virginia justice asked, "Have you personally made any investigation of Carrie Buck and her ancestry with a view of passing upon the probable heredity of her descendants?"[58] Estabrook "made a brief study" of the Buck women (Carrie and her mother, Emma) and found "the evidence points to the fact that Emma Buck is a feeble-minded woman . . . [who] has had three feeble-minded children by unknown fathers."[59] Estabrook reminded the justices that Emma Buck had not married and was thus predisposed to commit deviant sexual acts. According to Estabrook, present deviancy reliably predicted future devolution. The Bucks already had seemingly borne this out: first with Emma, then with Carrie, and finally with Vivian. Hence, Virginia authorities made the proper decision to sterilize Carrie Buck to prevent further decline.[60]

Harry Laughlin also appeared before the Supreme Court to defend Virginia's law and testify against Buck. He concurred with Estabrook: the Buck women "belong to the shiftless, ignorant, and worthless class of anti-social whites of the South whose parentage cannot be determined."[61] Carrie Buck simply confirmed her "life long record of moral delinquency" when she had "born one child illegitimately."[62] As troublingly for Laughlin, Buck's parentage was a mystery, and he wondered whether her family was purely white or if miscegenation had occurred long ago. Without visual evidence of racial mixing, she required an inscription, or a way to physically mark and define what was otherwise nebulous and unknown. And since miscegenation could not definitively be proven without knowing one's parentage, Laughlin advocated sterilization as an effective way to "mitigate race degeneracy."[63]

Put differently, the surgical procedure registered Carrie Buck as an official purveyor of racial deterioration, but it also halted further decline. If Estabrook's facts of history had proven Anglo-Saxon supremacy, he nevertheless conceded that history could sometimes be reversed. Carrie Buck and the mongrel Virginians evidenced sexual deviancy, miscegenation, and poverty as the chief ways to undo the achievements of an otherwise formidable race. As in Indiana, Virginia authorities perceived themselves amid an epidemic of de-

"Triple mixtures" (Caucasian-Indian-Negro) in Robeson County, North Carolina, from Arthur Estabrook's scrapbook of field photographs. Courtesy of the Arthur Estabrook Collection, SUNY Albany.

generacy and acted accordingly. After the *Buck* decision, Virginians stepped up their efforts in what historian Edwin Black has called "mountain sweeps," targeting "hillfolk" throughout the southwestern corner of the commonwealth.[64]

Virginia's efforts exposed the tenuousness of purity and revealed the fragile fault line between supremacy and decay. But the quest for Anglo-Saxon purity implied an earnest belief that there existed such a concept with which to begin; for the efforts to work, there needed to be a population for whom the state's policies protected and strengthened. And rather than fixate solely on the failures—the Bucks, the Wins, the Ishmaels, or the countless other families who hailed from the upland South—some thought it necessary to showcase examples of successful preservation. Here again, John Powell emerged as an instrumental actor. After successfully lobbying the state legislature to pass the Racial Integrity Act of 1924, he returned to his first passion: music. In the expanse of the Blue Ridge Mountains, Powell searched for the folk music that his European rivals claimed did not exist. The music of the hills, Powell believed, exhibited unadulterated Anglo-Saxon culture. He wanted to prove the naysayers wrong and display the artistic contributions of these men and women before it was too late.

A John Powell Reprise: From the Halls of the Capitol to the Hills of "Old Virginny"

The professional music community greeted Powell's political advocacy with ambivalence. Some wondered if he could sustain a career as both a composer and a white supremacist. One writer for the *Musical Courier* wrote that Powell had compromised his status as an elite musician with his divergence into Virginia politics. Powell retorted, "There are matters which are of more importance than the personal welfare and career of any individual. If the work of the Anglo-Saxon Clubs should demand the sacrifice of my musical career—which is highly improbable—I trust that I shall not hesitate to meet the demand."[65] After Virginia legislators passed the legislation he had ardently lobbied for and the Supreme Court upheld sterilization, Powell began his next project and returned to music.

Powell long held that "The beauty of Anglo-Saxon folk music surpasses any other in the whole wide world"; now that he had completed his work on racial integrity, he had the time to prove it.[66] In the western corner of Virginia, Powell believed he had found music that "embraced all historical periods of the race from Lord Randall . . . of the Teutonic migrations to the Green Mossy Banks of the Lea," to North American colonization.[67] These men and women offset some of the impact of amalgamation, and for Powell they provided the strongest evidence of Anglo-Saxon supremacy. He decided that a music and arts festival was the best way to bring attention to the hills and advertise his findings. The composer chose Virginia's second highest peak, Whitetop Mountain in Grayson County, as the setting for a celebration of all that was refined and beautiful about those who had retained their "racial composite."[68]

Much to his dismay, like the missionaries who arrived in the southern mountains over thirty years earlier, Powell found that poverty and bad behavior infused much of Grayson County's population. He still hoped that music "remedied" the "alien and uncouth" mountaineers.[69] Aside from their lowly condition, Powell certified that they had the "innate musical gift of our race . . . which, consequently, is reattainable by us, their descendants."[70] Curiously then, Powell imposed on those who should have already possessed a superior culture that which he *expected* to find. In effect, he created an "authentic" Anglo-Saxon culture in the absence of one. And far from building on local customs from the bottom up, the festival developed into a grotesque spectacle, what historian David Whisnant has referred to as "cultural manipulation" from the top down.[71]

Held among scenic overlooks, the festival grounds offered majestic views of the Blue Ridge Mountains as they soared over Virginia, North Carolina, and Tennessee. First called the Interstate or Tri-State Music Festival, Powell settled on the name, White Top Folk Festival (named after the nearby fifty-two-hundred-foot peak, Whitetop Mountain).[72] The event ran from 1931 through 1939. Powell cancelled the festival in 1940 after heavy rains flooded the site and made it unsuitable for the gathering. To finance the festival, Powell required assistance from real estate speculator John Blakemore; he solicited the folklorist and mountain enthusiast Annabel Morris Buchanan for artistic and production assistance. Like Powell, Blakemore held white supremacist beliefs, but he was foremost a businessman who wanted to develop the festival grounds and the five-thousand-foot mountain into a destination for East Coast vacationers.[73] His interest in a music festival went as far as it produced still more lucrative opportunities. As the Great Depression deepened throughout the 1930s, the festival failed to spur the tourism Blakemore had anticipated, and he eventually rescinded support. And while the music festival never approached the numbers that the three organizers had originally envisioned, it nevertheless drew tens of thousands of people from the upland South and beyond. It also gained some high praise along the way.[74]

Powell had two goals for the festival. Primarily, he "organized [it] in 1931, as an endeavor to discover and preserve the best Anglo-Saxon music, balladry, arts, and traditions."[75] Second, Powell conceived of the festival as a corrective to the surging popularity of what the nascent recording industry called "hillbilly music." Upon signing lucrative contracts with OKeh and Document Records, Ernest Stoneman, Dock Boggs, the Carter Family, and Al Hopkins and his Hillbillies, among others, became overnight sensations. Record executives in New York City and Chicago packaged and sold this music to a growing base of middle-class consumers.[76] These hillbilly musicians displayed a bucolic folk aesthetic that contravened 1920s opulence and anticipated Depression-era populism. But for Powell, they bolstered stereotypes of rural, white southerners as uneducated simpletons with poor taste and little talent. With their hayseed image and lack of sophistication, they offended the classical musician's sensibilities. Most of all, though, Powell believed they were unbefitting heirs to the vaunted Anglo-Saxons. In response to such vulgarity, he demanded that all performances at his festival "be traditional, of real worth (no 'hill-billy' music permitted)."[77] Ironically then, Powell's festival simply exchanged and reproduced one fabricated tradition for another.

Just as Carrie Buck sullied Anglo-Saxon womanhood with her deviant behavior, the singing hillbilly misrepresented the noble southern mountaineer's heritage, according to Powell. To the composer, Yankee businessmen profited from the singing hillbillies and romanticized the apparent backwardness of the upland South. At the same time, they ignored the supposed achievements of its people. Crude stereotypes, promoted and marketed by those without knowledge of western Virginia's distinguished history, obscured the "direct and unestranged" link these men and women shared with "the original English settlers."[78] "Our race, from the earliest of times, has shown the true mark of genius," Powell theorized. Hillbilly music, on the other hand, displayed man's base instincts and lacked artistic merit.[79]

Hence the festival served Powell's pedagogical and ideological aims. It reconnected native-born whites to their true, if forgotten, identity. The future of the country depended on the success of the festival, Powell proclaimed. "We have seen that our only hope for a nation in America," the musician added with urgency, "lies in our grafting the stock of our culture on the Anglo-Saxon root." Further, Powell wanted the festival to rekindle "our racial psychology."[80] Still with a chip on his shoulder, he recalled his experience in Europe: "The Anglo-Saxon peoples had been looked down upon as the most unmusical of civilized races."[81] But if the festival succeeded, "this misconception was not only dispelled, but it was manifested that the Anglo-Saxons possessed the richest, most varied, and most profoundly beautiful folk music in the world."[82] The festival's performers then needed to fulfill the lofty expectations Powell established with his promotional rhetoric.

Tents and stages greeted patrons as they entered the festival grounds. Crowds gawked at fiddle and dance competitions, Elizabethan era plays, and balladeering youngsters and elders alike. Attendees who desired a more interactive experience could enroll in onsite courses such as "Emotional and technical quality of Anglo-Saxon Folk Music" or "Old English Native Dance."[83] In addition to performances and workshops, Powell organized a conference with some of the era's leading folklorists, journalists, and race theorists. The formality of this event signaled Powell's intention to make the festival as much an intellectual and academic experience as it was entertainment. He wanted all in attendance to bear in mind the serious considerations in the midst of the daily pageantry.

Powell's 1933 keynote address conveyed how important it was for the tri-state area of western Virginia, eastern Kentucky, and East Tennessee to ward off miscegenation and degeneracy. Only then was it "possible for us to draw inspiration from this great treasure of folk music that is at our disposal."[84] Powell concluded, "Deep in the mountains of Virginia, North Carolina, Kentucky, and Tennessee, where dwell the descendants of the purest Anglo-Saxon stock in America, also lies their simple expression in ballads and folk tunes, constituting the fundamental impulse of native white America."[85] Later, he echoed Ralph Waldo Emerson's "double-distilled" thesis. The musician proclaimed Anglo-Saxons had evolved further in the United States than they had elsewhere and composed the better race than those who stayed in England: "The mountaineer is freer in his manner, more alert, and less inarticulate than his British prototype and bears no trace of the obsequiousness of manner which, since the enclosure Acts robbed him of his independence and made of him a hired laborer."[86] In the expanse of "10,000 square miles . . . larger than England, Scotland and Wales [combined]," Powell's mountaineer pacified the wilderness and improved on an already strong "racial composite."[87]

This historical interpretation of the southern mountains recalled Emerson, but it also parroted Theodore Roosevelt, Ellen Churchill Semple, and Nathaniel Southgate Shaler. These figures emphasized how the circumstances that greeted the Anglo-Saxon in North America—the frontier and its readily available land, coupled with the incessant wars of conquest against Native Americans—ensured the virility and manly independence of the upland southerner and explained his unwillingness to succumb to wage labor. By locating the White Top Folk Festival amid these tropes, Powell articulated a familiar refrain. He also attached a transcendent purpose to the week of amusements and frivolity.

And indeed, Powell's work paid off. The festival, at least in its early years, was well attended. Between 1931 and 1935, White Top garnered crowds in the thousands; it peaked in 1933 when Powell invited Eleanor Roosevelt as a guest of honor.[88] Attendees and critics alike praised Powell's event. One reviewer witnessed "the joys and tragedies of Anglo-Saxon history . . . epitomized in the folk tunes and dances . . . by the bearers of the Southern tradition."[89] The reporter beamed, "The White Top Festival [created] a true appreciation of beautiful music—a combative influence to jazz—and to save for posterity those ancient tunes that sprang from the native emotions of our race."[90] To this critic, the festival succeeded precisely because it disavowed music closely associated with African Americans.

Likewise, another critic, Vanderbilt University's George Pullen Jackson, asked his readers in the *Southern Literary Messenger:* "Is American folk music beautiful?"[91] The professor replied, "A definite denial was given by White Top experiences to cynical and unwarranted doubts as to the innate musicality of the Anglo-Saxon racial composite in America."[92] These critics praised the festival for capturing an increasingly rare and unadulterated culture, and they credited Powell with challenging the ascendant genres of jazz and hillbilly music. Not coincidentally, these genres exemplified the two looming threats to Anglo-Saxons: miscegenation in the case of jazz and degeneracy in the case of hillbilly music. Finally, in the aftermath of the Racial Integrity Act of 1924 and the resolution of *Buck v. Bell* (1927), the festival issued a glimpse into what a purified Virginia might look like if the damage wrought by years of mongrelization could be reversed.

Whitetop Mountain and Its Environs: Myths and Realities

Even though Powell's festival hinged on pseudoscientific notions of race and biology, the Whitetop Mountain area was a surprisingly diverse corner of the commonwealth. The actual demographics of Virginia's Blue Ridge and the surrounding mountain communities undermined what Powell had so elaborately forged. In this regard, Powell joined William Wallace Harney, Mary N. Murfree, John Fox Jr., and many others who had etched the southern mountains into the nation's imaginary as an isolated reserve of Anglo-Saxon innocence. As historian Kenneth Noe has reminded us, enslaved people built many of the railroads in southwestern Virginia, and many freedmen lived there well after the Civil War.[93] David Whisnant has pointed out in his study of the festival that several African American families had lived in Grayson County for generations.[94]

More recently, some scholars have claimed that Melungeons—a hybrid population of Mediterranean, Sephardic Jewish, North African, and Roma ethnicities—may have peopled the very hills that perplexed Estabrook and enamored Powell.[95] Proponents of this thesis suggest that a forgotten and even lost community of East Europeans, Anatolians, and North Africans had arrived as early as the sixteenth century and settled in southern Appalachia. Neither Anglo-Saxon nor Teutonic, these settlers were ethnically mixed and culturally vibrant, leaving an indelible imprint on American culture.[96] In addition, folklorist Cecelia Conway has excavated the banjo's long history and traced it from West Africa to the Mississippi River Delta of the American South; only after several decades did it make its way into the mountains, where poor whites embraced it. At least a handful of black banjo players probably lived in and around the same hollows where Powell recruited musicians. Undoubtedly, black mountaineers shaped Powell's very conception of Anglo-Saxon folk music, as well as the culture that he so brazenly appropriated.[97] This was but one irony of Powell's obsession with the color line. Much of the music he lauded as authentic bore the influences of over three hundred years of cultural exchange, or what Estabrook would have uncomfortably referred to as mongrelization.

While Powell disavowed this history, others did acknowledge the mountains' diversity. Annabel Morris Buchanan recognized the contributions African Americans made to the region's music and proposed to include black performers in the festival. She wrote in a letter to Powell, "Everyone knows your views on racial integrity, but . . . we owe it to our negro musicians to pay some attention to what they are doing, especially because they're doing considerably better choral work than anybody else in Virginia."[98] Powell refused. "Negro music," he exclaimed, "when analyzed is almost as meager and monotonous as the Red Indian music."[99] He added, "Many of the best known negro songs are now known to be compositions of white men, as, for example Stephen Foster's songs. And the Negro spirituals, it has now been discovered, are also chiefly European in their origins."[100] John Blakemore sided with Powell's assessment over Buchanan's request for the limited inclusion of African Americans. When asked if he would include "Negro spirituals," Blakemore curtly replied, "No Negro contestants are permitted and there have never been any on the mountain."[101] Blakemore, like Powell, was more determined to uphold the fantasy of White Top than to showcase the region's multicultural reality. This was not surprising since both men never intended the festival to celebrate Virginia's true demographics. Indeed, they desired to do quite the opposite; theirs was a mission of racial rejuvenation predicated upon the dubious fiction of Anglo-Saxon purity and supremacy.

However, though Blakemore may have shared Powell's ideology, as an investor he was more concerned with the festival's profitability. And by the late 1930s, interest waned and ticket sales slumped.[102] In 1940 Blakemore abandoned his plan to turn the rural mountain into a tony resort; shortly thereafter he withdrew his funding. Powell had to look elsewhere. Ever persistent, the musician secured money from Chicago's Wrigley Company. He sent out a press release to radio stations around the country and announced that Wrigley Gum "proudly sponsored the White Top Folk Festival . . . Preserving the best of Anglo-Saxon traditions, August 15–17, 1940."[103] Powell moved forward with the event, booked performers, and organized the annual conference; by all appearances, the festival was poised to enter a new decade, albeit without the quixotic buzz it commanded ten years earlier.

Unfortunately for both Powell and his new sponsor, rain fell relentlessly on the mountaintop, and the grounds turned into a swampy, treacherous mud pit as the date drew near. The 1940 flood forced Powell to cancel; making matters worse the famous chewing gum manufacturers opted out of their sponsorship. By early 1941, after he failed to court benefactors, Powell's festival lay moribund. At one point, he even contacted the eminent British historian and diplomat John Wheeler-Bennett. As a man who hobnobbed with looming twentieth-century figures like Winston Churchill, Leon Trotsky, and Benito Mussolini, Wheeler-Bennett also wrote the official biography of King George VI. In Powell's mind this made him something of an Anglo-Saxon extraordinaire.[104] Powell presumably met Wheeler-Bennett when both men were briefly at the University of Virginia. There, the historian evidently grew enamored with the American South and the institution of slavery.[105] It is not clear how well the two knew each other, but Powell was at least comfortable enough to request that Wheeler-Bennett exert his clout and lobby the British parliament to sponsor the festival. The native Virginian cajoled the British historian, "Of all such ties, that which lie closest to my heart and possess potentially the most compelling emotional appeal is the common heritage of folk music . . . the supreme embodiment of the fundamental emotional and cultural oneness of all English-speaking peoples."[106] In the midst of increasing belligerency in Europe and the Pacific, Powell believed his festival would solidify the transatlantic bond between the two nations.

More likely, these same tensions relegated the festival to an afterthought for John Bennett-Wheeler and other Britons who may have supported Powell under different circumstances. As the Nazi Blitz terrorized Londoners over the first months of 1941, a festival in rural Virginia was not among anyone's top priorities, except of course a composer who had earnestly believed that Anglo-Saxon folk music could save civilization. Nonetheless, neither the Parliament of Great Britain nor Wrigley Gum saved White Top. Moreover, music festivals, a hallmark of the late 1920s and 1930s, lost much their popularity as the world fell into another catastrophic war. The White Top Folk Festival and its peer events tapped a national anxiety over the Great Depression. Each of the festivals—typically set in rural locations with atmospherics reminiscent of a religious revival—harkened back to an era free from the oscillations of industrial capitalism.[107] Folklorist Percy MacKaye believed White Top and other festivals like it represented a social movement, what he referred to as "the age of the folk against the machine."[108] But by decade's end, the populism of the Depression Era had faded into the nationalist fervor of war and militarism.

More basically, the war effort ensured that Anglo-Saxons served alongside Italian Americans, Irish Americans, Polish Americans, Jews, and others upon whom Powell looked with suspicion. Given this context, it seems unlikely that audiences would have continued to flock to a festival built so explicitly on a narrow definition of white supremacy. Whatever the reasons, Powell's fantasyland—channeled through the seemingly innocuous medium of a music festival—ended with the opening of the new decade. Alarmingly, however, the eugenics movement that Powell had so enthusiastically embraced spread to points far beyond the Virginia hills with consequences more horrific than the musician may have foreseen.[109] But throughout, the fascination with the southern mountains and rural music endured. And to Powell's disappointment, regional stereotypes such as that of the hillbilly continued to challenge his favored image of Elizabethan era fiddlers.

Still, with its contrived meddling and manipulated spectacles, the White Top Folk Festival served its promoters' purposes, as deceptive as they may have been. At a time when racial hierarchies exhibited many vexing inconsistencies, the festival assured all in attendance that there not only existed an exceptional Anglo-Saxon culture but also a preserve of strong blood to restore Virginia, and maybe even the nation, from a biological collapse that seemed to have steadily unfolded for over a generation. Powell's uncontaminated musician had avoided the sexual improprieties of someone like Carrie Buck, as well as the miscegenation that necessitated the Racial Integrity Act of 1924. But then again, this same White Top performer was susceptible to degeneracy. Thus, these fragile men and women required both the protection and veneration of the state.

Powell's festival never garnered the notoriety of either *Buck v. Bell* or the Racial Integrity Act of 1924. His vision of Anglo-Saxon folk music never exceeded the popularity of hillbilly music or jazz. But the festival responded to them all. It was a referendum on the home region of Boone, Crockett, and other lauded frontiersmen. Interwar Virginia also reopened a host of familiar questions. Would the state's western hills be identified with singing hillbillies? Or would they be regarded as John Fox Jr. and John Powell had proposed: an endangered bastion of Anglo-Saxon innocence? Did the era's leading eugenicists rediscover deep in the Blue Ridge a salve for a nation wracked by degeneracy and miscegenation? Or did Carrie Buck, along with Arthur H. Estabrook's "mongrel Virginians," signal that they had arrived too late? For nearly a decade, summers on Whitetop Mountain provided more than a setting for a folk festival. The grassy bald that offered panoramic views of three states from a towering fifty-five hundred feet thus doubled as an ideological battleground where such questions could be contested and negotiated. Few had convincing answers.

Legacies of the US American Eugenics Movement

As a grim postscript to this and the previous chapter, as well as to segue into the next, let us recall Harry H. Laughlin's trip to Nazi Germany. A colleague of Estabrook's at the Eugenics Record Office, Laughlin had drafted Virginia's Sterilization Act. Like Estabrook, he too testified against Carrie Buck. His theories circulated throughout the United States and informed Powell's event well before an infamous Austrian extended eugenics to its appalling extreme.[110] For certain, the brutal machinations of the Third Reich made Powell's attempt to construct a utopia in western Virginia appear comparatively benign if deeply offensive to our present-day judgment. That said, aside from their outcomes and aesthetics, Hitler's laws to "protect German blood," Harry Sharp's Indiana Plan, Harry H. Laughlin's *Model Eugenical Sterilization Law,* and John Powell's White Top Folk Festival shared a common ideological foundation of flawed scientific assuredness, biological determinism, and virulent racism.[111]

In the tragic wake of the Nazi Holocaust—a campaign explicitly designed to "cleanse" Germany of its alleged impurities and contaminants in ways more assertive and violent than racial integrity legislation, immigration restriction, and sterilization—the American eugenics movement and its intellectual standard bearers rightly fell from the graces of acceptable science and political thought. But they fell only so far. And although Laughlin never received the official recognition in the United States that the Nazis bestowed upon him, many states in his native country clung to their sterilization laws, and they continued to deploy the procedure well after the atrocities committed by Hitler's regime came to light.[112] It took several more decades before the Supreme Court dismantled Virginia's Racial Integrity Act of 1924 and its accompanying ban on interracial marriage in the landmark case *Loving v. Virginia* (1967). As noted, Indiana kept its sterilization laws on the books until they were quietly repealed in 1974.[113]

However, even as states and the federal government slowly overturned such laws, dispelling the faulty logic behind them was a more difficult task. In fact, when Richard Herrnstein and Charles Murray published their controversial collaboration, *The Bell Curve,* in 1994, the ideas of Laughlin, Estabrook, and Davenport received another hearing.[114] The *New York Times* bestseller resuscitated theories about the supposed genetic underpinnings of poverty. Critically, it was even introduced as evidence to further weaken the nation's floundering welfare state. A must-read among Newt Gingrich's Republican colleagues after they swept both chambers of Congress in the 1994 midterm elections, Herrnstein and Murray's study repackaged and updated many of the conclusions that the ERO had reached over seventy years earlier, namely that there existed a correlation among one's intelligence, socioeconomic status, and race.[115]

Led by Gingrich, the 104th Congress used the contentious findings in *The Bell Curve* as well as Murray's earlier work *Losing Ground* to promote the Personal Responsibility and Work Opportunity Act of 1996, commonly referred to as "welfare reform."[116] If poverty resulted from the cultural and embodied pathologies of maladjusted men and women, then statist solutions proposed by midcentury liberals were bound to fail. To the contrary, the federal government's policies had actually incentivized laziness and eroded poor peoples' work ethic, Gingrich proposed. The legislation, signed by Bill Clinton, reduced federal assistance to many of the nation's poorest families. With rather striking efficiency and sweeping implications, the Republican-controlled Congress and Clinton's Democratic administration overturned some key New Deal and Great Society era public policies. The new law supplanted Aid for Families with Dependent Children (AFDC) with a more stringent program known as Temporary Assistance for Needy Families (TANF). With stricter requirements to receive assistance, eligibility predictably shrank; this led President Clinton to famously declare the "end of welfare as we know it."[117] Historians have more recently concluded that TANF, while indisputably cutting the welfare rolls, has put financial pressure on poor people and has disproportionately affected women and single mothers. As poverty rates have increased over the past two decades, welfare reform has locked millions of poor women and men into a low-wage work force that has proven exceedingly difficult to exit.[118]

Herrnstein, Murray, and the 104th Congress undoubtedly exercised more caution in their conclusions about the poor than did the earlier generation of eugenicists. While the thesis of *The Bell Curve* sounded familiar to historians of the American eugenics movement, the two authors mostly avoided the contention that Nordics, Teutonics, or Anglo-Saxons had demonstrated superior intelligence and behavior.[119] Instead, *The Bell Curve* opted for a broader, more complex conception of whiteness, one that has evolved over the past half-century to encompass the mosaic of "white ethnics" that were once regarded with suspicion. Likewise, the two researchers never singled out a specific American region for its supposed purity. Still, Herrnstein and Murray affirmed that economic inequality and what they described as cultural dysfunction were reflections of "ethnic differences in cognitive ability."[120] The influential argument thus reignited the proposition that innate racial differences more actively shaped one's social mobility than did the entrenched legacies of racism, sexism, classism, and ableism.[121]

John Powell. Library of Congress.

The Bell Curve's success also illustrated the sway that deterministic arguments still held, even as the heyday of eugenics receded further into the past.[122] However, to bridge the work of Powell and Laughlin's generation to that of Herrnstein and Murray skips a step. Sustained economic growth occurred throughout much of the nation during the post–World War II decades, but not in the upland South. Consequently, politicians and journalists were again taken aback by a startling reappearance of Anglo-Saxon collapse. So while these chapters have presented some responses to the jarring paradox of poverty during the first half of the twentieth century, it remained unresolved well into the second half.

The next chapters reconsider the domestic policies and popular culture of the postwar era in light of what we have uncovered thus far. In a climactic moment, Lyndon Johnson declared a war on poverty in 1964. He did so on the heels of a highly publicized tour through West Virginia and eastern Kentucky, where he met an unemployed mill worker named Tom Fletcher. The porch of Fletcher's home in Inez, Kentucky, provided the backdrop for many memorable photographs of Johnson's trip. Nestled in the Cumberland Mountains, Fletcher's abode was about equidistant between Whitetop Mountain in Grayson County, Virginia, and Switzerland County, Indiana. If Fletcher's family had relocated across the Ohio River to Indiana sixty years earlier, as had thousands of other eastern Kentuckians, it is plausible that they too may have attracted the attention of Indiana's Committee on Mental Defectives. If his family had instead chosen to move southeast to Virginia, perhaps they might have been the subjects of Arthur H. Estabrook's study or recruited by Powell for his festival. But in a different time and space, Fletcher and his family stood at the center of a photo op with a US president who personally assured him that his life would improve.

Times had certainly changed. But as we will see, some well-known postwar liberals made assumptions similar to those who authored Indiana's sterilization laws and the Virginia Racial Integrity Act of 1924 and organized the White Top Folk Festival. Obviously there are profound differences between prewar and postwar movements to rescue and strengthen a racially illustrious population. However, as chapter 4 attests, the commonalities are too often overlooked and deserve some critical attention.

CHAPTER 4

WEST VIRGINIA MOUNTAINEERS, KENTUCKY FRONTIERSMEN, AND THE RHETORIC OF POSTWAR LIBERALISM

These farmers, miners, and mechanics from the mountains and meadows of the mid-South—with their fecund wives and numerous children—are, in a sense, the prototype of what the "superior" American should be, white Protestants from early American, Anglo-Saxon stock; but on the streets of Chicago they seem to be the American dream gone berserk.
—Albert N. Votaw, 1958[1]

Writing for *Harper's Magazine,* Albert Votaw announced that a dangerous multitude of poor whites had invaded Chicago. More generally, his article referred to the mass migration of 3.2 million white southerners to industrial cities in the North and West in the years surrounding World War II.[2] These men and women reshaped the urban fabric of neighborhoods like Chicago's Uptown, the Briggs section of Detroit, and Cincinnati's Over-the-Rhine district. Considerable numbers of upland southerners also flocked to smaller cities like Columbus, Dayton, and Indianapolis.[3] As Votaw suggested, longtime city dwellers did not always welcome these newcomers, and some migrants never quite adjusted to the culture and pace of city life.

James Maxwell, a journalist for the cosmopolitan, New York-based magazine, the *Reporter,* anticipated Votaw's piece by a few months. But rather than Chicago, Maxwell detailed Indianapolis, a hometown of Oscar McCulloch and the Tribe of Ishmael. He interviewed a woman who "was not a New Yorker denouncing Puerto Ricans or a San Franciscan belaboring Mexicans" but was instead a native-born Hoosier troubled by the corrosive influence of "hillbillies."[4] Maxwell found the woman's admission remarkable because these same people were "usually considered to be the most favored in American society—

the white Anglo-Saxon Protestants."[5] Reminiscent of what CMD researchers found fifty years earlier, Maxwell estimated that "one out of every four persons born in Kentucky" ended up in Indiana; their "moral standards," he wrote, "would shame an alley cat."[6] A few years later, Jean Shepherd, one of postwar America's trenchant humorists, claimed in his best-selling, semiautobiographical story collection *In God We Trust: All Others Pay Cash,* "Indiana is full of primeval types who've drifted up from the restless hills of Kentucky and the gulches of Tennessee." These violent and tempestuous "hillbillies," according to Shepherd, used dynamite to celebrate, feud, and fish; it was their "milk of life."[7]

Maxwell, Shepherd, and Votaw reached familiar conclusions about the southern mountains and called to mind familiar contradictions that had long characterized the region's people. Their respective tones, whether delivered in humor or horror, echoed the ambivalence of not only the Indiana eugenicists who sought to repair the state's racial hygiene but also Theodore Roosevelt's *The Winning of the West.* As we know, Roosevelt and some of his outspoken colleagues had theorized that Kentucky backwoodsmen were a stalwart race who kept the flame of the frontier burning brightly.[8] They evolved "to grapple with the wilderness and to hew out of it a prosperous commonwealth."[9] But Roosevelt also loathed poor southern whites and described them as crackers and squatters who spread the "seeds of vicious, idle pauperism and semicriminality."[10] With confusion bordering on indignation, postwar observers voiced a cognitive dissonance that Roosevelt may well have recognized. The latter's conception of "hardy backwoods stock" wavered uneasily between racial strength and semicriminality. Over fifty years later, a journalist for *Harper's* witnessed the "American Dream gone berserk," and the *Reporter* feared that the "most favored in American society" had been reduced to brusque hillbillies.[11]

The troubling paradox of a superior population mired in economic, cultural, and biological malaise thus extended into the 1950s and 1960s.[12] And as the next two chapters attest, the paradox continued to have great consequences for the nation's public policy and popular culture. The resurgent perception of racial and manly deterioration helped foster the impetus for the War on Poverty and rallied a new generation of reform-minded public servants and intellectuals around issues of identity and economic inequality. Indeed, as Theodore Roosevelt and other Progressive Era figures perceived the declension of virile white men, so too did midcentury liberals like John F. Kennedy, Michael Harrington, Harry M. Caudill, Lyndon B. Johnson, and others. The strategies to address this decline had changed drastically, but Progressives such as Roosevelt and liberals like Kennedy both shared the conviction that the state had the duty to prevent destitution among a venerable population.

Historians have studied the racialized and gendered contours of postwar liberalism. Jill Quadagno, Michael B. Katz, and Martin Gilens have explained how racism undermined the War on Poverty, especially as images of so-called undeserving African Americans dominated the media by the late 1960s and 1970s.[13] Another prevalent narrative has positioned white liberals as comfortable allies with the civil rights movement and has emphasized how African American activists worked at the local level with sympathetic politicians at the federal level to dismantle Jim Crow from the bottom up and battle poverty.[14] Other studies have focused on the Democratic Party and the sectional realignment of the two major political parties that occurred after the passage of the Civil Rights Act of 1964.[15]

However, historians who have proposed that the War on Poverty responded to unresolved problems in black America are most relevant to this argument. From their perspective, white liberals in the 1960s fashioned policies to correct the shortcomings of the New Deal. One eminent historian of modern liberalism, Ira Katznelson, has written, "When President Johnson in 1964 announced a 'Great Society' effort to eradicate poverty and complete the New Deal, it was widely understood to be an effort directed at black poverty and the exclusion of African Americans from the middle-class mainstream."[16] Another widely cited study, Allen J. Matusow's *The Unraveling of America*, provides a social and a political history of the 1960s. According to Matusow, sociologists Lloyd Ohlin and Richard Cloward's theories to mitigate juvenile delinquency in New York City presaged innovative components of the War on Poverty, namely the Community Action Programs.[17] Ultimately, contends Matusow, "The war on poverty began, in short, because the civil rights movement was educating whites to the realities of black deprivation and because deprived blacks were mute no longer."[18] Without question, the Civil Rights and Economic Opportunity Acts of 1964 empowered millions of poor people of color; however, as Matusow later concedes, this was an unintended consequence of the poverty program, as not even Johnson, let alone most white voters, approved of, desired, or even understood the implications of community action.[19]

James L. Sundquist, a leading advocate for antipoverty legislation and an adviser to Presidents Kennedy and Johnson, captured this point when he argued, "The War on Poverty did not arise, as have many great national programs, from the pressure of overwhelming public demand; the poor had no lobby."[20] Nevertheless, the ambitious legislation yielded electoral vindication. Not even three months after Johnson signed the Economic Opportunity Act of 1964 into law, he and his fellow Democrats consolidated power in one of the most lopsided elections in modern US history. The party captured sixty-eight seats in the US Senate and nearly three hundred in the House of Representatives; Johnson won 61 percent of the popular vote.[21] That the Democratic sweep occurred not quite a year after the assassination of John F. Kennedy suggests that liberals benefited from a national tragedy still weighing upon the electorate. In addition, Barry Goldwater's brand of insurgent conservatism had little draw beyond disaffected segregationists and required a few decades to gestate before it crystallized into modern GOP orthodoxy.[22] These considerations aside, voters clearly responded to Johnson's promise to complete what his predecessor had begun. Yet scholars of the period have neglected the key images and rhetoric that led many Americans to embrace liberalism in the 1950s and early 1960s. In the process, they have also failed to connect the continuities of race, culture, and reform from the first half of the century to the second.

Here, the influential arguments of Matusow and Katznelson are instructional, if flawed. Given the rhetoric of several white liberals in the postwar decades, as well as the long-running concerns with Anglo-Saxon collapse examined thus far, it is overly optimistic and perhaps quixotic to accept their desire to be "educated" by the civil rights movement or to assume that the War on Poverty was "widely understood" to target African Americans and complete the New Deal. If anything, most poverty warriors fixated on white men, particularly that American "prototype" from the southern mountains whom Votaw, Maxwell, and Shepherd had thoroughly scorned.

What follows here is neither a policy history of the War on Poverty nor an exploration of the relationship between white liberals and black activists in the civil rights movement. There are many terrific studies on those topics, but this chapter instead critiques the rhetorical and visual representation of poverty. It explains how racialized and gendered anxieties, conveyed through the ambivalent cultural legacy of frontier masculinity, molded the political discourse of the late 1950s and early 1960s in ways historians have not adequately considered. Set against the backdrop of pre–World War II notions of race and identity, this chapter reframes how celebrated white liberals approached poverty and why they concluded that it was a national crisis. It also reconfigures our understanding of how and why the War on Poverty originated and under what conditions it received support.[23] As long as economic inequality had a white face, liberals could speak authoritatively about class, quietly ally with moderate civil rights activists, and maintain an electoral mandate, albeit briefly.

First, this chapter details the postwar "rediscovery" of poverty by journalists, academics, and politicians. Next, it positions John F. Kennedy's 1960 primary campaign in West Virginia as a pivotal moment in the making of postwar liberalism, one that built on a preexisting discourse of white masculine restoration. Throughout the state's depressed mining towns, Kennedy articulated a vision that later became the Area Redevelopment Act of 1961 (ARA). Notwithstanding its limitations, the ARA was an important harbinger of the War on Poverty. The chapter then analyzes the work of Michael Harrington and Harry Caudill, two prominent antipoverty activists. Harrington's *The Other America: Poverty in the United States* (1962) and Caudill's *Night Comes to the Cumberlands: A Biography of a Depressed Area* (1963) were widely read within the Kennedy and Johnson administrations, respectively. Beyond others, these books informed the policies of the 1960s and issued stunning indictments of an economic system that left many behind. This chapter concludes with President Johnson's symbolic trip to Tom Fletcher's home in Inez, Kentucky. The April 1964 visit to the unemployed lumber-mill worker was central to Johnson's high-profile lobbying effort on behalf of the Economic Opportunity Act; he signed the bill into law four months later.[24] Throughout the 1960s, West Virginia mountaineers and Kentucky frontiersmen were symbolic figures on which the national discussion on race, gender, and economic inequality pivoted. With few exceptions, the paradox of purity and the fear of racial collapse hung over these discussions.

The Rediscovery of Poverty and the Making of a President

Not all journalists shared Votaw and Maxwell's vitriol. Some had sympathy for poor whites from the upland South, and few more so than two-time Pulitzer Prize-winning *New York Times* reporter Homer Bigart. During the late 1950s and early 1960s, he wrote extensively about the transformation of the coal industry in Appalachia.[25] His first piece on the topic appeared on the front page of the *New York Times* on January 11, 1959. The headline read, "Depression Rivaling '30s Grips Kentucky-Virginia Coal Area." Bigart detailed the Harlan County, Kentucky, workforce that had contracted from nearly thirteen thousand to five thousand men. Mechanization and stagnant wages threw over ten thousand "destitute" individuals in the county onto an ill-equipped relief system.[26] A month later Bigart traveled to West Virginia, where he uncovered more of the same. Across the Cumberland Mountains, unemployment was seldom under 15 percent, he reported. Forty-five thousand miners had run through their unemployment benefits, and as many as three hundred thousand people throughout West Virginia and eastern Kentucky relied on "mollygrub," the locals' term for "the monthly dole of Federal surplus foods."[27]

The crisis brought with it crimes of desperation. Some hard-pressed men found prison an acceptable alternative to unemployment since it ensured public assistance for their families. A sheriff in West Virginia remarked, "A man who can't support his wife can do it by going to jail."[28] To Bigart, there was something particularly troublesome about a man who deliberately broke the law to provide for his wife and children, especially in southern Appalachia, where coal mining was among the manliest of professions and where the miner had long maintained a rugged persona, deeply embedded in the unforgiving landscape. Bigart lamented, "Gone is the frontier bravado, the sense of adventure, the self-reliance that once marked the Kentucky mountaineer."[29] These men extracted from the hills the very resources that fueled an industrial revolution and propelled the United States into a global superpower. That they now resorted to petty crime exposed the weaknesses of the welfare system. In a nation where affluence had spread to nearly all corners, noted Bigart, the Appalachian miner was conspicuously left out.

Of course, upland southerners were not the only ones who failed to participate in the postwar boom. As a correspondent for the *New York Times* and a resident of that newspaper's city, Bigart did not need to travel five hundred miles to find a story about poverty. He could have walked mere blocks to find conditions rivaling the misery of the southern coalfields. In Harlem and the South Bronx, for example, poor blacks and Latinos faced unemployment of over 30 percent, and about half of the population lived in poverty.[30] More generally, between 1959 and 1963, nonwhites across the United States suffered chronic unemployment consistently above 10 percent, and the poverty rate exceeded 40 percent.[31] Bigart never explained what drew him to Appalachia, and nothing suggests that he was indifferent to the impact of economic despair on people of color. Regardless, Bigart's emphasis struck a chord, and the spectacle of white poverty gripped the media.[32]

As Bigart wrote about the depression in coal country, Harry W. Ernst and Charles H. Drake coauthored a piece entitled "The Lost Appalachians: Poor, Proud and Primitive" for the *Nation*. Ernst and Drake indicted the coal industry for recklessly exploiting West Virginia's natural resources while offering hardship to the people. "Although white Protestants of old American stock," the article contended, Appalachian migrants to northern cities "face the same prejudice that traditionally has made life uncomfortable for strangers in new lands."[33] Not long after, the *Saturday Evening Post* ran its own cover story, "The Strange Case of West Virginia." Journalist Roul Tunley detailed the crushing poverty in the state but quickly reminded readers of what he believed was West Virginia's strongest asset: its demographics. He interviewed several West Virginians, one of whom told the reporter that in spite of its impoverishment, "There's nothing wrong with the people. . . . They're intelligent and conscientious and want to give a day's work for a day's pay." Tunley agreed and added, "Largely native born, Anglo-Saxon stock, [West Virginians] strike the visitor as gentle, proud, polite and full of kindness to strangers."[34] Writing about West Virginia apparently required, as it had for so long, at least one reference to the exalted legacy of the state's people.

Later that year, the *Washington Post* ran its own feature story about the southern mountains; this one concluded with a call to action. Like the *New York Times,* the *Post* sent a well-regarded journalist, Julius Duscha, to cover "the country's worst blighted area, the Appalachian Region." On cue, Duscha informed his readers, "Relief has become a way of life for once proud and aggressively independent mountain families." He reasoned, "many of them [are] descendants of pioneer American families," and they were "victims of a modern civilization that is often as heartless as it is efficient." Duscha described the same problems that Bigart had detailed: the mechanization of the coal industry; the exploitation of natural resources by outside corporate interests; rampant unemployment among men, young and old; and the inability or unwillingness of the rural population to leave for better opportunities elsewhere. And here again the reporter reminded his readers that the mountains "were settled 200 and more years ago in pre–Revolutionary War times, primarily by Anglo-Saxon immigrants from the Eastern Seaboard." Duscha concluded that some industry had come back to the "proud hills," but not enough to shore up the faltering economy. As a result, he implored "the Federal Government as well as the states in the area . . . to establish a special relief program" for older people and public works programs for younger, jobless men.[35]

Ernst, Drake, Tunley, and Duscha reiterated what many had believed and anticipated what others would soon propose about West Virginia. Jennings Randolph, the state's senior US senator, repeatedly made claims about the exceptionalism of his constituents. After witnessing coal operators lay off hundreds of miners, Senator Randolph spoke before the Senate Subcommittee on Production and Stabilization in a March 1959 hearing in Beckley, West

Virginia. He chastised the state's business leaders and politicians: "The men and women of West Virginia are descendants of a stalwart race of pioneers . . . who valued the free life for the opportunities it offered the individual to develop his own latent powers. Their descendants today prize the same values." They just needed some vocational training and programs to connect to prospective employers.[36] Amid a heated Democratic primary in early 1960, many party leaders, including Randolph, had become proponents of a federally administered antipoverty program. By reminding their audience that whites were poor and cloaking any potential response to the economic crisis in the language of uplift, some emphasized the necessity of rehabilitating a "pioneer race" endangered by a rapidly changing economy. This rhetoric dramatically framed the incongruity of poverty in the midst of the sustained economic growth.

No one, however, mobilized the rhetoric and images of white poverty as effectively as did John F. Kennedy during the early months of 1960. As the

John F. Kennedy talks with miners in West Virginia during the Presidential Primary campaign. Courtesy of the President's Collection, John F. Kennedy Presidential Library and Museum, Boston.

senator from Massachusetts commenced his presidential bid, the West Virginia mountaineer took center stage. It was well known that Kennedy needed support from the state in both the primary and the general elections, and he was prepared to spend ample time, energy, and money there. His success hinged on his ability to court the very people whom Randolph had called "a stalwart race of pioneers." The primary campaign initiated a relationship between the eventual occupant of the White House and West Virginians that culminated in some of the era's notable legislation. Above all, the campaign demonstrated Kennedy's willingness to attach some of his policy objectives to the mission of revitalizing white manhood.

The Democratic primaries went into high gear that spring, and the dramatic plotline involved the race among John F. Kennedy, Hubert H. Humphrey, and Lyndon B. Johnson. If Kennedy proved viable in the South, his path to the nomination became considerably easier. Overwhelmingly Protestant and working class, West Virginians were said to be suspicious of a Catholic from an elite New England family. *Time* succinctly claimed that "mountaineer Protestants [were] likely to be wary of a Roman Catholic candidate."[37] To win, Kennedy needed votes from the same people who sent Robert Carlyle Byrd, a former member of the Ku Klux Klan, to the US Senate. Byrd, avowedly anti-Catholic and a segregationist, urged West Virginians to reject Kennedy and cast their votes for the Texas-born Protestant, Lyndon B. Johnson. (Johnson's name, however, never actually appeared on the state's primary ballot.) Meeting the culture clash head-on, Kennedy dug in and practically took up residency in West Virginia. After campaigning lightly in March and extensively throughout April and early May, Kennedy, to the surprise of many, won the May 10 primary with a decisive 60 percent of the vote.[38]

It took more than a ubiquitous presence in West Virginia to win the state's delegates, though. Equally crucial were the messages Kennedy delivered and the promises he made. With a press corps documenting each speech, the Massachusetts senator stressed the hard times that had recently befallen the population. But still he always reminded them that they were heirs to laudable frontiersmen, steeped in a history of patriotic service to the country. He urged West Virginians to move beyond their religiously informed skepticism, address the environmental damage wrought by the "blindness of men," and entrust him with rehabilitating the state's proud "heritage."[39] The *New York Times* reported, "Mr. Kennedy hammered at the theme of Federal neglect of a staunch and worthy people."[40] He stressed to the swelling crowds, "It was West Virginians who led the American forces to France in World War I. Thousands of your citizens fought and bled on the far-flung battlefields of World War II. . . . And West Virginia again led the nation in Korea, where a higher proportion of West Virginians shed their blood in the fight against Communism than those from any other state."[41]

After delivering these lines, the senator spoke of the need to award additional defense contracts to the state. "Of all the 50 states," Kennedy refrained, "your State is last in defense payrolls, last in defense employment and last in the amount of money spent by the Defense Department. . . . As a result, many of West Virginia's plants lie idle, your skilled and vigorous men are out of work, and your resources are untapped."[42] If the mountaineer had so willingly served overseas and fought in the nation's great conflicts, he reasoned, it was only fair to fully incorporate him into the military-industrial complex at home.

The candidate highlighted these themes at each campaign stop. Speaking in Glenwood Park, a small town in Mercer County, centrally located among rocky, unproductive soil and decommissioned coal mines, the senator accused Republicans of sending "overseas under our surplus food disposal program, beef, chicken, turkeys, ducks, pork, sausage, potatoes, milk, orange juice, peaches, cherries and other fruits and vegetables," while West Virginians ate "only flour, rice and corn-meal."[43] Such a paltry diet could not "maintain the strength of your men," Kennedy said as he proposed a new food-assistance program.[44] He concluded his speech by reciting lyrics to an old folk song, "Give me men to match my mountains."[45] Kennedy observed that, luckily, "West Virginia already has men to match her mountains—men of vigor and courage and determination—men who have contributed to America's strength in the past and who will contribute again in the future."[46] Kennedy and the press repeatedly employed such adjectives as *staunch, worthy, vigorous,* and *proud* to describe the poor whites of the southern mountains. This language implicitly contrasted with those who were presumably not worthy, or who lacked vigor and were lame, inadequate, and inferior. This subtle tripling of race, manliness, and service was the bedrock of Kennedy's campaign message; it was also a powerful position from which to advocate a poverty program for the Mountain State.[47]

Before increasingly large and enthusiastic crowds, Kennedy sharpened his message in the days leading up to the election. Speaking in the state capital, Charleston, he declared, "Of course West Virginians are not asking for handouts—for charity—or for special treatment. The people of West Virginia are a proud and independent people—typical of the best of American life."[48] At another stop the presidential hopeful castigated Dwight D. Eisenhower for his outspoken concern with poverty in seemingly remote places like China and India but his failure to address the problem in the United States. The Democrat suggested, "Mr. Eisenhower should come here [to West Virginia] after he has seen Asia and see that good American citizens need help also."[49] Kennedy thus indulged many Americans' isolationist impulse and their wariness of foreign and humanitarian aid, particularly since hardship persisted among so many at home. These speeches also afforded Kennedy another opportunity to confer a privileged citizenship upon West Virginians that, because of their so-called heritage, entitled them to defense contracts, food assistance, wage supports, job training, and educational funding. The benefits he proposed would place a socioeconomic floor that "worthy" mountaineers, "typical of the best in American life," could not fall below.

Only at the margins did Kennedy cautiously broach juvenile delinquency, African-American poverty, and civil rights, opting instead to focus on West Virginia and the plight of poor whites. *Jet* magazine writer, Simeon S. Booker, registered his frustration with Kennedy's detachment from the black community during the campaign and his early presidency. Booker, among the most well-connected and respected black reporters in the United States, "had no contact with the Kennedys" before the campaign. He recalled, "I had covered Washington . . . about ten years and the Kennedys just never crossed those areas that I covered, civil rights, human rights."[50] Booker felt that JFK "wasn't conversant in civil rights, in all of the sectional sides of it. He wasn't familiar."[51] After all, Kennedy had voted with the Mississippi segregationist James O. Eastland in rendering the 1957 Civil Rights Act unenforceable.[52] To Booker and others involved in the fledgling movement, the Massachusetts senator was far from an ally, approaching something closer to an obstructionist if not a reactionary.

Throughout the 1950s Kennedy was more divided over civil rights than was his eventual presidential competitor, Richard M. Nixon. And the Democratic campaign, Booker reported, was "very, very dull. . . . There was no emphasis on Negroes here or there."[53] "The Negro wasn't part of the technical machinery of the primary," Booker argued, and Kennedy gained little from directly courting the civil rights movement. Kennedy did not want to alienate the southern wing of the party.[54] In contrast, Booker remembered, "Nixon had won a lot of respect in the Negro community." Unlike Kennedy, Booker remembered, Nixon had "joined the NAACP [National Association for the Advancement of Colored People]; he had gone around and spoke to Negro groups; he'd gone to Africa."[55] The vice president, rather than the Massachusetts senator, appeared poised to continue Eisenhower's precedent and cautiously introduce federal power, if necessary, to desegregate the South. With a strong contingent of Dixie-crats flanked by a sizable cohort of northern Democrats who were indifferent towards racial equality, a civil rights alliance between African Americans and white liberals within the Republican Party seemed plausible at the onset of the 1960 campaign.

So it was at least somewhat surprising that Kennedy skillfully moved be-yond his lackluster record and won 68 percent of the nonwhite vote. To his credit, Kennedy pledged to advance the Democratic Party's national platform and support civil rights, which he eventually did. Furthermore, his famous mid-October phone call to Coretta Scott King, voicing support for her impris-oned husband, was reported widely in the black press and evidently compelled many to give the Democrat a second look. Overall, Kennedy dexterously molli-fied white southerners, many of whom were undoubtedly segregationists, while he slowly approached the moderate goals of the civil rights movement. In one of the closest elections in US history, Kennedy edged Nixon by just over one hundred thousand votes among the 68 million ballots cast. And even though he won only 38 percent of the Protestant vote nationally, Kennedy secured key southern states like Georgia, the Carolinas, Missouri, and Arkansas, in addi-tion to West Virginia; choosing rival Lyndon B. Johnson as a running mate ensured Democratic success in Texas. Weaker numbers in any of these demo-graphic groups or states would have ushered Nixon into the White House.[56]

Given the time and effort Kennedy devoted to West Virginia, his victory there ranks near the top of his political achievements: it established the senator as a formidable campaigner and an acceptable choice for non-Catholic voters, and it gave him the appearance of being a fierce advocate for the rural poor. Pulitzer Prize-winning journalist and psychiatrist Robert Coles explained it clearly: "In 1960 John F. Kennedy went before Appalachia's poor rural Protes-tant people to ask their help in his quest for the Presidency. They said yes to him, those 'hillbillies' did, with their long bodies and craggy faces and their Prot-estant Anglo-Saxon heritage."[57] Daniel Patrick Moynihan, one of Kennedy's closest advisers, agreed. He described the West Virginians whom Kennedy met during the campaign as "a decent, but impotent, people of impeccable pioneer origin," and he challenged his fellow Catholic to pass "the crucial test," win the primary and then the presidency, and, finally, restore the dignity of the state's esteemed population.[58] Moynihan believed the primary had a trans-formative impact on his friend and colleague: "Commitments were made in West Virginia and, just as important, impressions were gained that remained with the Kennedy administration throughout."[59] Both Coles and Moynihan understood how essential it was to gain the support of poor whites in West Virginia; they also knew that the campaign rhetoric would require legislative action and a bold agenda once Kennedy won the nomination and, eventually, the presidency.

More important, Coles, Moynihan, and the rest of the Kennedy team learned how racialized and gendered liberalism delivered a politically advantageous opportunity to engage the nation in a frank (if vastly incomplete) discussion about the chronic problem of poverty and inequality. They also tapped into a rich seam of American nostalgia and mythology. Two months after leaving the Mountain State a victor, Kennedy trekked west to officially receive his party's nomination at the Democratic National Convention in Los Angeles. Here, the campaign's rhetoric of manly pioneers and courageous frontiersmen came to a rousing crescendo as the newly minted nominee paid homage to the nation's history of settler colonialism:

> I stand tonight facing west on what was once the last frontier.
> From the lands that stretch three thousand miles behind me,
> the pioneers of old gave up their safety, their comfort and
> sometimes their lives to build a new world here in the West. . . .
> Their motto was not "every man for himself"—but "all for the
> common cause." They were determined to make that new world
> strong and free, to overcome its hazards and its hardships, to
> conquer the enemies that threatened from without and within.[60]

By locating a communal spirit within the pioneers, Kennedy contravened Frederick J. Turner's myth of the West as the proving ground for American individualism. But Kennedy also celebrated the frontier as the primordial space where an exceptional American identity, forged through the righteous conquest of enemies, came to fruition. Some enemies were dangerous rogue settlers (from within); others were presumably hostile Indians or nations (from without). Both, however, had to be eliminated.

Kennedy's metaphor clarified and brought purpose to his agenda. He at once celebrated the conquest of the continent by heroic settlers, but he also wanted to conquer a "New Frontier." This one, "the frontier of the 1960s," would not be subdued with six shooters and the US Cavalry. Instead, it required a sustained engagement with "the uncharted areas of science and space, unsolved problems of peace and war, unconquered pockets of ignorance and prejudice, unanswered questions of poverty and surplus." But, Kennedy urged, like the pioneers of past centuries, his fellow citizens should conceive of themselves as "pioneers on that New Frontier." The campaign revealed how Kennedy had internalized the mythology of the frontier and defined his policies as a continuation of a longer colonial project. He had, after all, structured the most important speech he had ever given in his career to that point around the very iconography that had served him so well in West Virginia. Pioneers and frontiersmen were thus the gift that kept on giving for the Kennedy campaign.[61]

By affixing such potent symbolism to his candidacy and indeed to his party's platform, Kennedy accomplished something else as well. Whether or not it was a concerted strategy, the senator's celebration of white manhood was rivaled only by his clear enunciation of its vulnerabilities. Such an ambivalent evaluation then opened a space from which questions of economic justice and federal involvement could be considered apart from the civil rights movement. Therefore, addressing structural inequality and the maldistribution of wealth and power meant primarily rescuing poor white men and their families from entrenched poverty and despair; civil rights, on the other hand, could be framed as an issue of basic political fairness, void of any redistributive measures and benignly (and conveniently) separated from the solutions sought by the movement's more radical activists. In other words, as long as "those craggy Anglo-Saxons" were the most visible actors on this new frontier, liberals risked little political capital—they may have actually gained some—as they engaged issues of class and inequality in ways not seen since the 1930s.

Policy, Poverty Warriors, and the Progressive Tradition

Once in the White House, Kennedy fulfilled some of his campaign promises. On May 1, 1961, he signed the Area Redevelopment Act, a flagship domestic program of his New Frontier agenda. It provided up to $75 million annually to "help areas of substantial and persistent unemployment and underemployment to take effective steps in planning and financing their economic redevelopment."[62] The ARA was not a new idea; it was a revised version of the Depressed Areas Act written by Senator Paul H. Douglas, a Democrat from Illinois, and sponsored by Kennedy but vetoed three times by President Eisenhower.[63] Critics noted that funding for area redevelopment fell more generously on the congressional districts where Kennedy had nourished indispensable political alliances.[64] Pennsylvania, Kentucky, and West Virginia had the highest concentrations of the 114 "areas" considered economically depressed.[65]

The ARA did not solve the problems associated with deindustrialization and chronic impoverishment in the designated areas, including within those counties and municipalities it targeted in the southern mountains. From its outset the act faced accusations from conservatives that it was socialistic and lacked a cohesive vision. With resources spread thinly across so many districts, the Area Redevelopment Administration quickly devolved into an ineffectual, poorly run bureaucracy. Ill equipped to handle the breadth of the region's economic problems and unable to gather the necessary political support to enact substantive changes, the ARA achieved few results.[66] In response, the Conference of Appalachian Governors lobbied Kennedy to create a separate program focused on rural poverty in the mountain South. At first reluctant, Kennedy eventually acquiesced, and in 1963 he created the President's Appalachian Regional Commission (PARC). That year, representatives from Ohio, Pennsylvania, Maryland, West Virginia, Kentucky, Tennessee, North Carolina, South Carolina, Virginia, Alabama, and Georgia discussed the problems unique to the region and proposed solutions.[67]

Later in 1962, the Ford Foundation funded a study that accompanied the establishment of the PARC. Edited by Thomas R. Ford and entitled *The Southern Appalachian Region,* the book collected contributions by leading academics and folklorists, and it fleshed out what was allegedly exceptional about the region, the issues it faced, and how best to confront them.[68] Ford argued that "the fierce independence and proud self-reliance of the highlander, a heritage of frontier life" presented at once great hopes and challenges best administered by a federal agency.[69] Another contributor, University of North Carolina sociologist Rupert B. Vance, explained, "Certainly the history of settlement offers no indication that people were shunted into the mountains nor that they were of inferior stock." He added that one could "impute no unworthiness to the populations involved."[70] Meanwhile, W. D. Weatherford and novelist Wilma Dykeman reinforced the belief that mountain southerners were "pioneers . . . who came first, remained stronger than the wilderness, and never let go of their grip on hope and courage."[71] "The dominating strain was Scotch," they contended; this accounted for the apparent tenacity and independence of the southern mountaineer.[72]

Overall, the study reminded its readers that southern Appalachia had always been rich in natural resources and acclaimed for its folk culture. However, its population of fertile Anglo-Saxon and Scotch women on the one hand and muscular, resourceful men on the other hand, was perhaps its greatest resource of all. Still, in terms of its popularity and the degree to which it informed public debate, the Ford study could not match two other momentous works appearing that same year. By the end of 1962, Michael Harrington had published *The Other America: Poverty in the United States,* and Harry Caudill released *Night Comes to the Cumberlands: A Biography of a Depressed Area.* Reaching a national readership, these works expanded the nation's fascination with poverty and decisively linked the fate of the decade's liberalism to the spectacle of downtrodden white mountaineers.[73]

The Other America is usually remembered as an early contribution to the postwar debate on poverty and inequality. But given the attention that journalists and politicians had already paid to the problem, Harrington's book arrived fairly late on the scene. Its release in March 1962 received little fanfare until literary critic Dwight Macdonald favorably reviewed it for the *New Yorker* in early 1963. Macdonald first discussed the "insular poverty of those who live in the rural South or in depressed areas like West Virginia."[74] Much of the review provided an in-depth statistical analysis of poverty that Macdonald believed Harrington had omitted. If he was short on statistics, Harrington nevertheless vividly detailed the dire economic straits that millions faced, including rural whites, migrants, and those most disproportionately affected, African Americans and the elderly. Harrington's biographer, Maurice Isserman, has noted that Harrington timed his study impeccably well, tapping into the burgeoning interest in poverty that arrived on the heels of Kennedy's West Virginia primary. Macdonald thus found a sympathetic audience to pitch Harrington's exposé.[75]

Even as Harrington analyzed inequality more comprehensively than others, he used precisely the same descriptive language as Kennedy and the contributors to the Ford study. Harrington introduced his readers to the other America with a portrayal of the southern mountains as a bucolic outpost of pioneer culture. To Harrington, the beautiful but remote hollows offered an escape "from the strains and tensions of the middle class."[76] He then intimated, "It is not just the physical beauty that blinds the city man to the reality of these hills." Rather, Harrington counseled, "They are of old American stock, many of them Anglo-Saxon, and old traditions still survive among them. Seeing in them a romantic image of mountain life as independent, self-reliant, and athletic, a tourist could pass through these valleys and observe only quaintness."[77] Hence what made poverty in this other America so pernicious was not its total invisibility but rather how it veiled itself in a shroud of rusticity. Those who traveled through the southern mountains, Harrington feared, might incorrectly conclude that the region's unfortunate people had chosen scarcity as a lifestyle. Indeed, it would have been unusual for Anglo-Saxons to live in squalor and destitution without some reasonable explanation. But that was exactly what Harrington witnessed. Far from admirably disavowing the trappings of bourgeois consumerism, the nation's "old American stock" teetered on the brink of collapse. The poor whites he encountered may have escaped the ennui of the suburban middle class, as well as the reckless opulence of the leisure class, but they did so by stubbornly resisting modernity. This attitude effectively neutralized any advantage the mountaineer may have accrued over the generations. But it nevertheless made them a worthy target of federal assistance.

Harrington, however, only began his book with a chapter on the mountain South, and overall the study assessed the complexities of poverty with incisive skill. Not all liberals matched Harrington's scope and content, and likely none believed as passionately in the redemption of white masculinity as much as Harry Caudill. A native of Whitesburg, Kentucky, Caudill left the Bluegrass State to serve in the army during World War II. Upon his return, he successfully ran for office as a state representative, a post he held for three terms. As an elected official, Caudill traveled throughout his district and state, and he grew outraged over what he perceived to be a rapacious coal industry's wholesale exploitation of Kentucky's environment and its people. More insidious still, alleged Caudill, was how thoroughly the industry appeared to have corrupted state government and turned it into an appendage of corporate control. In response, Caudill penned *Night Comes to the Cumberlands,* or what he described as "a biography of a depressed area," detailing the "rape" of his beloved Kentucky hills.[78]

Initially *Night Comes to the Cumberlands* received more acclaim than did *The Other America.* Caudill wrote what could be called a populist manifesto, situated comfortably within the nation's vibrant tradition of democratic and environmental activism, but, troublingly, it also evoked the biological determinism of Progressive Era racial theorists like Theodore Roosevelt and Madison Grant. Roosevelt heralded the trans-Appalachian West as the space where white men evolved by productively channeling their violent impulses toward the conquest of nature and people. Armed with a flawed understanding of natural selection, Roosevelt constructed elaborate social hierarchies and argued that Kentuckians were descendants of a Nordic race that spread south from Scandinavia to Scotland and then England. Eventually, the Nordics crossed the Atlantic and settled in North America; through brutal conflict with both the people and the environment of the new continent, their stock improved even further. Roosevelt categorized this new and superior breed of man alternatively as a Kentucky, backwoods, or American race.[79]

Writing at the end of the nineteenth century, Roosevelt's historical analysis prefigured some of the eugenicists' theories. And as discussed, one of its leading proponents, Madison Grant, secured federal protection for the declining bison population on the Great Plains, later worked to preserve the California Redwoods from the timber industry, and eventually took a lead role in the establishment of the Bronx Zoo.[80] Grant authored *The Passing of the Great Race* in that same spirit of preservation; it achieved widespread acclaim and greatly influenced the eugenics movement. Even more than Roosevelt's *Winning of the West,* Grant's magnum opus articulated the Teutonic Thesis as he argued that Teutonic, Nordic, and Anglo-Saxon men, naturally predisposed to conquer distant lands and people, had evolved into the world's strongest races. But Grant also feared that the descendants of these men had come into contact with lower-order people and faced a serious threat of contamination. Consequently, Grant, along with several others, proposed anti-immigration and anti-miscegenation measures to reverse the damaging effects of racial pollution.[81]

Caudill never adopted the primary tenets of the eugenics movement, and his political ideology departed significantly from those who did. Yet, he shared with them a rather vulgar understanding of evolution and biology, as well as a commitment to preserve what they regarded as endangered populations. In contrast to Grant and Roosevelt, Caudill believed racial mixing yielded new and exciting combinations of men, and Kentucky was ideal for this process to unfold. White settlers "fought the Indian as a beast," Caudill wrote, and they "unhesitatingly mated with the red man's squaws."[82] He continued, "White women and girls were frequently in short supply and great demand, and the frontier standards of beauty could not be high. . . . Great numbers of dusky aborigine women found their way into the pole cabins of the borderers—to bear broods of unruly half-breed children."[83] This sexually charged environment was "the spawning ground of such heroic American scouts as Daniel Boone, Simon Kenton, John Colter, Kit Carson, Jim Bridger, and others, who in buckskin jacket and leggings, with butcher knife, tomahawk and rifle, marked the trails for a century of westward migration."[84]

Caudill's Kentucky half-breed, a curious progeny of unholy bonds, was therefore a new race "spawned" from the white settlers' dual conquest of the wilderness on the one hand and indigenous womanhood on the other. The irony of Caudill's argument is as unmistakable as it is tragic. While he extended a rape metaphor to describe the coal industry's impact on the land and people, Caudill failed to acknowledge how sexual violation and domination, indeed rape, were central to the broader project of white-settler colonialism, the virtues of which he otherwise confidently extolled. Disturbingly, then, rather than problematize the brutality of sexual exploitation and patriarchal dominance, Caudill simply incorporated them into his narrative of evolution and manly triumph in North America.[85]

Like Kennedy, Caudill had updated a trope about the upland South that dated back to the late nineteenth century. Theodore Roosevelt once claimed that Kentuckians were pioneers, "intensely American stock" who had staged their violent conquest of the continent from the hills and valleys of Appalachia.[86] Caudill also echoed Nathaniel Southgate Shaler, whose writings, one recalls, deeply influenced Roosevelt. As Shaler argued that the Kentucky backcountry furnished men who were "a strength to Virginia in the Revolution, and their children gave character to the army of [Thomas J. "Stonewall"] Jackson in the Civil War," Caudill, in turn, reminded his readers of the selfless courage the Kentuckians had displayed during more recent conflicts.[87] "In the war of 1898 and again in 1917 thousands of boys 'jined the army,'" he wrote; "nineteen years later Breathitt County provided so many volunteers that it was the only county in the United States in which the draft never became operative."[88] Perhaps hyperbolically, Caudill claimed some men walked nearly two hundred miles from the easternmost hollows of the commonwealth to Lexington to volunteer, further illustrating how "the mountaineer was ardently patriotic."[89] These actions supplied indisputable proof to Caudill that Kentuckians had contributed more than any other people had to the rise of US supremacy. In sum, Kentucky frontiersmen settled the West, fending off native people and preparing the wilderness for private ownership; next, they valiantly fought and secured independence from a tyrannical crown; a few generations later they took up arms against misguided brothers and saved the Union; and since then, they labored in the coal mines and extracted the carbon-based nourishment for a mighty industrial economy.

Caudill's celebratory interpretation of history made the mountaineer's decline unacceptable and fueled his indignation. Indeed, the true Kentucky tragedy, he surmised, was that in the years after World War II an exceptional population had lost the outlet through which it had historically exhibited independence and masculinity. "Bit by bit," Caudill admonished, "[the Kentuckian's] self-reliance and initiative deteriorated into self-pity. . . . He became in countless cases, a Welfare malingerer."[90] A negligent coal industry reversed nature's course and effectively relegated the vaunted descendants of Boone, Crockett, Carson, and Jackson to a state of unemployed dependency. Rather than quelling the frontier and evolving further, these modern-day mountaineers appeared emasculated and could do little more than accept demoralizing "handouts." Outraged, Caudill determined that "condescending charity in any form is harmful to the moral fiber of a people," and cash assistance only kept them "on the dole."[91]

In response to these injustices, Caudill proposed several initiatives to put Kentuckians back to work. Most immediately, he advocated New Deal-style public works programs. Reminiscent of Oscar McCulloch's claim, the fate of race and manliness to Caudill was demonstrably linked to muscular work; confining otherwise virile white men to idleness invited dire consequences. Here again Caudill voiced concerns similar to those not only of McCulloch but also of Madison Grant and Theodore Roosevelt. The latter famously warned of the dangers from failing to live a "strenuous life," and Grant proposed that devolution was a deleterious side effect of advanced bureaucratic societies.[92] Grant also maintained that while the innate intelligence and analytical skills of Anglo-Saxon and Nordic men qualified them for middle and upper management, such work drained them of the very impulses that had strengthened the race in the first place. "The refusal of the [racially superior] native American to work with his hands when he can hire or import serfs to do manual labor for him is the prelude to his extinction, and the immigrant laborers are now breeding out their masters and killing by filth and by crowding as effectively as by the sword," Grant claimed.[93] The sedentary life of the managerial bureaucrat had led many native-born white men to contract neurasthenia, threatening them with permanent lameness and inadequacy.[94]

Likewise, Caudill feared that without muscular toil the mountaineer might languish to the point of extinction. Whether he tamed the wilderness, saved the Union, or mined coal, the Kentuckian had historically demonstrated his masculinity through one form of physical work or another. Now, in the absence of a frontier and at the mercy of coal barons, Kentucky men had become alienated from the source of their identity. Fittingly, Caudill's assessment was phallic in its allusions. The coal industry increasingly resorted to blasting the tops off of mountains (a method also known as strip mining and akin to contemporary mountaintop removal), at once exposing and easing access to the rich seams of bituminous coal while drastically reducing the need for costly, labor-intensive longwall mining.[95] And as operators stripped the southern mountains of their peaks, miners lost their vitality and their spiritual manhood, rendered impotent by an industry that no longer valued or required their labor. With well-positioned sticks of dynamite, operators accomplished what once required hundreds of miners working underground with pick and axe.

Consequently, Caudill urged the federal government "to organize projects on which idle men could work."[96]

Overall, Caudill's highly fictionalized and sentimentalized history of Kentucky, coupled with his deterministic understanding of race and biology reminiscent of those who wrote in a previous era, armed him with a dynamic set of rhetorical tools to craft an effective emotional appeal. Accordingly, the arguments of *Night Comes to the Cumberlands* successfully bridged the lamentable side of the Progressive Era with early 1960s liberalism like no other statement of the decade. Caudill's book also tapped the same zeitgeist as Kennedy's campaign, area redevelopment, Harrington's *The Other America,* and the Ford survey. Beyond simply lobbying for jobs, each hoped to achieve at least some level of racial and masculine restoration and feared that the revered Anglo-Saxon had fallen into disrepair; the state had the responsibility to intervene.

Since Caudill's emphasis on racial decline, manly labor, and military service artfully distilled Kennedy's campaign message, it should come as no surprise that the president's cabinet and closest advisers read the work and regarded it highly. Two examples included William L. Batt, an administrator for the Area Redevelopment Administration, and Theodore Sorenson, Kennedy's speechwriter and head counsel.[97] Secretary of the Interior Stewart L. Udall wrote the foreword to Caudill's book. Udall's background in a small Mormon community in rural Arizona rivaled Kennedy's in its cultural and social contrast to eastern Kentucky. Still, Udall shared Caudill's concern with industry's reckless environmental exploitation. And Udall, too, believed that it was unacceptable for upland southerners to live in dire poverty. "This is Daniel Boone country," the secretary proclaimed in the opening pages of *Night Comes to the Cumberlands,* "where Indians and then fiercely independent frontiersmen found in these isolated valleys the elements that sustained vigorous life." He continued, "Yet it is one of the ironies of our history that many of their descendants live there today in bleak and demoralizing poverty almost without parallel on this continent."[98]

What Udall described as an irony had once again become a full-blown national crisis, and it was time for action. As long as the public looked upon impoverished white people with consternation and sympathy, Kennedy was emboldened to raise them from the despair of broken-down mines and desolate hollows. True, the preferred tactics of men like Arthur H. Estabrook, Harry H. Laughlin, and Madison Grant lost favor; expanding a benevolent welfare state was a radically different approach than sterilization, the Indiana Plan, or "racial purging." But at root, the white-led reform movements of the twentieth century's first half and, subsequently, the postwar decades aspired to strengthen a heralded people from a prized American region. The methods certainly changed, but the goals and even some of language remained the same.

Toward a War on Poverty

By the end of 1963, as the Appalachian governors had forecasted, the Area Redevelopment Act of 1961 failed to achieve meaningful results in most of the districts it targeted. However, national attention was elsewhere as grief over the assassination of John F. Kennedy gripped the country. On the evening of November 22, minutes after doctors pronounced the thirty-fifth president dead, Lyndon B. Johnson, standing beside a widowed Jacqueline Kennedy, famously took the oath of office aboard Air Force One. As he did, Johnson inherited an agenda that a nation in mourning would overwhelmingly support, as well as one that he was determined to expand and make his own. Over the next year, the Johnson administration brainstormed new policies, bureaucracies, and legislation that culminated in the War on Poverty. Johnson based some of the programs on Kennedy's New Frontier, but others were altogether separate from what his predecessor might have pursued.[99]

Veterans of the Kennedy team, many of whom continued to work under Johnson, never forgot how the campaign images provided an urgent, emotional gloss to otherwise complicated and convoluted policy debates. Some felt the rhetoric of fallen whiteness was critical to stewarding legislation through Congress and sustaining its popular support. Adam Yarmolinsky, an architect of the War on Poverty, noted, "The original picture of the poverty program in the public eye was Appalachia."[100] He recalled defending the War on Poverty against critics who believed it provided undue benefits to African Americans: "Planners expected the poverty programs to offer very little for the blacks" because "most poor people are not black, [and] most black people are not poor." "If anything," Yarmolinsky concluded, "color it Appalachian if you were going to color it anything at all."[101] He later circulated a memorandum among Lyndon Johnson's poverty task force entitled, "Why the Poverty Program Is Not a Negro Program."[102] The memo reminded critics: "The poverty problem in Appalachia and the Ozarks was almost entirely a white problem and in the Deep South it was a white as well as a Negro problem."[103] Yarmolinsky instinctively recognized that any federal initiative the public believed assisted African Americans more than whites faced an uncertain future; he corrected anyone who concluded as much.

A few years later Yarmolinsky candidly revealed, "The crisis of the northern ghetto was simply not foreseen in anything like its present critical character by the draftsmen of the [War on Poverty] program."[104] One wonders what shape the decade's liberalism might have taken if the urban crisis had occurred at the beginning of the 1960s rather than at the middle and end. But statements from Yarmolinsky and Udall clarify the degree to which policy makers seemed primarily concerned with and responsive to economic hardship when it could be portrayed as falling undeservingly on white men from the upland South.

At the same time, however, poverty warriors rallied against the disenfranchisement and displays of terror that plagued the Jim Crow South. Most aligned themselves, at least tepidly, with a burgeoning civil rights movement.[105] And once it came to fruition, the War on Poverty led to an upsurge of black and Latino activism in northern and western cities, as well as in the South. Yet stemming the further decline of a historically privileged population, one that key political figures claimed had contributed to the nation's ascendance and military dominance, infused new urgency and meaning into postwar liberalism. Additionally, sustaining the emphasis on this population fomented the will to push a bold domestic agenda. West Virginia mountaineers and Kentucky frontiersmen, those rugged descendants of Daniel Boone and David Crockett, were thus ideal symbols to rally a nation around a novel set of social and economic policies.

Four years after John F. Kennedy campaigned across West Virginia for the votes that established his candidacy, Lyndon B. Johnson trekked across the Tug Fork River to Kentucky. There, he visited Tom Fletcher in Inez and then spoke in Paintsville, the next hollow to the west. Crowds lined his motorcade route, ten thousand people gathered for his speech in Paintsville, and nearly two thousand more greeted him in Inez; dozens of journalists and photographers also documented the president's so-called poverty tour. From the porch of Fletcher's modest home, Johnson urged Congress to pass the Economic Opportunity Act, which was then stalled in Congress.[106] Johnson, like Homer Bigart, needed only to stroll down his street to find impoverishment as severe as that on display for his photo op in eastern Kentucky. Similarly deplorable conditions persisted among broad swaths of the black population in Washington DC; thousands of impoverished Washingtonians lived within walking distance of the White House. That Johnson traveled more than five hundred miles, press in tow, rather than a few city blocks, was a simple political calculation. Symbols of a faded frontier, white people from the upland South also embodied a rustic folksiness, and they supposedly retained, in flesh and blood, a cherished link to the past. As bulldozers made way for more interstate high-ways and vapid housing developments, the affluent society could at least offer some assistance to the downtrodden pioneers who once occupied the apex of racial citizenship.

Daniel Boone had given way to Tom Fletcher. This startling and incongruous proposition ensured that economic inequality would receive a thorough public hearing in the early 1960s. It was not the first time that poverty exposed a crisis of white masculinity and raised the possibility of Anglo-Saxon collapse. Theodore Roosevelt called on a like-minded coalition of Progressives to save the "American race," supposedly found at its purest in Kentucky.[107] His distant cousin with the same last name, a rather popular president in his own right, proposed a New Deal that often displayed the faces of migrant Okies, Arkies, and miners as the people who would receive immediate and deserved aid.[108] We should locate the "rediscovery" of poverty in the upland South in this context. Historicizing the cultural legacy of frontier masculinity and the accompanying racial discourse in which it was embedded reconfigures our understanding of the origins of the War on Poverty and casts the decade's liberalism in fresh if unsettling light.

But politics were only one side of the coin. And as we have seen, culture weighed as heavily on the public's perception of race and poverty as did any stump speech by a presidential candidate or book written by a journalist or novelist. Indeed, culture and politics informed one another and composed a symbiotic relationship. If Tom Fletcher and the laid-off coal miners of southern West Virginia exemplified the need for relief, there also existed a countervailing image of southern whiteness. As the nation rediscovered poverty, *The Real McCoys, The Andy Griffith Show, The Beverly Hillbillies, Green Acres,* and *Petticoat Junction* amassed millions of primetime viewers. Aside from their differences, each program presented a romanticized, if at times troubling view of white southern identity. Writers, producers, and television executives explored the upland South more exhaustively than at any time since the local color movement, and they again used the region and its people as a vehicle to critique modern American life. For certain, no evidence suggests that the producers of these programs conspired with Michael Harrington or Harry Caudill, let alone the Kennedy or Johnson administrations, to craft their portrayals of southerners. Nevertheless, the political rhetoric of the late 1950s and early 1960s collided with popular culture. The confluence of the two shaped postwar liberalism; perhaps even more important, they sowed the seeds of its demise.

CHAPTER 5

PRIMETIME HILLBILLIES

Upland Southern Whiteness and Popular Culture in the Civil Rights Era

> Each week millions of Americans gather around their sets to watch this combination [*The Beverly Hillbillies, Green Acres*, and *Hee Haw*] which has to be the most intensive effort ever exerted by a nation to belittle, demean, and otherwise destroy a minority people within its boundaries. Within the three shows on one night hillbillies are shown being conned into buying the White House, coddling a talking pig, and rising from a corn-patch to crack the sickest jokes on TV.
>
> —James Branscome, 1971[1]

While Native Americans and African Americans might dispute Branscome's oft-cited, hyperbolic assessment of the Columbia Broadcasting System's (CBS) Tuesday evening line-up, his words have garnered affirmation from many scholars of the upland South.[2] To Branscome, an anti–strip mining activist who came of age with the environmental movement, the images that CBS beamed into millions of homes during the 1960s had proven that those who lived in or came from the southern mountains remained acceptable targets of ridicule. Others tempered their critiques but registered strong disapproval nonetheless. David E. Whisnant has likened the images of poor southern whites to "cultural imperialism"; John Egerton and Frye Gaillard objected to Al Capp's depiction of white southerners in his famous *Li'l Abner* comic strip as "pig-sty-wallowing ignoramuses."[3] Despite the mostly vulgar, exploitative representation of the region and its people, the stereotypical hillbillies brought ratings and revenue to television networks and newspapers across the nation.[4]

Since it premiered over fifty years ago, *The Beverly Hillbillies* is still one of the most acclaimed situation comedies in the history of television.[5] Likewise, *TV Guide* recently placed *The Andy Griffith Show* ninth on its list of the "Top 50 shows," noting that it never fell below seventh in the Nielson ratings; the program enjoyed its peak viewership during its final season in 1968.[6] *Petticoat Junction* and *Green Acres* capitalized on the same rural aesthetic as the other two with slightly less success. These programs gained popularity throughout the 1960s as Al Capp's *Li'l Abner* entered its third decade and became one of the longest-running, most beloved comic strips. The superlatives attached to all of these are aptly warranted, notwithstanding the opinions of their detractors, this author among them.[7] Still, the question remains: why did fictional characters from the upland South, including the Clampetts from the Ozarks, the McCoys from West Virginia, as well as denizens from fictional towns like Mayberry and Hootin' Holler, North Carolina, and Dogpatch, Kentucky (or maybe Arkansas), capture the imagination of the American public in the 1950s and 1960s?

This chapter proposes that the portrayal of white upland southerners offered a counterweight to the upheaval of the postwar decades. During the local color movement of the late nineteenth century and the folk festivals of the late 1920s and 1930s, white men and women from the rural South were seen as relics of racial innocence and symbols of familial and social stability. They allayed fears of immigration, miscegenation, and imperial expansion. Likewise, during the tumult of the late 1950s and 1960s, the hardscrabble lives of white southern characters, emblematic of the entrenched poverty with which many of these real-life men and women were forced to contend, offered a powerful plot device for writers, directors, and producers. By embracing normative notions of gender and sexuality, as well as exulting the pious conservatism of the white South, these characters and programs supplied opposition to the movement culture of the sixties, even as these same programs affirmed some of the goals of the Great Society welfare state. That their popularity peaked alongside the advance of liberalism—and waned with its decline—must not be overlooked.[8]

And while they were regarded as family-friendly, apolitical entertainment, these rural comedies proliferated in highly divisive years. Indeed, each presented, to varying degrees, romantic notions of a white South that stood as a bulwark against the perceived excesses of an increasingly pluralistic, diverse nation. Aside from the unflattering, hayseed image that they usually evoked, rural white southerners such as the McCoys and the Clampetts endorsed a period in the not-so-distant past of uncontested white rule and bucolic simplicity. In fact, if we accept the premise that the War on Poverty attracted middle-class voters partly because liberals had successfully framed the issue of economic inequality through the lens of southern masculinity in distress, the popularity of *The Beverly Hillbillies, The Andy Griffith Show, Green Acres,* and *Petticoat Junction* becomes more legible. After all, the subtle (and at times, not so subtle) iconography and performances that typified these programs overlapped with the debates surrounding the War on Poverty and offered the backdrop from which the decade's liberalism took shape.[9]

This chapter thus expands on what media critic Horace Newcomb has proposed about the omnipresence of hillbilly stereotypes. Newcomb largely agreed with his fellow critics as he recognized "the imperialistic, conservative, exploitative functions of television images of Appalachia." But he asserted that the shows and characters "also suggest other functions," making "it possible to demonstrate that the larger populace has historically used Appalachia for that liminal ground on which to criticize its own values, to challenge the 'acceptable' way of life with other attitudes."[10] Newcomb's liminal ground referred to the shifting sociopolitical terrain of postwar America. Accordingly, this chapter positions the comedic hillbilly of the 1950s and 1960s, that exemplary figure of Appalachia but also the Ozarks, as merely the latest paradoxical delegates of a region long characterized by its vexed relationship to the nation *writ large*. It then grafts these fictional white southerners onto some of the determinative events of the civil rights era and rejoins them to a broader context. The characters who appeared in comic strips and situation comedies offer another way to gauge the public perception of race and identity at a pivotal juncture of the century. The chapter concludes with CBS's so-called rural purge in the early 1970s, the sudden cancellation of nearly every show set in the upland South or about white southerners. This moment symbolized the retrenchment of mountaineers from their prominent, sometimes lead roles in popular and political culture.[11]

Literary and Comedic Precursors to the Televised Hillbilly

By the end of World War II, stereotypes of poor whites from the upland South were firmly embedded in the national imagination. These depictions wavered between the isolated, pure Anglo-Saxon and the quarrelsome hillbilly. Or, more commonly, the stereotypes encompassed a combination of the two. Simultaneously targets of admiration, derision, and fascination, and almost always emblematic of rural simplicity, the mountaineer disrupted notions of American modernity. Famous writers like Henry Louis (H. L) Mencken and Erskine Caldwell had long maligned poor whites from the South as depraved holdouts from a more primitive time. In the literary genre known as southern gothic, other writers also portrayed the so-called white trash of the Deep South, as well as the coastal and upland South, as sinister and endemically violent. For Mencken and Caldwell, but also for Harper Lee, Flannery O'Connor, and William Faulkner, among others, impoverished whites were arguably the most dysfunctional people in what had become the most dysfunctional American region. Indeed, many of the greatest writers of the midcentury found in the South a particularly riveting setting for their fiction.[12]

Mencken, according to historian Anthony Harkins, lamented "the loss of the antebellum southern aristocracy during the Civil War and the emergence of a society dominated by 'the poor white trash' in whose veins flowed 'some of the worst blood of western Europe.'"[13] Not to be outdone, Caldwell published *Tobacco Road, We Are the Living,* and *God's Little Acre,* all of which explored the contours of white poverty and moral declension in his home state of Georgia. Caldwell's wretched characters invited little sympathy; like Mencken, he believed that antebellum slavery had deformed and irreparably damaged the South, leaving it without a stable middle class. After the Civil War there was a vacuum in southern leadership; despite their high numbers, poor whites, with their deplorable customs, were ill equipped to inherit and organize a society in shambles. Mencken and Caldwell joined Arthur Estabrook, John Powell, and Mandel Sherman as authorities on the topic of race and poverty in the rural South. While the latter three wrote what passed as social science, all these men grew enamored with the apparent contradictions of southern whiteness. Some, like Powell, fetishized its alleged authenticity, while others such as Estabrook, troubled by what they perceived as the dangerous encroachment of racial pollution, offered a more cautious assessment. Collectively, however, these studies upheld the region as a peculiar outpost in the midst of national crises like depression and then war. And moreover, these writers strengthened the foundation on which still greater interest in the upland South would be built.[14]

The southern mountaineer was a fixture in more than literature and dubious scientific studies. The unlikely medium of the comic strip strongly shaped the representation of rural men and women from West Virginia to Arkansas. Paul Webb's *The Mountain Boys,* Billy DeBeck's character Snuffy Smith (introduced in the comic strip *Barney Google*), and Al Capp's *Li'l Abner,* debuted within months of each other in 1934 and remained popular for several decades.[15] As a cartoonist for *Esquire,* Webb portrayed mountaineers as dallying young men: uneducated, lazy, and lacking footwear, they were more interested in drinking moonshine and wallowing in squalor than they were in performing an honest day's work. Webb never validated the precise whereabouts of his mountain boys, but the illustrations intimated an isolated hollow deep among the hilly southern backcountry. Webb, like others who profited from portraying the South as a poor backwater, lived in the North (Pennsylvania). Even as the Great Depression ravaged nearly every corner of the United States, the backwardness of Webb's cartoon characters still seemed remarkable. But in contrast to the breadlines and Hoovervilles that dotted the urban landscape, *The Mountain Boys* were supposed to amass laughter and derision rather than pity.[16]

Not surprisingly, Webb's cartoons never delved into the wholesale exploitation of upland southern resources by powerful outside corporations; nor did Webb explain how this left the mountain population (whether in the Ozarks or the Appalachians) susceptible to booms, busts, and bouts of desperation. Absent this background knowledge, one might conclude that the cause and effects of the Great Depression fell deservedly upon a deficient population of barefooted hillbillies. To a predominantly middle-class readership, this sentiment elided the fundamental reasons for the collapse, including overproduction, reckless speculation, and the financial manipulation of markets and currency.[17]

As Webb's *Mountain Boys* hit the pages of *Esquire,* DeBeck's Snuffy Smith, an occupant of a fictional North Carolina mountain town known as Hootin' Holler, was introduced as a character in *Barney Google,* a strip DeBeck had created in 1919. In the late 1930s, as the character's popularity soared, the strip was renamed *Barney Google and Snuffy Smith* and focused increasingly on the North Carolina hillbilly. (Eventually, under DeBeck's successor, Fred Lasswell, Snuffy edged out the original title character almost completely.) Anthony Harkins has also expertly detailed DeBeck's contribution to hillbilly stereotypes and has proposed that *Snuffy Smith* closely hewed to the portrayals of Appalachians proffered by local color authors Mary N. Murfree and George Washington Harris. Though he hailed from Chicago, DeBeck studied the region's literature and tapped into its well-worn tropes. Snuffy Smith, a sturdy Anglo-Saxon cut from the frontier mold, was nonetheless frequently shown sleeping, drinking, and carrying on, thus exemplifying the paradox of poverty that had defined the mountain population since the end of the nineteenth century. As Harkins points out, "Snuffy Smith may be immoral, violent, lazy, and abusive, but he also represents the antielite attitudes, rugged independence, and physical prowess of mythic frontiersmen epitomized by Crockett and Boone." The comic strip, in more complex ways than Webb's *Mountain Boys,* further designated the upland South as an exceptional space in the public imagination. Harboring a keen sense of white supremacy and patriarchal dominance, DeBeck's character clumsily vacillated between all that was supposed to be celebrated about the region and all that was supposed to be feared.[18]

Webb and DeBeck aside, it was Alfred Gerald Caplin's (best known as Al Capp) *Li'l Abner* that exceeded the fame of *The Mountain Boys* and *Snuffy Smith.* In contrast to Webb's boorish clodhoppers or DeBeck's edgy mountaineer, Capp's characters, with their earnest naivety, commanded sympathy and respect, as well as millions of readers. The Yokums hailed from Dogpatch, an all-white community located in the rural upland South (there remains dispute over whether the setting was eastern Kentucky, the Arkansas Ozarks, or perhaps another location altogether). The fictional town became one of the most famous southern locales outside of Atlanta, New Orleans, Montgomery, and Birmingham. If by the 1950s the latter cities were synonymous with African American culture, as well as being epicenters of the civil rights movement, Dogpatch was its mirror opposite, demographically homogeneous and playfully tranquil, though distinctly southern nonetheless.[19]

Like Webb and DeBeck, Al Capp was also not from the South; nor had he spent significant time there. But luckily for the native New Englander, literary figures like John Fox Jr., Mary N. Murfree, and Harold Bell Wright had blazed a literary path for Capp to journey. All had presented the southern mountains as commodious and premodern; the people stood out by their innocence, virginal femininity, and chivalrous masculinity. Capp followed this model in some key ways but broke it in other ways. With a career spanning over four decades, the cartoonist tackled a dizzying array of topics and introduced dozens of characters—so many that a conclusive analysis of the comic strip lies beyond the scope of this study. Still, as Harkins has usefully written, while "Capp's storylines often wandered far afield, his hillbilly setting remained a central touchstone, serving as a microcosm and a distorting carnival mirror of broader American society."[20] Harkins might have added that Capp's hillbillies bolstered the image of the rural South in the public's mind as a reserve of undiluted whiteness amid pluralistic challenges to the postwar social order.

Capp's protagonist, Li'l Abner Yokum, is one example. The nineteen-year-old Abner, with his well-chiseled physique conjured a manly and racial ideal that Theodore Roosevelt would have admired. His mentality, however, more closely resembled a thoughtful, if naïve and reckless adolescent. Here, Abner's physical presence embodied the pinnacle of white masculinity, but he was still buffoonish enough to be easily identified as a hillbilly. This contradictory representation of mountain manliness was a central theme that coursed through the work of social scientists and prominent authors alike. As descendants of Boone and Crockett, the mountaineer supposedly stood at the apex of human evolution; however, degraded intelligence and behavior threatened to spoil the otherwise strong, effectual body.[21]

Daisy Mae, Dogpatch's voluptuous blonde, presented another variant on the themes of race, gender, and sexuality in the upland South. Endlessly vying for Abner's affection, Daisy Mae's sexualized persona undermined the historical trope of submissive femininity and southern white womanhood, but it affirmed still other stereotypes of mountain women. Overall, however, she served the narrative purposes of Capp's comics. Writers typically rendered female characters from the mountain South as innocent and pure on the one hand, but they also presented them as sexually available, at least to the proper suitor, on the other hand. As vessels through which male desire could pass or be acted upon, mountain women in the novels of John Fox Jr. and Mary N. Murfree for example, were seen as exotic objects of desire and conquest by outsiders. Northern men sought these young southern women because they had never encountered the perceived vice and prurience of the nation's cities, and they supposedly remained subservient within the mountains' rigid patriarchal social order. Cleverly, though, Capp flipped the script and positioned Daisy Mae as a boldly assertive woman who aggressively courted a man, in this case, Abner. Still, she was far from an icon of women's liberation, and Capp was even further from feminism. His depiction of Daisy Mae hinged largely on her identity as a sexual foil for male readers to gaze upon. But Capp had an additional purpose: the weekly comic strip required ongoing themes and running gags, and Daisy Mae's relentless, if at times futile pursuit of Abner fit the bill.[22]

Li'l Abner's success extended beyond the Depression and World War II years, reaching its largest audiences in the 1950s and 1960s. The comic strip's readership crested with the rising tide of social movements and civil rights agitation. Throughout, Dogpatch reflected the opinions of its creator and presented a façade of tranquility in the midst of open displays of white supremacy that occurred across the real South. Not one to withhold an opinion on current events, Capp praised Alabama's segregationist governor, George Wallace, calling him "more of a friend to blacks than John Lindsay or LeRoi Jones" (Lindsay was the mayor of New York City and a liberal on civil rights, and Jones—later known as Amiri Baraka—was a leading figure in the Black Arts movement).[23] As Denis Kitchen and Michael Schumacher have asserted, *Li'l Abner* never carried an overtly anti–civil rights message, but it did convey disdain toward student activists and figures associated with the counterculture and advocates of civil rights. In one notable comic strip, Capp presented a character named Joanie Phoanie.[24] An allusion to Joan Baez, Capp's Phoanie took advantage of the apparent simplemindedness and poor taste of the nation's youth to make money as a folk singer peddling an antiwar, pro-civil rights message. In another comic strip, Capp showed college students joining a left-wing organization known as Students Wildly Ignorant of Nearly Everything (SWINE).[25]

Not surprisingly, Capp's comedy drew praise from several high-profile conservatives; he even built casual friendships with Richard Nixon, Spiro Agnew, and Ronald Reagan.[26] And like those three, his popularity was based partly on a reactionary message and his opposition to the decade's social movements. Almost exclusively white, possibly segregated, and skeptical of a diverse and urban society, Capp's Dogpatch, defying its drab poverty and disreputable residents, was nevertheless a redoubt to the presumably corrosive encroachment of youth culture and political liberalism. Many of the comic strip's themes echoed the ascendant brand of politics that increasingly characterized the Republican Party during the Goldwater campaign and after.[27]

Significantly, however, the men and women of Dogpatch and Hootin' Holler prefigured the hillbilly characters of primetime television in the coming years. The representation of poor whites that followed on television broke little new ground and was largely derivative. Beyond the comic strips discussed above, the country-city shtick of *The Real McCoys* and *The Beverly Hillbillies* imitated the premise of *Ma and Pa Kettle*. The popular hillbilly couple, along with their fifteen children, left the farm for the city in the 1940s; millions of dollars in film revenue followed. And moreover, as we have seen, the cartoonists and prolific novelists of the 1930s and 1940s rehearsed many of the topics first proposed during the local color movement; so too did the sitcoms of the 1950s and 1960s.

But with the transformative medium of the television, coupled with the burgeoning civil rights movement and rising social disunity, a fictional upland South and its colorful cast of characters achieved even more success. The TV became a diversion from contemporary events and troubling times. The whiteness of televised entertainment and the prevalence of southern characters during the postwar decades then must not be seen as inert and void of meaning. Rather, these programs brought to the surface the submerged anxieties about race, gender, and power that had long preoccupied the American imagination. The situation comedy, laced with heavy doses of nostalgic imagery, celebrated a set of social relations and hierarchies that had begun to buckle, if not break. It was this context that upland southern whites reached unprecedented levels of ubiquity and continued their long, strange trip into our collective psyche.[28]

From the Comic Strip to Primetime Television

The first situation comedy to focus on the idiosyncratic lives of southern whites was *The Real McCoys*. Airing on ABC between 1957 and 1962, viewers watched the McCoys negotiate their move from "West Virginny" to "Californy." Like the family who infamously feuded with the Hatfields, the McCoys of primetime also rallied around their family patriarch, Grandpa Amos (Walter Brennan). But unlike the perpetrators of lawless violence in the late-nineteenth-century Appalachian feud, these McCoys provided a moral compass to a nation on the brink of unrest. The show's central tension involved the unrelenting encroachment of urban life upon traditional US American notions of independence, white rule, and patriarchal authority. Throughout *The Real McCoys,* family, neighbors, and friends sometimes challenged Grandpa Amos, but his time-honored wisdom almost always prevailed.[29]

The first episode, "Californy Here We Come," aired on October 3, 1957, and summoned the themes of race, class, and authority. In the first scene, the McCoys traveled in their jalopy (a symbol of itinerancy derived from the Great Migration and popularized by John Steinbeck in *The Grapes of Wrath* and later in *Ma and Pa Kettle;* writer Paul Henning adopted it for *The Beverly Hillbillies*) to their new home in the American West. Along the way, a police officer pulled the family over to return the spare tire that had fallen from the unsteady vehicle. The McCoys defensively asserted that they had done nothing wrong and chastised the officer for wrongfully detaining them; however, once the officer presented them with the tire and his intent became clear, the audience laughed and the tension was diffused. The family then went on their way, grateful for the watchful eye of the highway patrol. The brief exchange was revealing for two reasons. First, the family's suspicions of the police relied on the viewer's recognition that poor people, regardless of race, had been historically targeted as criminals and carried with them the presumption of guilt. Second, the officer's diffidence toward the McCoys, despite their irreverence, exhibited how differently law enforcement interactions played out, depending on the suspect's identity.[30]

The year that *The Real McCoys* premiered, Eugene "Bull" Connor became the Commissioner of the Birmingham Police Department, thus ushering in six years of open conflict between the city's white police force and many of its black residents, who fought to uphold court-ordered desegregation. As *The Real McCoys* aired, brutal scenes of civil rights activists attacked by police dogs and sprayed by high-pressure water hoses highlighted the longstanding racist procedures of many southern police departments. On September 23, 1957, just ten days before the first episode of *The Real McCoys,* Arkansas governor Orval Faubus deployed the state's national guard to thwart nine black students from desegregating Little Rock Central High School. The standoff between the 101st Airborne Division, sent by President Eisenhower, and Governor Faubus anticipated the ways in which other southern politicians would mobilize local and state firepower as a last-ditch effort to preserve Jim Crow. As the 1950s concluded and the 1960s wore on, the scope of police intimidation directed at black communities in both the North and South became evident, and it was at the root of dozens of urban rebellions.[31]

Beyond the memorable opening scene, the first episode contained other evocative moments. Once the McCoys settled into their West Coast home, they met one of their neighbors, a Mexican man named Pepino Garcia (played by Puerto Rican actor Tony Martinez). As Pepino introduced himself to the McCoys, Amos and his grandson, Luke (Richard Crenna), shielded the women of the family from the dark-skinned stranger; Amos whispered to Luke, "I left my gun in the car, but I've got my hand on my knife." Luke replied, "I believe he means us no harm. . . . It's a foreigner." Luke then tried to decipher Pepino's accent, reassuring his grandfather, "That there's English. He's done somethin' to it, but English was what it was." The exchange was lighthearted enough, given Luke McCoy's own drawl and difficulty with the English language. But by labeling Garcia a suspicious foreigner, the McCoys, who had just arrived, claimed California and naturalized themselves as the rightful occupants of the land.[32]

Hence, within minutes of the show's premiere, the family displayed the privileges and arrogance of settler colonialism. Indeed, it soon became clear that Pepino's primary role on the show was to serve as the McCoys' farmhand, supply comic relief, and offer timely morsels of folk wisdom derived from his identity as a Mexican. His culture was an alien spectacle to be consumed by a predominantly white audience. A racial "other," Pepino played a sympathetic and likable figure even as he bolstered stereotypes of migrant workers as servile to white authority and below the ranks of citizenship; he quickly took to referring to Amos McCoy as "Señor Grandpa." At the same time, Garcia's alacrity and simplemindedness suggested that he was both content with and too dim to pursue anything beyond the low-wage service occupation that he held.[33]

Two additional scenes demonstrate the above points. In the first, Grandpa Amos sulked on the front porch, feeling out of place in California. Pepino asked the other McCoys why Amos was despondent. Luke explained how Amos and his friends from West Virginia traded barbs to show affection toward each other, but he had not found anyone to connect with since they moved west. Pepino's eyes lit up, and he marched outside to greet Amos: "You got the ugliest face like I never did see." Amos, elated to return the favor, stared down Pepino and emphatically responded, "You ain't never looked in the mirror then cuz you got the ugliest, crookedest, most disgusting arrangement that ever got called a face." Pepino, not familiar with the game, failed to deliver a follow-up insult. Amos concluded that his new friend lacked the wit to banter back and forth with him. He patted Pepino on the head, appreciating the gesture but assuming that the farmhand had some intellectual shortcomings.[34]

By contrast, later in the episode, Amos shouted down another one of his neighbors, Florie MacMichael (Madge Blake), after some of her sheep had crossed onto the McCoy property. Amos soon found out that the sheep grazed on the land in return for access to water on the MacMichaels' property. By the time that Amos returned to the house, the MacMichaels had turned off the McCoys' water in retaliation. Luke realized the only way to get the water running again was for Amos "to apologize to some people." The irate grandfather refused. "It ain't people, it's a woman," Amos angrily proclaimed, "and I'm a McCoy. And no McCoy never crawled to a man let alone a woman." After Luke admonished his grandfather, Amos reluctantly set out to right the situation.[35]

Once the old man arrived at the MacMichaels' home, he impatiently explained to Ms. MacMichael that he was unaware that the sheep grazed on the property in exchange for access to water. MacMichael then claimed that it was her brother, George (Andy Clyde), who made the decision. Upset that he had almost apologized to a woman, Amos exclaimed, "You mean to tell me I degraded and humiliated myself for nothing. Where's this brother of yours at?"[36] Before Amos finished the question, George approached from the other room, aggressively gesticulating and hurling insults. To resolve the dispute, George challenged Amos to an arm wrestling match, which ended in a draw. Throughout the bizarre display of manly competition, it became clear to viewers that George and Amos were in fact bonding in the precise ways in which Pepino had tried and failed. Amos had finally met his equal in strength and intellect: an older white man who also spoke with a southern drawl and enjoyed spirited debates and arm wrestling.

The scene ended with Amos inviting George to throw horseshoes, and the audience was reassured that the cantankerous men had forged an alliance. But while Amos was at the MacMichaels' home making a new friend and restoring the water, the rest of the McCoys gathered in the living room. They feared that they had been too rough on their grandfather for his truculent ways and that perhaps he had abandoned them to return to West Virginia. Seconds later, Amos opened the front door and received an ebullient welcoming. As he sat down in his chair, the family gathered around. Pepino fetched him some "pipe water." Amos then requested that his daughter-in-law, Kate, "hand me my banjo, sugar babe."[37] The final credits rolled as "Señor Grandpa" picked his banjo and a grateful family sang and danced. Pepino joined in as an Appalachian hootenanny unfolded from the living room of a southern California home.[38]

While it was only the first of 224, the inaugural episode of *The Real McCoys* established several key themes that persisted throughout the series. For one, the program upheld a reverence for male authority, oftentimes propped up by crude stereotypes of women and Mexicans. The value placed on tradition and the patriarchal family, alongside the celebration of rural modes of subsistence—ranching, hunting, and farming—implicitly critiqued the trappings of middle-class suburban life. Whether he was trying to assuage Amos or fetch him water, Pepino, the only person of color to regularly appear on the show, reminded viewers that a man with dark skin was best suited to serve whites, remain obedient, and strive to assimilate. That Pepino Garcia and the McCoys got along so well under such terms suggested that adhering to established racial hierarchies was necessary to ensure social harmony.[39]

With the success of *The Real McCoys,* CBS launched its next rural comedy, *The Andy Griffith Show.* Set in the fictional, idyllic town of Mayberry, loosely based on Mount Airy, a small town in the northwest corner of North Carolina bordering Virginia. *The Andy Griffith Show* showcased the benevolent arm of law enforcement in the beloved character of Sheriff Andy Taylor (played by Griffith).[40] Premiering in October 1960, just months after the sit-in demonstrations at the Woolworth lunch counter in Greensboro, *The Andy Griffith Show* never broached the real-life events that occurred in North Carolina, let alone elsewhere in the nation. In contrast to the reality of violence across the South, Mayberry, like Dogpatch, was nearly all white, easygoing, and contained not a trace of unrest. As media critic Don Rodney Vaughan has argued, "Mayberry was immune from hard news."[41]

Nonetheless, the escapist, ostensibly apolitical, and socially removed plotlines of the show celebrated small-town justice and steered clear of the challenges posed by civil rights, feminism, and the antiwar movement. Set in a southern state, the show never featured an African American in a speaking role until the 215th episode.[42] However, there were occasional hillbilly characters. The most prominent to appear were the Darlings. Briscoe Darling (Denver Pyle), the head of a family of singing hillbillies, had four sons and a daughter named Charlene (Maggie Peterson); they drove from the mountains and into town on a jalopy reminiscent of the McCoys'.[43] Their trips into Mayberry —"the city," as Briscoe referred to it—ensured hijinks and inconvenience for Sheriff Andy Taylor and his deputy, Barney Fife (Don Knotts). Episodes featuring the Darlings entailed some combination of tortured romances, weddings gone awry, and unusual rituals, all of which presented rural mountaineers as superstitious relics from a bygone era. In spite of their antics and regardless of how absurd the situation, *The Andy Griffith Show* portrayed the county sheriff with compassion and patience.[44]

The Darlings made their first appearance during a third-season episode entitled "The Darlings Are Coming." Airing on March 18, 1963, the program opened with Briscoe attempting to fix his overheated truck by dumping water from a drinking fountain for horses into the vehicle's engine. The sight of four grown men in a broken-down pickup truck with another man collecting water in a broad-brimmed hat drew the attention of the sheriff. Bemused, Andy confronted the Darlings and explained to Briscoe that his actions violated two city ordinances. Andy then gently told Briscoe, "We believe in warning people first, especially strangers." After failing to jumpstart the truck, Sheriff Taylor directed the family to a motel for the night. Briscoe rented the cheapest room under the false pretense that he was alone. The rest of the Darlings then snuck into the small room, unpacked their instruments, and launched into a rousing and disruptively loud bluegrass jam session. Not surprisingly, the irritable desk clerk heard the ruckus and called the sheriff. After catching Charlene and her four brothers fleeing out of the back window, Andy took pity on the stranded family and invited them to stay with him. The episode concluded with Andy joining the Darlings on guitar for an impromptu concert at the sheriff's home.[45]

Briscoe unflinchingly led his family in all matters of consequence. He tried to arrange marriages for his daughter, sons, and even his infant granddaughter, though not without some trouble along the way.[46] Briscoe once found Charlene a suitable husband who "hardly ever hit" her and gave her a home with a "wood floor."[47] In another episode, Charlene's marriage fell apart, leading her to pursue Andy (for whom she had long harbored a crush). To secure her union with the sheriff, she initiated an elaborate ritual, apparently known only to hill folk. Before he understood what was going on, Andy had unwittingly become her husband. When he tried to reverse the ceremonial marriage, Briscoe and his sons trapped the sheriff and held him at gunpoint until he cautiously agreed to accept the young woman as his wife.[48] It was clear that Briscoe had orchestrated the ordeal, but his sons appeared willing and ready to leverage violence on the sheriff if directed. Eventually, Andy annulled the marriage and diffused the tense situation. By the end of the episode, he successfully reunited Charlene with her original husband, Dudley, another man from the hills.

A bit unpredictable, Briscoe was also noble and basically good natured. His character contrasted with the debased hillbilly Ernest T. Bass (Howard Morris). An eccentric, gun-toting bumpkin and symbol of Anglo-Saxon collapse if ever there was one, Bass lived alone among the hills and stirred up trouble with the Darlings. In the episode "Mountain Wedding," Bass, who had long courted Charlene, refused to recognize her marriage to Dudley. To prove his unrequited love for her, Bass stalked Charlene and threw love letters wrapped around rocks through the family's windows. At Briscoe's request, Andy and Barney traveled up the mountain to intervene in what they feared might escalate into a deadly showdown between Bass and the Darlings. Briscoe conceded to Andy, "I was gonna kill him." Calmly, Andy persuaded Briscoe to allow Bass to explain why he would make the best husband for Charlene. The unruly mountaineer declared, "I can do chin-ups. I'm the best rock thrower in the country, and I'm saving up for a gold tooth. I'm the man for you, Charlene, and you know it." Unconvinced, Charlene quickly dismissed Bass's bid. The episode came to a risible climax when Barney, after a rancorous debate with Andy, donned a wedding gown to bait Bass into kidnapping him rather than Charlene. Predictably, Bass sprung from the nearby bushes, shotgun in hand, and nabbed the disguised Barney. Once the disgruntled backwoodsman figured out that he had been tricked, the preacher had completed the ceremony and married Charlene and Dudley. Only then did Bass cease his attempts to coerce Charlene into marriage.[49]

While entertaining, the Darlings never appeared regularly on *The Andy Griffith Show;* they starred in only six episodes between 1963 and 1966. Yet, these episodes aired as interest in white poverty crested and public attention focused on the southern mountains.[50] Like Kennedy, Harrington, Caudill, and other poverty warriors who had fixated on the upland South, so too did the producers of *The Andy Griffith Show*. And like *The Real McCoys,* Sheriff Andy Taylor's relationship with the Darlings and Ernest T. Bass was noteworthy given the context. Even after the Darlings attempted to squat in the town and were thrown out of the motel for violating the terms of their stay, Andy treated them with empathy and generosity. When the Darlings threatened the sheriff at gunpoint, he continued his approach as a skilled negotiator and enforcer of the peace. Not once did the viewer believe that a deadly showdown between poor people and law enforcement was eminent, even when irascible mountaineers ran afoul of the sheriff.

The same could not have been said regarding the events in the nonfictional South. African Americans faced deadly reprisals, at times directed or condoned by county and state police departments, for their confrontation with Jim Crow at the very moments when the Darlings flagrantly, if laughably, disregarded law and order. Even the ease with which the Darlings traveled in and out of Mayberry illustrated the relative privilege from which even the poorest of whites had historically benefitted in the region; an ability to travel freely from one place to an another was certainly not a universally shared experience in the US South. *The Andy Griffith Show*'s success, regardless of whether or not the episodes included the Darlings, derived in part from its portrayal of an overwhelmingly white town in the South plagued primarily by trivial and indeed comical disturbances. Tellingly, these were resolved not by federal legislation or the National Guard but rather by a single sheriff and his bumbling deputy. Extended further, the very premise of the show celebrated the virtues of small-town southern justice administered by the county sheriff.[51]

Like other fictional towns in the South, Mayberry lacked any civil rights mobilization. Given the potent unrest in Mississippi, Georgia, Alabama, North Carolina, and elsewhere, those who watched *The Andy Griffith Show, The Real McCoys,* and the evening news may have sympathized with George Wallace, the Alabama governor who had delivered a speech advocating "segregation forever" in the early weeks of 1963.[52] As Wallace issued his now-infamous proclamation, primetime television affirmed the cultural authority of two white southern men. Amos McCoy left West Virginia and instantly laid claim to California while Andy Griffith remained in small-town North Carolina to keep the peace. But more important, their performances connected notions of social harmony, moral clarity, and comic levity to white rule and paternalistic hierarchies. And while *The Andy Griffith Show* and *The Real McCoys* never explicitly endorsed Jim Crow or transmitted a prosegregation message (Andy Griffith, for instance, was a liberal Democrat), many of the episodes presented a softer, gentler image of the South and its white population, one that belied the brutal images that saturated the daily news. These upland southerners—religiously and culturally conservative, as well as powerfully nostalgic, peaceful, and good-natured, if at times abrasive—reproduced the structural oppression that marred the first half of the century even as they curried favor with viewers. Still, *The Andy Griffith Show* and *The Real McCoys* were only a prelude to the decade's biggest hit, *The Beverly Hillbillies.*

Meet the Clampetts

The Andy Griffith Show and *The Real McCoys* aired alongside several other situation comedies and dramas. During the 1950s and 1960s, the three major networks (NBC, CBS, and ABC) dominated the airwaves and collectively fed an insatiable appetite that Americans had for televised entertainment. While programs like *The Honeymooners* and *I Love Lucy* supplied a more honest if humorous glimpse into the lives of working-class women and men, most of the comedies idealized nuclear, white, and middle-class families. Accordingly, wholesome suburbanites took center stage. At the height of the Cold War, television exhibited an affluent and united nation. Responsible fathers worked white-collar jobs, owned homes, provided for their families, and had the disposable income for the annual summer vacation at the seashore. This was the mold of such favorites as *The Adventures of Ozzie and Harriet, Father Knows Best, The Danny Thomas Show,* and *Leave It to Beaver.* But by the early and middle 1960s, the sitcom that had achieved the most success depicted not content lives of the middle-class suburban set, but the comparatively novel lives of a motley crew of Ozark hillbillies known as the Clampetts.[53]

Two years after the premiere of *The Andy Griffith Show,* a young writer from Independence, Missouri, named Paul Henning produced his first episode of *The Beverly Hillbillies* for CBS.[54] Millions tuned in to watch a family of southerners start their lives anew in California after having received a handsome payout for selling the oil beneath their property. Disregarding the mostly negative reviews from the press, Americans embraced *The Beverly Hillbillies,* and almost immediately it reached the top of the ratings.[55] It became the first sitcom to consecutively rank as the nation's most-watched program, claiming the top spot in 1962–63 and 1963–64.[56] Throughout its twelve seasons, only during its final two did it fail to achieve the highest ratings. Some episodes even set records for the most-watched television event; in the pre-Super Bowl era of ratings, Henning's *Hillbillies* were among the top.[57]

The show's popularity dovetailed with the rediscovery of the upland South and its people. In an interview, Henning recounted how he too had been fascinated with southern mountaineers and viewed their lifestyle as a quaint oddity, worthy of respect. As a Boy Scout, Henning camped in the Ozarks and traveled to Civil War battlefields in Maryland, Tennessee, and Virginia. During these excursions, he encountered people who he claimed had lived in the remotest places and had maintained their customs for over a hundred years. Henning's experience of the region's people led him to proclaim, "I just always admired hillbillies . . . and found their sense of humor hysterical." What would happen, Henning wondered, if someone could "transplant a real hillbilly family to a modern American city?" Given the changing nature of midcentury American life, with its superhighways and sprawling suburbs, there was no better concept for a sitcom, according to the young writer, than to take a family from the rural South, one with habits and a culture frozen in the nineteenth century, and uproot them to that most gaudy bastion of American consumerism and superficiality: Beverly Hills, California.[58]

Curiously though, Henning did not base his cast entirely on the people whom he encountered as a Boy Scout. Rather, he drew equal inspiration from Jack Kirkland's theatrical production of Erskine Caldwell's *Tobacco Road*. The play, which Henning had attended as a teenager growing up outside of Kansas City, was about a dysfunctional family from rural Georgia, known as the Lesters, who had mismanaged their land and squandered their wealth. Turning that narrative on its head, Henning's Clampetts were deeply impoverished until they accidentally discovered an oilfield below their feet; this catapulted the family into the elite. In further contrast to the Lesters, the Clampetts were far from the menacing breed of mountain whites Caldwell had written about. Instead, Henning's hillbillies aligned more with the accounts of many prominent liberals who had held southern mountaineers in high regard despite their troubling poverty and peculiar habits.[59]

The show presented the Clampetts with a quirky do-it-yourself ethic that endeared them to the public. Borrowing from *The Real McCoys,* among others, the family traveled over a thousand miles to southern California from their mountain hollow in an overstuffed jalopy. Jerry Scoggins, Lester Flatt, and Earl Scruggs wrote the famous theme, "The Ballad of Jed Clampett," a catchy two-minute bluegrass tune that explained the family's unlikely ascent from rags to riches as the opening credits rolled.[60] With the inclusion of Granny (Irene

Ryan), Henning's Clampetts went back one generation earlier than did the McCoys, thus more clearly establishing kinship to the rural folk and the venerable populations that had for so long captured the nation's attention. Notably, Henning did not cast Granny as the family's matriarch; instead, she played the dour mother-in-law. This positioned Jed (Buddy Ebsen) as the unwitting leader of the family. He toed a line between being hopelessly clueless of modern convenience and cleverly resourceful. Notwithstanding his completion of the sixth grade, an academic accomplishment surpassed by no other Clampett, Jed's nephew, Jethro (Max Baer Jr.), was the most gauche member of the family. Earnest and puerile, Jethro recalled both Li'l Abner and Luke McCoy. And like those two, his affable naivety was an endless source of comic material for Henning. Lastly, Elly May (Donna Douglas), Jed's daughter and only child, fulfilled the role of a mountain beauty, gracing television with her long blonde hair and well-proportioned body. Her appearance brought to mind female characters from the local color movement at the turn-of-the-century, but more recently she conjured Charlene Darling and Al Capp's Daisy Mae Yokum. Elly May's name, however, was lifted straight from the script of *Tobacco Road*.[61]

Aside from their distinctive traits, the Clampetts' acerbic critique of commercialism propelled them to stardom; with humor and wit, they dissected and simplified the complexities of modern American life. In doing so, the Clampetts' rural, southern whiteness conveyed a specific racial and cultural desirability before the mass audience. Their serendipitous arrival in the upper class brought with it a culture clash that Henning artfully exploited. *The Beverly Hillbillies* romanticized the perceived values of the rural South, but the program also lampooned the pretensions of the urban sophisticates as well as the vacuity of over-the-top consumerism, both of which received their highest expressions in the glitz and glamour of postwar California. Just as *Ozzie and Harriet* and *Leave It to Beaver* earned accolades for their respective portrayals of the suburban contentment that supposedly typified the 1950s, *The Beverly Hillbillies* nourished the perception of honest, hardworking poor whites; what they lacked in technological savvy and bourgeois style, they made up for with time-honored wisdom and backcountry gumption.[62]

But while the Clampetts were undoubtedly whimsical, they could also be quite reactionary. Their reverence for tradition at times clashed with their neighbors in Beverly Hills. The nouveau riche of sprawling Los Angeles apparently regarded their less fortunate countrymen and women with disdain and snubbed their noses at the modesty and frugality displayed by the Clampetts. In this regard, Henning satirized a subset of affluent white people who he believed had failed to engage the social contract. At the same time, the Clampetts, in their reluctance to adapt to a changing nation, challenged the wisdom of the decade's social movements. As an eminently likable family of white southerners with whom the nation was supposed to identify, the Clampetts advocated a lifestyle of thrift and simplicity in the face of conspicuous consumption on the one hand, and insurgent protest movements on the other hand. These characteristics, as white liberals like Kennedy and Caudill pointed out, made poor mountaineers, those who had *not* struck it rich with bubbling crude, the ideal targets of the welfare state.[63]

To illustrate the point, the Clampetts arrived in California—or, some might say, the show premiered—on September 26, 1962, around the same time that Harrington and Caudill released their respective studies and Kennedy signed legislation for area redevelopment. But news from Oxford, Mississippi dominated the headlines that week. On September 20, James Meredith, an African American man from Kosciusko, Mississippi, became the first black student to enroll for classes at the state's segregated flagship institution, the University of Mississippi. In violation of judicial and executive orders, Governor Ross Barnett had already twice denied Meredith admission, and he had planned to do so again. As a result, President Kennedy sent federal marshals to accompany Meredith and desegregate Ole Miss. Americans watched in anticipation to learn whether the *Brown* decision, reached eight years earlier, was unenforceable rhetoric, or whether it had truly provided the federal government with the authority to undo Jim Crow. Barnett, emboldened by support from many Mississippians, remained intractable and committed to segregation. Sporadic violence throughout September escalated into white riots by month's end; two people died and over a hundred more were injured in the uproar.[64] But on October 1, defying threats to his life, Meredith entered the campus lyceum flanked by troops. The Associated Press relayed, "Approximately 100 uniformed State Highway patrolmen and scores of sheriffs, deputies, plainclothesmen and policemen held back a crowd of 2,000 jeering students" as the black Mississippian ventured towards his first college class, US history.[65]

Like *The Andy Griffith Show*, *The Real McCoys*, and most other television programs, *The Beverly Hillbillies* seldom engaged current affairs. Through the first four seasons, the Clampetts' world never included Meredith's integration, the March on Washington, Kennedy's assassination, the murder of Medgar Evers, Freedom Summer, or the Gulf of Tonkin Incident; nor did Johnson's signing of the Civil Rights Act of 1964 and Voting Rights Act of 1965 receive mention. Still, its ratings soared. Henning insisted that at least some of the sitcom's popularity stemmed from the Clampetts' ability to avoid topics that might alienate any one segment of its viewers.[66] However, Henning's contention that the show harbored no ideology veiled its celebration of southern whiteness and its opposition to a changing society. Like the removed enclaves of Mayberry and Dogpatch, the Clampetts' mansion in Beverly Hills represented, albeit in comic relief, much of what the 1960s did not.

In the inaugural episode, "The Clampetts Strike Oil," viewers witnessed a very different experience of the early decade than what unfolded on the nightly news. The show first presented the family on their property in the Ozarks; they were instantly recognizable as backwards and poor. Soon after, Granny Clampett introduced herself to the audience by yearning for the Confederacy. Once they arrived in California, Jed mistakenly believed that the utility poles running adjacent to the neatly coiffed lawns of Beverly Hills were ready-made firewood, or "black ol' dead tree trunks," according to Elly May. Aware of the difference between utility poles and firewood, Granny disapprovingly uttered, "So help me Jefferson Davis."[67] Jed replied that he was no longer president, implying that Davis's tenure as the leader of the Confederacy was once legitimate but had simply lapsed. Granny curtly responded, "There'll be no more Yankee talk in this house."[68] The brief exchange was one of the first bits of dialogue and afforded a glimpse into the Clampletts' worldview. While Granny delivered her one-liner with innocuous intent and received audience laughter, she and her family affirmed a social order predicated upon racism. At the very moment of Granny's utterance, James Meredith and countless other African Americans throughout the South faced murderous reprisals in their efforts to dismantle a white supremacist society, one that the Clampetts wistfully celebrated.

The show's second episode, "Getting Settled," aired the day after Meredith integrated the University of Mississippi, and Oxford faced more violent demonstrations. On CBS the Clampetts took up residence in their new home and explored their neighborhood. Unfortunately, tension arose when Jed's cousin, Pearl (Bea Benaderet), stuck in the southern mountains, cautiously broached the idea of moving west. In a rare moment of solemnity, Pearl told Mr. Brewster (Frank Wilcox), the oil speculator who recommended that the Clampetts take their fortune and move to southern California, "I ought to be out there in Beverly Hills helping Cousin Jed." The opulent western oilman, unfamiliar with the prudent social graces of southern women, responded, "Well he certainly has plenty of room for you. This mansion has thirty-two rooms and fourteen baths." But size was not the issue; rural southerners had long crammed into tight mountain quarters. Rather, Pearl furled her brow and tersely explained to Brewster, "I wouldn't go without being asked." While the viewer knew that Jed had simply forgotten to extend the invitation in the haste of moving from one set of hills to another, a spurned Pearl believed otherwise. A split screen then showed Pearl sadly gazing out of a cabin window and Jed standing about his new mansion looking morose. Jed then longingly voiced, "I sure wish she [Pearl] was out here." Eventually Jed contacted his cousin, and the two straightened out the misunderstanding. By the episode's conclusion, Pearl had arrived in Beverly Hills at Jed's insistence.[69]

That these episodes aired as the University of Mississippi desegregated against the will of state lawmakers creates an opportunity to theorize how ideologies circulate, regardless of what Henning's intention may have been as he finalized the script. The famous literary critic, Mikhail Bakhtin, has usefully argued that the implications of language "will always be determined by the real conditions of its uttering and foremost, by the nearest social situation."[70] This of course did not mean that Pearl's wish to join her family in Beverly Hills was analogous to the "social situation" of James Meredith's integration. Nor should Bakhtin's theory issue license to attribute covert or cryptic motivations to Paul Henning and the cast of *The Beverly Hillbillies*. Rather, advocates of linguistic analysis challenge us to consider how context, encompassing as it does a matrix of discursive interactions, frames events, thus injecting them with meaning.[71] The Clampetts' resounding success generated a message and advanced an ideology that resonated in time and place. Pearl's refusal to impose on her cousin reflected submissiveness conversant with the behavioral expectations of white southern women. This depiction of feminine propriety and etiquette stood in diametric opposition to James Meredith, an African American man who was seen by advocates of Jim Crow as imposing on and threatening the traditional institutions of white male supremacy, in this case Mississippi's flagship university. On the day after Meredith's integration, the nation's highest-rated television program tacitly endorsed an entrenched system of white patriarchal dominance at a moment when it met a formidable challenge.[72]

It was Elly May, however, who gave Henning the strongest opportunities to reinforce conventional notions of womanhood and sexuality. As a stereotypical "Tomboy," Elly May repudiated acceptable female behavior; her coveralls, physical strength, and athleticism departed from how most women appeared on television during the 1950s and 1960s, especially those who lived among the upper class. But Elly May's performance was also a platform for Henning to affirm a gender hierarchy and vindicate male authority. In one example, Elly May put her cousin, Jethro, in a powerful sleeper hold; she relented only after

Jed demanded, "You turn him loose before I take the strap to both of you." Later in the episode, Jed sat down with Elly May and said, "You're getting too big to wrestle with boys. . . . You're a young lady now. You gotta start minding your manners and fixing yourself up real nice and wearin' dresses." Elly May protested, "Pa! Folks would call me sissy." The conversation then turned serious as viewers learned that Jed had always wanted a son, but his wife had died tragically many years earlier. A brokenhearted Jed explained to his daughter, "I raised you like a boy and I was wrong to do it. I reckon every man would like to have a son and you was my only young'un. . . . I just decided to turn you into a boy." Elly May, returning some levity to the dialogue, was evidently comfortable enough with the arrangement as she bragged about her ability to "outrun, outclimb, outfight, and outshoot" the boys. But now that she had matured, Jed believed such behavior "ain't fittin'. It ain't right for folks to go against nature. Now look at ol' Duke there [referring to the family's hound dog]. Reckon we could turn him into a cat?" Likewise, Jed reasoned, "Nature made you a girl."[73]

Jed's analogy, stretched as it was, diffused Elly May's subversive conduct and confirmed his standing as the commanding patriarch. Clampett required that his daughter adhere to sanctioned codes of female decorum, and he threatened to use force ("the belt") if she continued to deviate from them. In failing to adopt her father's rigid ideal of femininity, Elly May's behavior was "unnatural" and maybe even ungodly. As a result, her manliness necessitated intervention. Indeed, one of the show's recurring themes involved the efforts of Pearl and Mrs. Drysdale (Harriet E. MacGibbon) to teach Elly May how to act like a proper southern belle and leverage her good looks to entice wealthy men. But for the dynamic to work as comedy, Elly May had to be perceived as naturally beautiful yet naïve and perpetually confused by, or at least uninterested in, satisfying bourgeois expectations of female sexuality. Exploiting a well-established theme of Anglo-Saxon virginal purity, Henning expertly configured Elly May as an object of male desire, at once tantalizingly attractive but also nubile and girlish, rendering her allure vaguely taboo. Elly May's unrefined aesthetic also created a spectacle whereby viewers voyeuristically participated in her ambivalent struggle to meet the standards of middle- and upper-class womanhood. This required that her awkward sexuality be harnessed and reconfigured for the benefit of would-be male partners. She was thus a proverbial diamond-in-the-rough, a woman on the cusp of sexual and social respectability but one who needed some guidance along the way.[74]

These antics epitomized *The Beverly Hillbillies* during their near decade-long run and explained the ardor of their fan base. As the drama of the 1960s escalated and divisions along the lines of race, generation, and ideology grew ever more pronounced, the Clampetts' rags-to-riches story united the nation around the mythology of class mobility and the boundless possibilities of the American West. Henning's cast also provided weekly reminders that respect for tradition, authority, and family were necessary values to foster amid of the turbulence that existed just beyond Beverly Hills, and perhaps even within it. The Clampetts' negotiation of the fraught cultural and socioeconomic terrain of Beverly Hills was little more than a new twist on an old narrative, one with which we have become quite familiar. With their primordial ingenuity, *The Beverly Hillbillies* rekindled a fanciful pioneer spirit that had long enamored the nation and permeated popular culture. Like the writings of Theodore Roosevelt, Nathaniel Southgate Shaler, and Harry Caudill, Henning's hillbillies seemed predisposed to conquer the frontier and settle the West.[75]

Undoubtedly, they were very different from Daniel Boone and David Crockett, but nonetheless the Clampetts represented pioneers of another sort. In this iteration, they may not have blazed a trail through an unrelenting wilderness populated by hostile Native Americans, but Jed and his family did confront a hostile culture infused with the trappings of haughty affluence and aloof grandeur. Accordingly, before millions of viewers, the Clampetts conquered the suburbs, armed not only with bowie knives and Colt firearms (both of which they likely had in ample supply), but more important, with the homespun values and sturdy convictions they learned from having persevered in the southern mountains.

With the success of *The Beverly Hillbillies*, CBS executives encouraged Paul Henning to produce two more rural-themed comedies: *Petticoat Junction* and *Green Acres*. The former premiered in 1963 and the latter in 1965; both reaped high ratings as they accompanied the Clampetts and *The Andy Griffith Show* in primetime. By the fall of 1965, Columbia Broadcasting presented a veritable smorgasbord of white rural comedy.[76] In spite of their differences, each sitcom observed a rather formulaic script, and their respective characters evoked familiar and derivative stereotypes. All celebrated a highly romanticized past as they satirized the apparent moral bankruptcy and vice-ridden nature of the present. Uncle Joe Carson (Edgar Buchanan) of *Petticoat Junction* joined Jed Clampett and Sheriff Andy Taylor as lead protagonists on their respective programs. Clampett and Taylor stood out for their commitment to the male-headed family, rigorous labor, and unwavering Christian virtue. Uncle Joe Carson, on the other hand, took on the role of the "lazy hillbilly," reminiscent of the characters in Paul Webb's comics or Erskine Caldwell's novels.

Though he never approached the perfidiousness of the Lesters in *Tobacco Road* or the unwashed boorishness of *The Mountain Boys,* Carson's mostly affable demeanor was exceeded by his scheming and irreparably dilatory habits. As a counterpoint to the strong and decisive yet empathetic Sheriff Andy Taylor, Carson spent more time avoiding work than actually doing it.[77]

Of these shows' lead characters only Oliver Wendell Douglas (Eddie Albert) of *Green Acres* was not a natural-born southerner. Clampett, Carson, and Taylor (one might include Amos McCoy among these men as well) shared a penchant for exposing the folly of modern life; evidently this skill was the near-exclusive province of older white men from the upland South. In contrast, Douglas, named after the famous Supreme Court justice Oliver Wendell Holmes, was a wayward Yankee in search of a simpler life. An erstwhile lawyer who had abandoned his practice in New York City, Douglas purchased a farm in the fictional town of Hooterville, a nondescript outpost likely somewhere among the Ozarks. Here, he planned to start his life anew.[78] The ill-prepared Douglas was consistently in over his head and an inferior steward of the land. Even Arnold Ziffel, the show's communicative pig, fit in better than did the big city lawyer. Douglas never caught on to the vicissitudes of agriculture or the austerity it took to eke out a living from the land. He seldom performed any task correctly or without substantial assistance from a townsperson, of whom he asked begrudgingly and only after his own repeated failures. The ineffectual city slicker, while amiable for the most part, failed to earn the viewers' respect in the same way as his primetime counterparts. Regardless of Douglas's elite education and his former career in law, he depended on the "local yokels" and their inherent knowledge of the land to get by. If nothing else, *Green Acres* prematurely belied Frank Sinatra's famous claim. Mr. Douglas did in fact "make it" in New York though he could not so easily make it anywhere, or at least not in Hooterville.[79]

Tom Fletcher to Jed Clampett: Culture, Politics, and the Making of Postwar Liberalism

So far this book has explored an array of figures, real and fictional. But who among them personified the upland South in the second half of the twentieth century? Was it still Daniel Boone and David Crockett, if ever it truly was? How about Tom Fletcher, the man from eastern Kentucky who had lost his job amid the restructuring of his state's coal and lumber industry? This chapter has presented some additional options: fictional mountaineers from the Ozarks and West Virginia, a county sheriff from North Carolina, or maybe one of the other whimsical characters who appeared on primetime television or in popular comic strips. Until Jed Clampett moved his family west, he and Tom Fletcher lived in similar homes and settings. The poverty the two men had struggled to overcome buttressed one of the most persistent stereotypes of the region. At the same time, however, nostalgia for the frontier, associated as it was with the valorization of white masculinity, made Tom Fletcher and Jed Clampett predictable, if unwitting, representatives of the upland South. This, of course, was the legacy of favored pioneers like Boone and Crockett. At the height of *The Beverly Hillbillies'* popularity and in the aftermath of Johnson's poverty tour, Clampett and Fletcher loomed large on the nation's cultural and political stage.

But what message did journalists, politicians, and television producers send as they rehearsed yet more overwrought and inaccurate narratives about the upland South and its peoples? Their depictions of the region largely emphasized racial homogeneity, feminine purity, and pioneer masculinity. These themes echoed the local color movement at the turn of the century and found renewed interest in the folk revivals of the 1920s and the Great Depression; that they also coursed through the rhetoric of postwar liberalism and popular culture should not come as a surprise. It was, after all, a seductive account, steeped in the pathos of a national mythology. And if told properly, with the correct images and actors, it reliably shaped public opinion and achieved political results. The passage of the Area Redevelopment Act and the Economic Opportunity Act of 1964 on the one hand, and the revenue gleaned from CBS's primetime lineup on the other, had proven as much.

Still another story unfolded, and it too invites some questions. Did it matter beyond a coincidence that *The Beverly Hillbillies* and its rural-themed counterparts peaked in success just as the civil rights movement permeated the news on a daily basis? What impact did African Americans who had protested generations of violent, unequal treatment have on the direction of the decade's liberalism? By the late 1960s, civil rights and the black freedom movement eclipsed the quixotic portrayal of the upland South in the media. The harmonious lives of white people shown on television had always been rather detached from society writ large, and their popularity slowly waned. This blithe disconnect of network TV led Gil Scott-Heron in 1970 to famously proclaim, "The Revolution Will Not Be Televised."[80] The words of the black poet resonated. Fearing the irrelevancy of their programming, network executives soon pulled the plug on the rural lineup. Ratings had slumped, and the rediscovery of poverty and the legislation that accompanied it no longer garnered headlines.

Within two years of Scott-Heron's rap, on the eve of Richard Nixon's 1972 reelection, CBS completed its so-called rural purge and canceled every sitcom that featured the trials and tribulations of white southerners.[81] True, during that same year CBS introduced *The Waltons;* set in western Virginia, the family drama achieved acclaim and modest ratings over its nine-year duration. But overall, the "Country Broadcast System," as some had mockingly referred to CBS, rebranded itself and moved in another direction. Programming such as *Maude, M*A*S*H, The Bob Newhart Show, All in the Family,* and, later, *The Jeffersons* supplanted the hillbilly comedies of the sixties.[82]

However, the die may well have been cast as early as October 1962 when the Clampetts moved to Beverly Hills and James Meredith integrated the University of Mississippi. In hindsight, the month was a turning point worth deeper consideration. Outside the South, a predominantly sympathetic nation supported James Meredith's integration. And by the middle of the 1960s the oppressive and highly publicized nature of Jim Crow was a national embarrassment that many citizens wished to see overturned.[83] Civil rights activists made great strides in turning the public against the most flagrant violations of human rights in the South. As the elections of the first half of the decade indicated, a majority of voters did not believe that one's race should preclude him or her from drinking from a water fountain, sitting at a lunch counter, or participating in politics. Yet, as the next chapter demonstrates, public polling also documented the reservations about activists who traveled across the South to actually test the civil and voting rights legislation.

But as this chapter and the previous one have proposed, the representation of white poverty and the fixation upon upland southerners captured the public's attention and empathy, particularly regarding the thornier issues of economics. Scholars of Black Power have asserted that liberals readily offered "a mouthful of civil rights but not a mouthful of food."[84] One pollster noted that the *Brown* decision signaled the legal decline of Jim Crow, but over ten years after the ruling, seven out of ten white homeowners still resisted the integration of African Americans into "their" neighborhoods.[85] This obstinacy highlighted the thoroughly institutionalized nature of racism in the United States; it also portended the limits of liberalism.

Here again *The Beverly Hillbillies* is instructive. After striking oil, Jed Clampett purchased a home in a wealthy suburban neighborhood. In the process, he and his family illustrated the unspoken ways in which whiteness structured foundational aspects of everyday life. Purchasing a home, for example, was itself an activity animated by racial considerations. Home ownership proved illusive for millions of African Americans and other people of color who had been historically frozen out of the market by exclusionary methods like redlining and restrictive covenants. Suspending for a moment the fictional nature of the Clampetts, let us consider the real-life demographics of Beverly Hills, a neighborhood known as an exclusive enclave, synonymous with "swimming pools and movie stars." Nearly 98 percent of Beverly Hills' 30,817 residents were white, according to the 1960 census.[86] While the census never recorded how many poor whites moved into the neighborhood after having received millions of dollars from fortuitously misfiring a rifle into a field of "bubbling crude," one safely assumes the number was low.

Though their ascent to the elite was unlikely, the Clampetts nonetheless paralleled the impressive levels of white economic advancement that occurred throughout the 1950s and 1960s, even if they did so through stereotypical performances and derivative comedy. Yet the ascetic diligence of other upland southerners had for too long gone unrewarded, and many now faced dire economic straits. For them, liberals advertised a project that would, at a minimum, make life better in places like Inez, Kentucky. Only in the fictional context of primetime television did a family from the Ozarks land in Beverly Hills, but perhaps thousands of others might claim more modest suburban homes elsewhere and join the affluent society.

Johnson and advisors meet outside of Tom Fletcher's home In Inez, Kentucky, on April 24, 1964. Courtesy of the LBJ Presidential Library, Austin, Texas.

But as the decade progressed, viewers outgrew the hillbilly comedies, and more people concluded that the War on Poverty went too far beyond assisting men like Tom Fletcher and his family. As they did, support for the welfare state withered, and a new political alignment emerged from the discontent of the late 1960s and early 1970s. Considerations of race and gender, however, continued to inform public policy and popular culture. Upland southerners would make appearances in the next decades, though they starred in lead roles less frequently.[87] Meanwhile, as the War on Poverty channeled some resources to poor communities, activists launched increasingly pointed critiques of US policy at home and abroad. In fact, the impressive, if brief, ascendency of the civil rights and then the Black Power movements made it impossible for liberals to emphasize West Virginia mountaineers and Kentucky frontiersmen in the ways in which they had during the late 1950s and early 1960s. The changing optics of economic inequality as well as the ensuing dissolution of postwar liberalism, and what it wrought, conclude this book. And as such, we return once more to public policy and the field of politics and perceptions.[88]

CHAPTER 6

THE LIMITS OF LIBERALISM AND THE CHANGING FACE OF POVERTY

The Collapse of the Kennedy-Johnson Coalition

> No, nothing about the War on Poverty is commonplace. In
> the zeal of its administrators, in the freshness of their ideas, in
> the innovations of organization and policy approach, it stands
> alone—even in a period when many New Frontiers were being
> crossed and a Great Society was being born. No matter what
> may happen to the Office of Economic Opportunity and the
> Economic Opportunity Act, their influence upon American
> institutions will have been profound.
>
> —James L. Sundquist, 1969[1]

In late February 1964, Florida resident David Beard met Lyndon Johnson at a campaign event in Miami. An enthusiastic Beard arrived over an hour early to wait in line for a front-row seat; afterwards, he secured an autograph from the thirty-sixth president. Unfortunately, rushed by his handlers at the event's conclusion, Johnson absentmindedly wandered off with Beard's favorite Parker pen. Over six months later, the Floridian responded to the incident with an angry letter. To make amends, Juanita D. Roberts, one of Johnson's office managers, sent Beard a new pen emblazoned with the White House insignia. Roberts conceded, "It will not take the place of your Parker, but I hope you will accept it in the spirit with which it is sent." Beard never followed up.[2]

However, his letter suggested that something had bothered him beyond a stolen pen. In comments unrelated to the Miami encounter, Beard demanded "an explanation on why you are not as quick to call out troops to bring law and order in Harlem as President Kennedy was to call them out to bring law and order in Oxford, Mississippi."[3] "The riots in New York," he continued, "are far more serious than the riots brought on by Federal Marshals in Oxford."[4] Beard was referring to Kennedy's deployment of the 2nd Infantry Division, the 503rd Military Police Battalion, and the Mississippi Army National Guard to assist James Meredith's integration of the University of Mississippi a year earlier. That Beard blamed the Oxford riots on the presence of federal troops and integrationists rather than those who had resisted Meredith's admission revealed his sympathies.

While the letter stood out for the memorable encounter between a president and his one-time supporter, it was nevertheless indicative of thousands of others that the White House received during Johnson's second term. Collectively, they documented a growing antagonism toward the Democrat among many voters. These men and women felt that the administration had passively stood by as unrest and African American militancy gripped the nation. Worse, some concluded that Johnson and his congressional allies had even tacitly supported or given license to this behavior. To critics like Beard, the War on Poverty had fashioned liberals into enablers of sloth, excess, and, most ominously, black male insurrection.[5]

Beard also exemplified a brewing insurgency that gained steam through the latter half of the 1960s and would transform politics for decades. To Beard and others, Johnson had unacceptably deviated from the programs he had promoted a few years earlier. Thus, this chapter builds on the preceding argument that support for the War on Poverty was contingent on its ability to be interpreted as an effort to bolster whites who had failed to gain access to postwar prosperity. Heretofore this book has emphasized the words and actions of a hand-wringing white elite. These politicians, journalists, novelists, writers, and television producers invoked the upland South to explore the themes of racial and manly decline, economic inequality, and the shortcomings of the affluent society. The nostalgia and mythology they had attached to this contradictory region and its people made it an ideal backdrop for campaign events, investigative journalism, and even comic strips and several highly rated television sitcoms.

By contrast, this chapter inverts the focus and grants a view of the decade's politics and activism from the bottom up. It does so first by discussing a series of scandals and attacks on the poverty programs. Journalists and politicians increasingly noted the unintended effects that the War on Poverty had in communities of color across the urban North and West, as well as in the South. A chorus of detractors seized on several high-profile controversies to damage the reputation of the Office of Economic Opportunity. Opponents of the OEO then argued that the programs laid bare the inherent criminality of African Americans, as well as the latent perfidiousness of liberalism and the ineptitude of the welfare state.[6]

Next, this chapter uncovers the voices of middle- and working-class whites, men and women who shared Beard's frustrations. Most were suburbanites who never claimed an Anglo-Saxon identity; nor did they seem particularly enamored with the upland southerners who had transfixed liberals from Caudill to Kennedy to Henning. Instead, prosaic matters like economic competition, status anxiety, and crime motivated them. Here, the idealistic pronouncements by the elite at the beginning of the decade became subsumed by the explicit racism of a consciously embattled segment of the white population. Whereas earlier chapters concentrated on the power of rhetoric and visual representation, this one shifts gears to scrutinize the power of political demographics and petty resentments. As these resentments accumulated, the face of poverty in the popular imagination changed from rural, southern, and white to urban, northern, and black. In the process, the ideological basis of liberalism unraveled.[7]

Curiously, however, the changing perception of the War on Poverty, and liberalism more generally, obscured what it did and did not accomplish. Adversaries of the poverty programs portrayed them as ill-conceived social experiments, but the War on Poverty offered limited funding for organizers and activists to mitigate despair in some depressed communities. Notwithstanding some major victories, liberal legislation still did not markedly improve economic conditions for most poor people, especially people of color. Paradoxically, then, even as it lost support for supposedly subsidizing urban rebellion and encouraging laziness, the War on Poverty remained, as it had been advertised in the first place, an initiative that provided assistance to more white, male-headed families, as well as America's older citizens, than other demographics. That it produced uneven levels of success along lines of race, gender, and age should be viewed as consistent with the aims that the program's architects established from its outset.[8]

But more significantly, Johnson and Congress bowed to critics and responded to the narrative of urban crime and fears of black violence by rescinding or scaling back many of the poverty programs. Rather than double down and strengthen policies that had demonstrated some ability (or at least the potential) to alleviate hardship, President Johnson bolstered law enforcement and passed the opening round of punitive legislation that would facilitate a mass expansion of the nation's prison system.[9] He also expanded the war in Southeast Asia. And just as some liberals had used poor whites from the southern hills to gain traction for their policies in the early 1960s, other politicians have since presented images of poor blacks and urban disintegration to forge their own appeal. The gradual dismantlement of America's modest welfare state thus began before it was fully implemented. It was precipitated by the growing sense that federal assistance targeted not white people who deserved it but, rather, minorities who did not. James Sundquist's prescient claim that the War on Poverty would have "a profound impact" on American institutions was indeed accurate, though in ways far different from what he had envisioned.[10]

The Changing Perceptions and Dissolution of the War on Poverty

From its inception, the presentation and reality of the War on Poverty diverged. Adam Yarmolinsky's statement that "the original picture of the poverty program in the public eye was Appalachia. . . . [It] offered very little for blacks because most poor people are not black and most black people are not poor" highlights the storyline that many poverty warriors had invested in.[11] The ubiquity of poor whites in popular culture aligned with the initial popularity of the poverty programs and liberalism overall. By the early 1960s, largely due to the pervasiveness of hillbilly imagery, most everyone agreed that "the color" of Appalachia was white. They may have also known that it was a highly romanticized brand of whiteness, strengthened by cherished mythologies, and worth restoring despite its apparent problems. The second part of Yarmolinsky's claim, however, was simply incorrect. Perhaps he issued the statement for political purposes, but the War on Poverty offered more than "very little" to black communities, at least briefly. Furthermore, while most poor people may not have been black, most black people were indeed poor; the poverty rate among African Americans was 56 percent in 1960 and fell to 50 percent by 1965.[12] This fact alone undermined Yarmolinsky's "original picture" of the War on Poverty.[13]

Yarmolinsky's half-true proclamation reflected the skittishness that some poverty warriors had over assertions that the federal programs were directed at nonwhite populations. Most linkages between the War on Poverty and civil rights received tepid approval at best and more typically, vocal resistance. Ambivalence toward civil rights activists was on full display during the summer of 1964 when hundreds of college students, white and black, embarked upon Mississippi to register the state's disenfranchised black voters; the endeavor famously became known as Freedom Summer.[14] But as the registration drives ramped up, a Harris Survey concluded, "The American public, by an overwhelming 2 to 1 majority, views with disfavor the efforts of northern students to push for civil rights for Negroes in Mississippi."[15] The pollsters found that only 31 percent approved of the voter registration; 57 percent disapproved while 12 percent were not sure. Lyndon Johnson's special counsel, Lee White, opposed efforts to confront Jim Crow, urging the president to deny requests to send troops to protect the activists. White protested, "It is nearly incredible that those people who are voluntarily sticking their head into the lion's mouth would ask for somebody to come down and shoot the lion."[16] To White, the students were misguided and naïve, and they deserved whatever fate befell them.

Director of the Federal Bureau of Investigation (FBI) J. Edgar Hoover, known for his surveillance of civil rights activists, informed the *Clarion Ledger,* a Jackson, Mississippi–based newspaper, that his "organization most certainly does not and will not give protection to civil rights workers."[17] To the delight of Mississippi segregationists, the paper concluded: "Protection is in the hands of the local authorities."[18] The local protection Hoover advocated came under increasing scrutiny after James Chaney, Michael Schwerner, and Andrew Goodman, all of whom had participated in Freedom Summer, went missing and were later found murdered not far from Jackson.[19] The terrifying episode led the aging muckraker Upton Sinclair to write to President Johnson and criticize his administration's commitment to implementing civil rights throughout the South. Sinclair rationalized, "If murder is not a Federal crime, surely kidnapping is, and it is no quibble to say that the victims were kidnapped before they were murdered. . . . I think we are disgraced in front of the whole world if that horrid crime ends up as a mockery of the government."[20] Johnson replied to Sinclair: "I can assure you that the same intense effort that went into the investigation of this and other crimes related to civil rights will be made with respect to bringing a trial to those we think guilty."[21] Johnson's claim, though, was disingenuous; the federal government never brought the full weight of federal law enforcement to bear on the case, and authorities neither arrested nor questioned several known suspects. Only in 2005 did Edgar Ray Killen, a well-known white supremacist, alleged conspirator, and assailant in the murders face trial. He was convicted on three counts of manslaughter and is presently serving a sixty-year sentence in Mississippi.[22]

If Johnson failed to protect civil rights workers in the South, his administration deserves some credit for its innovative Community Action Programs (CAP), though it is not clear that the White House knew what the programs might engender. CAP proved far more inclusive than federal efforts hitherto and supplied a mechanism for many poor communities to access federal and state funding. These programs disbursed grants and fostered self-activity across the United States.[23] Herbert Hill, the NAACP's labor director, cautiously embraced community action even as he resisted the "extension of white welfare paternalism."[24] Still, Hill endeavored to "rescue the antipoverty program from the politicians who want merely a sterile and ineffective program that will mean little or nothing for the Negro community. . . . The NAACP favors a real war on poverty, not a symbolic encounter."[25] If the programs proved successful, Hill thought poor people could empower themselves, exert control over federal resources, and finally address the problems that plagued their neighborhoods. New and creative forms of activism occurred under the guise of community action, ones that were not foreseen by conservatives and many liberals alike.[26]

However, as more black-run organizations secured funding and created their own Community Action Agencies (CAA), opposition to the War on Poverty increased. The ordeal between white Mississippi Democrats and the Child Development Group of Mississippi (CDGM) was one example. The state's African American population was among the largest and most impoverished in the nation, and child welfare services were nonexistent in many cities and counties. Rather miraculously, given the context, the CDGM had operated intermittently for years without a consistent source of financial support. Its mission to administer daycare and early childhood education for kids of the working poor made the group an ideal recipient of aid through the OEO's Head Start Program. Various Mississippi community leaders worked collaboratively on a proposal and won a $1.5 million grant; it was the largest awarded during the summer of 1965. The money soon flowed to precarious daycare centers in the state, including the CDGM.[27]

Head Start's partnership with Mississippi's struggling childcare centers quickly became the model for federally funded, locally administered poverty programs. The group elected distinguished board members, including A. D. Beitell, former president of Tougaloo College (a historically black college); Marian Wright, a lawyer for the NAACP's legal defense fund; and Reverend James McCree, a charismatic preacher and longtime advocate of civil rights.[28] The board decided to headquarter the CDGM at Mary Holmes Junior College in West Point, Mississippi. Unfortunately, the black Mississippians who ran the organization immediately found themselves at odds with the state's notoriously bigoted government and congressional delegation. These lawmakers had correctly noted that blacks could bypass the openly white supremacist state government and directly access federal funding through Head Start.

Mississippi's white Democratic establishment believed this was an unacceptable proposition. Not long afterwards, a controversy broke out that sealed the fate of the CDGM and exposed the zeal with which many white southern legislators, at the state and federal level, opposed the War on Poverty's inclusiveness. Shortly after the childcare provider received its first infusion of federal dollars, Mississippi's two segregationist senators, John Stennis and James O. Eastland, accused the CDGM of "gross malfeasance and corruption."[29] They ordered an investigation of Head Start based on allegations that it laundered money on behalf of the Mississippi Freedom Democrats, the state's opposition Democratic Party that fought for equality. "Deceit and disorganization," Stennis claimed, typified the day-to-day machinations of the CDGM. He also concluded that Head Start was a front for subversive groups that advocated integration. The local press portrayed the childcare organization as a hive of "racial zealots and agitators" rather than as a nonprofit that handed out formula and offered shelter and education for poor children.[30]

As a concession to Stennis and the state legislature, the CDGM relocated their offices to Mississippi's capital city, Jackson, nearly 150 miles from West Point; the move cost thousands of dollars and hundreds of hours in labor. Still, Stennis, Eastland, and Mississippi governor Paul B. Johnson singled out the program for audits in an apparent intimidation campaign. The state hired men to rummage through the various daycare centers, nearly all of which were staffed by African American women. The auditors aggressively searched for anything that might be viewed as an inappropriate use of taxpayer money. Not surprisingly, they found "peculiarities" ranging from "excessive car rentals" to paid vacations; the CDGM argued that the car rentals were necessary to move from West Point to Jackson, and they disputed taking vacations. Stennis believed that "SNCC types"—a reference to the Student Nonviolent Coordinating Committee, a key civil rights group—had used CAP funds to infiltrate Mississippi and that they then used daycare funding to support extravagant lifestyles.[31] At the same time, Stennis and Johnson used the new civil rights law to penalize the daycare centers. One provision banned federal funding to segregated nonprofits; since black men and women had exclusively run eight centers, all of which were located in overwhelmingly black parts of the state, Senator Stennis and Governor Johnson proposed that they were segregated and thus ineligible for assistance unless they hired whites. The cynical strategies worked, and within a year the state's leadership had stripped 50 percent of the Head Start money bound for the state. In Congress, the senator proposed to eliminate the rest of the state's share of funding until its (white) leadership could exercise unchallenged oversight, effectively annulling the very concept of community action.[32]

Undeterred by the bureaucratic obstructionism of Mississippi's white Democrats, African Americans still managed to secure some limited funding. This persistent determination among black daycare workers and activists revealed that the War on Poverty remained the best and perhaps only hope to improve local conditions and circumvent a fortified power structure that had long relegated them to second-class citizens.[33] But as it turned out, the political battles that hobbled the CDGM were typical of other OEO initiatives. If anything, allegations over the misuse of public funds in Head Start paled in comparison to the explosive controversies that critics exploited elsewhere. Politicians, media, and law enforcement uncovered damning evidence that they claimed linked the War on Poverty to civil unrest. Some fabricated and some real, these controversies altered the perception of the War on Poverty as a benefit program to address the apparent decline of white men in the upland South to one that had nefariously financed nonwhite people intent on destruction within the nation's smoldering urban ghettos.[34] By recasting the federal government and the OEO as enablers of radicalism and criminality, conservatives found a platform to oppose the War on Poverty and liberalism more broadly.

One of the first of these incidents occurred in Harlem during the summer of 1965, just as the battles over Head Start in Mississippi heated up. Controversy broke out when a young black writer named LeRoi Jones (later and more famously known as Amiri Baraka) received funds through the OEO program Project Uplift. With the grant, Jones established the Black Arts Theater as the cultural auxiliary to Harlem Youth Opportunities Unlimited (HARYOU), another project that had received money. For over three years, the well-regarded psychologist and native New Yorker Kenneth Clarke had overseen the growth of HARYOU into one the city's largest job-training institutes.[35] Jones wanted to expand HARYOU to include theatrical productions and training in the arts and humanities. These would "explore, develop, extend, propagate, and preserve the dramatic arts and talents of the Afro-Americans" in Harlem, according to Jones.[36] He staged several plays, including *Experimental Death Unit, Black Ice,* and *Jello,* all of which delved into the weighty themes of racism, oppression, white violence, slavery, and genocide; they were also works of contentious political philosophy. But in contrast to liberal calls for civil rights and cultural pluralism, Jones articulated a more radical conception of black self-defense, separatism, and Afro-centrism. The playwright and poet had indeed taken the mission of HARYOU well beyond Clarke's rather paternalistic vision of vocational training.

As soon as OEO director Sargent Shriver learned of the performances, he shut the program down and subjected HARYOU to congressional review. Through the chorus of condemnation, Shriver assured skeptics that the OEO's support of Jones was an "embarrassment that would never happen again."[37] Notably, however, Harlem remained calm as rebellions broke out across dozens of American cities over the next three years.[38] Some observers have proposed that Jones's plays had a "cathartic" affect among Harlem residents who may have otherwise vented their dissatisfaction through violence as they had a year earlier, before the presence of Jones's experimental arts venue.[39] Shriver, for one, wondered if "they would have preferred a Watts" to the Black Arts Theater.[40] Though Jones lost federal funding for his performances, he continued work on several projects and with area youth. And while no single piece of evidence explains the relative peace in Harlem during the late 1960s, the continuity and strength of the black arts movement was likely one cause.

Following the Black Arts Theater controversy, Adam Clayton Powell, the civil rights advocate, New York representative, and member of the House Committee on Education and Labor, angrily watched as his colleagues from both parties tried to eliminate many OEO programs, including Project Uplift and Head Start. At one point, Powell accused Sam Gibbons, the senior ranking member on the education committee and a Democratic representative from Florida, of acting as the "chief assassin" of the War on Poverty and stirring the "hysteria of Black Power" to undermine it.[41] In an effort to defend the poverty programs, Powell, whose district was a predominantly African American and Latino section of Harlem, rehearsed Adam Yarmolinsky's claim. According to Powell, the programs mostly benefited poor whites: "There is a battle plan now forming against the War on Poverty to exterminate the future of 32,000,000 poor people, the vast majority of whom are white and I am here to fight for them—not for myself."[42] Tellingly, Powell thought the best way to fend off attacks on the OEO was to reiterate that the "vast majority" it served were white. The strategy was not new, and it recalled the way in which the programs were advertised in the first place.

By 1966 editorial boards and newsrooms from many of the nation's largest cities had voiced opposition to Johnson and the War on Poverty. The *Chicago Tribune*'s editorial page proclaimed that the OEO had "subsidized riots."[43] The *Roanoke Times* seconded the claim: "Militant misfits in the poverty war" received a "blank check . . . to stir up anti-white sentiment and open violence."[44]

Local newspapers, police, politicians, and, most notably, indignant white observers sensationalized and sometimes fabricated the link between urban violence and federal funding. After civil unrest broke out in Nashville during the
spring of 1967, the city's chief of police, John Sorace, testified before the Senate
Judiciary Committee. He blamed the uprising on "militant negroes" and the
white liberals in Washington who passed the Economic Opportunity Act of
1964.[45] "The Student Non-Violent Coordinating Committee," charged Sorace,
"is teaching Negro children pure, unadulterated hatred of the white race in a
summer school subsidized by the Federal Government."[46] He explained that
the OEO had issued $7,700 for a "liberation school" where students par-
ticipated in "racial rioting" and other activities the police chief described as
"anti-white."[47] Some of the money went towards teaching "Negro history and
culture and inspired pride in race among colored children." This, according
to Sorace, led to "hatred for the white man." He concluded, "We believe in
this instance, the Federal funds are helping to perpetuate the problems of our
cities."[48] Sorace failed to consider whether the resentment experienced by black
Nashvillians, those who had for generations faced legal segregation, police violence, and impoverishment, might have been at least equally accountable for
any rise in militancy. Instead, the police chief blamed the animus on those
he described as a radicalized and criminal element. These men and women,
mostly affiliated with SNCC, had apparently commandeered the tax dollars of
honest Americans and incited poor people to rebel.

Shriver and some liberals in Congress scrutinized Sorace's veracity. After
the uprising in Nashville, Sargent Shriver defended the role of the OEO: "In
the 27 cities that have had riots this summer, there are 12,128 persons who are
direct employees of OEO funded agencies. . . . In the same 27 cities, six of the
12,128 paid poverty workers were arrested and to date, none of the six have
come to trial and none have been convicted."[49] Property damage from the riots
approached $274 million; yet none of the OEO's 491 properties located in the
affected cities had been targeted, according to Shriver. Consequently, Shriver
concluded that OEO workers "resolved in conversation rather than in conflict,
in mediation rather than with Molotov cocktails."[50] Shriver's evidence, like the
presence of the Black Arts Theater in New York, suggests that despite the accusations of its opponents, the OEO may have improved community relations
in distressed cities.

Regardless, Shriver's assessment mattered little in the court of public opinion, and the perception that the War on Poverty led to black revolt rather than
white uplift grew. A 1967 study by White House Fellow J. Timothy McGinley

reported that nearly 70 percent of those polled believed that "the president had gone too far in the Civil Rights area."[51] Letters from concerned citizens like Mildred Griffen from Baltimore and Leo Stronczek from Fort Wayne, Indiana, captured the sentiment. Griffen felt the War on Poverty drove "the Negro . . . to expect handouts without any responsibility," and she implored her friends to protest whenever "we see our money go to the poor colored."[52] Stronczek agreed and demanded that Johnson repeal the War on Poverty, the Civil Rights Act of 1964, and the Voting Rights Act of 1965 "until we see that these people become civil."[53] Ardis Kuehne, another opponent of Johnson's policies, claimed to have "conclusive evidence that our tax money is being used to finance these riots staged by these people that supposedly are working for the OEO."[54] Pearl Laupert, a woman from Ellicot City, Maryland, argued that unruly black men started the riots in Baltimore after receiving taxpayer dollars; the "coloreds want to be the dictators of the United States," she declared.[55] Virginia Behnke, from Tampa, initiated a letter writing campaign on behalf of "Mr. Average Citizen."[56] Behnke was certain that Mr. Average Citizen wanted his taxes to pay police officers and the national guard, those "wonderful young men [who] protect our property and our lives . . . [and] open fire and kill off the first of these men" who gathered in the streets.[57] If Behnke, Laupert, Kuehne, Stronczek, and David Beard represented a composite of Mr. and Mrs. Average Citizen, the role that white ethnics and middle-class men and women played in turning the tide against Johnson and his policies becomes clear.[58] The majority of letters addressed to the White House disapproved of the president; most accused Johnson of weakness in the face of black crime and viewed him as naïve to assist a segment of the population that had acted so insubordinately.

Sorace's testimony on the Nashville riots, as well as the accusations of an untold number of observers, buttressed additional reports of violence linked to the poverty programs. One of the more alarming examples took place in Cleveland, Ohio. A 1966 uprising in the city's Hough neighborhood sent already tense race relations into a tailspin, and suspicion increased between the city's mostly white police department and its black citizens. The latter lived mostly in poor neighborhoods on the city's East Side, where unemployment and white flight had taken its toll. However, a nonprofit community improvement group, Cleveland: NOW!, led by the city's first black mayor, Carl B. Stokes, seemed uniquely situated to bridge the racial and class chasm that had divided Ohio's largest city. Stokes was determined to raise $1.5 billion over several years and use the proceeds for an ambitious urban renewal and revitalization effort. In the first year, Stokes received, among other donations, $1.6 million in federal matching funds through the Office of Economic Opportunity; this money was supposed to furnish small, minority-owned businesses with low-interest loans.[59]

The efforts of Cleveland: NOW! and the charismatic mayor to rebuild the city's battered economy and ease its social tensions ultimately failed. And pent-up resentments boiled over again on July 23, 1968, in the Glenville neighborhood. The spark that caused the conflagration remains nebulous, but all agree that a gunfight broke out between the police and a Black Power group known as the Republic of New Libya. The police contended that the group had "planned an ambush" on officers, but some black Clevelanders claimed that the police had instigated the shootout after they had provocatively confiscated a car that had belonged to a member.[60] Regardless, the pitched battle resulted in the deaths of three white officers and four African Americans, three of whom were allegedly connected to the Republic of New Libya; over a dozen other bystanders and officers were injured in the melee. During the ensuing four nights hundreds of black Clevelanders rebelled in response to what they believed was yet another example of heavy-handed police tactics. Looting occurred throughout the neighborhood, and the city's fire department handled over fifty calls.[61]

After the uprising subsided, the Cleveland Police Department alleged that Fred "Ahmed" Evans, an activist who had received over ten thousand dollars from Cleveland: NOW! to open a bookstore and community center known as the Afro Culture Shop, was among the armed militants who had shot an officer. Federal and local authorities had placed Evans and the Republic of New Libya under surveillance well before the confrontation and had suspected that he had amassed firearms and conceived of the bookstore as a staging ground for an insurrection.[62] The city's two daily newspapers, the *Cleveland Press* and the *Cleveland Plain Dealer,* presented circumstantial evidence that Evans had purchased the guns used in the shootout with money obtained through the mayor's nonprofit. Though these allegations were never proven, they stuck. Cleveland: NOW! and the OEO were tainted by their associations with the Republic of New Libya; the War on Poverty came under intense public scrutiny once again.[63]

J. Edgar Hoover's FBI quickly issued a statement that declared Evans and the Republic of New Libya "extremists and violent" as well as "a threat to the internal security of this country."[64] A reporter for the *Cleveland Press* summed up Cleveland: NOW! as a reckless attempt to "[pay] off those considered to be explosive elements."[65] In the aftermath of the uprising, Mayor Stokes removed white officers from neighborhood beats across the city's East Side and formed black-led community patrols; he also imposed a curfew and requested that the Ohio National Guard stand by in the event of more disturbances. The mayor's attempt to mediate between the city's black community and the police department seemingly alienated him from both, and his vision for a Cleveland renaissance never came to fruition. Evans, meanwhile, was taken into custody the day after the shootout. He was later convicted of murder and sentenced to death. The state eventually commuted his sentence to life without parole, though he died in prison ten years later.[66]

The intrigue surrounding the Republic of New Libya aside, neither the 1966 nor 1968 riots in Cleveland approached the destruction wrought by what occurred in Detroit during the summer of 1967. With estimates between $40 and $80 million in property damage, the uprisings that broke out across the Motor City that year were the costliest of the decade.[67] In response, the White House received hundreds of letters from angry men and women around the country demanding that the military occupy Detroit, dismantle the poverty programs, and kill or imprison any Detroiter who participated in the unrest. One irate observer, Hawthorne Lane, blamed "the Supreme Court, the Justice Department, the Congress and the Administration [for] tying the hands of law enforcement officials to a point where they are afraid to even fight back when being attacked."[68] The War on Poverty and civil rights, Lane continued, "made the negro think he is the ruler of the white people, therefore, he does what he pleases because the Federal Government upholds his actions."[69] Albert Turk, a man from the Detroit area, believed that the War on Poverty gave "negroes money to arm themselves" and seize the city, and eventually, the rest of the nation.[70] He wrote to Sargent Shriver and asked, "Why should taxpayers pay money to be murdered?"[71] James Andrews echoed these sentiments and mocked the unraveling of Johnson's presidency: "God must be laughing Himself to death at the problems raised by you liberals who have encouraged the negroes to think they can live without working."[72] To Andrews, divine intervention, not a war against poverty, was required for "lawless and uncivilized negroes" to achieve equality with white people.[73] He advised Johnson to fire his whole cabinet and appoint "men like Wallace of Alabama, Reagan of California, Goldwater of Arizona, and some other people who know that two and two equals four."[74] All three of the political figures Andrews named had earned the respect of segregationists and conservatives through their steadfast opposition to civil rights legislation and the War on Poverty.

Others who wrote the White House, like Warren H. Folks, also from Michigan, exceeded the vitriolic racism of Lane, Turk, and Andrews. Warren Folks condemned Kennedy and Johnson for cracking down on the Ku Klux Klan, "that all-American, pro-Christian organization," thus allowing African Americans "to achieve their racial integration, amalgamation and cross-breeding of the races."[75] Folks concluded, "Your ultra-liberal anti-poverty agenda may have some merits were it not for the proven fact that your American Negroes are so hungry and thirsty that whisky stores are the places first looted after their sniper and fire-bomb attacks."[76] Here, a resentful Folks depicted Johnson as a cowardly, ineffectual father figure who was unable or unwilling to exact authoritative and decisive discipline upon "his" violent, out of control children.

But Folks's letter was illustrative for another reason. He posed the damning questions: "Just how great is your Great Society? No, perhaps I should ask, HOW BLACK IS IT?"[77] This simple query neatly encapsulated the widespread and increasing antagonism directed towards the War on Poverty and the Office of Economic Opportunity. Not even three years in, a vocal and growing contingent of whites equated the programs with unrest and blackness. A poll conducted in 1966 reported that only 17 percent of the public approved of the War on Poverty and believed it was "doing a good job."[78]

Warren Folks thus articulated the widely held belief that the Great Society had become less "great" and too "black." The two, apparently, could not coexist; as such, the poverty programs had gone dangerously awry from the otherwise acceptable mission of supporting white, rural southerners into one that subsidized black, urban violence. To its ardent detractors, the War on Poverty seemed to be a zero-sum proposition: anything great could not be black, and federal funding that fell into the hands of disempowered black communities equated to a loss of power among taxpayers. The recurrent references to taxpayers connoted whiteness, but also a sense of responsibility and citizenship; urban African Americans were then seen as something less, tax-takers neither deserving nor capable of citizenship. Most of all, as petty as they were, these letters documented a deep-seated unease among the postwar middle class. Its members' status, privilege, and power appeared shaken by the unrest of the urban ghetto but perhaps more so by the alleged complicity of liberals who seemed comfortably ensconced in Washington's halls of power, far from the smoldering rubble.[79]

Discontent accelerated through Johnson's tenure as media outlets unearthed a steady stream of inflammatory stories from which to extend the narrative. For certain, some attributed the uprisings to generations of federal neglect and institutional racism. Edward Richardson wrote to the administration from Detroit; he believed the city's riots represented a "renewed thrust for freedom" and justly responded to police brutality, housing discrimination, and economic inequality.[80] "When we see the indifference to the rights and needs of some of the citizens of this country," as well as the "failure to respond to peaceful, dignified and rightful protest," Richardson reasoned, violence was imminent, a last resort born of necessity.[81] Michigan governor George Romney agreed with Richardson's assessment, evocatively confessing in 1968 that systemic housing discrimination in and around Detroit had acted as a "high income white noose" around the necks of black residents.[82] But if the White House correspondence files are an accurate indication, the declarations of thousands of others who demanded a change in policy towards the poor and the abandonment of the War on Poverty submerged the voices of an empathetic Michigander and his reflective governor.

Meanwhile, Johnson's support collapsed. The president's approval rating peaked at nearly 80 percent immediately after the assassination of John F. Kennedy and remained around 70 percent through the 1964 presidential campaign. But by the end of 1965, Johnson's popularity began to decline and only recovered slightly after he announced his decision to not seek reelection in 1968. During the summer of 1967, as riots in Detroit, Newark, and East St. Louis, Illinois rocked the nation, Johnson's approval dipped below 50 percent for the first time. The president's poll numbers fell to 35 percent after reports of the Tet Offensive splashed across the front pages of newspapers nationwide in late January and February 1968. The surprise offensive by the North Vietnamese and their Viet Cong allies drove American forces from Saigon and other key positions; it also called into question Johnson's handling of the conflict.

Two months after Tet, another round of urban rebellions broke out in response to the assassination of Martin Luther King Jr., further damaging the president's standing. [83] All told, according to historians Stephan and Abigail Thernstrom, 329 "important riots" took place across 257 cities between 1965 and 1968; over 300 people had died amid hundreds of millions in property damage. Within four years, Johnson looked increasingly ineffectual as images of black men like Ahmed Evans and urban rioters had supplanted downtrodden white mountaineers like Tom Fletcher as the beneficiaries of the War on Poverty. And with the changing face of poverty, both the Johnson presidency and its brand of liberalism unraveled.[84]

Perceptions and Reality: Evaluating the War on Poverty

Emphasizing the sensational events and the disaffection of outspoken white critics presents a distorted view of what the poverty programs did and did not accomplish, however. The War on Poverty, in practice, looked quite different from the generally held assumptions of men and women who believed that it had become too "black." Unlike the high-profile controversies surrounding the CDGM, LeRoi Jones, and Ahmed Evans, the programs assisted poor people and bolstered activists in numerous ways that went mostly unreported and sparked little outrage. And over the past decade scholars have stitched together a rich, bottom-up history of the War on Poverty; collectively they dispel many of the myths that took root during the late 1960s and 1970s. As historian Annelise Orleck has noted, "the War on Poverty years were extraordinary—in the upsurge of grassroots organizing, in democratic activism by people so poor and disenfranchised that they had never before been engaged, in community-created and -run service institutions."[85]

Beyond the CDGM's hard-fought battle for assistance, examples abound that affirm Orleck's argument. Historian Rhonda Y. Williams has demonstrated how activists still secured funds through the OEO for urgently needed urban housing in some of the nation's poorest cities, despite the obfuscation of their opponents. Women from Baltimore's deteriorating neighborhoods, Williams has found, navigated an arcane bureaucracy, accessed limited funding, and developed affordable housing alternatives.[86] Likewise, Noel Cazenave has shown how community organizers in New York used the CAP to develop childcare as well as tutoring, afterschool, and mentoring programs.[87] According to one government estimate, youth programs affiliated with the Upward Bound Program kept as many as three in four potential dropouts enrolled in public high schools.[88] Orleck's research has focused on Las Vegas, a city particularly dynamic for its collaborative activism in the late 1960s and 1970s. A multiracial coalition of black women, welfare rights lawyers, and other activists received federal grants to challenge and eventually overturn discriminatory policies within Nevada's welfare system.[89] These studies illustrate the quotidian though labor-intensive ways that dedicated women and men marshaled scant resources to improve the day-to-day material conditions of several poor communities. Far from making headline news, these activities required applying for grants, building community-based coalitions to lobby local, state, and federal lawmakers, organizing and leading neighborhood meetings and rallies, and spending countless hours in volunteer or low-paid positions to improve the lives of those at the margins of society.

These activities still do not convey the macro impact that the War on Poverty had on millions of poor and working people. Arguably, US citizens aged sixty-five and over benefited from the poverty programs more than any other single demographic. The Social Security Act of 1965, legislation that included Medicare and Medicaid, was a transformative and enduring achievement of the Eighty-Ninth Congress. The legislation supplied health insurance for older Americans as well as those with disabilities and some low-income children and adults. While the Veteran's Administration had long provided government-run healthcare for US veterans, the United States now joined other western democracies with a federally administered health insurance system for some of its civilian population.[90] The act also increased financial assistance to retired and disabled Americans. As a result, the poverty rate among citizens aged sixty-five and older declined from over 40 percent in 1960 to under 25 percent by 1970. In 1972 Richard Nixon signed into law a measure that reindexed social security and standardized eligibility under a new Supplemental Security Income (SSI) program.[91] The program took effect in 1974 and granted additional cash assistance for seniors; the poverty rate fell to a historically low 16 percent in the next two years, according to the Social Security Administration.[92]

The 1965 legislation also expanded the eligibility and raised payments for those who qualified for Aid to Families with Dependent Children (AFDC). For the first time, AFDC served African Americans throughout the South; because these men and women were formerly excluded, the program disbursed over 20 percent more in benefits than it had in earlier years.[93] Congress later enacted the earned income tax credit (EITC) in 1975; for most low-wage earners this effectively eliminated income taxes and transferred cash to working families near or below the poverty level.[94] So while 5 million people left the nation's poverty rolls during the first two years of the War on Poverty, a longer view, between 1960 and 1975, yielded a decline from 22 to 11 percent. Since then, the rate has hovered between 11 and 16 percent.[95]

Aside from the creation of new welfare programs and the expansion of others, poverty reduction occurred unevenly. Much of the War on Poverty's success, as well as its legacy, reflected its original emphasis on white men. If skeptics like Warren Folks wondered "how black" the War on Poverty was, they would have been surprised to learn that while 12 million fewer white "male-headed households" were officially poor by 1969, 11 million female-headed families remained impoverished. Historian James T. Patterson has found that by 1974, 6 percent of white, male-headed families and less than 10 percent of white men lived in poverty.[96] By contrast, 17 percent of nonwhite male-headed families and 27 percent of white female-headed families were poor. Fifty-five percent of nonwhite female-headed families were stuck in poverty throughout the 1960s and 1970s; thus, almost no statistical improvement occurred within this demographic even with the welfare programs and adjustments to the tax code.[97]

To complicate the picture further, although the war against poverty made progress among certain demographics, the Economic Opportunity Act of 1964 masked the persistence of economic hardship in a few significant ways. And when viewed through a broader scope that includes the totality of national spending and the nation's involvement in Vietnam, the War on Poverty appears less impressive. The Social Security Administration (SSA) had established an arbitrary, perhaps misleading means to calculate the official poverty level based primarily on the price of food, then estimated at seventy cents a day. The Bureau of Labor Statistics (BLS), meanwhile, proposed that a family of four required at least $6,960 in yearly household income to keep pace with inflation, as well as to cover the costs of essential food, clothing, shelter, and transportation.[98] This was over twice the dollar amount that the SSA had arrived at by emphasizing the relatively cheaper price of food instead of the more rapidly escalating costs of housing and transportation (the SSA thus considered a family of four poor in 1966 if the household income was below $3,355).[99] Using the BLS figures, roughly 33 percent of American households failed to exceed $7,000 in annual income between 1965 and 1970; this index located the poverty level nearly three times higher than the official figure used by the Social Security Administration to disburse welfare payments—though like the SSA, the BLS located the heaviest burden falling on female-headed families of color.[100]

In addition, any appraisal of the War on Poverty and 1960s liberalism must be tempered by some discussion of the decade's other, more infamous war. Most congressional liberals favored, albeit to varying degrees, US American involvement in Vietnam. While it is true that the Eighty-Eighth and Eighty-Ninth Congresses, both of which were under Democratic control, passed the Civil Rights Act of 1964, the Economic Opportunity Act of 1964, the Voting Rights Act of 1965, and the Social Security Act of 1965, it is also true that Congress in 1964 passed the Gulf of Tonkin Resolution. The ill-fated resolution called for military escalation in Southeast Asia based on a faulty accusation that the North Vietnamese had attacked the USS *Maddox*.[101] Soon afterwards, defense spending increased and averaged over $300 billion annually between 1965 and 1970. In comparison, the War on Poverty received about $30 billion. The Office of Economic Opportunity averaged $1.7 billion per year and accounted for a rather modest 1.5 percent of the federal budget in those same years.[102] The cost of war abroad thus consistently outpaced the nation's greatest antipoverty campaign by about one hundred to one.[103] Next to these figures Lyndon Johnson's famous 1964 declaration to "eliminate poverty" seems rather half-hearted.[104]

Furthermore, President Johnson's escalation of the Vietnam War led to short-term deficits and long-term debt, hampering the federal government's ability to fund ambitious domestic programs. Two years before the Gulf of Tonkin incident, Johnson's predecessor proposed one of the largest tax cuts since the implementation of a progressive income tax in 1913. President Kennedy's Revenue Act, adopted and signed by Johnson in early 1964, returned billions of dollars to the nation's highest earning corporations, businesses, and individuals. While the revamped tax code offered some relief for middle-income earners, in tandem with increased military spending it further increased the nation's debt.[105] Johnson's commitment to anticommunism, along with his enactment of the Kennedy tax cuts, calls into question what one of his biographers, Jeffrey Helsing, described as a "guns vs. butter dilemma." Johnson may have believed that the "two great streams in our national life converged—the dream of a Great Society at home and the inescapable demands of our obligations halfway around the world," but his thorough engagement with the latter undermined his ability to spread much butter.[106]

A War on Poverty Postscript: Liberalism without a White Face and the Rise of Law-and-Order Politics

So while support for the War on Poverty collapsed even as the funding for it never approached that spent on the war against Vietnam, its impact endures. The expansion of AFDC, EITC, Medicare, Medicaid, and the variety of other programs implemented or augmented by Johnson and Nixon remains the apogee of the nation's welfare state.[107] Millions accessed affordable housing, food, and healthcare; civil rights and voting rights increased political participation and representation among African Americans and sealed the fate of Jim Crow.[108] Undoubtedly, for these very reasons, millions of others had concluded that the War on Poverty had become "too black" and believed it had stoked the fires of urban rebellion and radicalism. To these disillusioned men and women, Johnson's Cold War liberalism transferred power and tax dollars from honest, hardworking whites to the unruly, darker-skinned denizens of the nation's troubled cities.

Further, there is little indication that poverty warriors and white liberals in the Kennedy and Johnson administrations anticipated the surge of democratic activism engendered by community action and maximum feasible participation. Men like James L. Sundquist, Ted Sorenson, Sargent Shriver, Daniel P. Moynihan, and Stuart Udall, among others, cautiously accepted the self-activity and local engagement that the Economic Opportunity Act of 1964 inspired, but they did so with significant reservations. The War on Poverty had unwittingly opened doors and led to new pathways of resistance for poor people, regardless of race, but they only opened so wide. And within a few years, these doors had already begun to shut. As they did, new ideas about politics and public policy came into view. The second half of the 1960s and first half of the 1970s offered a glimpse into what a multiracial, locally administered poverty program could look like, but neither the political will nor the vision was sustained.

Instead, by the end of his term, President Johnson heeded the calls for law and order coming from Beard, Folks, and other disaffected men and women who wrote to the White House. Although they rarely receive the same consideration as Lyndon Johnson's other signature initiatives, the Law Enforcement Assistance Act of 1965 and the Omnibus Crime Control and Safe Streets Act of 1968 were equally decisive pieces of legislation, ones that provide a fitting conclusion to this chapter. They signaled the willingness on the part of congressional liberals (the Ninetieth Congress was also led by Democrats) to at once feed the growing perception that crime was out of control and depart from the benevolent liberalism of the War on Poverty. Even though violent crime and homicides had actually declined or remained stable between 1935 and 1965, visuals of the riots undermined the statistics.[109] Johnson announced, "I signed the bill because it responds to one of the most urgent problems in America today—the problem of fighting crime in local neighborhoods and on the city street."[110] The 1968 act established a federal licensing system to monitor the sales and distribution of firearms; it also simplified the procedures for the FBI to obtain wiretaps.[111]

Most formatively, however, the legislation included the Law Enforcement Administration Assistance Act (LEAAA). This sent $75 million in federal funding to state and local law enforcement agencies to spend on personnel and equipment.[112] Heather Ann Thompson has relayed that this was only the beginning; the federal government spent "approximately 7.5 billion to beef up the nation's law and order apparatus in little more than a decade."[113] With the infusion of cash, police departments and other domestic security forces expanded their ranks, and they also updated their arsenals with military-grade equipment, a trend that has greatly accelerated in the past fifteen years.[114] Armed with assault weapons and tanks, the National Guard, according to many observers, proved to be an effective fighting force and deterrent on city streets. Hence, the Johnson administration and its congressional allies provided police departments with a similar level of firepower. Furthermore, the act signaled a bipartisan consensus on shepherding federal resources into urban surveillance and spatial control rather than the alleviation of poverty.[115]

And though Johnson's legislation beckoned more aggressive law enforcement, the Democratic Party had nevertheless fallen from the graces of many white voters. Republican Richard Nixon sensed an opportunity to connect liberalism and the War on Poverty to urban crime; in doing so, he won his party's nomination for the presidency. In August 1968 Nixon spoke before the Republican National Convention and argued that crime control and security must be atop the domestic agenda. His half-hour acceptance speech used the word "law" ten times and "order" eleven times. The newly minted candidate proclaimed, "For the past five years we have been deluged by Government programs for the unemployed, programs for the cities, programs for the poor, and we have reaped from these programs an ugly harvest of frustrations, violence and failure across the land." Nixon continued, "The nation with greatest tradition of the rule of law is plagued by unprecedented lawlessness."[116]

Nixon failed to acknowledge the legislation Johnson had signed to fund local police and security forces during the preceding three years. Still, Nixon's call for law and order gained traction through the campaign, and the Republican prevailed over his challenger, Hubert H. Humphrey. Further illustrating the white electorate's disillusionment with the apparent legacy of Kennedy and Johnson, segregationist candidate George Wallace garnered nearly 14 percent of the popular vote. Combined with Nixon's 43 percent, nearly six in ten voters rejected Humphrey, though he did have support from labor, African Americans, and Jews.[117] The Kennedy-Johnson coalition lay in ruins, and the "high tide" of liberalism had receded into the political abyss.[118]

Shortly after taking office, Nixon appointed a four-term congressman from Illinois named Donald Rumsfeld to administer the embattled OEO. As a young bureaucrat, Rumsfeld defended many of the OEO's programs, including community health and job-training centers. Rumsfeld's tenure lasted through Nixon's first term, and after winning reelection, the president abolished the OEO entirely. In its place, he created the Community Services Agency (CSA), administered by another future secretary of defense, Frank Carlucci. In contrast to the OEO, the newly formed CSA abandoned the community action programs and exposed Nixon's determination to dismantle the War on Poverty and forge what he referred to as New Federalism, a disparate set of policies that reflected the skepticism of the centralized planning that characterized much of the decade's liberalism.[119]

The precipitous rise of mass incarceration and the expansion of the nation's prison system also resulted from the emphasis on law and order policies and the retreat from the War on Poverty. Between 1972 and 1980, the number of incarcerated men in the United States nearly doubled to over four hundred thousand.[120] This trend continued under the presidential administrations of Gerald Ford and Jimmy Carter, but Ronald Reagan's presidency brought with it the strongest commitment to mass incarceration and notions of punitive justice.[121] During the 1980s Reagan escalated the so-called war on drugs first declared by Richard Nixon in 1970. Longer sentencing for the possession and sale of banned substances coupled with a greater financial commitment to wage this new war led to record numbers of incarcerated men and women. The FBI's antidrug funding increased from $8 million to $95 million, and the Defense Department's budget to battle the drug trade ballooned from $33 million to over $1 billion by the end of Reagan's second term.[122] Reagan's campaign never eliminated drugs from the streets, but it did result in millions more going to prison. By 1990 the nation's incarcerated population exceeded one million people, a trend that continued unabated through the next fifteen years. In California alone, historian Ruth Wilson Gilmore has noted, the state's population of incarcerated people increased 500 percent from 1982 through 2000.[123] By 2011, 2.5 million people were locked up, and nearly 5 million more were on probation or parole.[124] At present, 6 million others are formerly incarcerated, and as many as 65 million have criminal records; thus, at any given period over the past decade, between 20 and 30 percent of the nation is either incarcerated, formerly incarcerated, paroled, probated, or carries a criminal record.[125]

These figures, however, fail to reveal the devastating and disproportionate impact that mass incarceration and the politics of law and order have had on poor communities of color. Of the 2.5 million people incarcerated as of 2011, nearly 40 percent were black men; yet, African American males made up just over 6 percent of the general population. Over one in nine African American men between the ages of twenty and thirty-four were imprisoned.[126] Beyond those who have been incarcerated, a third of African American men have been convicted of a felony.[127] Both formerly incarcerated as well as nonserving convicted people must negotiate the stigmatizing and usually permanent label of "ex-con" and remain outside the ranks of full citizenship. Unemployment and poverty rates for this demographic are the highest throughout the nation, exceeding well over 50 percent in many regions. Fourteen states, eleven of them in the South, ban convicted felons from ever again voting.[128] According to the Department of Justice, by the end of the twentieth century, African American men were over six times more likely than white men to serve prison sentences, and Latino men were over twice as likely as whites.[129]

Given this turnaround in national priorities, James L. Sundquist's bold prediction that the Economic Opportunity Act would "profoundly influence" American institutions deserves a final comment. As an advisor to both Kennedy and Johnson, as well a member of the War on Poverty taskforce, Sundquist understood more than most the powerful forces that the federal government could bring to bear on the stubborn persistence of economic hardship. Yet he failed to grasp how these same forces could unravel and sow the seeds for a decidedly different approach towards poor people, one typified by the regulation of impoverished communities and the incarceration of millions of poor bodies. This chapter has argued that the unintended consequences of the poverty programs dislodged the ubiquitous images of white upland southerners from the forefront of popular and political culture. The predominant stereotype of poverty no longer consisted of nostalgia-laden, quaint rural white people. These men and women provided a stalking horse on which postwar liberalism could ride and gain considerable, if fleeting, traction. The derided hillbilly and the lauded pioneer, for all their differences, engrossed the public and were largely seen as acceptable recipients of federal assistance. To understand why these archetypes figured so prominently in the nation's modern history requires one to understand the contradictory and shifting locations that upland southern whiteness has occupied in the American imagination. This book has tried to tell that story.

By the end of the 1960s, however, the fear of black violence had displaced the fear of Anglo-Saxon decline as a central issue that state and federal governments had sought to address. But in a curious twist, the very apparatus that was initially put in place to curb the latter had allegedly fostered the former. The welfare state had failed, or so it seemed to millions of voters who adopted Richard Nixon's law-and-order politics. In ways that historians have not fully considered, the second half of this book has argued that the ascent and sustainability of postwar liberalism, that which Sundquist predicted would reshape the nation, hinged on a broader culture and veneration of whiteness. The upland South was the linchpin of this culture, and it provided an effective backdrop for retail politics. When the region and its people receded from view, the ideological potency and perhaps much of the legitimacy of liberalism receded with it. The conclusion briefly considers the rise of modern conservatism in relation to the decline of liberalism and the welfare state. Lastly, a brief reflection on the previous forty years shows how the upland South still plays a role in state and federal policy, albeit a significantly muted one. Gone are the days when politicians explicitly crafted policies to restore or cleanse the so-called Anglo-Saxon race of its perceived impurities; however, the region still feels the impact of state involvement. And indeed, it retains, even amid vast social, economic, and cultural changes, a sense of identity rooted in the mythologies we have explored thus far.

CONCLUSION

THE PERSISTENCE OF A REGION, THE POWER OF MYTHOLOGY

> In Chicago, they found a woman who holds the record. She used 80 names, 30 addresses, 15 telephone numbers to collect food stamps, Social Security, veterans' benefits for four nonexistent deceased veteran husbands, as well as welfare. Her tax-free cash income alone has been running $150,000 a year.
>
> —Ronald Reagan, 1976[1]

Though he never actually uttered her name in his speeches, the woman Ronald Reagan referenced during his 1976 primary campaign was Linda Taylor. Reagan, known for his folksy style and a tendency to embellish, got a few facts incorrect. Taylor had defrauded the Illinois Department for Public Aid (IDPA), but prosecutors found that she had eight aliases and collected the more modest sum of eight thousand dollars. Regardless, for Reagan and his proponents, Taylor embodied how egregious and prevalent welfare fraud had become. The *Chicago Tribune,* the paper that first reported Taylor's transgressions and indeed coined the phrase "welfare queen" (Reagan later adopted the phrase for his campaign), worked with Illinois legislators to publicize other fraudulent claims within the state's public-aid system during the mid-1970s. As other cities and states launched similar investigations, reports of fraud spread, and the public outcry grew louder. By the time of Reagan's 1976 campaign, stories of welfare cheats presented conservatives with an adversary to rally against. And to considerable effect, they honed this message over the next four decades. But for our purposes, Reagan's rhetoric is an ideal counterpoint to conclude this study. Although much of the speech registers some of the changes that have occurred in American politics since the 1960s, Reagan's pronouncements also suggest some continuity. In this regard, his 1976 primary campaign offers us a pathway to review the book's findings and ponder a few final observations that unsettlingly direct us back to where we began.[2]

Sixteen years after John F. Kennedy traveled through West Virginia and called for a robust poverty program to restore dignity and economic prosperity to the state's mountaineers, Reagan hit the campaign trail with a strikingly different message. And though both men were equally determined to secure their respective party's presidential nomination, the ideas they brought to the American electorate greatly diverged. Unlike Kennedy, who had won the nomination and election in 1960, the upstart Republican failed to capture his party's nomination in 1976. Yet his campaign resonated, and four years later Reagan's time had arrived. Far from being a political novice—he was already a well-known actor and pitchman, had campaigned for Barry Goldwater in 1964, and was governor of California from 1967 to 1975—Reagan in his first presidential run nonetheless solidified his national reputation as the charismatic leader of the GOP's conservative wing, the stalwart opposition to the moderate, eastern establishment. But tellingly, Reagan fashioned his first bid for the presidency on the very same issue that Kennedy and Johnson had used over a decade earlier: the role of government in addressing poverty and economic inequality. If liberals had advocated an activist state to respond to the crisis of poverty, Reagan had largely done the opposite. He and fellow conservatives made dismantling the War on Poverty a centerpiece of their platform.[3]

For all their differences, Kennedy, Johnson, and Reagan knew well the power of symbolism. Kennedy's trip to West Virginia showcased the travesty of men who he claimed were of pioneer origin but could not feed their families. Johnson mobilized similar imagery as he toured eastern Kentucky and lobbied for the Economic Opportunity Act from Tom Fletcher's front porch. Ronald Reagan, on the other hand, famously disparaged the federally led poverty initiative as he campaigned for Barry Goldwater in 1964: "We were told four years ago that 17 million people went to bed hungry every night. Well, that was probably true. They were all on a diet."[4] Twelve years later, some of Reagan's oft-repeated and most effective anecdotes involved "welfare queens" who drove Cadillacs and "strapping young bucks" who used their food stamps to buy T-bone steaks.[5]

These pronouncements highlighted the extent to which all three men had relied on the subtext of race and gender to strengthen their arguments. The two Democrats presented the face of white, rural poverty to win support for liberalism, and for a few years it worked. The legacy of honorable mountaineers and frontiersmen who had fallen on hard times presented the rationale for the poverty programs and stood as a raison d'être for postwar liberalism. Meanwhile, Reagan's 1976 campaign artfully played on the resentments of men like David Beard, Warren Folks, and others who angrily wrote to the Johnson White House several years earlier. By the 1970s it seemed that one way to curry favor with conservative voters was to present the face of black, urban poverty and articulate policies that would get tough on inner-city crime. This too worked. Black women such as Linda Taylor were usually depicted as unwed mothers; if they were men, or "strapping young bucks," they were viewed as surly, indolent, and possibly criminal. Reagan and his allies considered both types undeserving of assistance and portrayed these men and women as caricatures for all that had gone wrong with the experiment of liberalism during the 1960s and early 1970s.[6]

And while skilled politicians certainly understood the power of imagery and symbolism, they may not have recognized their real-time contributions to a discussion about race and poverty that had extended back for nearly a century. This book has excavated and tried to clarify part of that discussion. It has at times included but also transcended election-year politics and party affiliation. At its core, the discussion has shaped the very notion of what government at the state and federal level should do to address the entrenched problem of poverty and the perceived problem of racial decline. And indeed, poverty cannot be disentangled from questions of race, region, and popular culture, at least not in the United States. This is not an original observation, and there is no shortage of studies on the topics addressed here. Some have explored the discursive creation of the upland South as a distinct American region. Others have mapped the rise and fall of liberalism in the post–World War II years; still other scholars have detailed the ascent of modern conservatism over the past forty years. This book has tenuously adjoined each of these pursuits through its emphasis on the politics and cultural representation of the upland South.

The region assumed great significance when local color writers proposed that men and women of prized Anglo-Saxon, Teutonic, and Nordic extraction called the southern hills home; these mountaineers were said to be the descendants of pioneer heroes like Daniel Boone and David Crockett. However, they lived in severe poverty and evidently failed to adopt acceptable middle-class behavior and customs. This undermined the mountaineers' position atop the racial hierarchy and set into motion a paradox that fueled fascination with the region for generations. The first three chapters explained this paradox and explored how some prominent figures tried to resolve it. In Indiana, social workers, politicians, and academics concluded that sterilization was one solution to the problem of poor "hill people" who crossed the Ohio River from Kentucky and Tennessee. In Virginia, eugenicists turned Carrie Buck's sterilization into a cause célèbre and believed they had purged her from the race. In the process, they restored a proper Appalachian femininity based on broader considerations of Anglo-Saxon purity. John Powell's music festival, held high atop the Blue Ridge, conveyed precisely the same apprehensions as did the turgid prose of the era's leading academic theorists.

Aside from their differences, these spectacles expressed the tension of a supposedly esteemed race that had experienced a dramatic decline. But each also assumed that there was something worth preserving, despite the impoverishment and deficiencies of many whites from the upland South. Thus the hillbilly emerged as a most ambivalent and potent stereotype, emblematic of rural simplicity but also of racial collapse, or the threat thereof. Each failed attempt to restore those descendants of Boone and Crockett called into question some of the nation's foundational myths about race, culture, and citizenship. No set of policies or cultural manipulation, it appeared, produced the desired results: biologically strong and exceptional men and women who were credible heirs to the rugged pioneers of centuries past. For every Boone, Crockett, and virginal Anglo-Saxon heroine who appeared as the face of the upland South, seemingly endless tribes of Ishmael, Carrie Bucks, or other so-called defectives troubled the narrative.

Policy approaches towards poor whites changed significantly after World War II, but the stereotypes and rhetoric endured. The defeat of totalitarian regimes abroad blunted the biological determinism that had informed notions of race and ethnicity during the first half of the twentieth century. However, white people from the upland South still commanded far-reaching attention through the postwar years. But rather than being targeted for sterilization and investigated by eugenicists for their supposed depravity on the one hand and celebrated for their perceived Anglo-Saxon blood on the other, these same whites now legitimized the need for the War on Poverty. They became the symbols for liberals to rally around and advertise their domestic agenda. That said, negative stereotypes did not simply disappear; indeed, the television hillbilly gained preeminence during these same years. The upland South not only retained its visibility, but it may have even gained some.

Throughout the century, the region's contradictory identity wavered between supposedly positive attributes like genetic purity, virile masculinity, and virginal femininity and negative ones such as sexual depravity, cultural debasement, and economic impoverishment. But by the end of the 1960s the upland South no longer commanded such intrigue. After all, the marquee story of that decade was not found among the rural hills of Appalachia or in the remote hollows of the Ozarks. It unfolded elsewhere in the South as civil rights activists dismantled Jim Crow. With some trepidation, liberals allied with these activists and proposed a Great Society to rise from the ashes of nearly a century of segregation. But many on the left who had grown wary of liberalism relayed a keen sense of injustice and critiqued the very machinations of the US political and economic system. These men and women demanded change by any means necessary and held a vision rather different from the pluralism of the Kennedy-Johnson coalition.

As the 1960s progressed and Jim Crow fell apart, the endemic problems of the northern and western cities, shaped as they were by years of discriminatory public policies, federal and state neglect, and de facto segregation, came into stronger relief. Civil unrest led politicians, liberal and conservative alike, to call for law and order. When evidence surfaced that funding from the Office of Economic Opportunity had fallen into the hands of radicals, public outcry grew to a fever pitch. The majority of the white voting public believed this was unacceptable; to them it demonstrated that welfare instigated violent rebellion in the urban North and West more often than it provided support for the so-called deserving poor of the upland South.

Furthermore, the events of the late 1960s led some to fuse liberalism to a disparaging notion of "big government." Ronald Reagan, among others, gave voice to this idea with his famous proclamation: "The nine most terrifying words in the English language are: I'm here from the government, and I'm here to help." The sardonic dictum captured the disillusionment of millions of Americans who believed that the statist policies of the War on Poverty were ineffectual at best and mendacious transfers of wealth from hardworking white citizens to underserving minorities at worst. A bloated welfare bureaucracy, critics maintained, created a permanent class of pampered bureaucrats to administer benefits to a dependent class of Americans who lacked the initiative or the incentives to enter the labor force. Reagan used Linda Taylor to represent this latter demographic.[7]

Ronald Reagan's campaign also presaged the way in which the legacy of the 1960s would be continually debated for decades to follow. Race, in ways spoken and unspoken, has structured these debates. Poverty, of course, has long been stigmatized, but in contrast to the middle of the century and earlier, it has also come to signify nonwhiteness almost exclusively in national discourse since the 1970s. Accordingly, frank proposals to address economic inequality and rekindle the ambition of the Economic Opportunity Act have received little more than rancorous opprobrium and have not been pursued.[8]

And more critically, through their embrace of law and order legislation, politicians from both parties have increased surveillance of poor communities and contributed mightily to mass incarceration.[9] This has corresponded to the broader economic transformation that the United States has undergone in the past half-century. In the midst of deindustrialization and rising inequality, the expansion of the prison system has allayed middle-class fears of crime and unrest. At the same time, correctional facilities have provided stable work in many otherwise depressed towns. Between 1980 and 2000, according to the Urban Institute, 350 state prisons were built in rural areas; between 1992 and 1994 alone, over 60 percent of new prison construction occurred in nonmetropolitan areas.[10] Fueling an additional prison boom, Bill Clinton—with bipartisan support—signed the Violent Crime Control and Law Enforcement Act of 1994. The law issued $10 billion for prisons and allocated funding to local and state police departments to hire more officers and update their technology, firearms, and other equipment. In addition, state governments passed their own "get-tough" measures, and prison construction, as well as maintenance, became a steady growth industry throughout the 1980s and 1990s.[11]

Lest these forces remain overly abstract and apart from the concerns of this book, let us return a final time to western Virginia. Across the mountains and valleys, not too far from where Carrie Buck grew up, Arthur H. Estabrook located the Win tribe, and John Powell hosted his festival, there now sit three penitentiaries: Pocahontas State Correctional Facility (PSCF), Wallens Ridge State Prison, and Red Onion State Prison. Each was built after President Clinton signed his 1994 Law Enforcement Act and Virginia governor George Allen won a landslide election on a platform that included the abolition of parole. Allen fulfilled his campaign promise, and in early 1995 his Truth-in-Sentencing Act effectively dashed the hopes of thousands of incarcerated people in the Commonwealth of Virginia who had expected an early release.[12] Virginia's prisons quickly became overcrowded with inmates who might have otherwise received parole for relatively minor, nonviolent offenses or good behavior. In response, Allen received $500 million to augment the state's prison system; between 1995 and 2008, the commonwealth constructed fourteen facilities, including the three above.[13]

PSCF opened most recently in 2007 in the town of Pocahontas, located on the western edge of Tazewell County. It currently holds over nine hundred inmates; most have come to the institution after having served elsewhere for at least twenty years.[14] Red Onion State Prison and Wallens Ridge State Prison are located a hundred miles from PSCF on Route 19, also known as the

Trail of the Lonesome Pine. Opened in 1999, Wallens Ridge and Red Onion are identical maximum-security facilities located about thirty-five miles apart from one another in Wise County. Together, the two confine an inmate population of about twenty-five hundred men. Combined with PSCF, the three facilities employed over eleven hundred Virginians and had an annual payroll exceeding $30 million as of 2013.[15] They have largely supplanted coal mining and timber, and they rival tourism as the foundation of the western Virginia economy.

These forbidding institutions, built into one of the nation's more picturesque landscapes, contrast with the adjacent town of Big Stone Gap. Situated among the Cumberland Mountains, Big Stone Gap is just four miles from Wallens Ridge State Prison and about thirty miles from Red Onion. Its compact downtown features museums, specialty shops, and a theater, all of which highlight its contributions to the history of the southern mountains. Here, it would be difficult to miss the sights and references dedicated to Big Stone Gap's native son, John Fox Jr. A block from the town's main street, Wood Avenue, one stumbles upon the John Fox Jr. Museum, the refurbished former residence of the novelist. In this turn-of-the-century home, Fox penned *The Trail of the Lonesome Pine* and *The Little Shepherd of Kingdom Come*. One on-site placard makes the disputable claim that *The Trail of the Lonesome Pine* was the nation's first novel to sell over a million copies.[16] Reverence for the man and his celebrated opus are on display elsewhere as well. A scenic state highway bears the novel's name, and several roadside attractions remind travelers that they are in the "heart of Appalachia."[17]

Each summer volunteer actors even arrange a theatrical production of *The Trail of the Lonesome Pine* at the June Tolliver House and Folk Art Center, Big Stone Gap's open-air theater.[18] The performance has achieved such popularity that state lawmakers have recognized it as the "Official Outdoor Drama of the Commonwealth of Virginia."[19] Like the novel, the onstage interpretation of *The Trail of the Lonesome Pine* portrays the feud between the Tollivers and the Falins. The actors' lurid descriptions of the pristine environment—from the peaks of the Cumberland Mountains to the remote hollows around the gap— allegorized the isolated purity of the two families.[20] And although *The Trail of the Lonesome Pine* will probably not earn a spot on Broadway anytime soon, it faithfully translates the drama of the century-old novel. The mountaineers are as tempestuous and distrustful of outsiders as ever, and June Tolliver's romance with Jack Hale strikes the observer as being as illicit today as it was in 1908. Most of all, the message of the play remains resoundingly clear: modern life, with its heavy industry and excessive materialism, had finally reached western Virginia. As a result, the sanctity of the land and its people could no longer be guaranteed.[21]

To critics, the adaptation, like the novel, is a pulp romance that shamelessly exploits Appalachian stereotypes. And that judgment is not without merit. But in spite of its formulaic plot and predictable conclusion, *The Trail of the Lonesome Pine* remains prescient for reasons that its author certainly never intended. Its contemporary staging is set against the backdrop of yet another seismic socioeconomic change underway across the upland South and indeed, the nation. Like the deceased writer, Big Stone Gap's contemporary boosters have promoted the region as a vestige of a frontier culture basked in authentic Anglo-Saxon folklore. But predictably, western Virginia's new economy, as reliant on prisons as it is on such industrial staples as coal and lumber, receives no mention in the glossy tourist brochures.

Understandably, the region's natural beauty and its frontier history claim more attention. The town's boosters thus look askance at that which makes it viable in the present, while at the same time they stage for the world an illusory representation of its past. Hence, a powerful irony greets the throng of tourists who come to watch the Tollivers and Falins negotiate the rise of an economic order that has long since faded. With two super-maximum-security prisons looming amid the lush foliage of the hills, the audience is situated between a fictional portrayal of the past and the obscured reality of the present.

More than scenic roadways connect Big Stone Gap's theater to Wallens Ridge and Red Onion, though. In fact, the play and the prisons relate the respective economic configurations from which each one emerged. The play exhibits the tensions that accompanied the onset of industrial capitalism; prisons have flourished in its decline. Though both the play and the prison are at once contingent upon, as well as illustrative of, a series of mythologies that have proven as durable as they have mutable. *The Trail of the Lonesome Pine* celebrates a history rooted in notions of racial purity and cultural authenticity, and it laments the advent of the industrial age, precipitating as it did dangerous encounters with a diverse and unpredictable world. The prison, among other things, has functioned to restore the perception of peace and security to a populace that has grown fearful of those with darker skin and lower incomes.

As we have seen, however, this was not always the case. For much of the twentieth century, some of the most dangerous threats to the white republic came from within. Tactics ranging from the cultural to the political to the medicinal and scientific could not restore what was supposed to be an exceptional

American race. And by the end of the 1960s, Jed Clampett and Tom Fletcher seemed to have eclipsed Daniel Boone and David Crockett as the emblematic figures of a highly revered American region, even if the shadows cast by the latter two men continued to shape our impressions of it. Yet during the last half-century, a new set of priorities has fully materialized. These have resulted not in efforts to save the poor, rural, and white but have instead culminated in the mass incarceration of the poor, urban, and black. Thus, one wonders whether Theodore Roosevelt's so-called race history persists. A journey from Big Stone Gap up the windy road to Wallens Ridge or Red Onion State Prison suggests that though times have certainly changed, his words remain as relevant in our day as he believed they were in his.

NOTES

Introduction

1. Theodore Roosevelt, *The Winning of the West: An Account of the Exploration and Settlement of Our Country from the Alleghanies to the Pacific,* New Library Edition, Six Volumes in Three (1889–1896; repr., New York: G. P. Putnam's Sons, [1920]), vol. 1, pt. 1: 8. See also Theodore Roosevelt, "The Winning of the West: The Spread of English Speaking Peoples," excerpted in *The Man in the Arena: Selected Writings of Theodore Roosevelt; A Reader,* ed. Brian M. Thomsen (New York: Forge Books, 2003), 24; and Thomas G. Dyer, *Theodore Roosevelt and the Idea of Race* (Baton Rouge: Louisiana State University Press, 1992), quoted on p. 59.

2. For a discussion of Roosevelt's views on hunting, manliness and athletics, and public land use, see Theodore Roosevelt, *Outdoor Pastimes of an American Hunter* (New York: Charles Scribner's Sons, 1906), 374. See also Sarah Watts, *Rough Rider in the White House: Theodore Roosevelt and the Politics of Desire* (Chicago: University of Chicago Press, 2003), for more information on Roosevelt's conception of race, gender, and sexuality.

3. On Roosevelt's trip to the Badlands and his idea for the Boone and Crockett Club, see Roger L. Di Silvestro, *Theodore Roosevelt in the Badlands: A Young Politician's Quest for Recovery in the American West* (New York: Bloomsbury, 2011), 245; Edmund Morris, *The Rise of Theodore Roosevelt* (New York: Modern Library, 2001), 387–92; and Richard Slotkin, *Gunfighter Nation: The Myth of the Frontier in Twentieth Century America* (New York: Harper Perennial, 1992), 36–51. The Boone and Crockett Club remains a hunting and conservation society interested in many of the same ideas as its founders. For more information on the club, see its official website, http://www.boone-crockett. org/ (accessed November 5, 2013). For an early history of the club, written from an inside perspective, see Charles Sheldon, *A History of the Boone and Crockett Club* (Washington, DC: Boone and Crockett Club, 1931).

4. Jonathan Peter Spiro, *Defending the Master Race: Conservation, Eugenics, and the Legacy of Madison Grant* (Burlington: University of Vermont Press, 2008), 4–6.

5. Ibid.

6. See Morris, *Rise of Theodore Roosevelt;* Kathleen Dalton, *Theodore Roosevelt: A Strenuous Life* (New York: Vintage Press, 2004), 125–28. For an extended

discussion of Roosevelt's fears of immigration and his views on race, see Gary Gerstle, *American Crucible: Race and Nation in the Twentieth Century* (Princeton, NJ: Princeton University Press, 2002), 14–43.

7. On urban history and immigration, see Matthew Frye Jacobson, *Whiteness of a Different Color: European Immigrants and the Alchemy of Race* (Cambridge, MA: Harvard University Press, 1999); Daniel Rogers, *Coming to America: A History of Immigration and Ethnicity in American Life,* 2nd ed. (New York: HarperCollins, 2002), esp. pt. 2, "The Century of Immigration," 121–286; David R. Roediger, *Working towards Whiteness: How America's Immigrants Became White; The Strange Journey from Ellis Island to the Suburbs* (New York: Basic Books, 2006), esp. pts. 1–2, 3–132. On race in the post-Civil War Deep South, see Grace Elizabeth Hale, *Making Whiteness: The Culture of Segregation in the South, 1890–1940* (New York: Vintage, 1999), esp. 3–12, 75–84, 88–94; and Glenda Elizabeth Gilmore, *Gender and Jim Crow: The Politics of White Supremacy in North Carolina, 1896–1920* (Chapel Hill: University of North Carolina Press, 1996), 1–30. A standard treatment, first published in 1955, remains C. Vann Woodward, *The Strange Career of Jim Crow,* commemorative ed. with new afterword by William S. McFeely (New York: Oxford University Press, 2002), esp. 67–110.

8. Thomas F. Gosset, *Race: The History of an Idea in America* (1967; repr. New York: Oxford University Press, 1997), 116. For a foundational text on Appalachia in the context of western expansion, see John Anthony Caruso, *The Appalachian Frontier: America's First Surge Westward* (1959; repr. Knoxville: University of Tennessee Press, 2003).

9. I define the upland South as a subregion of the US South that includes southern Appalachia (or the Mountain South), the Bluegrass Region of Kentucky, Tennessee's Upper Cumberland, and the Arkansas and Missouri Ozarks. Despite many differences within these areas, they have retained a social, cultural, political, and economic coherence that has historically stood apart from the Deep South, the Coastal South, or, for that matter, the Midwest. Admittedly, this book emphasizes southern Appalachia, but with several explorations beyond, a more encompassing title is warranted.

10. For a collection of essays on the pervasive, damaging nature of Appalachian stereotypes, see Dwight B. Billings, Gurney Norman, and Katherine Ledford, eds., *Back Talk from Appalachia: Confronting Stereotypes* (Lexington: University of Press of Kentucky, 2000). See also J. W. Williamson, *Hillbillyland: What the Movies Did to the Mountains and What the Mountains Did to the Movies* (Chapel Hill: University of North Carolina Press, 1995), 86–89.

11. In answering the questions posed in this paragraph, I aim to address the concerns raised by Larry J. Griffin and Barbara Ellen Smith in articles published in the *Journal of Appalachian Studies* 10, nos. 1 and 2 (2004), an issue

dedicated to questions of race and whiteness. Smith argued that the southern mountaineer was "too often generic rather than gendered" and called for historians and sociologists to pay more attention to the interactive nature of race, class, and gender in Appalachia. Likewise, Larry J. Griffin claimed that "inquiry into white mountaineers as 'whites' remains infrequent." See Smith, "De-gradations of Whiteness: Appalachia and the Complexities of Race," 38–57 (quote on p. 42); and Griffin, "Whiteness and Southern Identity in the Mountain and Lowland South," 7–37 (quote on p. 7). James C. Klotter has raised some of these questions in his ranging study of Kentucky; see Klotter, *Kentucky: Portrait in Paradox, 1900–1950* (Frankfort: Kentucky Historical Society, 1996), 17–24.

12. Henry D. Shapiro, *Appalachia on Our Mind: The Southern Mountains and Mountaineers in the American Consciousness, 1870–1920* (Chapel Hill: University of North Carolina Press, 1986), 3–31; Allen Batteau, *The Invention of Appalachia* (Tucson: University of Arizona Press, 1990), 1–5, 38–39. These two works remain the strongest treatments of the discursive construction of Appalachia at the end of the nineteenth century. I extend the discussion beyond Appalachia proper to include the bluegrass region of Kentucky and Upper Cumberland of Middle Tennessee.

13. Alice O'Connor, *Poverty Knowledge: Social Science, Social Policy, and the Poor in Twentieth Century U.S. History* (Princeton, NJ: Princeton University Press, 2001), esp. 25–54.

14. Harry Sharp described his Indiana Plan in *Vasectomy: A Means of Preventing Defective Procreation* (Jeffersonville: Indiana Reformatory Print, 1909), 2–3.

15. Nathaniel Deutsch, *Inventing America's "Worst" Family: Eugenics, Islam, and the Fall and Rise of the Tribe of Ishmael* (Berkeley: University of California Press, 2009), 9–10.

16. The phrase "racial hygiene" was used by several eugenicists and was popularized by Indiana University professor Thurman Rice in his study entitled *Racial Hygiene: A Practical Discussion of Eugenics and Race Culture* (New York: Macmillan, 1929). This chapter joins some excellent recent scholarship on Indiana eugenics. In addition to Deutsch, *Inventing America's "Worst" Family,* see Stephen Ray Hall, "Oscar McCulloch and Indiana Eugenics" (PhD diss., Virginia Commonwealth University, 1993); and Alexandra Minna Stern, "'We Cannot Make a Silk Purse out of a Cow's Ear': Eugenics in the Hoosier Heartland," *Indiana Magazine of History* 103 (March 2007): 3–38 (declared by the editors to be the best article of the year to appear in the journal). See also Brent Ruswick, "The Measure of Worthiness: The Rev. Oscar McCulloch and the Pauper Problem, 1877–1891," *Indiana Magazine of History* 104 (March 2008): 3–35; and Elsa Kramer, "Recasting the Tribe of Ishmael," *Indiana Magazine of History* 104 (March 2008): 36–64.

17. Supreme Court Justice Oliver Wendell Holmes famously uttered the phrase as he delivered the majority opinion in the case. For a recent and definitive account of what occurred within the Supreme Court, see Paul Lombardo, *Three Generations, No Imbeciles: Eugenics, the Supreme Court, and* Buck v. Bell (Baltimore: Johns Hopkins University Press, 2008), 157–73.

18. Like Indiana, Virginia has also attracted much scholarly attention because of its outsized role in the eugenics movement. On John Powell, see Pippa Holloway, *Sexuality, Politics, and Social Control in Virginia, 1920–1945* (Chapel Hill: University of North Carolina Press, 2006), 33–40; and David E. Whisnant, *All That is Native and Fine: The Politics of Culture in an American Region* (Chapel Hill: University of North Carolina Press, 1983), 181–252. Whisnant's chapter on folk music in Virginia remains the standard treatment of the topic and an influence on this work.

19. A few notable texts widely publicized this so-called rediscovery, and none were more important than John Kenneth Galbraith, *The Affluent Society* (New York: Houghton Mifflin, 1958); Michael Harrington, *The Other America, Poverty in the United States* (New York: Scribner, 1962); and Harry Caudill, *Night Comes to the Cumberlands* (Boston: Little, Brown, 1963). Harrington and Caudill receive extended treatment in the fourth chapter.

20. The final chapters are much indebted to critiques of postwar liberalism. See Francis Fox Piven and Richard Cloward, *Regulating the Poor: The Functions of Public Welfare* (New York: Vintage, 1971), esp. pts. 2 and 3; William Kelso, *Poverty and the Underclass: Changing Perceptions of the Poor in America* (New York: New York University Press, 1994), 3–14; Michael B. Katz, *The Undeserving Poor: From the War on Poverty to the War on Welfare* (New York: Pantheon Books, 1989), esp. chaps. 3–5; and Ira Katznelson, *When Affirmative Action Was White: An Untold History of Racial Inequality in Twentieth-Century America* (New York: W. W. Norton, 2006), 15–24.

21. For an excellent discussion of these shows, see Anthony Harkins, *Hillbilly: A Cultural History of an American Icon* (New York: Oxford University Press, 2005), 173–204.

22. The literature on the Civil Rights Movement, the origins of the War on Poverty, and 1960s liberalism is extraordinarily vast. A few of the magisterial works that have been instructive for this study include Taylor Branch, *Parting the Waters: America in the King Years* (New York: Simon and Schuster, 1988); Branch, *Pillar of Fire: America in the King Years, 1963–1965* (New York: Simon and Schuster, 1998), esp. 210–11, 225–28, 289–97, 595–596; and Branch, *At Canaan's Edge: America in the King Years, 1965–1968* (New York: Simon and Schuster, 2006), 298–316. Charles M. Payne, *I've Got the Light of Freedom: The Organizing Tradition and the Mississippi Freedom Struggle* (Berkeley: University of California Press, 1996), provides one of the stron-

gest explorations of grassroots organizing in the South. For the purposes of these chapters, prominent works include Allen J. Matusow, *The Unraveling of America: A History of Liberalism in the 1960s* (New York: Harper and Row, 1984), esp. chap. 4, "The Origins of the War on Poverty," 97–127; Robert Korstad and James Leloudis, *To Right These Wrongs: The North Carolina Fund and the Battle to End Poverty and Inequality in 1960s America* (Chapel Hill: University of North Carolina Press, 2010); Kent Germany, *New Orleans after the Promise: Poverty, Citizenship, and the Search for a Great Society* (Athens: University of Georgia Press, 2007), esp. 38–58; James T. Patterson, *Grand Expectations: The United States, 1945–1974* (New York: Oxford University Press, 1996), esp. chaps. 13–19; Sidney M. Milkis, "Lyndon Johnson, the Great Society, and the 'Twilight' of the Modern Presidency," in *The Great Society and the High Tide of Liberalism*, ed. Sidney M. Milkis and Jerome M. Mileur (Amherst: University of Massachusetts Press, 2005), 1–50; and Nick Kotz, *Judgment Days: Lyndon Baines Johnson, Martin Luther King, Jr., and the Laws That Changed America* (Boston: Houghton Mifflin, 2005), 27, 89–111. On recent literature related to Lyndon Johnson, see Kent Germany, "Historians and the Many Lyndon Johnsons: A Review Essay," *Journal of Southern History* 75, no. 4 (2009): 1001–28.

23. Irwin Unger's *The Best of Intentions: The Triumph and Failure of the Great Society under Kennedy, Johnson, and Nixon* (New York: Doubleday, 1996) explores the question of intent and concludes, albeit for different reasons than this study does, that the War on Poverty unraveled by the 1970s. Still, according to Unger, its impact has been transformative.

24. Martin Gilens, *Why Americans Hate Welfare: Race, Media, and the Politics of Antipoverty Policy* (Chicago: University of Chicago Press, 1999), esp. 102–31; Jill Quadagno, *The Color of Welfare: How Racism Undermined the War on Poverty* (New York: Oxford University Press, 1994), esp. 4–17, 28–30, 40–59; Kenneth Neubeck and Noel Cazenave, *Welfare Racism: Playing the Race Card against America's Poor* (New York: Routledge, 2001), 121–30, 157–59. For another study that explores liberalism within a broader context of reform and racial thought, see Carol A. Horton, *Race and the Making of American Liberalism* (New York: Oxford University Press, 2005).

25. Numerous studies have traced the growth in economic disparities over the past generation. Perhaps none do so as comprehensively as does the noted sociologist G. William Domhoff in *Who Rules America? Challenges to Corporate and Class Dominance,* 6th ed. (New York: McGraw Humanities, 2009), 1–20. Domhoff also hosts a website through the University of California, Santa Cruz, at http://www2.ucsc.edu/whorulesamerica/power/wealth.html (accessed May 21, 2013), for additional statistics, figures, and analysis about the expanding levels of inequality over the past forty years.

26. Michelle Alexander, *The New Jim Crow: Mass Incarceration in the Age of Colorblindness* (New York: New Press, 2010), esp. 12–18 (first quote on p. 3). See also Heather Thompson, "Why Mass Incarceration Matters: Rethinking Crisis, Decline, and Transformation in Postwar American History," *Journal of American History* 97, no. 3 (2010): 703–58. While these studies have earned much-deserved attention, there are several other recent books and articles on the topic. Some of the strongest work includes Christian Parenti, *Lockdown America: Police and Prisons in the Age of Crisis* (New York: Verso, 1999); Ruth Wilson Gilmore, *Golden Gulag: Prisons, Surplus, Crisis and Opposition in Globalizing California* (Berkeley: University of California Press, 2007); Glenn Loury, *Race, Incarceration, and American Values* (Cambridge: MIT Press, 2008); and Jonathan Simon, *Governing through Crime: How the War on Crime Transformed American Democracy and Created a Culture of Fear* (New York: Oxford University Press, 2009).

27. On Indiana, see the studies mentioned in note 15, above. Given Virginia's significance in colonial and Revolutionary history, early national history, Civil War history, and modern southern history, there are likely more studies of the Old Dominion than of any other single state in the union.

28. Alan Trachtenberg, *The Incorporation of America: Culture and Society in the Gilded Age,* 25th anniversary ed. (1982; repr., New York: Hill and Wang, 2007), x.

29. Ibid.

Chapter 1

1. Edward A. Ross, *Social Control: A Survey of the Foundations of Order* (1901; repr., Cleveland: Press of Case Western Reserve University, 1969), 410. A version of this chapter was previously published as an article; see Ian C. Hartman, "Appalachian Anxiety: Race, Gender, and the Paradox of 'Purity' in the Age of Empire, 1873–1901," *American Nineteenth Century History* 13, no. 2 (2012): 229–55. I define the age of empire as the years encompassing roughly the final quarter of the nineteenth century and the first decade of the twentieth.

2. United States Census Office, *Twelfth Census of the United States, Taken in the Year 1900,* vol. 1, pt. 1, *Population* (Washington, DC: Government Printing Office, 1901), clxxxii, clxxxvii–clxxxviii. (Cited hereafter as *Twelfth Census, 1900.*)

3. For more on Ross, see Matthew Frye Jacobson, *Barbarian Virtues: The United States Encounters Foreign Peoples at Home and Abroad, 1876–1917* (New York: Hill and Wang, 2001), 64–65; Jacobson, *Whiteness of a Different Color,* 50; and Laura Lovett, *Conceiving the Future: Pronatalism, Reproduction, and the*

Family in the United States, 1890–1938 (Chapel Hill: University of North Carolina Press, 2007), 4–14, 76–109.

4. David Starr Jordan, *The Blood of the Nation: A Study of the Decay of Races through the Survival of the Unfit* (Boston: American Unitarian Association, 1906), 7. In contrast to many of his imperialist colleagues, Jordan was skeptical of foreign interventions insofar as he believed that war threatened many of the very people he believed were the strongest members of Anglo-Saxon society.

5. Roosevelt, *Winning of the West,* vol. 1, pt. 1: 8. See also Marilyn Lake and Henry Reynolds, *Drawing the Global Colour Line: White Men's Countries and the International Challenge of Racial Equality* (Cambridge, UK: Cambridge University Press, 2008), 6–14.

6. For a distillation of the Teutonic origins thesis and its impact of foreign policy as well as domestic political culture in the late 1890s, see Mark S. Weiner, "Teutonic Constitutionalism: The Role of Ethno-Juridical Discourse in the Spanish-American War," in *Foreign in a Domestic Sense: Puerto Rico, American Expansion, and the Constitution,* ed. Christina Duffy Burnett and Burke Marshall (Durham, NC: Duke University Press, 2001), 48–81.

7. Ross, *Social Control,* 15–16.

8. Amy Kaplan, *The Anarchy of Empire in the Making of U.S. Culture* (Cambridge, MA: Harvard University Press, 2002), 12.

9. For a discussion of the phrase "racial character" and its use by Roosevelt and Ross, see Lovett, *Conceiving the Future,* 7–8.

10. On defining the boundaries of the mountain South, Appalachia, and the southern mountains, see Richard Drake, *A History of Appalachia* (Lexington: University Press of Kentucky, 2001), v–xi; John Alexander Williams, *Appalachia: A History* (Chapel Hill: University of North Carolina Press, 2001), 1–18. In this book, I use the terms interchangeably.

11. For an example of writers who referred to the Anglo-Saxon stock in the Blue Ridge of Virginia but also parts of New England, see J. E. Chamberlain, "A Dream of Anglo-Saxondom," *The Galaxy: A Magazine of Entertaining Reading* 24 (1877): 789. Nell Irvin Painter, *A History of White People* (New York: W. W. Norton, 2010), is the best explanation of American Anglo-Saxonism; pages 190–255 provide an especially useful discussion of Ross and Roosevelt. See also Alexander Saxton, *The Rise and Fall of the White Republic: Class Politics and Mass Culture in Nineteenth Century America* (New York: Verso, 1991), 1–22, 343–44. Reginald Horsman, *Race and Manifest Destiny: The Origins of American Racial Anglo-Saxonism* (Cambridge, MA: Harvard University Press, 1981), was especially useful in formulating the ideas herein. On "Anglo-Saxon purity," see John C. Inscoe, "Race and Racism in Nineteenth-Century Southern Appalachia: Myths, Realities, and Ambiguities," in *Appalachia in*

the Making: The Mountain South in the Nineteenth Century, ed. Mary Beth Pudup, Dwight B. Billings, and Altina Waller (Chapel Hill: University of North Carolina Press, 1995), 106–10 (quote on p. 107).

12. Shapiro, *Appalachia on Our Mind,* 3–5; Batteau, *Invention of Appalachia,* 1–19. Whisnant's *All That is Native and Fine* remains the most imaginative treatment of culture in Appalachia during the early and mid-twentieth century. See also Harkin, *Hillbilly,* 13–14, 29–33; David C. Hsiung, "Stereotypes," in *High Mountains Rising: Appalachia in Time and Place,* ed. Richard A. Straw and H. Tyler Blethen (Urbana: University of Illinois Press, 2004), 101–13; and Inscoe, "Race and Racism,"103–31.

13. Frantz Fanon, *The Wretched of the Earth* (1961; repr., New York: Penguin, 2001), 58.

14. Richard White, *Railroaded: The Transcontinentals and the Making of Modern America* (New York: W. W. Norton, 2011), 47–87. For additional works that explore the railroad boom's connection to the economic panic, see Kenneth D. Ackerman, *The Gold Ring: Jim Fisk, Jay Gould, and Black Friday, 1869* (New York: Da Capo Press, 2005), 267–87; Ron Chernow, *The House of Morgan: An American Banking Dynasty and the Rise of Modern Finance* (New York: Grove Press, 2001), 27–40; John M. Lubetkin, *Jay Cooke's Gamble: The Northern Pacific Railroad, the Sioux, and the Panic of 1873* (Norman: University of Oklahoma Press, 2006), 3–14; Robert H. Wiebe, *The Search for Order, 1877–1920* (New York: Hill and Wang, 1966), 1–10; and Trachtenberg, *Incorporation of America,* 17–25.

15. Will Wallace Harney, "A Strange Land and Peculiar People," *Lippincott's Magazine,* October 12, 1873, 430–31. Harney's essay has been reprinted, along with several other indispensible primary sources relating to the southern mountains, in *Appalachian Images in Folk and Popular Culture,* ed. W. K. McNeil (Ann Arbor, MI: UMI Research Press, 1989), 45–58.

16. While Harney is considered among the first local color writers to depict Appalachia, David C. Hsiung has uncovered many earlier writers who arrived in the generation before the Civil War and developed the enduring stereotype of the southern Appalachians as an isolated and forgotten population. See Hsiung, *Two Worlds in the Tennessee Mountains: Exploring the Origins of Appalachian Stereotypes* (Lexington: University Press of Kentucky, 1997), esp. chap. 6, "The Creation of Appalachian Images," 162–82.

17. For an extended take on the significance of Fox's work, see Warren Irving Titus, *John Fox Jr.* (New York: Twayne, 1971).

18. John Fox Jr., *A Mountain Europa* (New York: Harper and Brothers, 1899).

19. Ibid., 11–12.

20. John Fox Jr., *The Trail of the Lonesome Pine* (New York: Charles Scribner's Sons, 1908). For an earlier novel with similar themes, see Fox, *The Kentuck-*

ians (New York: Charles Scribner's Sons, 1898). On how Fox contributed to Appalachian stereotypes, see Darlene Wilson, "A Judicious Combination of Incident and Psychology: John Fox Jr. and the Southern Mountaineer Motif," in Billings, Norman, and Ledford, *Back Talk from Appalachia,* 98–118.

21. Fox, *Trail of the Lonesome Pine,* 235.

22. Curiously, Darlene Wilson has found that early drafts of Fox's novels portray Appalachian characters as racially ambiguous and likely not white but rather "tri-racial isolates," or Melungeons; see Wilson, "The Felicitous Convergence of Mythmaking and Capital Accumulation: John Fox Jr. and the Formation of An(Other) Almost-White American Underclass," *Journal of Appalachian Studies* 1, no. 1 (1995): 27–29; and Katherine Vande Brake, *How They Shine: Melungeon Characters in the Fiction of Appalachia* (Macon: Mercer University Press, 2001), 228–35.

23. Caspar R. Whitney, John Fox, Jr., John R. Spears, et al., war correspondents, *Harper's Weekly,* May 28, 1898, 506.

24. Ibid., 507.

25. For more on the racial discourse surrounding Teutonics and their connections to Anglo-Saxons, see Painter, *History of White People,* 135, 316–17; Gossett, *Race,* esp. chap. 5, "The Teutonic Origins Theory," 84–122. As more evidence of the inconsistencies of racial science, some maintained that the Teutonic was Germanic, Nordic, and Alpine, while others saw the lineage move toward the Angles, Saxons, and Celts.

26. See Walter LaFeber, *The New Empire: An Interpretation of American Expansion, 1860–1898* (Ithaca, NY: Cornell University Press, 1998), for a particularly formative analysis of US imperialism, esp. pt. 2, "The Intellectual Formulation," 62–101.

27. For more on the intersection of Appalachian writers and empire, see Emily Satterwhite, "Romancing Whiteness: Popular Appalachian Fiction and the Imperialist Imagination at the Turn of Two Centuries," in *At Home and Abroad: Historicizing Twentieth-Century Whiteness in Literature and Performance,* ed. La Vinia Delois Jennings (Knoxville: University of Tennessee Press, 2009), 93–119; and Wilson, "The Felicitous Convergence," 26–31.

28. On the justifications of expansion and the way in which domestic culture reflected these justifications, see Richard Drinnon, *Facing West: The Metaphysics of Indian Hating and Empire Building* (Norman: University of Oklahoma Press, 1990), esp. pt. 4, "Civilizers and Conquerors," 219–351, and pt. 5, "Children of Light," 355–467; and Eric T. Love, *Race over Empire: Racism and U.S. Imperialism* (Chapel Hill: The University of North Carolina Press, 2004), 1–26. On the way in which notions of gender contributed to US expansion, see Kristin L. Hoganson, *Fighting for American Manhood: How Gender Politics Provoked the Spanish-American and Philippine-American Wars*

(New Haven: Yale University Press, 2000); and Gail Bederman, *Manliness and Civilization: The Cultural History of Gender and Race in the United States, 1880–1917* (Chicago: University of Chicago Press, 1996).

29. Julian Ralph, "Where Time has Slumbered," *Harper's New Magazine,* September 1894, 613–630 (quote on p. 616).

30. United States Census Office, *Report on Population of the United States at the Eleventh Census: 1890* (Washington, DC: Government Printing Office, 1895), pt. 1, cxix. (Cited hereafter as *Eleventh Census, 1890.*)

31. Ibid.

32. Wilma Dunaway, *The First American Frontier: The Transition to Capitalism in Southern Appalachia* (Chapel Hill: University of North Carolina Press, 1996), 24–26. Dunaway demonstrates that "precapitalist modes of production" concluded with the onset of English hegemony in the Ohio Valley by the late eighteenth century. For an older study on the early lumber and timber industry in Appalachia, see Roy B. Clarkson, *Tumult on the Mountain: Lumbering in West Virginia, 1770–1920* (Parsons, WV: McClain Printing, 1964).

33. Kenneth W. Noe, *Southwest Virginia's Railroad: Modernization and the Sectional Crisis* (1994; repr., Tuscaloosa: University of Alabama Press, 2003), 9–21.

34. See population volumes of *Eleventh Census, 1890; Twelfth Census, 1900;* and United States Bureau of the Census, *Thirteenth Census of the United States, Taken in the Year 1910* (Washington, DC: Government Printing Office, 1912).

35. For the now-classic works on the labor history and industrialization of Appalachia, see David Alan Corbin, *Life, Work, and Rebellion in the Coal Fields: The Southern West Virginia Miners* (Urbana: University of Illinois Press, 1981); and Ronald D. Eller, *Miners, Millhands, and Mountaineers: Industrialization of the Appalachian South, 1880–1930* (Knoxville: University of Tennessee Press, 1982). On the racial and ethnic composition of Appalachia, see Joe William Trotter Jr., *Coal, Class, and Color: Blacks in Southern West Virginia, 1915–1932* (Urbana: University of Illinois Press, 1990); and Ken Fones-Wolf and Ronald L. Lewis, eds., *Transnational West Virginia: Ethnic Communities and Economic Change* (Morgantown: West Virginia University Press, 2003).

36. Ronald L. Lewis, *Transforming the Appalachian Countryside: Railroads, Deforestation, and Social Change in West Virginia* (Chapel Hill: University of North Carolina Press, 1998), 50–54.

37. For insightful analyses of Native Americans and slavery, see Celia Naylor, *African Cherokees in Indian Territory: From Chattel to Citizens* (Chapel Hill: University of North Carolina Press, 2008); Tiya Miles, *Ties That Bind: The Story of an Afro-Cherokee Family in Slavery and Freedom* (Berkeley: University of California Press, 2006); and Miles, *The House on Diamond Hill: A Cherokee Plantation Story* (Chapel Hill: University of North Carolina Press, 2010).

38. John C. Inscoe, *Mountain Masters: Slavery and Sectional Crisis in Western North Carolina* (Knoxville: University of Tennessee Press, 1989), 84–86.

39. Wilma Dunaway, *Slavery in the Mountain South* (New York: Cambridge University Press, 2003), 241–43.

40. One of the earliest and highly consequential texts to have conclusively overturned the myth of Appalachian whiteness was this essay collection: William Turner and Edward Cabbell, eds., *Blacks in Appalachia* (Lexington: University Press of Kentucky, 1985).

41. For a recent overview of the literary history of Appalachia, see Emily Satterwhite, *Dear Appalachia: Readers, Identity, and Popular Fiction since 1878* (Lexington: University Press of Kentucky, 2011). See esp. chap. 1, "Charm and Virility," 27–54.

42. Painter explicates turn-of-the-century race theory in *History of White People,* 72–190.

43. See the ASA website for a brief biography of each of the organization's presidents. Ross's may be found at http://www2.asanet.org/governance/Ross.html (accessed on May 21, 2013).

44. Roosevelt, *Winning of the West,* vol. 1., pt. 1. Roosevelt's views on race are explored in Dyer, *Theodore Roosevelt and the Idea of Race.* See also Horsman, *Race and Manifest Destiny: Origins of American Racial Anglo-Saxonism,* 301–5, for some discussion of Roosevelt's racial attitudes and beliefs along with the intellectual context in which he operated. A definitive biography of Roosevelt remains Edmund Morris, *Theodore Rex* (New York: Modern Library, 2002); on race, see pp. 52–53, 314. On the role of race, desire, and sexuality, see Watts, *Rough Rider in the White House,* 6–13.

45. Roosevelt, *Winning of the West,* vol. 1, pt. 2: 108–9.

46. Ibid., vol. 1, pt. 1: 119.

47. Ibid., 195–22.

48. Ibid., 120.

49. Ross, *Social Control,* 370–75.

50. Roosevelt, *Winning of the West,* vol. 1, pt. 1: 119.

51. This was the topic of Roosevelt's famous 1899 Chicago speech entitled "The Strenuous Life." It was reprinted in Theodore Roosevelt, *The Strenuous Life and Other Essays and Speeches* (New York: Century Company, 1900), 1–22. For Roosevelt's discussion of heroic frontiersmen, see Roosevelt, *Winning of the West,* vol. 1, pt. 1: 117–56.

52. Roosevelt discussed the wartime contributions of his favored pioneers throughout the work. See his discussion of "the Backwoodsman" in *Winning of the West,* vol. 1, pt. 1: 117–56, for a few examples.

53. Theodore Roosevelt, *The Winning of the West: An Account of the Exploration and Settlement of Our Country from the Alleghenies to the Pacific, Book II* (New

York: G.P. Putnam's Sons, 1889), vol. 1, pt. 2: 34–65. This chapter, "Boon [*sic*] and the Settlement of Kentucky," deals with Daniel Boone's exploits during the Revolutionary period and the role of manliness in the construction of a mythic West.

54. Roosevelt, *Winning of the West,* vol. 2, pt. 1: 95; also quoted in Watts, *Rough Rider in the White House,* 69.

55. Roosevelt, *Winning of the West,* vol. 2, pt. 1: 96.

56. Semple's formulation of anthropogeography has been largely discredited, and it is now understood more accurately as environmental determinism. In its place, the study of human and cultural geography has materialized. These disciplines pay closer attention to the ways in which social, economic, and cultural forces interact with both natural and human-made geography. For contemporary studies in the field, see David Harvey, *Justice, Nature, and the Geography of Difference* (New York: Blackwell, 1996); and Edward Soja, *Postmodern Geographies: The Reassertion of Space in Critical Social Theory* (London: Verso, 1989).

57. Ellen Churchill Semple, "The Anglo Saxons of the Kentucky Mountains: A Study in Anthropogeography," *Geographical Journal* 17 (June 1901): 588–613.

58. Ibid. (quotes on pp. 589 and 591).

59. Ibid., 594.

60. For a recent discussion on Semple and the significance of race and whiteness in eastern Kentucky, see Anne E. Marshal, "Civil War Memory in Eastern Kentucky is 'Predominantly White:' the Confederate Flag in Unionist Appalachia," in *Reconstructing Appalachia: The Civil War's Aftermath,* ed. Andrew Slap (Lexington: University Press of Kentucky, 2010), 353–55.

61. Roosevelt, Semple, and Ross focused primarily on the alleged impact of frontier masculinity in Appalachia, but others would later find much objectionable about impoverished white women. The infamous *Buck v. Bell* case put the threat of racial decline on center stage. After the Supreme Court ruled in favor of Virginia, the state increasingly targeted poor women in the Blue Ridge for coercive sterilization See Lombardo, *Three Generations, No Imbeciles,* 7–29; and Holloway, *Sexuality, Politics, and Control in Virginia,* 52–76.

62. See Amy Kaplan and Donald Pease, eds., *Cultures of United States Imperialism* (Durham, NC: Duke University Press, 1994), for several essays on ideology, culture, and US empire, including Vicente L. Rafael, "White Love: Surveillance and Nationalist Resistance in the U.S. Colonization of the Philippines," 185–219. See also Alfred McCoy and Francisco Scarano, eds., *Colonial Crucible* (Madison: University of Wisconsin Press, 2009); and Susan Brewer, *Why America Fights: Patriotism and War Propaganda from the Philippines to Iraq* (New York: Oxford University Press, 2011), esp. chap. 1, "The "Divine Mission": War in the Philippines," 14–45.

63. Painter, *History of White People,* 161–62. For more on Emerson's racial theory, see Ralph Waldo Emerson, *English Traits* (Boston: Philips, Samson, 1856), 47–75.

64. Painter, *History of White People,* 162.

65. Bederman, *Manliness and Civilization,* esp. chap. 3, "Teaching Our Sons to Do What We Have Been Teaching the Savages to Avoid," 77–120 (quote on p. 11). See also Watts, *Rough Rider in the White House,* 115–18.

66. Bederman, *Manliness and Civilization,* 130.

67. Neurasthenia was also known as "American Nervousness," a phrase first coined by George Beard in *American Nervousness: Its Causes and Consequences* (New York: G. P. Putnam's Sons, 1881). See pp. iii–xviii for a summary of the affliction.

68. It was not lost upon observers such as Roosevelt, Shaler, and Ross that the alleged racial composition of both the so-called Kentuckian and the victims of neurasthenia was mostly the same.

69. Shaler's relationship to Roosevelt is discussed in Dyer, *Theodore Roosevelt and the Idea of Race,* 5–7; Douglas Brinkley, *The Wilderness Warrior: Theodore Roosevelt and the Crusade for America* (New York: HarperCollins, 2009), 100–104; and Evan Thomas, *The War Lovers: Roosevelt, Lodge, Hearst, and the Rush to Empire* (New York: Little, Brown, 2010), 77–87 (in these pages, Thomas mistakenly refers to Nathaniel Shaler as Norman Shaler).

70. Nathanial Southgate Shaler, *American Commonwealths: Kentucky, a Pioneer Commonwealth* (Boston: Houghton Mifflin, 1884), 11.

71. Ibid. (quotes on pp. 18 and 34).

72. Historians, especially John C. Inscoe, have long debunked the myth of Appalachian Union loyalty. See Inscoe, *Mountain Masters,* 177–210; and Inscoe, *The Heart of Confederate Appalachia: Western North Carolina and the Civil War* (Chapel Hill: University of North Carolina Press, 2003), 12–29. See also Kenneth W. Noe, "'Deadened Color and Colder Horror': Rebecca Harding Davis and the Myth of Unionist Appalachia," in Billings, Norman, and Ledford, *Back Talk from Appalachia,* 67–85; and Slap, *Reconstructing Appalachia,* especially Tom Lee's essay on East Tennessee, "The Lost Cause That Wasn't: East Tennessee and the Myth of Unionist Appalachia," 293–322.

73. These findings echo the persuasive arguments advanced by Richard Slotkin in his magisterial work on violence and the American West: *Regeneration through Violence: The Mythology of the American Frontier, 1600–1860* (Norman: University of Oklahoma Press, 1973), 369–93.

74. On race, empire, and Anglo-Saxonism, see these essays in Kaplan and Pease, *Cultures of United States Imperialism:* Richard Slotkin, "Buffalo Bill's 'Wild West' and the Mythologization of the American Empire," 174–75; Amy Kaplan, "Black and Blue on San Juan Hill," 228–30; and Kevin Gaines,

"Black Americans' Racial Uplift Ideology as 'Civilizing Mission': Pauline E. Hopkins on Race and Imperialism," 435–50. See also Laura Briggs, *Reproducing Empire: Race, Sex, Science, and United States Imperialism in Puerto Rico* (Berkeley: University of California Press, 2002), 82–83; and Martha Hodes, "Fractions and Fictions in the United States Census of 1890," in *Haunted by Empire: Geographies of Intimacy in North American History*, ed. Ann Laura Stoler (Durham, NC: Duke University Press, 2006), 240–70.

75. Albert J. Beveridge, *The Meaning of the Times and Other Speeches* (Indianapolis: Bobbs Merrill, 1908), 113. See also Gosset, *Race*, 84–112, for an explanation of Anglo-Saxon racial identity and its connections to imperialism.

76. Beveridge, *Meaning of the Times*, 114.

77. Here it is necessary to point out that not all racial theorists upheld the value of foreign interventions. David Starr Jordan's *The Blood of the Nation* expressed such concerns, as did men such as Andrew Carnegie and Henry Ford.

78. Altina L. Waller, *Feud: Hatfields, McCoys, and Social Change in Appalachia, 1860–1900* (Chapel Hill: University of North Carolina Press, 1988), 18–22.

79. On how the post-Civil War violence has contributed to notions of feuding and fed perceptions of so-called lawless hillbillies and white trash, see Waller, *Feud*, 18–33; *Blood in the Hills: A History of Violence in Appalachia*, ed. Bruce E. Stewart (Lexington: University Press Kentucky, 2012); William Lynwood Montell, *Killings: Folk Justice in the Upland South* (Lexington: University Press of Kentucky, 1986), xxv–xvi; T. R. C. Hutton, *Bloody Breathitt: Politics and Violence in the Appalachian South* (Lexington: University Press of Kentucky, 2013); T. R. C. Hutton, "UnReconstructed Appalachia: The Persistence of War in Appalachia," in Slap, *Reconstructing Appalachia*, 71–103; and Kathleen M. Blee and Dwight Billings, "Where 'Bloodshed is a Pastime': Mountain Feuds and Appalachian Stereotyping," in Billings, Norman, and Ledford, *Back Talk from Appalachia*, 119–37.

80. For more on the racial perceptions of missionaries in Appalachia, see Deborah Vansau McCauley, *Appalachian Mountain Religion: A History* (Urbana: University of Illinois Press, 1995), 25–29.

81. Introduction to the Annual Report of the American Missionary Association (AMA). Holdings accessed at the University of Illinois at Urbana Champaign's History, Philosophy, and Newspaper Library and Archives.

82. Washington Gladden, "Christian Education in the South," *American Missionary*, December 1883.

83. Ibid.

84. For the strongest comparison in the rhetoric of black poverty in the Deep South and white poverty in the southern mountains, see James C. Klotter, "The Black South and White Appalachia," *Journal of American History* 66, no. 4 (1980): 832–49.

85. George W. Phillips, "Report on Mountain Work," *American Missionary,* December 1884, 374. Also quoted in Henry Hartshorne, *Friends' Review: A Religious, Literary, and Miscellaneous Journal* 38 (1885): 341.

86. Ibid.

87. "Address of Prof. C. G. Fairchild," *American Missionary,* February 1883, 392.

88. Ibid. Beyond his association with the AMA, Charles Grandison Fairchild also taught at Berea College in Kentucky and was the son of the school's first president, Edward Henry Fairchild. For more on Berea and the Fairchilds, see Richard D. Sears, *A Utopian Experiment in Kentucky: Integration and Social Equality at Berea, 1866–1904* (Westport, CT: Greenwood Publishing, 1996), 50, 98–101.

89. On religion and masculinity, see Charles H. Lippy, *Do Real Men Pray? Images of the Christian Man and Male Spirituality in Protestant America* (Knoxville: University of Tennessee Press, 2005).

90. Oliver Otis Howard, "The Folk of the Cumberland Gap," *Munsey's Magazine,* July 1902, 508. Also quoted in Klotter, "Black South and White Appalachia," 843.

91. W. E. Barton, "Work Among the American Highlanders," *American Missionary,* March 1898, 179.

92. Ibid.

93. "The Independent Religious Intelligence," *American Missionary,* vol. 26, November 1, 1894.

94. Ibid.

95. See Painter, *History of White People,* 165–83, for an effective discussion of these contradictions.

96. Frederick Jackson Turner, "The Significance of the Frontier in American History," address before the American Historical Association, Chicago, 1893. The full text is available online courtesy of the University of Virginia at http://xroads.virginia.edu/~HYPER/TURNER/ (accessed May 22, 2013). For an analysis of the Turner thesis and its impact on US intellectual history, see Trachtenberg, *Incorporation of America,* 11–18, 26–30; and Slotkin, *Gunfighter Nation,* 26–61.

97. Morris, *Rise of Theodore Roosevelt,* 387–92. See also Slotkin, *Gunfighter Nation,* 36–51. Jonathan Peter Spiro also discusses the Boone and Crockett Clubs in *Defending the Master Race,* 4–6.

98. Matt Wray, *Not Quite White: White Trash and the Boundaries of Whiteness* (Durham, NC: Duke University Press, 2006), esp. chap. 1, "Lubbers, Crackers, and Poor White Trash," 21–47, for an extended discussion on the conditions of poor whites in the Upland South. See also Grady McWhiney, *Cracker Culture: Celtic Ways in the Old South* (Tuscaloosa: University of Alabama Press, 1988), 1–22.

99. Rebecca Harding Davis, "Qualla," *Lippincott's Magazine of Popular Literature and Science,* November 1875, 25.
100. Ibid.
101. For more on Davis's attitudes regarding Appalachia, see Noe, "'Deadened by Color and Colder Horror," 67–84.
102. Midcentury liberals such as Michael Harrington and John F. Kennedy used the phrase "pocket of poverty" to describe not only poor whites in Appalachia but also black poverty in urban areas and poverty among Native American reservations. See Harrington, *The Other America,* 11–12.
103. See Dwight Billings, introduction to Billings, Norman, and Ledford, *Back Talk from Appalachia,* 3–20, for a response to and brief analysis of these stereotypes.
104. This process began almost instantly as missionaries lobbied Congress to support measures that constructed some level of a safety net for the poorest citizens.

Chapter 2

1. Harry H. Laughlin, *Eugenical Sterilization in the United States* (Chicago: Municipal Court Psychiatric Institute, 1922), 454.
2. Harry Bruinius, *Better for All the World: The Secret History of Forced Sterilization and America's Quest for Racial Purity* (New York: Vintage, 2007), 294.
3. On Laughlin's trip to Germany, see Bruinius, *Better for All the World,* 293–99; Stefen Kuhl, *The Nazi Connection: Eugenics, American Racism, and German National Socialism* (New York: Oxford University Press, 1994), 49–50, 87; and Spiro, *Defending the Master Race,* 373. Jason McDonald explores Laughlin's diplomatic endeavors and his internationalist vision in his article, "Making the World Safe for Eugenics: The Eugenicist Harry H. Laughlin's Encounters with American Internationalism," *Journal of the Gilded Age and Progressive Era* 12, no. 3 (2013): 379–411.
4. Spiro, *Defending the Master Race,* xi, 357.
5. Elof Axel Carlson, *The Unfit: A History of a Bad Idea* (Cold Spring Harbor, NY: Cold Spring Harbor Laboratory Press, 2001), 161–83.
6. Edwin Black, *War against the Weak: Eugenics and America's Campaign to Create a Master Race* (New York: Dialog Press, 2003), 122–23.
7. Kuhl, *Nazi Connection,* 3–27.
8. For more on eugenics in the United States, see Nancy Ordover, *American Eugenics: Race, Queer Anatomy, and the Science of Nationalism* (Minneapolis: University of Minnesota Press, 2003); Alexandra Minna Stern, *Eugenics Nation: Faults and Frontiers of Better Breeding in Modern America* (Berkeley: University of California Press, 2005); Evelynn M. Hammonds, *The Nature*

of Difference: Sciences of Race in the United States from Jefferson to Genomics (Cambridge, MA: MIT Press, 2009); and Paul Lombardo, *Three Generations, No Imbeciles: Eugenics, the Supreme Court, and* Buck v. Bell (Baltimore: Johns Hopkins University Press, 2010). Perhaps most instrumental is Paul Lombardo, ed., *A Century of Eugenics in America: From the Indiana Experiment to the Human Genome Era* (Bloomington: University of Indiana Press, 2011), which contains these two essays on Indiana: Elof Axel Carlson, "The Hoosier Connection: Compulsory Sterilization as Moral Hygiene," 11–25; and Jason S. Lantzer, "The Indiana Way of Eugenics: Sterilization Laws, 1907–1974," 26–44. This chapter was especially influenced by the following studies: Hall, "Oscar McCulloch and Indiana Eugenics"; Deutsch, *Inventing America's "Worst" Family;* Ruswick, "The Measure of Worthiness"; Brent Ruswick, *Almost Worthy: The Poor, Paupers, and the Science of Charity in America, 1877–1917* (Bloomington: Indiana University Press, 2013), 143–78; and Kramer, "Recasting the Tribe of Ishmael," 36–64. However, Stern's "We Cannot Make a Silk Purse out of a Sow's Ear" has shaped my own thinking as I position the Ishmaels as an example of perceived Anglo-Saxon collapse.

9. On the threat of racial contamination and the fear of immigrants, see Jacobson, *Whiteness of a Different Color,* 139–70; Mae Ngai, *Impossible Subjects: Illegal Aliens and the Making of Modern America* (Princeton, NJ: Princeton University Press, 2005), 94–95, 242–45; Ariela Gross, *What Blood Won't Tell: A History of Race on Trial* (Cambridge, MA: Harvard University Press, 2010), 16–47; and David R. Roediger, *How Race Survived U.S. History: From Settlement and Slavery to the Obama Phenomenon* (New York: Verso, 2010), esp. 95–127.

10. Minna Stern, *Eugenics Nation,* 6–13; Paul Lombardo, introduction, "Looking Back at Eugenics," to Lombardo, *Century of Eugenics,* 1–11; Gregory Michael Dorr and Angela Logan, "'Quality, Not Mere Quantity, Counts': Black Eugenics and the NAACP Baby Contests," in Lombardo, *Century of Eugenics,* 68–94. To be clear, immigrants and African American were indeed targets of the eugenics movement in a variety of other contexts. For an authorative treatment on the eugenics movements and its connection to racism and birth control, see Carole R. McCann, *Birth Control Politics in the United States, 1916–1945* (Ithaca, NY: Cornell University Press, 1994). McCann's account correctly locates Margaret Sanger at the center of the story.

11. See Deutch, *Inventing America's "Worst" Family,* 44–52, for an explanation of how the term "tribe" became affixed to the poor whites in the Midwest.

12. Roosevelt, *Winning of the West,* vol. 1, pt. 1: 117. See also Dyer, *Theodore Roosevelt and the Idea of Race,* 28.

13. Oscar McCulloch, *The Tribe of Ishmael: A Study in Social Degradation* (Indianapolis: Charity Organization Society, 1888).

14. Ruswick, *Almost Worthy,* 14–15.
15. For others who have, in my view, mistakenly disassociated race from pauperism in recent historiography, see Joel Schwartz, *Fighting Poverty with Virtue: Moral Reform and America's Urban Poor, 1825–2000* (Bloomington: Indiana University Press, 2000), 161–65; and Nicholas Eberstadt, "Prosperous Paupers and Affluent Savages," *Society* 33, no. 2 (1998): 17–25. Thomas Sowell misses the specific racial connection to pauperism as he writes about a population of "Irish and Italian paupers" in *Ethnic America: A History* (New York: Basic Books, 1981), 28.
16. Lantzer, "Indiana Way of Eugenics," 26.
17. This chapter focuses on the Ishmaels, but researchers located other troublesome families elsewhere. For an overview of the family studies that helped launch the eugenics movement, see Nicole Hahn Rafter, *White Trash: The Eugenic Family Studies, 1877–1919* (Boston: Northeastern University Press, 1985), 1–31. For the two works usually regarded as the earliest and more consequential of the family studies, see Richard Louis Dugdale, *"The Jukes": A Study in Crime, Pauperism, Disease and Heredity also; Further Studies of Criminals* (New York: G. P. Putnam's Sons, 1877); and McCulloch, *Tribe of Ishmael.* Dugdale's subjects lived in rural upstate New York and McCulloch's in Indianapolis. For another authoritative text on the eugenics movement, see Daniel J. Kevles, *In the Name of Eugenics: Genetics and the Uses of Human Heredity* (Berkeley: University of California Press, 1985), 90–95, 100–110. Some of McCulloch's sermons and speeches were recorded and compiled by his wife, Alice, in *The Open Door: Sermons and Prayers by Oscar C. McCulloch, Minister of Plymouth Congregational Church, Indianapolis, Indiana,* ed. Alice McCulloch (Indianapolis: Press of W. B. Buford, 1892). See also Painter, *History of White People,* 260–66, for supplementary commentary on McCulloch's relationship to racial theorists such as Dugdale and Roosevelt.
18. Oscar McCulloch diary, May 22, 1877, Oscar McCulloch Papers (hereafter cited as OMP), box 2, folder 1, Indiana State Library, Indianapolis.
19. Genevieve C. Weeks, *Oscar Carleton McCulloch, 1843–1891: Preacher and Practitioner of Applied Christianity* (Indianapolis: Indiana Historical Society Printing, 1976), 35–37.
20. McCulloch diary, January 9, 1877, OMP, box 2, folder 1.
21. Weeks, *Oscar Carleton McCulloch,* 21. See also McCulloch diary entries for August 1, 1877, and July 4, 1891, OMP, box 2, folder 1. Additional entries in folders 1–3 convey similar sentiments.
22. McCulloch diary, July 3, 1877, OMP, box 2, folder 1.
23. Ruswick, "The Measure of Worthiness," 8.
24. Weeks, *Oscar Carleton McCulloch,* 57–60; W. R. Holloway, *Indianapolis, A Historical and Statistical Sketch of the Railroad City: Its Social, Municipal,*

Commercial, and Manufacturing Progress (Indianapolis: Indianapolis Press Journal, 1870), 109–25.

25. For an overview of the strike, see David O. Stowell, *Streets, Railroads, and the Great Strike of 1877* (Chicago: University of Chicago Press, 1999).

26. Weeks, *Oscar Carleton McCulloch,* 59; Emma Lou Thornbrough, *Indiana in the Civil War Era, 1850–1880* (Bloomington: Indiana University Press, 1965), 274–310.

27. Weeks, *Oscar Carleton McCulloch,* 59–60.

28. United States Census Office, *Statistics of the Population of the United States at the Tenth Census (June 1, 1880)* (Washington, DC: Government Printing Office, 1883), 477.

29. *Twelfth Census, 1900,* 524.

30. Gregory Rose, "Upland Southerners," in *The Encyclopedia of Indianapolis,* ed. David J. Bodenhamer and Robert G. Barrows (Bloomington: Indiana University Press), 1376–77.

31. Deutsch, *Inventing America's "Worst" Family,* 21.

32. Ibid. Though both states remained in the Union, Kentucky nonetheless sent thousands of troops to fight for the Confederacy.

33. Oscar McCulloch diary, January 20, 1878, OMP, box 2, folder 3.

34. Ibid.

35. Oscar McCulloch diary, n.d., OMP, box 2, folder 4. See also Hall, "Oscar McCulloch and Indiana Eugenics," 109–15.

36. Roosevelt, *Winning of the West,* vol. 1, pt. 1: 3. See also Madison Grant, *The Passing of the Great Race,* pt. 2, "The European Races in History." For two explanations of Roosevelt's articulation of the so-called Teutonic Theory, see Dyer, *Theodore Roosevelt and the Idea of Race,* 2–11; and Watts, *Rough Rider in the White House,* 156–67. See also Painter, *History of White People,* 301–27, for an excellent explication of Grant's thesis and the leading proponents of white supremacy at the turn of the century.

37. Oscar McCulloch diary, March 24, 1878, OMP, box 2, folder 2.

38. McCulloch, *Tribe of Ishmael,* 1.

39. Ibid.

40. Ibid.

41. Ibid.

42. Patricia Dean, "Charity Organization Society," in Bodenhamer and Barrows, *Encyclopedia of Indianapolis,* 402–3.

43. McCulloch, *Tribe of Ishmael,* 1.

44. Quoted in Ruswick, "Measure of Worthiness," 27.

45. McCulloch diary and scrapbook, February 3, 1878, OMP, box 2, folder 2.

46. McCulloch diary, July 20, 1885, OMP, box 4, folder 1.

47. McCulloch diary, October 31, 1885, OMP, box 4, folder 1.

48. McCulloch diary, December 20, 1885, OMP, box 4, folder 1.
49. Ibid.
50. Ibid.
51. McCulloch diary, February 12, 1888, OMP, box 4, folder 1.
52. Ruswick, "Measure of Worthiness," 25–30.
53. McCulloch diary, n.d., OMP, box 4, folder 1.
54. Quoted in Ruswick, "Measure of Worthiness," 25. See also McCulloch diary, OMP, box 4, folder 1, 1887.
55. Ruswick, "Measure of Worthiness," 25.
56. For more on Evangelical Protestantism and the Progressive Era reformers, see Keith A. Zahniser, *Steel City Protestant Laity and Reform in the Progressive Era* (New York: Routledge, 2013), 1–27; John L. Thomas, *Alternative America: Henry George, Edward Bellamy, Henry Demarest Lloyd, and the Adversary Tradition* (Cambridge, MA: Harvard University Press, 1983), 13–17, 61–62; and Michael McGerr, *A Fierce Discontent: The Rise and Fall of the Progressive Movement in America* (New York: Free Press, 2005), 64–67.
57. For effective overviews of the Progressive Era, see Nell Irving Painter, *Standing at Armageddon: The United States, 1877–1917* (New York: W. W. Norton, 1987), esp. 253–82; and McGerr, *A Fierce Discontent,* esp. pt. 2, "Progressive Battles," 77–182. Jackson Lears, *Rebirth of a Nation: The Making of Modern America, 1877–1920* (New York: HarperCollins, 2010), 276–326, nicely considers the role of empire and imperialism in ways the former two do not. The foundational texts on the period remain Richard Hofstadter, *The Age of Reform* (New York: Vintage, 1960); and Robert H. Wiebe *The Search for Order, 1877–1920* (New York: Hill and Wang, 1966).
58. Quoted in Ruswick, *Almost Worthy,* 143. Ruswick, "Measure of Worthiness," 25–30, also elaborates on the tension between McCulloch's ideas regarding heredity and his involvement in the labor movement.
59. McCulloch speech before National Conference on Charities and Corrections, in McCulloch diary, n.d. (ca. winter 1888), OMP, box 4, folder 1.
60. Ruswick, "Measure of Worthiness," 19–35; Ruswick, *Almost Worthy,* 143–45.
61. The authoritative biography of Eugene V. Debs remains Nick Salvatore, *Eugene V. Debs: Citizen and Socialist* (Urbana: University of Illinois Press, 1984).
62. *Indiana Bulletin of Charities and Corrections,* collected editions, 1908–1912, 30–31.
63. Ibid.
64. For the 1896 figure, see *Indiana Bulletin of Charities and Corrections,* Twelfth Annual Exhibit of State Charitable and Correctional Institutions (1900), 14. For the 1907–08 figure, see *Indiana Bulletin of Charities and Corrections,* collected editions, 1908–1912, 30–31.

65. Both Hurty and Sharp believed the procedure was a virtual cure-all for the seemingly disparate—if fictive—problems. See *Practical Eugenics in Indiana, J. N. Hurty Reprint from the Ohio State Medical Journal, February 1912,* Dr. John N. Hurty Papers, box 3, folder 1, Indiana State Archives.

66. Ibid.

67. Ibid.

68. Ibid.

69. For a more detailed explanation of eugenic thought, see Kevles, *In the Name of Eugenics,* 84–104.

70. See *Practical Eugenics in Indiana, J. N. Hurty Reprint from the Ohio State Medical Journal, February 1912,* Hurty Papers, box 3, folder 1.

71. Deutsch, *Inventing America's "Worst" Family,* 9.

72. For another interpretation of Harry Sharp's career, see Angela Gugliotta, "'Dr. Sharp with His Little Knife': Therapeutic and Punitive Origins of Eugenic Vasectomy-Indiana, 1892–1921," *Journal of the History of Medicine* 53 (October 1998): 371–406. Harry Sharp refers to the plan in Sharp, *Vasectomy,* 2–3.

73. Most obviously, this refers to Jim Crow in the U.S. South but also to the Chinese Exclusion Laws passed by Congress in 1882 and renewed in 1902.

74. In practice Harry Sharp had been illegally carrying out the procedure for at least ten years.

75. Indiana State Law, chap. 215, approved March 9, 1907, 377–78.

76. Ibid.

77. For other works that document the shift that occurred on poverty policy during the late nineteenth and early twentieth centuries, see James T. Patterson, *America's Struggle against Poverty, 1900–2000* (Cambridge, MA: Harvard University Press, 2000), 3–36; Michael B. Katz, *In the Shadow of the Poorhouse: A Social History of Welfare in America* (New York: Basic Books, 1996), 60–87; and Walter Trattner, *From Poor Law to Welfare State: A History of Social Welfare in the United States* (New York: Free Press, 1998), 108–273. See also Steven Noll, *Feeble-Minded in Our Midst: Institutions for the Mentally Retarded in the South, 1900–1940* (Chapel Hill: University of North Carolina Press, 1995), for an account of the emergence of southern institutions for people with disabilities.

78. See Rice, *Racial Hygiene,* 1–14, for a discussion of the phrase and Rice's determination that a failure to act would ensure a "dying race."

79. On the organization of the BCS, see *The First Report of the Board of State Charities made to the Legislature of Indiana for One Year and Eight Months, Commencing March 1st, 1889, and Ending October 31st, 1890* (Indianapolis: William B. Buford, Contractor for State Publishing and Binding, 1890).

80. Deutsch, *Inventing America's "Worst" Family,* 116–24, gives an explanation of Estabrook's activities in Indianapolis. McCulloch's collaborator, James Wright, penned most of the notes. Estabrook went through Wright's notes

and made hundreds of visits and conducted hours of research in what would have been an exhaustive study had he published it. However, for reasons unclear, the findings were never made public, and the inchoate manuscript is held with Estabrook's papers at the State University of New York at Albany.

81. Helen Reeves to Arthur Estabrook, April 16, 1921, Correspondence of Helen T. Reeves, Records of the Board of State Charities (hereafter BSC), State Institution for Feeble-Minded Mental Defectives, Photograph Collection, box 4, Indiana State Archives.

82. *Mental Defectives in Indiana: A Second Report of the Indiana Committee on Mental Defectives; To the Governor* (Indianapolis: William Buford, Contractor for State Printing and Binding, 1919), 24–25.

83. Ibid.

84. Ibid.

85. State Institution for Feeble-Minded Mental Defectives, Photograph Collection for Delaware County Folder, Records of the BSC, box 4.

86. Ibid.

87. All quotes in this paragraph are from *Mental Defectives in Indiana: A Second Report of the Indiana Committee on Mental Defectives,* 44–45.

88. State Institution for Feeble-Minded Mental Defectives, Photograph Collection for Delaware County Folder, Records of the BSC, box 4.

89. Ibid.

90. Deutsch, *Inventing America's "Worst" Family,* 17.

91. *Mental Defectives in Indiana: A Second Report,* 8.

92. Quoted in Stern, "'We Cannot Make a Silk Purse out of a Sow's Ear,'" 20. See also Hansford, "A Social Study of Mental Defectives," 23; Estabrook, "The Work of the Indiana Committee"; "Kentucky Hill-Folk in Indiana," County Surveys, Records for the Committee on Mental Defectives, BSC, box 1.

93. *Mental Defectives in Indiana: A Second Report,* 16.

94. Ibid. For a discussion on the sexual and moral connotations of "mental defectiveness" and its connections to the epithet "white trash," see Wray, *Not Quite White,* 83–85.

95. For additional analysis, see Stern, "'We Cannot make a Silk Purse out of a Sow's Ear,'" 13–21.

96. For more on McCulloch's work at the end of his life, see Ruswick, *Almost Worthy,* 143–78.

97. O'Connor, *Poverty Knowledge,* 25–54. O'Connor illustrates how solutions to poverty were intellectualized and bureaucratized among an academic elite over several generations at the end of the nineteenth and into the twentieth century.

98. On the class position of the reformers, see Rafter, *White Trash,* 12–23; and Wray, *Not Quite White,* 69–85.

99. For a timeline of the Indiana eugenics movement, see Hall, "Oscar McCulloch and Indiana Eugenics," 214–21.

100. Statistics available through Indiana's state website: http://www.in.gov/judiciary/citc/cle/eugenics/index.html. In 2007 the state issued a formal apology and launched the conference "Reflections on 100 Years of Eugenics." Historian of eugenics Paul Lombardo delivered the keynote address.

Chapter 3

1. Annabel Morris Buchanan, foreword to "White Top Folk Tales," unpublished manuscript in the Annabel Morris Buchanan Papers (hereafter AMB), series 3.1, folder 348, Southern Historical Collection, Wilson Library, University of North Carolina at Chapel Hill.

2. See Stephen Jay Gould, *The Mismeasure of Man*, rev. and exp. ed. (New York: W. W. Norton, 1996), 365–66; Mark Largent, *Breeding Contempt: the History of Coerced Sterilization in the United States* (New Brunswick, NJ: Rutgers University Press, 2008), 99–102; and Lombardo, *Three Generations, No Imbeciles*, esp. 1–30.

3. Lombardo, *Three Generations, No Imbeciles*, 2–7.

4. See Oliver Wendell Holmes, "Delivering the Majority Statement in the Supreme Court Case," *Buck v. Bell*, 274, U.S. (200), 1927. For more on the decision, see the University of Virginia's online exhibit, "Eugenics: Three Generations, No Imbeciles; Virginia, Eugenics, and *Buck v. Bell*," through the Claude Moore Health Sciences Library, http://www.hsl.virginia.edu/historical/eugenics/ (accessed May, 17 2013). Justice Pierce Butler, a devout Catholic, cast the lone dissenting vote. In response, Oliver Wendell Holmes claimed that Butler's religious beliefs had interfered with his judgment. See Ashley K. Fernandez, "The Power of Dissent: Pierce Butler and *Buck v. Bell*," *Journal for Peace and Justice Studies* 12, no. 1 (2002): 115–34.

5. The majority of the sterilizations took place between 1927 and 1955, with most occurring during the 1930s. The numbers remain disputed. See Gregory M. Dorr, "Defective or Disabled? Race, Medicine, and Eugenics in Progressive Era Alabama and Virginia," *Journal of the Gilded Age and Progressive Era* 5, no. 4 (2006): 382.

6. Gregory Michael Dorr, *Segregation's Science: Eugenics and Society in Virginia* (Charlottesville: University of Virginia Press, 2008), 10–13.

7. California was the only state to sterilize more people than did Virginia; it had, by 1910, a far larger population than Virginia as well. For a detailed account of the eugenics movement in the American West, see Minna Stern, *Eugenics Nation*.

8. *Buck v. Bell*, 274, U.S. 200 (1927), Holmes's majority opinion is available online courtesy of Cornell University at http://www.law.cornell.edu/

supremecourt/text/274/200 (accessed November 12, 2014). Laughlin, *Eugenical Sterilization in the United States,* 445–452. The law partly inspired the wording of the national immigration law known as the Johnson-Reed Act. See Aristide Zolberg, *A Nation by Design: Immigration Policy in the Fashioning of America* (Cambridge: Harvard University Press, 2006), 260–63; and Ngai, *Impossible Subjects,* 24–25.

9. Virginia targeted nonwhites for sterilization as well. Gregory Michael Dorr has concluded that over 20 percent of those who underwent the procedure were African Americans. This was proportionate to the commonwealth's black population. See Dorr, *Segregation's Science,* 381–83. However, the argument here is that authorities believed sterilization responded to specific problems *within* an otherwise superior race. These fallen whites caused particular alarm among the eugenicists.

10. On Virginia during the interwar years, see Whisnant, *All That Is Native and Fine,* 181–252; Holloway, *Sexuality, Politics and Social Control in Virginia, 1920–1945,* 21–77; and Dorr, *Segregation's Science,* 137–95. See esp. J. Douglas Smith, *Managing White Supremacy: Race Politics, and Citizenship in Jim Crow Virginia* (Chapel Hill: University of North Carolina Press, 2002), 76–106, for a discussion of Powell and "The Campaign for Racial Purity."

11. A few works have explored the life and career of John Powell. See Ronald David Ward, "The Life and Works of John Powell (1882–1963)" (PhD diss., Catholic University of America, 1970); and Pocahontas Wright Edmunds, *Virginians Out Front* (Richmond: Whittet & Shepperson, 1972), esp. "John Powell: Native Musician," 4–10, 338–45. For more critical explorations of Powell and his notions of race and culture, see Whisnant, *All That Is Native and Fine,* chap. 3, "This Folk Work and the 'Holy Folk': The White Top Folk Festival, 1931–1939," 181–250; David Z. Kushner, "John Powell: His Racial and Cultural Ideologies," *Min-Ad: The Online Journal of the Israel Musicology Society* 5, no. 1 (2006), 1–15. The article is available at http://www.biu.ac.il/hu/mu/min-ad/06/John_Powell.pdf (accessed November 17, 2014); Karen Elizabeth Adam, "'The Nonmusical Message will Endure With It:' The Changing Reputation and Legacy of John Powell (1882–1963)" (masters thesis, Virginia Commonwealth University, 2012); and Smith, *Managing White Supremacy,* 76–83.

12. Quoted in Whisnant, *All That is Native and Fine,* 220.

13. John Powell, "How America Can Develop a National Music," *Etude,* May 1927, 34, AMB, ser. A, folder 148.

14. *Richmond Time Dispatch,* March 31, 1931, JPP, box 36, folder 9.

15. ASCoA Constitution, Adopted at the Convention, October 13, 1923, JPP, box 38, folder 4.

16. Ibid.

17. A standard text on US American nativism remains John Higham, *Strangers in the Land: Patterns of American Nativism* (1955; repr., New Brunswick, NJ: Rutgers University Press, 2002), esp. chap. 10, "The Tribal Twenties," 264–99. See also Smith, *Managing White Supremacy,* 12, 68–80.

18. ASCoA Constitution.

19. Ibid.

20. John Powell to *Richmond Times Dispatch,* July 22, 1923, "Is White America to Become a Negroid Nation?" JPP, box 38, folder 4.

21. John Powell, "The Price of Pollution," *Richmond News Leader,* June 5, 1923, JPP, box 43, folder 4.

22. Ibid.

23. Ibid.

24. For the text of Virginia's 1924 Racial Integrity Act of 1924, see http://www2. vcdh.virginia.edu/encounter/projects/monacans/Contemporary_Monacans/ racial.html (accessed October 25, 2013). See also Dorr, *Segregation's Science,* 149.

25. John Powell, "The Last Stand: The Necessity of Race Integrity Legislation in Virginia as Shown by an Ethnological Survey of the State by Congressional Districts," unpublished, JPP, box 38, folder 10.

26. Ibid.

27. Ibid.

28. John Powell's notes for "The Last Stand," JPP, box 38, folder 26.

29. John Powell, "Homogenous America," transcripts of speech, n.d., n.p., JPP, box 38, folder 43.

30. *Richmond Times Dispatch,* June 15, 1924, JPP, box 38, folder 13.

31. Ibid.

32. Madison Grant to John Powell, February 1, 1924, JPP, box 39, folder 18.

33. See Lothrop Stoddard in response to a request by the ASCoA that he endorse the petition for Racial Purity on February 1, 1924, JPP, box 39, folder 100. See also Lothrop Stoddard to Powell, April 23, 1927, JPP, box 39, folder 19.

34. For a listing of operational Anglo-Saxon Clubs of America in Virginia during the 1920s, see JPP, box 64, folder 71. See also, Smith, *Managing White Supremacy,* 84–86. Curiously, during these same years, the College of William and Mary recruited Arthur Matsu to play quarterback. Matsu, the son of a Japanese man and Scotch woman, was the first student of Asian descent to enroll at the college. According to one southern newspaper, he was an "able, consistent punter, good ball carrier, and sure tackler, the Japanese makes up in brains and speed what he lacks in poundage. Unlike many of his race, Matsu is tall and thin." See "College Picks Jap to Captain Gridiron Team," *Evening Independent,* February 6, 1926, 7–10.

35. Charles Davenport and Arthur H. Estabrook, *The Nam Family: A Study in Cacogenics* (Cold Spring Harbor, NY: Eugenics Record Office Press, 1912).

36. Ibid., 2–4.

37. Arthur H. Estabrook, *The Jukes in 1915* (Washington, DC: Carnegie Institution of Washington, 1916), 2. Richard Dugdale published his trailblazing study of rural poverty in upstate New York in 1877. Estabrook wanted to issue a follow-up study in the mold of his work on McCulloch's Ishmaels. See Dugdale, *The Jukes.*

38. Ibid.

39. For more on Estabrook in Virginia, see Dorr, *Segregation's Science,* 153–55.

40. For more on the Isshies and how mongrelization allegedly occurred, see Estabrook and McDougle, "Triple Crosses in the South," abstract, June 14, 1924, Arthur H. Estabrook Papers (hereafter AHE), box 1, folder 9, M. E. Grenander Department of Special Collections and Archives, University at Albany, SUNY. See also Arthur H. Estabrook and Ivan E. McDougle, *Mongrel Virginians: The Win Tribe* (Baltimore: Williams and Wilkins, 1926).

41. McDougle to Estabrook, May 3, 1924. AHE, box 1, folder 3.

42. See McDougle's notes for May 10, 1924. AHE, box 1, folder 3.

43. Estabrook and McDougle, "Triple Crosses in the South," abstract, June 14, 1924. AEH, box 1, folder 9.

44. "Notes on Nams and Wins: Key Indexes to Places in Guilder Hollow," AHE, box 1, folder 9.

45. Estabrook and McDougle, *Mongrel Virginians,* 131–35.

46. For additional discussion on this point, see Deutch, *Inventing America's "Worst" Family,* 49–72.

47. Mandel Sherman and Cora B. Key, "The Intelligence of Isolated Mountain Children," *Child Development* 3, no. 4 (1932): 279.

48. Ibid.

49. Ibid., 289.

50. Mandel Sherman and Thomas Henry, *The Hollow Folk,* vol. 1 (Boston: Thomas Y. Crowell, 1933).

51. Grant, *Passing of the Great Race,* 39.

52. Horace Kephart was among the region's ardent defenders. He lobbied to preserve what would become the Great Smoky Mountains National Park. See Kephart, *Our Southern Highlanders: A Narrative of Adventure in the Southern Appalachians and a Study of the Life Among the Mountaineers* (New York: Macmillan, 1922); and John C. Campbell, *The Southern Highlander and His Homeland* (1921; repr., Lexington: University Press of Kentucky, 2004).

53. Campbell, *Southern Highlander and His Home,* 8.

54. Ibid., 70.

55. Estabrook and McDougle, *Mongrel Virginians,* 199.

56. Ibid., 202.

57. Lombardo, *Three Generations, No Imbeciles,* 31–40.

58. Proceedings for the Supreme Court of Appeals at Staunton, Virginia, September Term, 1925, 84–85, AHE, ser. 9, box 1, folder 43.

59. Ibid.

60. Dorr, *Segregation's Science,* 132.

61. Ibid.

62. Supreme Court of Appeals at Staunton, Virginia, September Term, 1925, 84–85. See also Lombardo, *Three Generations, No Imbeciles,* 134.

63. Supreme Court of Appeals at Staunton, Virginia, September Term, 1925, 5.

64. Black, *War against The Weak,* 3–9.

65. Powell answered his critics regarding his involvement in the Anglo-Saxon Club activities in "Anglo-Saxon Club Activities No Tax on Artist's Ability," January 11, 1925, JPP, box 6, folder 20. Also quoted in Adam, "'The Nonmusical Message Will Endure With It,'" 16.

66. John Powell, "Beauties of the Anglo-Saxon Folk Song," AMB, ser. A, folder 148 ("Articles by and about John Powell"). This document was published as "Music and the Nation," *Rice Institute Pamphlet* 10, no. 1 (1923): 127–63, available online at http://scholarship.rice.edu/bitstream/handle/1911/8712/article_RI103127.pdf?sequence=7 (accessed November 18, 2013).

67. Powell, "Beauties of the Anglo-Saxon Folk Song."

68. Ibid.

69. Ibid.

70. Ibid.

71. Whisnant, *All That Is Native and Fine,* 208. Whisnant's account of the festival in chapter 3, "'This Folk Work' and the 'Holy Folk': The White Top Folk Festival, 1931–1939" (pp. 181–252), remains definitive.

72. Note that White Top refers to the festival, and Whitetop refers to the actual mountain in Grayson County, Virginia.

73. Ibid., 210–14.

74. John Blakemore calculated the attendance in 1933 at 16,143 and in 1934, when Eleanor Roosevelt appeared, at over 20,000. See the John A. Blakemore Papers, 1928–1980 (hereafter JAB), box 1, folder 117, Southern Historical Collection, Wilson Library, UNC–Chapel Hill.

75. National Federation of Music Clubs press release for Fifth Annual White Top Folk Festival, 1935, AMB, ser. A, folder 146.

76. Bill C. Malone and David Strickland, *Southern Music/American Music,* 2nd ed. (Lexington: University of Kentucky Press, 2003), 58–71.

77. National Federation of Music Clubs press release for Fifth Annual White Top Folk Festival, 1935, AMB, ser. A, folder 146.

78. "And the Mountains Sing with Joy, White Top Musical Festival," *Southern Magazine* 2, no. 1 (April 1935), AMB, ser. A, folder 146.

79. John Powell, address before White Top Folk Festival Conference, August, 1933. Several notes and drafts of the address are available in AMB, ser. A, folder 144.

80. Powell, "How America Can Develop a National Music," 349.

81. John Powell, "Powell Sees Bond of Sympathy Between England-America," unknown publication and date, JPP, box 44, folder, 22.

82. Ibid.

83. "Real Southerner and the White Top Folk Festival," *Southern Literary Messenger,* June 1939, AMB, series A, folder 147.

84. Powell, address before White Top Conference, AMB, ser. A, folder 144, 1932–33.

85. John Powell, "Folk Music," *Richmond Times Dispatch,* July 29, 1935, JPP, box 37, folder 8.

86. John Powell, "Treasure Recovered (Folk Music)," *Home and Garden Review,* July–August, 1934, 5, AMB, ser. A (1934), folder 145.

87. Ibid.

88. Whisnant, *All That Is Native and Fine,* 191–95.

89. Robert Nelson, miscellaneous news clippings, AMB, ser. A, folder 146 (1935).

90. Ibid.

91. George Pullen Jackson, "Ballad Art Revived at White Top Festival," *Musical America,* September 1934, JPP, box 27, folder 34.

92. Ibid.

93. Kenneth Noe, "'A Source of Great Economy'? The Railroad and Slavery's Expansion in Southwest Virginia, 1850–1860," in *Appalachia and Race: The Mountain South From Slavery to Segregation,* ed. John C. Inscoe (Lexington: University Press of Kentucky, 2001), 101–15. See also Noe, *Southwest Virginia's Railroad,* 67–84.

94. Whisnant, *All That Is Native and Fine,* 244–46.

95. Historians have written substantively on Melungeons over the past ten years. See Wayne Winkler, *Walking Toward the Sunset: The Melungeons of Appalachia* (Macon, GA: Mercer University Press, 2004); Tim Hashaw, *Children of Perdition: Melungeons and the Struggle of Mixed America* (Macon, GA: Mercer University Press, 2007); Donald N. Yates and Elizabeth C. Hirschman, "Toward a Genetic Profile of Melungeons in Southern Appalachia," *Appalachian Journal* 38, no. 1 (2010): 92–111; and Melissa Schrift, *Becoming Melungeon: Making an Ethnic Identity in the Appalachian South* (Lincoln: University Nebraska Press, 2013). In addition, Darlene Wilson and others have compiled a wealth of material for the website melungeons.org.

96. According to at least a few historians, Elvis Presley, Ava Gardner, and Abraham Lincoln are among the most famous Melungeons. See N. Brent Kennedy and Robyn Vaughan Kennedy, *The Melungeons: The Resurrection of a Proud People* (Macon, GA: Mercer University Press, 1996).

97. Cecelia Conway, *African Banjo Echoes in Appalachia* (Knoxville: University of Tennessee Press, 1995), esp. 120–59; Karin Linn, *That Half-Barbaric Twang: The Banjo in American Culture* (Urbana: University of Illinois Press, 1994), 116–42.

98. AMB to Powell, March 23, 1932, AMB, folder 118, series A.

99. Powell, "How America Can Develop a National Music," 349.

100. Ibid.

101. Quoted in Whisnant, *All That Is Native and Fine,* 244.

102. JAB, box 1, folder 102.

103. The John A. Blakemore Papers, 1928–1980, Southern Historical Collection, Wilson Library, UNC-Chapel Hill box 1, folder 102.

104. For some background on Wheeler-Bennett, see Nicholas J. Cull, *Selling War: The British Propaganda Campaign against American Neutrality in World War II* (New York: Oxford University Press, 1995), 30–31, 99.

105. Powell to John Wheeler-Bennett, June 12, 1941. JPP, box 40, folder 40.

106. Ibid.

107. For more on the folk festivals of the 1920s and 1930s, see Ronald Cohen, *A History of Folk Festivals in the United States: Feasts of Musical Celebration* (Lanham, MD: Scarecrow/Rowman and Littlefield, 2008), 1–25; Rudy Abramson and Jean Haskell, eds., *Encyclopedia of Appalachia* (Knoxville: University of Tennessee Press, 2006), 860–61.

108. Miscellaneous article, AMB, ser. A, folder 144 (1932–33).

109. For some work on the eugenics movement beyond the United States, see Jennifer Robertson, "Blood Talks: Eugenic Modernity and the Creation of New Japanese," *History and Anthropology* 13, no. 3 (2002): 191–216; and Diana Wyndham, *Eugenics in Australia: Striving for National Fitness* (London, UK: The Galton Institute, 2003). As it relates to Great Britain, see Kevles, *In the Name of Eugenics,* 3–20; Carlson, *The Unfit,* 247–64; and Michael Bulmer, *Francis Galton, Pioneer of Hereditary Biometry* (Baltimore: Johns Hopkins University Press, 2003), 79–98.

110. Carlson, *The Unfit,* 279–383.

111. For further information on the Nazi Nuremberg Laws and the regime's implementation of a race-based legal system, see Eric Ehrenreich, *The Nazi Ancestral Proof: Genealogy, Racial Science, and the Final Solution* (Bloomington: Indiana University Press, 2007).

112. Black, *The War on the Weak,* 411–44.

113. Indiana University–Purdue University Indianapolis (IUPUI) has digitized several documents relating to the period between 1907 and 1974. See their website for articles, sources, and figures relating to the "Indiana Plan": http://www.iupui.edu/~eugenics/ (accessed March 26, 2013).

114. Richard Herrnstein and Charles Murray, *The Bell Curve: Intelligence and Class Structure in American Life* (New York: Free Press, 1994).

115. Eric Alterman, *What Liberal Media? The Truth about Bias and the News* (New York: Basic Books, 2004), 33.

116. James T. Patterson concludes with this explicit connection in *America's Struggle against Poverty,* 240–42.

117. For coverage on Bill Clinton's signing of the landmark legislation, see Barbara Vobejda, "Clinton Signs Welfare Bill Amid Division," *Washington Post,* April 23, 1996, available online at http://www.washingtonpost.com/wp-srv/politics/special/welfare/stories/wf082396.htm (accessed March 21, 2013).

118. The case against Bill Clinton's welfare reform is well documented. See Francis Fox Piven and Richard A. Cloward, *Breaking of the American Social Compact* (New York: Free Press, 1998), esp. pt. 3, 169–243; and, more recently, Sharon Hays, *Flat Broke with Children: Women in the Age of Welfare Reform* (New York: Oxford University Press, 2004).

119. Here I say "mostly" because the introduction of *The Bell Curve* issued only a tepid condemnation of the eugenics movements while at the same time staking out the precise deterministic ground that the movement had so long occupied. For the book's only reference to the so-called Nordic race, see page 5 and the discussion of World War I intelligence testing.

120. Herrnstein and Murray, *The Bell Curve,* 269.

121. Ibid. For the clearest articulation of this in Herrnstein and Murray, *The Bell Curve,* see the chapter entitled "Ethnic Differences in Cognitive Ability," 269–317.

122. *The Bell Curve,* not surprisingly, received withering criticism from scholars across the political spectrum. The strongest critique is Steven Fraser's edited volume, *The Bell Curve Wars: Race, Intelligence, and the Future of America* (New York: Basic Books, 1995). The collection includes essays by, among many others, Henry Louis Gates Jr., Jacqueline Jones, Orlando Patterson, and Thomas Sowell. For additional critiques of biological determinism, see Michael Lind, *Up from Conservatism: Why the Right Is Wrong for America* (New York: Free Press, 1996), 180–83; and Sydney Blumenthal, *The Rise of Conservative Ideology* (New York: Times Books, 1986), 292–95. See also Gould, *The Mismeasure of Man,* 367–90; indeed Gould's expanded and revised text includes a chapter entitled "Critique of the Bell Curve."

Chapter 4

1. Albert N. Votaw, "The Hillbillies Invade Chicago," *Harper's Magazine,* February 1958, 64. Votaw's article echoed what anthropologist Oscar Lewis had just termed, "the culture of poverty"; see Lewis, *Five Families: Mexican Case Studies in the Culture of Poverty* (New York: Basic Books, 1959), for the first extended treatment of the thesis. Lewis argued that economic inequality was largely due to cultural factors. For additional analysis of Votaw's article, see

Harkins, *Hillbilly,* 176–78; and Allen W. Batteau, *The Invention of Appalachia* (Tucson: University of Arizona Press, 1990), 146. On Appalachian migrants in Chicago, see Todd Gitlin and Nanci Hollander, *Uptown: Poor Whites in Chicago* (New York: Harper and Row, 1970). On Appalachian stereotypes, see Billings, Norman, and Ledford, eds., *Back Talk from Appalachia.* Ronald D. Eller, *Uneven Ground: Appalachia Since 1945* (Lexington: University Press of Kentucky, 2008), provides analysis of the chain of events detailed in this chapter; on Appalachians in Chicago and other cities in the Midwest, see pp. 20–29. My thanks to the editors and reviewers of the *Journal of Southern History,* where a version of this chapter first appeared; see Ian C. Hartman, "West Virginia Mountaineers and Kentucky Frontiersmen: Race, Manliness, and the Rhetoric of Liberalism in the Early1960s," *Journal of Southern History* 80, no. 3 (2014): 651–78.

2. James N. Gregory *The Southern Diaspora: How the Great Migration of Black and White Southerners Transformed America* (Chapel Hill: University of North Carolina Press, 2005), 12–15. Gregory notes that while most southern migrants moved north, in 1970 California residents included roughly 1.7 million whites and nearly six hundred thousand African Americans born in the South.

3. Chad Berry, *Southern Migrants, Northern Exiles* (Urbana: University of Illinois Press, 2000), 110. See also Thomas Kiffmeyer, "Looking Back to the City in the Hills: The Council of Southern Mountains and a Longer View of the War on Poverty in the Appalachian South, 1913–1970," in *The War on Poverty: A New Grassroots History,* ed. Annelise Orleck and Lisa Gayle Hazirjian (Athens: University of Georgia Press, 2011), 359–86. For more on white migration into the Midwest, see John Hartigan, *Odd Tribes: Toward a Cultural Analysis of White People* (Durham, NC: Duke University Press, 2005), 205–30; Kathryn M. Borman and Phillip J. Obermiller, eds., *From Mountain to Metropolis: Appalachian Migrants in American Cities* (New York: Bergen and Garvey, 1994); and Phillip J. Obermiller, Thomas E. Wagner, and E. Bruce Tucker, eds., *Appalachian Odyssey: Historical Perspectives on the Great Migration* (Westport, CT: Praeger, 2000).

4. James Maxwell, "Down from the Hills and into the Slums," *Reporter* (New York City), December 13, 1956, 27–29 (quote on p. 27). See Harkin, *Hillbilly,* 176–77, for additional analysis.

5. Maxwell, "Down from the Hills and into the Slums," 27.

6. Ibid.

7. Jean Shepherd, *In God We Trust: All Others Pay Cash* (New York: Doubleday, 1966), 129. Shepherd's troublesome Kentuckians and Tennesseans settled in northern Indiana rather than in Indianapolis.

8. Roosevelt, *Winning of the West,* vol. 1, pt. 2: 34–65. This chapter, entitled "Boon [*sic*] and the Settlement of Kentucky," deals explicitly with Daniel

Boone's exploits during the Revolutionary Period and the role of manliness in the West.

9. Roosevelt, *Winning of the West,* vol. 2, pt. 1: 96.

10. Ibid., 95. See Horsman, *Race and Manifest Destiny;* Saxton, *The Rise and Fall of the White Republic;* and Dyer, *Theodore Roosevelt and the Idea of Race.* See also Morris, *Theodore Rex,* 52–53, for discussions of Roosevelt, race, and Anglo-Saxonism.

11. The conflation of white poverty with "white trash" and discussion of the latter as both a racial and cultural identity has received treatment by several scholars. See Hartigan, *Odd Tribes,* 59–108; and Wray, *Not Quite White,* 21–47. For a polemical text, see Jim Goad, *The Redneck Manifesto: How Hillbillies, Hicks, and White Trash Became America's Scapegoats* (New York: Simon and Schuster, 1998).

12. For the best book-length treatments of Appalachia as a culturally constructed space, see Harkins, *Hillbilly;* Batteau, *Invention of Appalachia;* Shapiro, *Appalachia on Our Mind;* Whisnant, *All That Is Native and Fine;* and Hsiung, *Two Worlds in the Tennessee Mountains.* For edited collections, see Straw and Blethan, *High Mountains Rising;* and Pudup, Billings, and Waller, *Appalachia in the Making.*

13. Quadagno, *Color of Welfare,* 4–15; Katz, *Undeserving Poor,* 60–83; Gilens, *Why Americans Hate Welfare,* 102–10.

14. Branch's volumes *Parting the Waters* and *Pillar of Fire* and Payne's *I've Got the Light of Freedom* have all influenced this study. For more on the War on Poverty at the local level, see Orleck and Hazirjian, *War on Poverty.*

15. Patterson, *Grand Expectations,* esp. chaps. 13–19; Milkis and Mileur, *Great Society and the High Tide of Liberalism,* 1–59; Kotz, *Judgment Days,* 89–111. On recent literature related to Lyndon Johnson, see Kent Germany, "Historians and the Many Lyndon Johnsons: A Review Essay," *Journal of Southern History* 75, no. 4 (2009): 1001–28. Germany presents a thoughtful review of Randall B. Woods, *LBJ: Architect of American Ambition* (Cambridge, MA: Harvard University Press, 2007); however, he also offers a good overview of other works, as well as a general summary of 1960s liberalism.

16. Katznelson, *When Affirmative Action Was White,* 14.

17. Matusow, *Unraveling of America,* esp. chap. 4, "The Origins of the War on Poverty," 97–127. See also O'Connor, *Poverty Knowledge,* 10–22. O'Connor positions the War on Poverty in the context of a longer tradition of an activist state. For studies that emphasize the role of community action, see Premilla Nadasen, *Welfare Warriors: The Welfare Rights Movement in the United States* (New York: Routledge, 2005); Noel Cazenave, *Impossible Democracy: The Unlikely Success of the War on Poverty Community Action Programs* (Albany: State University of New York Press, 2007); and Annelise Orleck, *Storming Caesar's*

Palace: How Black Mothers Fought Their Own War on Poverty (Boston: Beacon Press, 2006).

18. Matusow, *Unraveling of America,* 120.

19. Ibid., 122–26. On the unforeseen effects of community action and maximum feasible participation—two components of the Economic Opportunity Act, see Nadasen, *Welfare Warriors,* 33–45. For other recent treatments of the War on Poverty's origins, see Korstad and Leloudis, *To Right These Wrongs;* and Germany, *New Orleans after the Promise.*

20. James L. Sundquist, "Origins of the War on Poverty," in *On Fighting Poverty: Perspectives from Experience,* ed. James L. Sundquist, vol. 2 of *Perspectives on Poverty* (New York: Basic Books, 1969), 7.

21. For more on the results of the 1964 election, see Mary C. Brennan, *Turning Right in the Sixties: The Conservative Capture of the GOP* (Chapel Hill: University of North Carolina Press, 1995), 102–4.

22. In addition to Brennan's *Turning Right in the Sixties,* see Rick Perlstein, *Before the Storm: Barry Goldwater and the Unmaking of the American Consensus* (New York: Nation Books, 2001). Perlstein's book is an effective treatment of the 1964 election; it details the internal shift within the Republican Party through the lens of the Goldwater candidacy and teases out its implications beyond the 1960s.

23. David E. Whisnant, *Modernizing the Mountaineer: People, Power, and Planning in Appalachia,* rev. ed. (Knoxville: University of Tennessee Press, 1994), is the strongest treatment of local, state, and federal policy, as well as voluntarism in the region, particularly from the New Deal through the 1960s, esp. 43–153.

24. Johnson had several events and meetings planned in West Virginia and Kentucky as part of his April 24, 1964, visit. For a list of his appearances and engagements that day, see the Lyndon Johnson Daily Diary, April 24, 1964, LBJ Presidential Library and Museum, Austin, TX, available online at http://www.lbjlibrary.net/assets/lbj_tools/daily_diary/pdf/1964/19640424.pdf (accessed October 26, 2013).

25. For more on Bigart's life, his career at the *New York Times,* and his accomplishments, see Richard Severo, "Homer Bigart, Acclaimed Reporter, Dies," *New York Times,* April 17, 1991, available online at http://query.nytimes.com/gst/fullpage.html?res=9E0CEEDE103AF934A25757C0A967958260 (accessed October 26, 2013).

26. Homer Bigart, "Depression Rivaling '30s Grips Kentucky-Virginia Coal Area," *New York Times,* January 11, 1959. Bigart reported similarly large numbers on relief in Virginia; according to the Virginia State Board of Welfare, almost nine thousand families and thirty-eight thousand individuals were on relief.

27. Homer Bigart, "West Virginia Grim," *New York Times,* March 16, 1959.

28. Ibid.

29. Homer Bigart, "Kentucky Miners: A Grim Winter," *New York Times,* October 20, 1963.

30. Bureau of Labor Statistics and Bureau of the Census, *Social and Economic Conditions of Negroes in the United States* (Washington, DC, 1967), 22–30; C. Michael Henry, introduction, "Historical Overview of Race and Poverty from Reconstruction to 1969," to *Race, Poverty, and Domestic Policy,* ed. C. Michael Henry (New Haven: Yale University Press, 2004), 1–56, esp. 5–6.

31. Ibid.

32. See Eller, *Uneven Ground,* 66–67, for additional analysis of Bigart's trip through the region.

33. Harry W. Ernst and Charles H. Drake, "Lost Appalachians: Poor, Proud and Primitive," *Nation,* May 30, 1959, 492.

34. Roul Tunley, "The Strange Case of West Virginia," *Saturday Evening Post,* February 6, 1960, 19–20, 64–66 (quotes on p. 65).

35. Julius Duscha, "A Long Trail of Misery Winds the Proud Hills," *Washington Post,* August 7, 1960. See also Eller, *Uneven Ground,* 64–65.

36. "Statement of Senator Jennings Randolph before the Senate Subcommittee on Production and Stabilization," March 5, 1959, 4–5, Pre-Presidential Papers, Presidential Campaign Files, 1960, Papers of John F. Kennedy, ser. 13:3, folder "Randolph, Sen. Jennings: Speeches," John F. Kennedy Presidential Library and Museum, Boston (hereafter cited as JFK Library), available online at http://www.jfklibrary.org/Asset-Viewer/Archives/JFKCAMP1960-989-20.aspx (accessed October 10, 2012).

37. "National Affairs: Tough Testing Ground," *Time,* March 28, 1960, 25. See also Louis Harris's poll as discussed in "The Campaign: The Religion Issue (Cont'd)," *Time,* May 2, 1960, 15–16.

38. Edmund F. Kallina Jr., *Kennedy v. Nixon: The Presidential Election of 1960* (Gainesville: University of Florida Press, 2010); W. J. Rorabaugh, *The Real Making of the President: Kennedy, Nixon, and the 1960 Election* (Lawrence: University of Kansas Press, 2009), 51–57; Gary A. Donaldson, *The First Modern Campaign: Kennedy, Nixon, and the Election of 1960* (Lanham, MD: Rowman and Littlefield, 2007). All three note Kennedy's reliance upon West Virginia but fail to historicize the racial undertones of the campaign. Theodore H. White's *The Making of the President, 1960* (New York: Harper Perennial, 1961) is a journalist's account of the election but has little analysis of Kennedy's campaign in West Virginia.

39. "Remarks of Senator John F. Kennedy at Mullens, West Virginia," April 26, 1960, West Virginia Archives and History Online Exhibit, http://www.

wvculture.org/history/1960presidentialcampaign/jfklibrary/19600426 mullenssp.html (accessed April 6, 2014).

40. Richard J. H. Johnston, "Kennedy Pledges West Virginia Aid; Says Republicans Neglect Economically Depressed Portions of the State," *New York Times,* April 26, 1960.

41. John F. Kennedy, "West Virginia—The State Which the Pentagon Forgot," speech given in Wheeling, WV, April 19, 1960, subseries 13:3, Pre-Presidential Papers, Presidential Campaign Files, 1960, Papers of John F. Kennedy, JFK Library, http://www.jfklibrary.org/Asset-Viewer/Archives/JFKCAMP1960– 989–18.aspx (accessed October 15, 2012).

42. Ibid.

43. John F. Kennedy, remarks given at Glenwood Park, WV, April 26, 1960, pp. 2–5, John F. Kennedy Speeches, JFK Library Digital Collections, http:// www.jfklibrary.org/Asset-Viewer/T_7MiG5JOU2ZlWyBacobFQ.aspx (accessed November 21, 2012).

44. Ibid., 3.

45. Ibid., 4.

46. Ibid., 5.

47. Kennedy's campaign tactics in West Virginia further revealed how US politicians and the public viewed poor people as either deserving or undeserving of assistance, a centuries-old idea. Michael Katz elaborates on how this bifurcation emerged during the War on Poverty, though clearly Kennedy had skillfully mobilized the language and image of "worthy assistance" a few years earlier. Katz, *Undeserving Poor,* chaps. 1 and 3.

48. John F. Kennedy, "A Program for West Virginia," speech given in Charleston, WV, April 20, 1960, p. 5, John F. Kennedy Speeches, JFK Library Digital Collections, http://www.jfklibrary.org/Asset-Viewer/JK-0jg1N_katCOPr-1BA7aA.aspx (accessed on November 21, 2012).

49. Richard J. H. Johnston, "Kennedy Hailed in Mining Region," *New York Times,* April 27, 1960.

50. Simeon Booker, oral history interview, recorded by John Stewart, April 24, 1967, pp. 1–2, John F. Kennedy Oral History Collection, JFK Library Digital Collections, http://www.jfklibrary.org/Asset-Viewer/Archives/JFKOH-SSB-01.aspx (accessed on November 14, 2012).

51. Ibid., 3–4.

52. For additional analysis of Kennedy's opposition to civil rights in 1957, see Michael O'Brien, *John F. Kennedy: A Biography* (New York: Thomas Dunne Books, 2005), 457–60.

53. Booker interview, 9.

54. Ibid., 1.

55. Ibid., 3.

56. These figures are from Gallup polling for the 1960 election and remain comprehensive in their demographic information. See "Election Polls—Vote by Groups, 1960–1964," http://www.gallup.com/poll/9454/election-polls-vote-groups-19601964.aspx (accessed September 3, 2012).

57. Robert Coles, "Rural Upheaval: Confrontation and Accommodation," in Sundquist, *On Fighting Poverty,* 103–26 (quote on p. 103).

58. Daniel P. Moynihan, "The Professors and the Poor," in *On Understanding Poverty: Perspectives from the Social Sciences,* ed. Daniel P. Moynihan, vol. 1 of *Perspectives on Poverty* (New York: Basic Books, 1969), 3–35 (quote on p. 6).

59. Ibid., 6.

60. John F. Kennedy, "Address of Senator John F. Kennedy Accepting the Democratic Party Nomination for the Presidency of the United States," Los Angeles, CA, July 15, 1960, American Presidency Project, http://www.presidency. ucsb.edu/ws/?pid=25966 (accessed May 12, 2014).

61. Ibid.

62. Area Development, sec. 1, Public Law 87–27, approved May 1, 1961. For the full text of the law, see Oklahoma State University Electronic Publishing Center, http://digital.library.okstate.edu/kappler/vol6/html_files/v6p0922. html (accessed April 7, 2014).

63. William L. Batt oral history interview, recorded by Larry J. Hackman, October 26, 1966, 4–9, 29–30, JFK Oral History Collection, JFK Library Digital Collections, http://www.jfklibrary.org/Asset-Viewer/Archives/ JFKOH-WLB-01.aspx (accessed April 12, 2014).

64. See Matusow's discussion of Area Redevelopment in *Unraveling of America,* 101–2.

65. "114 Areas Listed For Jobless Help: U.S. Names First Distressed Regions Eligible for Aid," *New York Times,* June 10, 1961.

66. For a critical analysis of the Area Redevelopment Act in southern Appalachia, see Eller, *Uneven Ground,* 51–71; Whisnant, *Modernizing the Mountaineer,* 70–91; and Gregory S. Wilson, *Communities Left Behind: The Area Redevelopment Administration, 1945–1965* (Knoxville: University of Tennessee Press, 2009), 83–104.

67. Using PARC's report, Congress passed the Appalachian Regional Development Act of 1965, which created the Appalachian Regional Commission (ARC). The PARC findings are contained in *Appalachia: A Report by the President's Appalachian Regional Commission, 1964* (Washington, DC, 1964), available online at http://www.arc.gov/about/ARCAppalachiaAReportbythe PresidentsAppalachianRegionalCommission1964.asp (accessed November 17, 2014) For a comprehensive study of the ARC, see Glen Edward Taul, "Poverty, Development, and Government in Appalachia: Origins of the Appalachian Regional Commission" (PhD diss., University of Kentucky, 2001).

68. Thomas R. Ford, ed., *The Southern Appalachian Region: A Survey* (Lexington: University Press of Kentucky, 1962).

69. Ford, "The Passing of Provincialism," in Ford, *Southern Appalachian Region,* 9–34 (quote on p. 12).

70. Rupert B. Vance, "The Region: A Survey," in Ford, *Southern Appalachian Region,* 1–8 (quote on p. 3).

71. W. D. Weatherford and Wilma Dykeman, "Folk Arts in Transition: Literature since 1900," in Ford, *Southern Appalachian Region,* 259–71 (quotes on pp. 260, 262).

72. Ibid., 264.

73. Both men published articles that previewed the arguments they soon elaborated on in their respective books; see Michael Harrington, "Our Fifty Million Poor: Forgotten Men of the Affluent Society," *Commentary* 28, no. 1 (1959): 19–27; and Harry Caudill, "The Rape of the Appalachians," *Atlantic Monthly,* April 1962, 37–41.

74. Dwight Macdonald, "Our Invisible Poor," *New Yorker,* January 19, 1963, 82–132 (quote on p. 82), available online at www.newyorker.com/archive/1963/01/19/ 1963_01_19_082_TNY_CARDS_000075671 (accessed October 29, 2012).

75. Maurice Isserman, *The Other American: The Life of Michael Harrington* (New York: Public Affairs, 2000), 156, 180–83, 195.

76. Harrington, *The Other America,* 3–4.

77. Ibid., 41.

78. Caudill, *Night Comes to the Cumberlands;* see chap. 19, "The Rape of the Appalachians." Caudill first used the phrase in an earlier article that anticipated many of his arguments in *Night Comes to the Cumberlands;* see Caudill, "Rape of the Appalachians," 37–42. For a detailed account of Caudill's life and activism, see John Cheves and Bill Estep, "Fifty Years of Night," *Lexington Herald-Leader,* 2013. This yearlong series provides a brief biography of Caudill and reflects on the impact that *Night Comes to the Cumberlands* had on the decade's politics and public policy.

79. See Nell Irving Painter's instructive chapter, "Roosevelt, Ross, and Race Suicide," in *History of White People,* 245–56, for a useful summary of Roosevelt's Teutonist leanings and how they related to the Kentuckian. See also Dyer, *Theodore Roosevelt and the Idea of Race,* 2–11.

80. Spiro, *Defending the Master Race,* xii, 61–67, chap. 2, chap. 11.

81. Grant, *Passing of the Great Race,* esp. 89–94, 167–212. For the role of expansion and conquest upon race, see chap. 10, "The Nordic Race Outside of Europe," 223–26.

82. Caudill, *Night Comes to the Cumberlands,* 13. Here, one might extend the territory into western Virginia as many of Caudill's favorite settlers spent as much time in the Virginia Mountains as they did in Kentucky.

83. Ibid., 90.

84. Ibid., 13.

85. For an instructive work on sexual violence on the western frontier, see chap. 3, "Sex and Conquest: Domination and Desire on Ethnosexual Frontiers," in Joane Nagel, *Race, Ethnicity, and Sexuality: Intimate Intersections, Forbidden Frontiers* (New York: Oxford University Press, 2003), 63–90.

86. Roosevelt, *Winning of the West,* vol. 1, pt. 1: 119.

87. Shaler, *American Commonwealths,* 18.

88. Caudill, *Night Comes to the Cumberlands,* 90.

89. Ibid., 90.

90. Ibid., 280.

91. Ibid., 374.

92. Roosevelt articulated his notion of manliness and the strenuous life before the Hamilton Club in Chicago on April 10, 1899. He defined the strenuous life as one of "toil and effort, of labor and strife." Theodore Roosevelt, "The Strenuous Life," in Roosevelt, *The Strenuous Life: Essays and Addresses* (New York: Bartleby Publishing, 1900), 3–22 (quote on p. 3).

93. Grant, *Passing of the Great Race,* 11–12.

94. See Gail Bederman, *Manliness and Civilization,* 84–88, and esp. chap. 5, "Theodore Roosevelt, Nation, and 'Civilization'," 170–215, for an instructive treatment of Anglo-Saxon masculinity in the Progressive era.

95. For an overview of the history and transformation of the coal industry, see Curtis Seltzer, *Fire in the Hole: Miners and Managers in the American Coal Industry* (Lexington: University Press of Kentucky, 1985).

96. Caudill, *Night Comes to the Cumberlands,* 371–76 (quote on p. 392).

97. William L. Batt, oral history interview, recorded by Larry J. Hackman, May 10, 1967, p. 186, JFK Library Oral History Collection, JFK Library Digital Collections, http://archive1.jfklibrary.org/JFKOH/Batt,%20William%20L/JFKOH-WLB-03/JFKOH-WLB-03-TR.pdf (accessed April 12, 2014).

98. Stewart L. Udall, foreword to Caudill, *Night Comes to the Cumberlands,* vii–viii (quotes on p. vii). For a biographical sketch and remembrance of Udall, see Keith Schneider and Cornelia Dean, "Stewart L. Udall, Conservationist in Kennedy and Johnson Cabinets, Dies at 90," *New York Times,* March 21, 2010.

99. For a compelling treatment of the aftermath of the Kennedy assassination and Johnson's first moments after being sworn in, see Steven M. Gillon, *The Kennedy Assassination—24 Hours After: Lyndon B. Johnson's Pivotal First Day as President* (New York: Basic Books, 2009), 87–112. For the definitive sources on the immediate days and months after the Kennedy assassination, see the first six volumes of *The Presidential Recordings: Lyndon B. Johnson,* published by W. W. Norton, New York. Volumes 1–3, *The Kennedy Assassination and the Transfer of Power, November 1963–January 1964,* were edited by

Max Holland, Robert David Johnson, David Shreve, and Kent B. Germany and published in 2005. Volumes 4–6, *Toward the Great Society, February 1, 1964–May 31, 1964,* were edited by Robert David Johnson, Kent B. Germany, David Shreve, and Guian A. McKee and published in 2007.

100. Adam Yarmolinsky, "Poverty and Urban Policy: Conference Transcript of 1973 Group Discussion of the Kennedy Administration Urban Poverty Programs and Policies," Brandeis University, June 16–17, 1973, in *The John F. Kennedy Presidential Oral History Collection,* pt. 1 (Frederick, MD: University Publications of America, 1988), 162–63.

101. Quoted in Katz, *Undeserving Poor,* 85–86.

102. Adam Yarmolinsky, "The Beginnings of the OEO [Office of Economic Opportunity]," in Sundquist, *On Fighting Poverty,* 34–51 (quote on p. 42).

103. Ibid., 42–44.

104. Ibid., 50.

105. There remains much debate, however, over what led to the Civil Rights Act of 1964 and the Voting Rights Act of 1965. On the role of the Cold War and the fear of Soviet propaganda, see Thomas Borstelmann, *The Cold War and the Color Line: American Race Relations in the Global Arena* (Cambridge, MA: Harvard University Press, 2001); and Mary L. Dudziak, *Cold War Civil Rights: Race and the Image of American Democracy* (Princeton, NJ: Princeton University Press, 2000). For another treatment, see Michael J. Klarman, *From Jim Crow to Civil Rights: The Supreme Court and the Struggle for Racial Equality* (New York: Oxford University Press, 2004), 182–83, 443–68.

106. According to the diary's notes, Johnson spoke before eighteen hundred people at his helicopter landing site, twelve hundred at the courthouse in Inez, and as many as ten thousand in Paintsville. The itinerary and notes are available through the LBJ Library and Museum at http://www.lbjlibrary.net/assets/lbj_tools/daily_diary/pdf/1964/19640424.pdf (accessed April 12, 2014). For an example of national reporting on the trip, see Marjorie Hunter, "President Hailed on 5–State Tour of Poverty Areas," *New York Times,* April 25, 1964.

107. For thorough investigations of racial thought in the Progressive Era, see Dyer, *Theodore Roosevelt and the Idea of Race,* 6–7 (quote on p. 7); Jacobson, *Barbarian Virtues,* esp. 139–72; and Jacobson, *Whiteness of a Different Color,* 39–90.

108. To note but two famous examples, see James Agee and Walker Evans, *Let Us Now Praise Famous Men* (1939; repr., New York: Mariner Books, 2001); and John Steinbeck, *The Grapes of Wrath* (New York: Viking Press, 1939). For an analysis of these and other New Deal–era examples, see Cara A. Finnegan, *Picturing Poverty: Print Culture and FSA Photographs* (Washington DC: Smithsonian Institution, 2003). Linda Gordon, *Dorothea Lange: A Life Beyond Limits* (New York: W. W. Norton, 2009), is an award-winning biography of the famous New Deal photographer.

Chapter 5

1. James Branscome, "Annihilating the Hillbilly: The Appalachians' Struggle with America's Institutions," *Katallagete* 3 (Winter 1971): 25; also quoted in Horace Newcomb, "Appalachia on Television: Region as Symbol in American Popular Culture," *Appalachian Journal* 7, nos.1 and 2 (Autumn–Winter 1979–80), 156 (repr. in *Appalachian Images in Folk and Popular Culture,* ed. W. K. McNeil, 317. For a discussion of the so-called Golden Age of Television, see Horace Newcomb, *Television: The Critical View* (1976; repr., New York: Oxford University Press, 2000), 14–16.

2. John Shelton Reed, *Southern Folk, Plain and Fancy* (Athens: University of Georgia Press, 1986), 43–44. See also Robert Schenkkan, *The Kentucky Cycle* (New York: Dramatist Play Services, 1993). For additional analysis of Schenkkan's play, see Dwight B. Billings, introduction to Billings, Norman, and Ledford, *Back Talk from Appalachia,* 6–9. For additional analysis of Branscome's piece, see Newcomb, "Appalachia on Television," 155–64; Sandra L. Ballard, "Tracing the Sources of the Comic Hillbilly Fool in Literature," in Billings, Norman, and Ledford, *Back Talk from Appalachia,* 138–39; Drake, *History of Appalachia,* 128; Smith, "De-Gradations of Whiteness," 48–49; Harkins, *Hillbilly,* 203; and M. Thomas Inge, "Li'l Abner, Snuffy, and Friends: The Appalachian South," in *Comics and the U.S. South,* ed. Brannon Costello and Qiana J. Whitted (Jackson: University Press of Mississippi, 2012), 22.

3. Quoted in Inge, "Li'l Abner, Snuffy and Friends," 22. See also David E. Whisnant, "Ethnicity and the Recovery of Regional Identity in Appalachia," *Soundings* 56 (Spring, 1973): 124–38; and John Egerton and Frye Gaillard, "The Mountaineer Minority," *Race Relations Reporter,* March 1974, 8–13.

4. The comical and buffoonish depiction of poor whites from the southern mountains was an ongoing trope in US popular culture; the "hillbilly" is perhaps the most famous iteration of this stereotype. For the longer history of the word and the culture that it purported to represent, see Harkins, *Hillbilly;* Williamson, *Hillbillyland,* 1–17; and McWhiney, *Cracker Culture,* 23–50. For the etymology the word, see Michael Montgomery, *From Ulster to America: The Scotch-Irish Heritage of American English* (Belfast, Northern Ireland: Belfast Historical Foundation, 2006), xvii–xx.

5. Harkins, *Hillbilly,* 210.

6. "TV Guide Names Top 50 Shows," CBS News, February 11, 2009, available online at http://www.cbsnews.com/2100-207_162-507388.html (accessed June 15, 2013).

7. On Capp and Li'l Abner, see Michael Schumacher and Denis Kitchen, *Al Capp: A Life to the Contrary* (New York: Bloomsbury, 2013), esp. 25–35.

8. Harkins, *Hillbilly*, 193–212; James Roman, *From Daytime to Primetime: The History of American Television Programs* (Westport, CT: Greenwood Press, 2008), 108–11.

9. This argument has benefited from the critiques of television and culture advanced by Harkins, *Hillbilly*, esp. chap. 6, "The Hillbilly in the Living Room," 173–204; J. W. Williamson, *Hillbillyland*, esp. chap. 2, "Comedies: The Hillbilly as Fool," 21–72; Steven Classen, *Watching Jim Crow: The Struggles over Mississippi TV, 1955–1969* (Durham, NC: Duke University Press, 2004), 107–39; Susan J. Douglas, *Where the Girls Are: Growing Up Female with the Mass Media* (New York: Three Rivers, 1995), 196–98; and Lynn Spigel and Michael Curtin, *The Revolution Wasn't Televised: Sixties Television and Social Conflict* (New York: Routledge, 1997), 1–17.

10. Newcomb, "Appalachia on Television," 156.

11. For the purposes of this chapter, I define "hillbilly situation comedy" as any comedic programming with lead characters whose personal and social development reflected, at least to some degree, their identity as white southerners.

12. For a discussion of the grip that the South had among writers, as well the southern gothic genre, see Stephen A. Smith, *Myth, Media, and the Southern Mind* (Fayetteville: University of Arkansas Press, 1985), 100. For an overview of the southern literary tradition, see James C. Cobb, *Away Down South: A History of Southern Identity* (New York: Oxford University Press, 2005), 130–63.

13. H. L. Mencken, "The Sahara of the Bozart," *Prejudices: Second Series* (New York: Octagon Books, 1920), 143, 147 (quoted in Harkins, *Hillbilly*, 110).

14. Sylvia Jenkins Cook, *Erskine Caldwell and the Fiction of Poverty: The Flesh and the Spirit* (Baton Rouge: Louisiana State University Press, 1991); W. J. Cash, *Mind of the South*, with a new introduction by Bertram Wyatt Brown (1941; repr., New York: Vintage, 1991), 376–78. For another work on poor whites in the rural South, see Erskine Caldwell and Margaret Bourke-White, *You Have Seen Their Faces*, foreword by Alan Trachtenberg (1937; repr., Athens: University of Georgia Press, 1995).

15. For additional analysis of *The Mountain Boys, Li'l Abner*, and *Snuffy Smith*, see Brooks Blevins, *Arkansas/Arkansaw: How Bear Hunters, Hillbillies, and Good Ol' Boys Defined a State* (Fayetteville: University of Arkansas Press, 2009), 96–100.

16. Harkins, *Hillbilly*, 103–11.

17. On the causes of the Great Depression, see Robert S. McElvaine, *The Great Depression: America 1929–1941* (New York: Random House, 1984), 25–50. For another influential treatment, see John Kenneth Galbraith, *The Great Crash of 1929* (New York: Houghton Mifflin, 1954), 1–23.

18. Harkins, *Hillbilly*, 113–20 (quote on p. 117).

19. For more on Capp and *Li'l Abner,* see Harkins, *Hillbilly,* 124–36; Blevins, *Arkansas/Arkansaw,* 98–99; Inge, "Li'l Abner, Snuffy, and Friends," 3–28; Arthur Asa Berger, *Li'l Abner: A Study in American Satire* (New York: Twayne Publishing, 1969); and, more recently, Kitchen and Schumacher, *Al Capp.*

20. Harkins, *Hillbilly,* 125.

21. For an investigation of *Li'l Abner,* race, and masculinity, see Jan Peterson Roddy, "Country-Queer: Reading & Rewriting Sexuality in Representations of the Hillbilly," in *Negotiating Sexual Idioms: Image, Text, Performance,* ed. Marie-Luise Kohlke and Luisa Orza (New York: Rodopi, 2008), 40–41.

22. Inge, "Li'l Abner, Snuffy, and Friends," 6–16.

23. Al Capp, interview in *Penthouse,* January 1973 (quoted in Kitchen and Schumacher, *Al Capp,* 242).

24. Kitchen and Schumacher, *Al Capp,* 202–3.

25. Al Capp, *Li'l Abner,* November 13, 1965, News Syndicate Company.

26. Kitchen and Schumacher, *Al Capp,* ix, 242.

27. Ibid., 31.

28. For an exemplary treatment of how white racial identity has formed in relationship to blackness, see Toni Morrison, *Playing in the Dark: Whiteness and the Literary Imagination* (New York: Vintage, 1992).

29. For further analysis of *The Real McCoys,* see Harkins, *Hillbilly,* 178–80; Graham, *Framing the South,* 113; Sara K. Eskridge, "Rube Tube: CBS, Rural Sitcoms, and the Image of the South, 1957–1971" (PhD diss., Louisiana State University, 2013), 140–52; and David Marc and Robert J. Thompson, *Prime Time, Prime Movers: From* I Love Lucy *to* L.A. Law—*America's Greatest TV Shows and the People Who Created Them* (1992; repr., Syracuse, NY: Syracuse University Press, 1995), 108–11.

30. Irving Pincus, "Californy Here We Come," *The Real McCoys,* aired October 3, 1957 (Los Angeles, CA: Inception Media Group, 2012), DVD.

31. On Bull Connor and civil rights in Birmingham during the late 1950s and early 1960s, see Branch, *Parting the Waters,* 187–90, 420–445. See also William A. Nunnelley, *Bull Connor* (Tuscaloosa: University of Alabama Press, 1991); and Diane McWhorter, *Carry Me Home: Birmingham, Alabama, the Climactic Battle of the Civil Rights Revolution* (New York: Simon and Schuster, 2001). On civil rights in Little Rock and the desegregation of Little Rock Central High School, see John A. Kirk, *Redefining the Color Line: Black Activism in Little Rock, Arkansas, 1940–1970* (Gainesville: University of Florida Press, 2002).

32. All quotes from Pincus, "Californy Here We Come," *The Real McCoys.*

33. Ibid. While Tony Martinez's character was undeniably based on a stereotypical portrayal of a Mexican farm worker the very presence of a Latino actor was itself notable for the time. Martinez, along with Desi Arnaz in *I Love*

Lucy, was among the first Latin American actors to hold a regular role on television. For a brief biography and remembrance of Martinez's life, see Dennis McLellan, "Tony Martinez, 'Pepino' On 'Real McCoys,' Dies At 82," *South Florida Sun-Sentinel,* September 22, 2002, available online at http://www.latinamericanstudies.org/cine/tony-martinez.htm (accessed April 20, 2014).

34. Pincus, "Californy Here We Come."
35. Ibid.
36. Ibid.
37. Ibid.
38. Ibid.
39. On Mexican identity in the West after World War II and the representation of migrant workers as "illegal aliens" and perpetual foreigners outside the boundaries of normative racial citizenship, see Mae M. Nai, *Impossible Subjects: Illegal Aliens and the Making of Modern America* (Princeton, NJ: Princeton University Press, 2004), 127–66.
40. Richard Kelly, *The Andy Griffith Show* (Winston-Salem, NC: John F. Blair Publishers, 1981), 48.
41. Don Rodney Vaughan, "Why *The Andy Griffith Show* Is Important to Popular Cultural Studies," *Journal of Popular Culture* 38, no. 2 (2004): 398.
42. Ibid., 414.
43. The bluegrass group the Dillards, comprising Doug Dillard, Rodney Dillard, Dean Webb, and Mitch Jayne, played the four sons.
44. For more on *The Andy Griffith Show,* the Darling family, and the context of civil rights, see Harkins, *Hillbilly,* 182–86; Newcomb, *Appalachia on Television,* 158–64; Darrell Y. Hamamoto, *Nervous Laughter: Television Situation Comedy and Liberal Democratic Ideology* (New York: Praeger, 1991), 53–54; and Marc and Thompson, *Prime Time Prime Movers,* 111.
45. James Fritzell and Everett Greenbaum, "The Darlings Are Coming," *The Andy Griffith Show,* season 3, episode 25, directed by Bob Sweeney, aired March 18, 1963. Available on *The Andy Griffith Show: The Complete Series* (Hollywood, CA: Paramount Home Video, 2005), DVD.
46. For the episode featuring Charlene's marriage and divorce, see James Fritzell and Everett Greenbaum, "Divorce, Mountain Style," *The Andy Griffith Show,* season 4, episode 25, directed by Jeffrey Hayden, aired March 30, 1964. Briscoe arranges to get his sons married in Arnold Margolin, Jim Parker, and Lee Phillips, "The Darling Fortune," *The Andy Griffith Show,* season 7, episode 6, directed by Lee Phillips, aired October 17, 1966. For Briscoe's attempt to arrange a future marriage between his granddaughter and Griffith's son, Opie, see James Fritzell and Everett Greenbaum, "The Darling Baby," *The Andy Griffith Show,* season 5, episode 12, directed by Howard Morris, aired

December 7, 1964. These episodes are available on the DVD set *The Andy Griffith Show: The Complete Series,* as is the episode cited in the note below.

47. James Fritzell and Everett Greenbaum, "Mountain Wedding," *The Andy Griffith Show,* season 3, episode 31, directed by Bob Sweeney, aired April 29, 1963.

48. Fritzell and Greenbaum, "Divorce, Mountain Style."

49. Fritzell and Greenbaum, "Mountain Wedding."

50. Harkins, *Hillbilly,* 184. For additional extended analysis on *The Beverly Hillbillies,* see Tim Hollis, *Ain't That a Knee Slapper: Rural Comedy in the Twentieth Century* (Jackson: University Press of Mississippi, 2008), 172–200; Eskridge, "Rube Tube," 135–46; and Marc and Thompson, *Prime Time Prime Movers,* 30–45.

51. For a very different case study in North Carolina law enforcement and its relationship to the civil rights movement, see Timothy B. Tyson, *Radio Free Dixie: Robert F. Williams and the Roots of Black Power* (Chapel Hill: University of North Carolina Press, 1999). Tyson explores the tradition of armed self-defense among African Americans in North Carolina in response to the county sheriffs who typically worked with white supremacist groups such as the Ku Klux Klan and the local Democratic Party organizations, among others.

52. "Inaugural Address of Governor George Wallace, which was delivered at the Capitol in Montgomery, Alabama on January 14, 1963," available online at http://digital.archives.alabama.gov/cdm/singleitem/collection/voices/id/2952/rec/5 (accessed July 20, 2013).

53. Stephen Cox, *The Beverly Hillbillies: A Fortieth Anniversary Wing Ding* (Nashville: Cumberland House, 2003), xiii. According to Cox, "No other [television program] reached the number one spot as quickly." For a history of television in the 1950s, see Lynn Spigel, *Make Room for TV: Television and the Family Ideal in Postwar America* (Chicago: University of Chicago Press, 1992). For a more theoretical examination of television and politics, see Anna McCarthy, *The Citizen Machine: Governing Television in 1950s America* (New York: New Press, 2010).

54. Before writing and producing *The Beverly Hillbillies,* Henning had made a name for himself working on the radio program *Fibber McGee and Molly,* as well as *The George Burns and Gracie Allen Show.* See Cox, *The Beverly Hillbillies,* 93–95, 172.

55. For one example of a negative review of *The Beverly Hillbillies,* see "The Beverly . . . What?" *TV Guide,* January 18, 1964, 12–13.

56. Hamamoto, *Nervous Laughter,* 52.

57. Cox, *Beverly Hillbillies,* 152–53.

58. Paul Henning, interview by Bob Claster, Toluca Lake, CA, September 3, 1997, available online courtesty of the Archive of American Television at

http://www.emmytvlegends.org/interviews/people/paul-henning# (accessed August 6, 2013).

59. Ibid. Parts 5–7 of the interview provide Henning's explanation of the Clampetts, his influences, and his experiences in the South.

60. While Scoggins, Flatt, and Scruggs performed the song, Paul Henning penned the now-famous lyrics; see Henning, "The Ballad of Jed Clamplett," performed by Jerry Scoggins, Lester Flatt, and Earl Scruggs (New York: Columbia Records, 1962).

61. On the influence of Li'l Abner and Al Capp on Paul Henning's hillbillies, see Gerard Jones, *Honey, I'm Home! Sitcoms: Selling the American Dream* (New York: St. Martin's Press, 1992), 163–65; and Hamamoto, *Nervous Laughter,* 52–53. See also Caldwell, *Tobacco Road.*

62. For more on Henning's intention with his characters, see his interview with Claster.

63. Harkins, *Hillbilly,* 196–202; Eskridge, "Rube Tube," 158–59, 168–70.

64. See Charles W. Eagles, *The Price of Defiance: James Meredith and the Integration of Ole Miss* (Chapel Hill: University of North Carolina Press, 2009), 340–70, for a thorough account of the riots. See also William Doyle, *An American Insurrection: The Battle of Oxford, Mississippi, 1962* (New York: Doubleday, 2001); and Mary Stanton, *Freedom Walk: Mississippi or Bust* (Jackson: University Press of Mississippi, 2003).

65. Claude Sitton, "Negro Rejected at Mississippi U.; U.S. Seeks Writs," *New York Times,* September 23, 1962.

66. Harkins, *Hillbilly,* 192–95; Henning, interview by Claster.

67. Paul Henning, "The Clampetts Strike Oil," *The Beverly Hillbillies,* season 1, episode 1, directed by Ralph Levy, aired September 26, 1962. Available on DVD: *Paul Henning's* The Beverly Hillbillies: *The Ultimate Collection,* vol. 1 (Orland Park, IL: MPI Home Video, 2005).

68. Ibid.

69. All quotes from Paul Henning, "Getting Settled," *The Beverly Hillbillies* season 1, episode 1, directed by Richard Whorf, aired October 2, 1962 (available on *Paul Henning's* The Beverly Hillbillies, DVD).

70. Valentin Voloshinov, *Marxism and the Philosophy of Language* (Cambridge, MA: Harvard University Press, 1986), 101. Most believe that Mikhail Bakhtin wrote this work under his colleague Voloshinov's name.

71. For an introduction on linguistic anthropology and context analysis, see Alessandro Duranti and Charles Goodwin, eds., *Rethinking Context: Language as an Interactive Phenomenon* (New York: Cambridge University Press), 1–43.

72. Hamamoto, *Nervous Laughter,* 61–63; Harkins, *Hillbilly,* 197–99.

73. All the dialogue in this paragraph appeared in Henning, "The Clampetts Strike Oil."

74. On gender performance and identity, the classic treatment remains Judith Butler, *Gender Trouble: Feminism and the Subversion of Identity* (New York: Routledge, 1990), 8–18. See also Joan Wallach Scott, *Gender and the Politics of History,* rev. ed. (New York: Columbia University Press, 1999), 28–52.

75. For certain, the national fascination with programming purporting to depict the Old West remained. In fact, *Bonanza* provided *The Beverly Hillbillies* with some of its stiffest competition in the ratings. *Gunsmoke* also remained popular throughout these years as well.

76. At one point, these shows all aired on Tuesday evenings.

77. On Carson and *Petticoat Junction,* see Eskridge, "Rube Tube," 177–79; and Harkins, *Hillbilly,* 199.

78. As with other fictional towns, the show's writers and producers never explicitly stated where Hooterville was located. Given Henning's fondness for the Ozarks, it is reasonable to conclude that the show took place amid the hills of southern Missouri, northern Arkansas, or perhaps even more centrally located in Oklahoma or southern Illinois, abutting the upland South. For clues, see Henning's interview with Claster; parts 5–7.

79. In addition to his guide to *The Beverly Hillbillies,* Stephen Cox has also authored *The Hooterville Handbook: A Viewer's Guide to Green Acres* (New York: St. Martin's Griffin Press, 1993). They are not scholarly interpretations, but Cox's books present useful primers to both programs. See also Hollis, *Ain't That a Knee Slapper,* 186–93; and Eskridge, "Rube Tube," 151–54.

80. Gil Scott-Heron, "The Revolution Will Not Be Televised," *Small Talk at 125th and Lenox* (New York: Flying Dutchman/RCA, 1970; remastered by RCA on CD, 1990).

81. Roman, *From Daytime to Primetime,* 109.

82. Hollis, *Ain't That a Knee Slapper, 1*91; Eskridge, "Rube Tube," 151. Notably, *The Waltons* engaged historical events such as the Depression, Pearl Harbor, and other events surrounding World War II.

83. For some recent works on the fall of Jim Crow, see Borstelmann, *The Cold War and the Color Line;* Dudziak, *Race and the Image of American Democracy;* and Klarman, *From Jim Crow to Civil Rights.*

84. See for example, Kwame Ture and Charles Hamilton, *Black Power: The Politics of Liberation* (New York: Vintage, 1967); Robert Blauner, *Racial Oppression in America,* (New York: Harper and Row, 1972); Robert L. Allen, "Reassessing the Internal (Neo)Colonialism Theory," *Black Scholar* 35, no. 1 (2005): 2–11; Robert Staples, "White Racism, Black Crime, and American Justice: An Application of the Colonial Model to Explain Crime and Race," *Phylon* 36, no. 1 (1975): 14–22; and Nan Elizabeth Woodruff, *American Congo: The African American Freedom Struggle in the Delta* (Cambridge, MA: Harvard University Press, 2003).

85. "Black Power/White Backlash," CBS News, September 27, 1966. The figure comes from the findings of Louis Harris, pollster for *Newsweek.*

86. United States Bureau of the Census, *1960 Censuses of Population and Housing: Report No. 82—Los Angeles Standard Metropolitan Statistical Area* (Washington, DC: Government Printing Office, 1961), 84. The census does count 649 "negroes."

87. Aside from *The Waltons* television program, the film *Deliverance* was the most high-profile production about white southerners in the 1970s (though the latter presented the region far differently from the former). The movie depicted depraved men from Georgia stalking a party of suburban travelers. For some excellent analysis of *Deliverance,* see Hartigan, *Odd Tribes,* 135–46.

88. On race and perceptions of welfare recipients, see Gilens, *Why Americans Hate Welfare,* 6, 102–33; Quadagno, *Color of Welfare,* 10–16; and Neubeck and Cazenave, *Welfare Racism,* 11–15.

Chapter 6

1. James L. Sundquist, introduction, *On Fighting Poverty,* 3.

2. David Beard to Lyndon B. Johnson, July 27, 1964. The Papers of Lyndon Baines Johnson at the Johnson Presidential Library, University of Texas at Austin, Human Relations (hereafter LBJ/HR), box 26.

3. Ibid.

4. Ibid.

5. For influential studies of the urban crisis, see Thomas Sugrue, *The Origins of the Urban Crisis: Race and Inequality in Postwar Detroit* (Princeton, NJ: Princeton University Press, 2005), 264–68; Heather Ann Thompson, *Whose Detroit? Politics, Labor, and Race in a Modern American City* (Ithaca, NY: Cornell University Press, 2004), 32–36; and Gerald Horne, *Fire This Time: The Watts Uprising and the 1960s* (Charlottesville: University of Virginia Press, 1995), 179–80.

6. This chapter builds on recent works about black masculinity; see Riche Richardson, *Black Masculinity and the U.S. South: From Uncle Tom to Gangsta* (Athens: University of Georgia Press, 2007), 17–18, 87–88. While not dealing with the 1960s, two studies—Andrew B. Leiter, *In the Shadow of the Black Beast: African American Masculinities in the Southern and Harlem Renaissances* (Baton Rouge: Louisiana State University Press, 2010); and Geoffrey C. Ward, *Unforgivable Blackness: The Rise and Fall of Jack Johnson* (New York: Vintage Press, 2006)—are theoretically instructive.

7. For studies that have demonstrated how conservatives have mobilized the fear of black crime to advance racialized notions of law and order, see Robert O. Self, *All in the Family: The Realignment of American Democracy since the 1960s*

(New York: Hill and Wang, 2012); Jefferson Cowie, *Stayin' Alive: The 1970s and the Last Days of the Working Class* (New York: New Press, 2010), 131–32; and Michael W. Flamm, *Law and Order: Street Crime, Civil Unrest, and the Crisis of Liberalism in the 1960s* (New York: Columbia University Press, 2007), esp. 162–78.

8. On the outcomes of the War on Poverty, see Frank Stricker, *Why America Lost the War on Poverty—And How to Win It* (Chapel Hill: University of North Carolina Press, 2007), 61–82; and Herbert Gans, *The War against the Poor: The Underclass and Antipoverty Policy* (New York: Basic Books, 1995), 24–26.

9. The phrase "opening round" is central; future presidents followed Johnson's lead. This chapter takes seriously Vesla Weaver's articulation of a "frontlash." In contrast to a backlash, the very existence and perseverance of the decade's social movements posed such a threat to white rule that new strategies culminating in mass incarceration arose in tandem with civil rights rather than strictly as a response to them. See Vesla Weaver, "Frontlash: Race and the Development of Punitive Crime Policy," *Studies in American Political Development* 21 (September 2007): 230–67. For more on the topic, see Amy E. Lerman and Vesla M. Weaver, *Arresting Citizenship: The Democratic Consequences of American Crime Control* (Chicago: University of Chicago Press, 2014); *Joseph Lowndes, From the New Deal to the New Right: The Southern Origins of Modern Conservatism* (New Haven, CT: Yale University Press, 2008), 1–10; Lowndes argues that historians should "move beyond the backlash thesis" (3). One of the first comprehensive studies to propose a backlash and its potential implications on national politics was Kevin P. Phillips, *The Emerging Republican Majority* (New York: Arlington House, 1969). For additional works that explore the idea, see Michael J. Klarman, "How *Brown* Changed Race: The Backlash Thesis," *Journal of American History* 81, no. 1 (1994): 81–118. See also Lisa McGirr, *Suburban Warriors: The Origins of the New American Right* (Princeton: Princeton University Press, 2001), 13–17. McGirr argues against the idea of a backlash, esp. 133–35, 203–18. Finally, see Rick Perlstein, *Nixonland: The Rise of a President and the Fracturing of America* (New York: Scribner, 2008), 366–68, for additional commentary.

10. For supplementary critiques of liberalism in the 1960s and a few explanations of the shortcomings of the War on Poverty, see Piven and Cloward, *Regulating the Poor,* 343–397; Katz, *Undeserving Poor,* 33–35; Katz, *In the Shadow of the Poorhouse,* 283–300; Quadagno, *Color of Welfare,* 9–14; and Kelso, *Poverty and the Underclass,* 4–15.

11. Yarmolinsky, "Poverty and Urban Policy," 162–63. Also quoted in Katz, *The Undeserving Poor: America's Enduring Confrontation with Poverty,* 2nd ed. (New York: Oxford University Press, 2013), 108.

12. Dylan Matthews, "Poverty in the 50 years since 'The Other America,' in 5 charts," *Washington Post,* July 11, 2012, "Wonkblog," available online at http://www.washingtonpost.com/blogs/wonkblog/wp/2012/07/11/poverty-in-the-50-years-since-the-other-america-in-five-charts/ (accessed May 21, 2014).

13. Interview with Adam Yarmolinsky conducted by Michael Gillette, October 21, 1980. The Lyndon B. Johnson Oral History Project, the Oral History Interviews of Adam Yarmolinisky, Interview 2, White House Central Files, Papers of LBJ.

14. See Doug McAdam, *Freedom Summer* (New York: Oxford University Press, 1988), for a definitive account of the ambitious project.

15. Harris Survey regarding Public Opinion on the Federal Protection of Students Participating in Freedom Summer, July 6, 1964. LBJ/HR box 26.

16. Lee C. White to Lyndon B. Johnson, June 17, 1964. LBJ/HR, box 26.

17. J. Edgar Hoover to the *Clarion Ledger,* July 11, 1964. LBJ/HR, box 26.

18. Ibid.

19. Payne, *I've Got the Light of Freedom,* 395–97; Bruce Watson, *Freedom Summer: The Savage Season That Made Mississippi Burn and Made America a Democracy* (New York: Viking, 2010), 75–97.

20. Upton Sinclair to Lyndon B. Johnson, December 17, 1964. LBJ/HR, box 27, folder 2.

21. Lyndon B. Johnson to Upton Sinclair, January 6, 1965. LBJ/HR, box 27, folder 2.

22. Watson, *Freedom Summer,* 293–96.

23. The War on Poverty was first represented as a vehicle of white uplift, but the policy did indeed prove to be quite inclusive in its implementation. The Community Action Programs illustrate this tendency. This analysis at once problematizes early perceptions of the War on Poverty as well as its planners' goals. At the same time, however, I acknowledge the relationship that activists at the local level nevertheless forged with the OEO and recognize how men and women used the poverty programs to achieve some notable objectives. On Community Action and Maximum Feasible Participation, see Daniel P. Moynihan, *Maximum Feasible Misunderstanding: Community Action and the War on Poverty* (New York: Free Press, 1969); and Daniel Knapp and Kenneth Polk, *Scouting the War on Poverty: Social Reform in the Kennedy Administration* (Lexington, MA: Heath/Lexington Books, 1971).

24. Bennet Schiff and Stephen Goodell, "The Office of Economic Opportunity during the Administration of President Lyndon B. Johnson; Volume One, November 1963–January 1969," unpublished history archived in Community Service Administration, Records of the Office of Economic Opportunity, Records of the Office of Planning, Research, and Evaluation, History of the OEO during the Johnson Years, 109, box 106 B entry 14, National Archives II, College Park, MD.

25. Ibid.

26. Cazenave, *Impossible Democracy,* 1–18.

27. For more on the CDGM, see Schiff and Goodell, "Office of Economic Opportunity," 45–59; and Polly Greenberg, *The Devil Has Slippery Shoes: A Biased Account of the Child Development Group of Mississippi* (New York: Macmillan, 1969). Greenberg was among the more involved with the group through its final years.

28. Schiff and Goodell, "Office of Economic Opportunity," 55–58.

29. Ibid.

30. Ibid., 50–59.

31. Ibid.

32. Ibid.

33. Ibid. See also J. Todd Moye, *Let the People Decide: Black Freedom and White Resistance in Sunflower County, Mississippi, 1956–1986* (Chapel Hill: University of North Carolina Press, 2004), 162–68.

34. Margaret Weir, *Politics and Jobs: The Boundaries of Employment in the United States* (Princeton, NJ: Princeton University Press, 1993). See also Weir, "From Equal Opportunity to 'the New Social Contract': Race and the Politics of the American Underclass," in *Racism, the City, and the State,* ed. Malcolm Cross and Michael Keith (London: Routledge, 1993), 93–108; and Gilens, *Why Americans Hate Welfare,* 110–21.

35. Daniel E. Crow in *Organizing Black America: An Encyclopedia of African American Associations,* ed. Nina Mjagkij (New York: Garland Publishing, 2010), 225.

36. LeRoi Jones on the mission of the Black Arts Theatre, quoted in Schiff and Goodell, "Office of Economic Opportunity," 77.

37. Ibid.

38. Harlem did, of course, experience urban rebellions in the summer of 1964. Jones partly attributed the relative calm in the neighborhood in the years afterwards to Black Arts Theatre. On the riots of 1964, see Sharifa Rhodes-Pitts, *Harlem Is Nowhere: A Journey to the Mecca of Black America* (New York: Little, Brown, 2011), 216–17.

39. Schiff and Goodell, "Office of Economic Opportunity," 81.

40. Quoted in correspondence, Jack Williams to Edgar May, March 3, 1966, in LBJ/HR, box 26. For an overview of the Black Arts Theatre and the broader movement in New York, see James Edward Smethurst, *The Black Arts Movement: Literary Nationalism in the 1960s and 1970s* (Chapel Hill: University of North Carolina Press, 2005), 100–178.

41. Press Release, U.S. House of Representatives Committee on Education and Labor, Adam C. Powell, N.Y., Chairman, September 15, 1966, Records of the Community Service Administration (hereafter CSA/OEO), Office of Eco-

nomic Opportunity, "Public Reaction to OEO Programs," box 5, National Archives II, College Park, MD.

42. Ibid.

43. "Subsidized Riots?" *Chicago Tribune,* date unknown, CSA/OEO, box 5.

44. "Militant Misfits in the Poverty War," *Roanoke Times,* August 10, 1967, CSA/ OEO, box 5.

45. Associated Press Reports, August 3, 1967, Lyndon B. Johnson Papers, White House Central Files (WHCF), box 27, folder 2.

46. Ibid.

47. Ibid.

48. Ibid.

49. Sargent Shriver before the Committee on Education and Labor, U.S. House on July 31, 1967, CSA/OEO, box 5.

50. Ibid.

51. See Margaret Weir, "From Equal Opportunity to the New 'Social Contract'," in Cross and Keith, *Racism, the City, and the State,* 97–99. McGinley allegedly circulated the results widely within the White House and top advisers all grew familiar with the study's conclusions.

52. Mildred M. Griffen to Johnson, July 28, 1967, Baltimore, MD, Papers of LBJ, President, 1963–1969, Human Relations. General Files 2/ St 22 (Michigan) July 28, 1967, Box 35 (hereafter LBJ/HR/General).

53. Leo Stronczek to Johnson, July 25, 1967, Fort Wayne, IN, LBJ/HR/General.

54. Ardis Kuehne to Johnson, January 22, 1968, no address, LBJ/HR/General.

55. Pearl Laupert to Johnson, July 25, 1967, Ellicot City, MD, LBJ/HR/General.

56. Virginia Behnke to Johnson, July 28, Tampa, FL, LBJ/HR/General.

57. Ibid.

58. One obvious display of the movement of Midwest ethnic whites toward an explicitly white supremacist agenda was found in the stunning success that George Wallace had during the midterms and primaries of 1965–66 in Michigan, Wisconsin, and Indiana. See Michael Rogin, "Wallace and the Middle Class: Backlash in Wisconsin," *Public Opinion Quarterly* 30, no. 1 (1966): 98–108.

59. For more on Carl Stokes and Cleveland: Now!, see Leonard N. Moore, *Carl B. Stokes and the Rise of Black Political Power* (Urbana: University of Illinois Press, 2002), 61–78. For a strong study on the urban history and contestation of public space in Cleveland in the postwar decades, see Stephanie Seawell, "The Black Freedom Movement and Community Planning in Urban Parks in Cleveland, Ohio, 1945–1977" (PhD diss., University of Illinois at Urbana-Champaign, 2014), 291–308.

60. Estelle Zannes, *Checkmate in Cleveland: The Rhetoric of Confrontation during the Stokes Years* (Cleveland: Press of Case Western Reserve, 1972), 133; Moore, *Carl B. Stokes,* 79–99.

61. For a full explanation of the Glenville Uprising, see Louis H. Masotti and Jerome Corsi, *Shootout in Cleveland: Staff Report Establishing a National Commission on the Causes and Prevention of Violence* (Washington, DC: Government Printing Office, 1969), 20–23; and Seawell, "The Black Freedom Movement and Community Planning in Urban Parks in Cleveland, Ohio," 311–22. For the court records on the event and the Republic of New Libya, see *Donald Williams v. Federal Bureau of Investigation,* No. 94–5373, November 14, 1995. Testimony available online at https://law.resource.org/pub/us/case/reporter/F3/069/69.F3d.1155.94-5373.html (accessed August 26, 2013).

62. Masotti and Corsi, *Shootout in Cleveland,* 23.

63. Bob Modic, "'Cleveland Now' Cash Bought Riot Arsenal, Evans Says," *Cleveland Press,* July 24 1968; Donald Sabath, "City Admits Ahmed Got $10,000," *Cleveland Plain Dealer,* July 26, 1968; Donald Sabath, "Probe Ahmed's Fund Pipeline," *Cleveland Plain Dealer,* July 26, 1968. See also Seawell, "Black Freedom Movement," 321.

64. Masotti and Jerome Corsi, *Shootout in Cleveland,* 23. See also *Williams v. Federal Bureau of Investigation.*

65. Bob Modic, "Critics Call Funds to Evans 'Bribery'," *Cleveland Press,* July 26, 1968, available online at http://web.ulib.csuohio.edu/speccoll// (accessed August 26, 2013).

66. For a detailed account of the uprising and its aftermath, see Leonard N. Moore, *Carl B. Stokes and the Rise of Black Political Leadership* (Urbana: University of Illinois Press, 2002), esp. 61–99.

67. On the uprising, see Sugrue, *Origins of the Urban Crisis,* 259–72.

68. Hawthorne Lane to Lyndon B. Johnson, July 28, 1967, LBJ/HR/General.

69. Ibid.

70. Albert Turk to Sargent Shriver, August 18, 1967, CSA/OEO.

71. Ibid.

72. James Andrews to Lyndon Johnson, July 28, 1967, LBJ/HR/General.

73. Ibid.

74. Ibid.

75. Warren H. Folks to Lyndon Johnson, July 28, 1967, LBJ/HR/General.

76. Ibid.

77. Ibid (emphasis in the original).

78. Weir, "From Equal Opportunity to the New 'Social Contract'," in Cross and Keith, *Racism, the City, and the State,* 97–99.

79. On the role that racial fear, crime, and anxiety had on shaping white middle-class political participation, see McGirr, *Suburban Warriors,* 187–216; and David Harry Bennett, *The Party of Fear: From the Nativist Movements to the New Right in American History* (Chapel Hill: University of North Carolina Press, 1988), 390–408. This last statement should not be taken literally.

Washington, D.C., experienced riots in these same years; they occurred just blocks from the Capitol.

80. Edward Richardson to Lyndon Johnson, July 28, 1967, LBJ/HR/General.

81. Ibid.

82. Nikole Hannah-Jones, "Living Apart: How Government Betrayed a Landmark Civil Rights Law," *ProPublica,* October 29, 2012, available online at http://www.propublica.org/article/living-apart-how-the-government-betrayed-a-landmark-civil-rights-law (accessed May 22, 2014). Hannah-Jones's article is part of the series, "Investigating America's Racial Divide." Housing discrimination is a topic explored in Ta-Nahesi Coates, "The Case for Reparations," *Atlantic,* May 21, 2014, available online at http://www.theatlantic.com/features/archive/2014/05/the-case-for-reparations/361631/ (accessed November 15, 2014).

83. For more on the politics and violence of the year, see Self, *All in the Family,* 18–74; Mark Kurlansky, *1968: The Year That Rocked The World* (New York: Random House, 2005); and Jeremi Suri, *Power and Protest: Global Revolution and the Rise of Détente* (Cambridge, MA: Harvard University Press, 2005), 164–212.

84. The statistics and extent of urban rioting were compiled by Stephan Thernstrom and Abigail Thernstrom, *America in Black and White: One Nation, Indivisible,* 2nd ed. (New York: Touchstone, 1999), 159. For a mapping of Johnson's approval ratings as tracked by Gallup, see the the University of Connecticut's Roper Center Public Opinion Archives at http://www.ropercenter.uconn.edu/CFIDE/roper/presidential/webroot/presidential_rating_detail.cfm?allRate=True&presidentName=Johnson (accessed November 15, 2014).

85. For a summary of the poverty programs and their impact, see Annelise Orleck, introduction, "The War on Poverty from the Grass Roots Up," to *The War on Poverty: A New Grassroots History, 1964–1980,* ed. Annelise Orleck and Lisa Gayle Hazirjian (Athens: University of Georgia Press, 2011), 1–30 (quote on p. 4). This is a comprehensive volume detailing the myriad ways in which the War on Poverty directed resources to poor communities.

86. Rhonda Williams, *The Politics of Public Housing: Black Women's Struggles against Urban Inequality* (New York: Oxford University Press, 2004), 138–56.

87. Cazenave, *Impossible Democracy,* 170–81.

88. Goodell and Schiff, "Office of Economic Opportunity," 93.

89. Orleck, *Storming Caesar's Palace,* 112–17.

90. France and Britain both deployed the state as a comprehensive healthcare provider immediately following World War II, while the Scandinavian countries followed suit shortly thereafter.

91. Edward D. Berkowitz and Larry DeWitt, *The Other Welfare: Supplemental Security Income and U.S. Social Policy* (Ithaca, NY: Cornell University Press,

2013), 1–13. As Berkowitz and DeWitt note, the expansion of social security under SSI was a conservative alternative to Nixon's Family Assistance Plan (FAP), a bill that proposed a guaranteed income set at about $1,600 for American households.

92. Milkis and Mileur, *The Great Society*, 320–51; Patterson, *America's Struggle against Poverty*, 158–59.

93. Patterson, *America's Struggle against Poverty*, 171.

94. John Fitzgerald, *The Effects of the Marriage Market on AFDC Benefits on Exit Rates from AFDC* (Madison: University of Wisconsin Institute of Research on Poverty Discussion Paper 878–89, 1989), 1–43.

95. For another meticulous breakdown of these figures and statistics see the University of Michigan's National Poverty Center website: http://www.npc. umich.edu/poverty/ (accessed February 3, 2011).

96. For these statistics, see Patterson, *America's Struggle against Poverty*, 159–62; and Mink and O'Connor, *Poverty in the United States*, 37–39.

97. Patterson, *America's Struggle against Poverty*, 155.

98. Andrew Karch, *Early Start: Preschool Politics in the United States* (Ann Arbor: University of Michigan Press, 2013), 78–81.

99. Patterson, *America's Struggle against Poverty*, 158.

100. Ibid., 159–60.

101. Errol Morris, *The Fog of War: Eleven Lessons from the Life of Robert S. McNamara* (Culver City, CA: Sony Pictures Classics, 2003), DVD. This documentary is a starting point for understanding the misinformation campaign that the Johnson Administration launched in the mid-1960s. See also H. R. McMaster, *Dereliction of Duty: Lyndon Johnson, Robert McNamara, the Joint Chiefs of Staff, and the Lies That Led to Vietnam* (New York: HarperCollins, 1997), 107–79.

102. Patterson, *America's Struggle against Poverty*, 147.

103. Seymour Melman, *The Permanent War Economy: American Capitalism in Decline* (New York: Simon and Schuster, 1976), 120–22; Errol Anthony Henderson, "Military Spending and Poverty," *Journal of Politics* 60, no. 2 (1998): 503–20.

104. See Johnson's 1964 State of the Union address for one of the first expressions of this. The transcript, video, photographs, and some analysis of the speech are available online through the LBJ Presidential Library at http://www. lbjlibrary.org/press/civil-rights-tax-cuts-and-the-war-on-poverty (accessed November 16, 2014).

105. For more on the Revenue Act of 1964, see Howard A. Winant, *Stalemate: Political Origins of Supply-Side Policy* (Westport, CT: Praeger, 1988); and Larry J. Sabato, *The Kennedy Half-Century: The Presidency, Assassination, and Lasting Legacy of John F. Kennedy* (New York: Bloomsbury, 2013), 264–66.

106. Jeffrey Helsing, *Johnson's War/Johnson's Great Society: The Guns vs. Butter Trap* (Westport: Praeger, 2000), 11–13.

107. Ibid., 166–67.

108. Katznelson, *When Affirmative Action Was White,* 25–51.

109. Thompson, "Why Mass Incarceration Matters," 327–30.

110. Quoted in Thompson, "Why Mass Incarceration Matters," 330.

111. For the full text of the law, see http://transition.fcc.gov/Bureaus/OSEC/library/legislative_histories/1615.pdf (accessed Novemeber 16, 2014).

112. Parenti, *Lockdown America,* 8–9.

113. Thompson, "Why Mass Incarceration Matters," 731.

114. Radley Balko, *Rise of the Warrior Cop: The Militarization of America's Police Forces* (New York: Perseus Books, 2013). See also Julilly Kohler-Hausmann, "Militarizing the Police: Officer John Burge, Torture, and War in the 'Urban Jungle,'" in *Challenging the Prison Industrial Complex: Activism, Arts, and Educational Alternatives,* ed. Stephen John Hartnett (Urbana: University of Illinois Press, 2010), 43–71.

115. Davis, *City of Quartz,* esp. chap. 4, "Fortress L.A.," 221–65.

116. Richard Nixon, "Acceptance Speech Delivered Before the Republican National Convention," August 8, 1968, available online at http://www2.vcdh.virginia.edu/HIUS316/mbase/docs/nixon.html (accessed June 2, 2014).

117. Walter LaFeber, *The Deadly Bet: LBJ, Vietnam, and the 1968 Election* (New York: Rowan and Littlefield, 2005), 165–79.

118. The 1968 election and its implications on the political landscape is detailed in Maurice Isserman, *America Divided: The Civil War of the 1960s* (New York: Oxford University Press, 2011), esp. 195–248; and Charles Kaiser, *1968 in America: Music, Politics, Chaos, Counterculture, and the Shaping of a Generation* (New York: Grove Press, 1988), 169–78. Though Nixon easily prevailed in the Electoral College, his margin of victory in the popular vote was quite narrow. He tallied roughly 500,000 more votes than Humphrey among the more than 73 million ballots that were cast.

119. For more on Rumsfeld's tenure in the Nixon administration, see Bonnie Leftkowitz, *Community Health Centers and the People Who Made it Happen* (New Brunswick, NJ: Rutgers University Press, 2007), 11–14. For some analysis of Nixon's first and second terms and how they differed in both tone and policy, see James Reichly, *Conservatives in an Age of Change: The Nixon and Ford Administrations* (Washington, DC: Brookings Institution Press, 1982), 232–49.

120. Thompson, "Why Mass Incarceration Matters," 703–58.

121. Alexander, *New Jim Crow,* 45–55; Gilmore, *Golden Gulag,* 37–42.

122. Gilmore, *Golden Gulag,* 3–11. For more on mass incarceration, see Marc Mauer, *Race To Incarcerate,* The Sentencing Project Series (New York: New

Press, 1999); and Glenn Loury, *Race, Incarceration, and American Values* (Cambridge, MA: MIT Press, 2008).

123. Gilmore, *Golden Gulag,* 3.

124. These figures are from the United States Bureau of Justice study authored by Laura M. Maruschak and Erika Parks, "Probation and Parole in the United States, 2011," available online at http://www.bjs.gov/index.cfm?ty=pbdetail &iid=4538 (accessed November 20, 2013).

125. These are based on figures from studies conducted by the National Employment Law Project, the American Civil Liberties Union, and the Bureau of Justice. For a summary of the findings, see Kai Wright, "Boxed In: How a Criminal Record Keeps You Unemployed for Life," *Nation* (November 25, 2013), available online at http://www.thenation.com/article/177017/boxed-how-criminal-record-keeps-you-unemployed-life?page=0,0 (accessed November 24, 2013).

126. Gilmore, *Golden Gulag,* 3. See also N. C. Aizenman, "New High In U.S. Prison Numbers: Growth Attributed to More Stringent Sentencing Laws," *Washington Post,* February 28, 2008; Alexander, *New Jim Crow,* 49–95.

127. Wright, "Boxed In."

128. See the Sentencing Project for a more detailed analysis of these trends at http://www.sentencingproject.org/template/index.cfm (accessed September 10, 2013). See also Nell Irvin Painter, *Creating Black Americans: African-American History and Its Meanings, 1619 to the Present* (New York: Oxford University Press, 2005), 351–53.

129. Prison and male inmate figures and statistics are available online through the Bureau of Justice Statistics at http://www.bjs.gov/content/pub/pdf/p12tar9112.pdf (accessed October 5, 2013).

Conclusion

1. Ronald Reagan, "Campaign Speech," 1976, quoted from "The Truth Behind the Lies of the 'Welfare Queen'," National Public Radio, aired on December 20, 2013, available online at http://www.npr.org/templates/transcript/transcript.php?storyId=255819681 on (accessed May 26, 2014). Beyond the welfare fraud, Taylor was also alleged to have committed more serious crimes, including child trafficking. Curiously, these allegations were typically not included in Reagan's narrative.

2. "'Welfare Queen' Becomes Issue in Reagan Campaign," *New York Times,* January 15, 1976. See also Julilly Kohler-Hausmann, "'The Crime of Survival': Fraud Prosecutions, Community Surveillance, and the Original 'Welfare Queen,'" *Journal of Social History* 41, no. 2 (2007): 329–54. For surveys on the rise of modern conservatism, see Michael Schaller and George Rising, *The*

Republican Ascendency: American Politics, 1968–2001 (Wheeling, IL: Harlan Davidson, 2002); and Michael Shaller, *Right Turn: American Life in the Reagan-Bush Era, 1980–1992* (New York: Oxford University Press, 2006).

3. Patterson, *America's Struggles against Poverty*, 204–16; Sean Wilentz, *The Age of Reagan: A History, 1974–2008* (New York: Harper Perennial, 2008), 41–47; Marisa Chapell, *The War on Welfare: Family, Poverty, and Politics in Modern America* (Philadelphia: University of Pennsylvania Press, 2010), 199–240.

4. Ronald Reagan, "A Time for Choosing." The speech was given in support of Barry Goldwater's presidency on October 27, 1964, in Los Angeles. Available online at http://www.reagan.utexas.edu/archives/reference/timechoosing.html (accessed June 1, 2014).

5. Wilentz, *Age of Reagan*, 41–47; Dan T. Carter, *From George Wallace to Newt Gingrich: Race in the Conservative Counterrevolution, 1963–1994* (Baton Rouge: Louisiana State University Press, 1996), 30–31; Ian Haney Lopez, *Dog Whistle Politics: How Coded Racial Appeals Have Reinvented Racism and Wrecked the Middle Class* (New York: Oxford University Press, 2014), 4–5, 55–76 (quote on p. 4).

6. Gilens, *Why Americans Hate Welfare*, 102–32. See also Lopez, *Dog Whistle Politics*, 55–76; and Neubeck and Cazenave, *Welfare Racism*, 117–31.

7. For a strong account of how the Reagan administration leveraged antigovernment rhetoric to court voters, see David Stockman, *The Triumph of Politics: The Inside Story of the Reagan Revolution* (New York: Avon, 1987), 19–47 (quote on p. 37). Stockman was Reagan's budget director and a key figure in his cabinet.

8. Quadagno, *The Color of Welfare*, 191–201; Gilens, *Why Americans Hate Welfare*, esp. 154–73; James R. Kluegel and Eliot Smith, *Beliefs about Inequality: America's Views about What Is and What Ought to Be* (New York: Aldine Transaction, 1986), 158–59; Theda Skocpol, *Social Policy in the United States: Future Possibilities in Historical Perspective* (Princeton, NJ: Princeton University Press, 1995), 297–312.

9. Michael Tonry, *Punishing Race: A Continuing American Dilemma* (New York: Oxford University Press, 2012), esp. chaps. 1–2, 1–51.

10. Eric J. Williams, *The Big House in the Small Town: Prisons, Communities and Economics in Rural America* (Santa Barbara, CA: Greenwood, 2011), 2–5.

11. Shahid M. Shahidullah, *Crime Policy in America: Laws, Institutions, and Programs* (Lanham, MD: University Press of America, 2008), 15–18. The law was best known for its ten-year moratorium on the sale of most assault weapons, including semiautomatic firearms.

12. For a brief summary of the impact, see Shahidullah, *Crime Policy in America*, 31–33.

13. Jon Ozmint, "Adopting 'No Parole' Requires Paying for its Consequences," *Charleston (SC) Post and Courier,* January 30, 2008. Available online at http://www.postandcourier.com/article/20080130/ARCHIVES/301309949 (accessed September 17, 2013). As the prison population continues to increase, the state has estimated that five more facilities may be required to avoid overcrowding.

14. This information is publically available online through the Commonwealth of Virginia Department of Corrections website, http://vadoc.virginia.gov/facilities/western/pocahontas/ (accessed November 6, 2013).

15. Craig Timburg, "At Virginia's Toughest Prison, Tight Controls," *Washington Post,* April 18, 1999, available online at http://www.washingtonpost.com/wp-srv/local/daily/april99/supermax18.htm (accessed September 17, 2013). See also Virginia's Department of Corrections website for maps and prison statistics at http://www.vadoc.virginia.gov (accessed September 20, 2013). PSCF employs about three hundred; Wallens Ridge and Red Onion employ over eight hundred.

16. Several other novels and books have sold more copies and more quickly than *The Trail of the Lonesome Pine.* Harriet Beecher Stowe's *Uncle Tom's Cabin* and Stephen Crane's *The Red Badge of Courage* are two examples. See Cindy Weinstein, ed., *The Cambridge Companion to Harriet Beecher Stowe* (Cambridge, UK: Cambridge University Press, 2004), xii, 5.

17. Indeed, the "Heart of Appalachia" is one of Virginia's officially designated regions, along with the Blue Ridge Highlands, Shenandoah Valley, and six others. See http://www.virginia.org/regions/HeartOfAppalachia/ (accessed November 12, 2013).

18. For additional information on other attractions and events at the house, see http://www.junetolliverhouse.com/ (accessed November 5, 2013).

19. See the Big Stone Gap's official state website for various tourist attractions in the area, including information on the town's production of *The Trail of the Lonesome Pine* at http://www.bigstonegap.org (accessed November 16, 2014).

20. Fox, *Trail of the Lonesome Pine,* 231.

21. For more on Fox, see Darlene Wilson, "A Judicious Combination of Incident and Psychology: John Fox Jr. and the Southern Mountaineer Motif," in Billings, Norman, and Ledford, *Back Talk from Appalachia,* 98–118.

BIBLIOGRAPHY

Primary Sources

Archival Sources

Indiana State Archives, Indianapolis.
    Board of State Charities. Records.
    Hurty, Dr. John N. Papers.
Indiana State Library, Indianapolis.
    McCulloch, Oscar. Papers.
United States National Archives and Records Administration. National Archives II, College Park, MD.
    Office of Economic Opportunity/Community Service Administration. Records.
    ———. Lyndon Baines Johnson Presidential Library and Archives, University of Texas at Austin.
    White House Central Files and White House Central Files (Confidential).
University at Albany, SUNY. M. E. Grenander Department of Special Collections and Archives.
    Estabrook, Arthur H. Papers, 1908–1962.
University of North Carolina at Chapel Hill. Southern Historical Collection, Wilson Library.
    Blakemore, John A. Papers. 1928–1980.
    Buchanan, Annabel Morris. Papers, 1902–1972.
University of Virginia, Charlottesville. Albert and Shirley Small Special Collections Library.
    Powell, John. Papers, 1882–1963.

Census Records

United States Bureau of the Census. *Thirteenth Census of the United States, Taken in the Year 1910*. Volume 1, *Population*. Washington, DC: Government Printing Office, 1912.
    ———. *1960 Censuses of Population and Housing: Report No. 82—Los Angeles Standard Metropolitan Statistical Area*. Washington, DC: Government Printing Office, 1961.
United States Census Office. *Report on Population of the United States at the Eleventh Census: 1890*. Part 1. Washington, DC: Government Printing Office, 1895.
    ———. *Statistics of the Population of the United States at the Tenth Census (June 1, 1880)*. Washington, DC: Government Printing Office, 1883.

——. *Twelfth Census of the United States, Taken in the Year 1900.* Volume 1, part 1, *Population.* Washington, DC: Government Printing Office, 1901.

DVDs
Alexander, David, Hy Averbeck, Charles Barton, and Sheldon Leonard. *The Real McCoys: Season 1.* Los Angeles, CA: Inception Media Group, 2012.

Griffith, Andy, Dean Hargrove, and Donna Colabella, et al. *The Andy Griffith Show: The Complete Series.* Hollywood, CA: Paramount Home Video, 2007.

Morris, Errol. *The Fog of War: Eleven Lessons from the Life of Robert S. McNamara.* Culver City, CA: Sony Pictures Classics, 2003.

Paul Henning's The Beverly Hillbillies: *The Ultimate Collection.* Volume 1. Orland Park, IL: MPI Home Video, 2005.

Online Archives
Indiana Eugenics: History and Legacy. 1907–2007. http://www.iupui.edu/~eugenics/.

Johnson, Lyndon Baines. Oral Histories. http://www.lbjlib.utexas.edu/johnson/archives.hom/biopage.asp.

Kennedy, John F. Presidential Library and Archives Oral Histories. http://www.jfklibrary.org/Search.aspx?nav=N:4294963148.

Other Primary Sources
Agee, James, and Walker Evans. *Let Us Now Praise Famous Men.* 1939. Reprint, Boston: Mariner Books, 2001.

Aizenman, N. C. "New High In U.S. Prison Numbers: Growth Attributed to More Stringent Sentencing Laws." *Washington Post,* February 28, 2008.

The American Missionary Association. The Independent; Religious Intelligence, Volume 26. New York: American Missionary Association Publishing, 1886.

Barton, W. E. "Work Among the American Highlanders." *American Missionary,* March 1898.

Beard, George Miller. *American Nervousness: Its Causes and Consequences.* New York: G. P. Putnam's Sons, 1881.

Beveridge, Albert. *The Meaning of the Times and Other Speeches.* Indianapolis, IN: Bobbs Merrill, 1908.

Bigart, Homer. "Depression Rivaling '30s Grips Kentucky-Virginia Coal Area." *New York Times,* January 11, 1959.

——. "Kentucky Miners: A Grim Winter." *New York Times.* October 20, 1963.

——. "West Virginia Grim." *New York Times,* March 16, 1959.

Bishop, Bill and Roberto Gallardo, "Daily Yonder: The Geography of Disability." *Kentucky Forward,* December 9, 2011.

Branscome, James. "Annihilating the Hillbilly: The Appalachians' Struggle with America's Institutions." *Katallagete* 3 (Winter 1971): 25–32.

Caldwell, Erskine. *Tobacco Road*. 1932. Reprint, Athens: University of Georgia Press, 1995.

Caldwell, Erskine, and Margaret Bourke-White. *You Have Seen Their Faces*. Foreword by Alan Trachtenberg. 1935. Reprint, Athens: University of Georgia Press, 1995.

Campbell, John C. *The Southern Highlander and His Homeland*. 1921. Reprint, Lexington: University Press of Kentucky, 2004.

Chamberlain, J. E. "A Dream of Anglo-Saxondom." *The Galaxy: A Magazine of Entertaining Reading* 24 (1877).

Caudill, Harry. *Night Comes to the Cumberlands: A Biography of a Depressed Area*. Boston, MA: Little, Brown, 1963.

——. "The Rape of the Appalachians." *Atlantic Monthly,* April 1962.

Davenport, Charles, and Arthur H. Estabrook. *The Nam Family: A Study in Cacogenics*. Cold Spring Harbor, NY: Eugenics Record Office Press, 1912.

Davis, Rebecca Harding. *Bits of Gossip*. Boston: Houghton Mifflin, 1904.

——. "Qualla." *Lippincott's Magazine of Popular Literature and Science,* November 1875.

Dubois, W. E. B. *The Souls of Black Folk: Essays and Sketches*. Chicago: A. C. McClurg, 1903.

Dugdale, Richard Louis. *"The Jukes": A Study in Crime, Pauperism, Disease and Heredity also; Further Studies of Criminals*. New York: G. P. Putnam's Sons, 1877.

Duscha, Julius. "A Long Trail of Misery Winds the Proud Hills." *Washington Post,* August 7, 1960.

Egerton, John, and Frye Gaillard. "The Mountaineer Minority." *Race Relations Reporter,* March 1974.

Emerson, Ralph Waldo. *English Traits*. Boston: Philips, Samson, 1856.

Ernst, Harry W., and Charles H. Drake. "Lost Appalachians: Poor, Proud and Primitive." *Nation,* May 30, 1959.

Estabrook, Arthur. *The Jukes in 1915*. Washington, DC: Carnegie Institution of Washington, 1916.

Estabrook, Arthur, and Ivan E. McDougle. *Mongrel Virginians: The Win Tribe*. Baltimore: Williams and Wilkins, 1926.

The First Report of the Board of State Charities Made to the Legislature of Indiana for One Year and Eight Months, Commencing March 1st, 1889, and Ending October 31st, 1890. Indianapolis: William B. Buford, Contractor for State Publishing and Binding, 1890.

Ford, Thomas, ed. *The Southern Appalachian Region: A Survey*. Lexington: University Press of Kentucky, 1962.

Fox, John, Jr. *A Mountain Europa*. New York: Harper and Brothers, 1899.

——. *The Trail of the Lonesome Pine*. New York: Charles Scribner's Sons, 1908.

Frost, William Goddell. "Our Contemporary Ancestors in the Southern Mountains." *Atlantic Monthly,* March, 1899.

Galbraith, John Kenneth. *The Affluent Society.* New York: Houghton Mifflin, 1959.

Gladden, Washington. "Christian Education in the South," *American Missionary,* December 1883.

Grant, Madison. *The Passing of the Great Race, or the Racial Basis of European History.* New York: Charles Scribner's Sons, 1916.

Harrington, Michael. "Our Fifty Million Poor: Forgotten Men of the Affluent Society." *Commentary* 28, no. 1 (1959): 19–27.

————. *The Other America, Poverty in the United States.* New York: Scribner, 1962.

Harney, Will Wallace. "A Strange Land and Peculiar People." *Lippincott's Magazine,* October 1873.

Hartshorne, Henry. *Friends' Review: A Religious, Literary, and Miscellaneous Journal,* Volume 38. Philadelphia, PA: American Printing House, 1885.

Holloway, W. R. *Indianapolis, A Historical and Statistical Sketch of the Railroad City.* Indianapolis, IN: Indianapolis Journal Print, 1870.

Indiana Bulletin of Charities and Corrections. Collected editions, 1908–1912.

————. Twelfth Annual Exhibit of State Charitable and Correctional Institutions, 1900.

Indicators of Welfare Dependence: Annual Report to Congress, 2008. Washington, DC: U.S. Department of Health and Human Services. Available online at http://aspe.hhs.gov/hsp/indicators08/.

Johnston, Richard J. H. "Kennedy Hailed in Mining Region: Crowds are Large and Enthusiastic." *New York Times.* April 27, 1960.

————. "Kennedy Pledges West Virginia Aid; Says Republicans Neglect Economically Depressed Portions of the State." *New York Times.* April 26, 1960. Jordan, David Starr. *The Blood of the Nation: A Study of the Decay of Races through the Survival of the Unfit.* Boston: American Unitarian Association, 1906.

Kephart, Horace. *Our Southern Highlanders; a Narrative of Adventure in the Southern Appalachians and a Study of the Life among the Mountaineers.* 1922. Reprint, Knoxville: University of Tennessee Press, 1976.

Knapp, Daniel, and Kenneth Polk. *Scouting the War on Poverty: Social Reform in the Kennedy Administration.* Lexington, MA: Heath/Lexington Books, 1971.

Laughlin, Harry. *Eugenical Sterilization in the United States.* Chicago, IL: Psychopathic Laboratory of the Municipal Court of Chicago, 1922.

Lewis, Oscar. *Five Families: Mexican Case Studies in the Culture of Poverty.* 1958. Reprint, New York: Basic Books, 1979.

Macdonald, Dwight. "Our Invisible Poor." *New Yorker,* January 19, 1963.

Masotti, Louis, and Jerome Corsi. *Shootout in Cleveland: Staff Report Establishing a National Commission on the Causes and Prevention of Violence.* Washington, DC: Government Printing Office, 1969.

Maxwell, James. "Down from the Hills and into the Slums." *The Reporter* (New York City). December 13, 1956.

McCulloch, Alice, ed. *The Open Door: Sermons and Prayers by Oscar C. McCulloch, Minister of Plymouth Congregational Church, Indianapolis, Indiana.* Indianapolis: Press of W. B. Buford, 1892.

McCulloch, Oscar. *The Tribe of Ishmael: A Study in Social Degradation.* Indianapolis: Charity Organization Society, 1888.

Modic, Bob. "Critics Call Funds to Evans 'Bribery.'" *Cleveland Press,* July 26, 1968.

Moynihan, Daniel P. *Maximum Feasible Misunderstanding: Community Action and the War on Poverty.* New York: Free Press, 1969.

———, ed. *On Understanding Poverty: Perspectives from the Social Sciences.* Volume 1 of *Perspectives on Poverty.* New York: Basic Books, 1969.

Nyden, Paul. "McDowell County Fighting Long-term Decline." *Charleston (WV) Gazette,* February 9, 2013.

Ozmint, Jon. "Adopting 'No Parole' Requires Paying for its Consequences." *Charleston (SC) Post and Courier,* January 30, 2008.

Phillips, George W. "Report on Mountain Work." *American Missionary,* December 1884.

Ralph, Julian. "Where Time Has Slumbered." *Harper's Weekly,* September, 1894.

Rice, Thurman. *Racial Hygiene: A Practical Discussion of Eugenics and Race Culture.* New York: Macmillan, 1929.

Roosevelt, Theodore. *Outdoor Pastimes of an American Hunter.* New York: Charles Scribner's Sons, 1906.

———. *The Strenuous Life and Other Essays and Speeches.* New York: Century Company, 1900.

———. *The Winning of the West: An Account of the Exploration and Settlement of Our Country from the Alleghanies to the Pacific.* New Library Edition. Six Volumes in Three. 1889–1896. Reprint, New York: G. P. Putnam's Sons, [1920].

Ross, Edward A. *Social Control: A Survey of the Foundations of Order.* 1901. Reprint, Press of Case Western Reserve University, 1969.

Schiff, Bennet, and Stephen Goodell. "The Office of Economic Opportunity during the Administration of President Lyndon B. Johnson; Volume One, November 1963–January 1969." Unpublished history archived in the Community Service Administration, Records of the Office of Economic Opportunity and the Office of Planning, Research, and Evaluation. History of the OEO during Johnson Years. Box 106B, Entry 14, National Archives II, College Park, MD.

Scott-Heron, Gil. "The Revolution Will Not Be Televised." *Small Talk at 125th and Lenox.* New York: Flying Dutchman/RCA, 1970. LP recording, remastered by RCA on CD, 1990.

Semple, Ellen Churchill. "The Anglo Saxons of the Kentucky Mountains: A Study in Anthropogeography." *Geographical Journal* 17 (June 1901): 588–613.

Shaler, Nathanial Southgate. *American Commonwealths: Kentucky, a Pioneer Commonwealth.* Boston: Houghton Mifflin, 1884.

Sharp, Harry. *Indiana Bulletin for the Board of State Corrections.* Thirty-third quarter, June 1898.

———. *Vasectomy: A Means of Preventing Defective Procreation.* Jeffersonville: Indiana Reformatory Print, 1909.

Sheldon, Charles. *A History of the Boone and Crockett Club.* Washington, DC: Boone and Crockett Club, 1931.

Shepherd, Jean. *In God We Trust: All Others Pay Cash.* New York: Doubleday, 1966.

Sitton, Claude. "Negro Rejected at Mississippi U.; U.S. Seeks Writs." *New York Times.* September 23, 1962.

Steinbeck, John. *The Grapes of Wrath.* New York: Viking Press, 1939.

Stockman, David. *The Triumph of Politics: The Inside Story of the Reagan Revolution.* New York: Avon, 1987.

Sundquist, James L., ed. *On Fighting Poverty: Perspectives from Experience.* Volume 2 of *Perspectives on Poverty.* New York: Basic Books, 1969.

Timburg, Craig. "At Virginia's Toughest Prison, Tight Controls." *Washington Post,* April 18, 1999.

Tunley, Roul. "The Strange Case of West Virginia." *Saturday Evening Post,* February 6, 1960.

Turner, Frederick Jackson. "The Significance of the Frontier in American History." Address before the American Historical Association. Chicago, 1893.

Votaw, Albert. "The Hillbillies Invade Chicago." *Harper's Magazine,* February 1958.

Whitney, Caspar R., and John Fox Jr., John R. Spears, et al., War Correspondents, *Harper's Weekly,* May 28, 1898.

Secondary Sources

Ackerman, Kenneth D. *The Gold Ring: Jim Fisk, Jay Gould, and Black Friday, 1869.* New York: Da Capo Press, 2005.

Adam, Karen Elizabeth. "'The Nonmusical Message Will Endure With It:' The Changing Reputation and Legacy of John Powell (1882–1963)." Masters thesis, Virginia Commonwealth University, 2012.

Alexander, Michele. *The New Jim Crow: Mass Incarceration in the Age of Colorblindness.* New York: New Press, 2010.

Allen, Robert L. "Reassessing the Internal (Neo)Colonialism Theory." *Black Scholar* 35, no 1 (2005): 2–11.

Allen, Theodore. *The Invention of the White Race: Racial Oppression and Social Control.* New York: Verso Press, 1994.

Altena, Bert, and Marcel van der Linden, eds. *De-Industrialization: Social, Cultural, and Political Aspects.* New York: Oxford University Press, 2002.

Alterman, Eric. *What Liberal Media? The Truth about Bias and the News.* New York: Basic Books, 2004.

Anderson, Benedict. *Imagined Communities: Reflections on the Origins and Spread of Nationalism.* London: Verso Press, 1991.

Anderson, Kay, Mona Domosh, Steve Pile, and Nigel Thrift, eds. *The Handbook of Cultural Geography.* New York: Sage Publications, 2002.

Bakhtin, Mikhail. *The Dialogic Imagination: Four Essays.* Austin: University of Texas Press, 1982.

Balko, Radley. *Rise of the Warrior Cop: The Militarization of America's Police Forces.* New York: Perseus Books, 2013.

Batteau, Allen. *The Invention of Appalachia.* Tucson: University of Arizona Press, 1990.

Bauman, Robert. *Race and the War on Poverty: From Watts to East L.A.* Norman: University of Oklahoma Press, 2008.

Bartels, Larry M. *The Unequal Democracy: The Political Economy of the New Gilded Age.* Princeton, NJ: Princeton University Press, 2010.

Bederman, Gail. *Manliness and Civilization: The Cultural History of Gender and Race in the United States, 1880–1917.* Chicago: University of Chicago Press, 1996.

Bennett, David Henry. *The Party of Fear: From the Nativist Movements to the New Right in American History.* Chapel Hill: University of North Carolina Press, 1988.

Berkowitz, Edward D., and Larry DeWitt. *The Other Welfare: Supplemental Security Income and U.S. Social Policy.* Ithaca, NY: Cornell University Press, 2013.

Berger, Arthur Asa. *Li'l Abner: A Study in American Satire.* New York: Twayne Publishing, 1969.

Berry, Chad. *Southern Migrants, Northern Exiles.* Urbana: University of Illinois Press, 2000.

Bhaba, Homi. *The Location of Culture.* New York: Routledge, 1994.

Billings, Dwight B., Gurney Norman, and Katherine Ledford, eds. *Back Talk from Appalachia: Confronting Stereotypes.* Lexington: University Press of Kentucky, 2000.

Black, Edwin. *War on the Weak: Eugenics and America's Campaign to Create a Master Class.* New York: Four Walls Publishing, 2004.

Blauner, Robert. *Racial Oppression in America.* New York: Harper and Row, 1972.

Blevins, Brooks. *Arkansas/Arkansaw: How Bear Hunters, Hillbillies, and Good Ol' Boys Defined a State.* Fayetteville: University of Arkansas Press, 2009.

Bloom, Harold. *The American Religion*. 2nd edition. New York: Chu Hartley Publishers, 2006.

Blumenthal, Sydney. *The Rise of Conservative Ideology*. New York: Times Books, 1986.

Blumer, Michael. *Francis Galton, Pioneer of Hereditary Biometry*. Baltimore: Johns Hopkins University Press, 2003.

Bodenhamer, David J., and Robert Graham Barrows, eds. *The Encyclopedia of Indianapolis*. Bloomington: Indiana University Press, 1994.

Borman, Kathryn M., and Phillip J. Obermiller, eds. *From Mountain to Metropolis: Appalachian Migrants in American Cities*. New York: Bergen and Garvey, 1994.

Borstelmann, Thomas. *The Cold War and the Color Line: American Race Relations in the Global Arena*. Cambridge, MA: Harvard University Press, 2001.

Branch, Taylor. *At Canaan's Edge: America in the King Years, 1965–1968*. New York: Simon and Schuster, 2006.

———. *Parting the Waters: America in the King Years, 1954–1963*. New York: Simon and Schuster, 1988.

———. *Pillar of Fire: America in the King Years, 1963–1965*. New York: Simon and Schuster, 1998.

Brennan, Mary C. *Turning Right in the Sixties: The Conservative Capture of the GOP*. Chapel Hill: University of North Carolina Press, 1995.

Brewer, Susan. *Why America Fights: Patriotism and War Propaganda from the Philippines to Iraq*. New York: Oxford University Press, 2011.

Briggs, Laura. *Reproducing Empire: Race, Sex, Science, and United States Imperialism in Puerto Rico*. Berkeley: University of California Press, 2002.

Brinkley, Douglas. *The Wilderness Warrior: Theodore Roosevelt and the Crusade for America*. New York: HarperCollins, 2009.

Bruinius, Harry. *Better for All the World: The Secret History of Forced Sterilization and America's Quest for Racial Purity*. New York: Vintage, 2007.

Bulmer, Michael. *Francis Galton, Pioneer of Hereditary Biometry*. Baltimore: Johns Hopkins University Press, 2003.

Butler, Judith. *Gender Trouble: Feminism and the Subversion of Identity*. New York: Routledge, 1990.

Carey, Jane, and Claire McLisky. *Creating White Australia*. Sydney, Australia: Sydney University Press, 2009.

Carlson, Elof Axel. *The Unfit: A History of a Bad Idea*. Cold Spring Harbor, NY: Cold Spring Harbor Laboratory Press, 2001.

Carter, Dan T. *From George Wallace to Newt Gingrich: Race in the Conservative Counterrevolution, 1963–1994*. Baton Rouge: Louisiana State University Press, 1996.

Caruso, John Anthony. *The Appalachian Frontier: America's First Surge Westward*. 1959. Reprint, Knoxville: University of Tennessee Press, 2003.

Cash, W. J. *The Mind of the South.* Introduction by Bertram Wyatt-Brown. 1941. Reprint, New York: Vintage, 1991.

Cazenave, Noel. *Impossible Democracy: The Unlikely Success of the War on Poverty Community Action Programs.* Albany: State University of New York Press, 2008.

Chapell, Marisa. *The War on Welfare: Family, Poverty, and Politics in Modern America.* Philadelphia: University of Pennsylvania Press, 2010.

Chernow, Ron. *The House of Morgan: An American Banking Dynasty and the Rise of Modern Finance.* New York: Grove Press, 2001.

Clarkson, Roy B. *Tumult on the Mountain: Lumbering in West Virginia, 1770–1920.* Parsons, WV: McClain Printing, 1964.

Classen, Steven. *Watching Jim Crow: The Struggles over Mississippi TV, 1955–1969.* Durham, NC: Duke University Press, 2004.

Coates, Ta-Nahesi. "The Case for Reparations." *Atlantic,* May 21, 2014.

Cobb, James C. *Away Down South: A History of Southern Identity.* New York: Oxford University Press, 2005.

Cohen, Ronald. *A History of Folk Festivals in the United States: Feasts of Musical Celebration.* Lanham, MD: Scarecrow/Rowman and Littlefield, 2008.

Conway, Cecelia. *African Banjo Echoes in Appalachia.* Knoxville: University of Tennessee Press, 1995.

Corbin, David Alan. *Life, Work, and Rebellion in the Coal Fields: The Southern West Virginia Miners, 1880–1922.* Urbana: University of Illinois Press, 1981.

Costello, Brannon, and Qiana J. Whitted, eds. *Comics and the U.S. South.* Jackson: University Press of Mississippi, 2012.

Cowie, Jefferson. *Capital Moves: RCA's 70–Year Quest for Cheap Labor.* New York: New Press, 2001

———. *Stayin' Alive: The 1970s and the Last Days of the Working Class.* New York: New Press, 2010.

Cox, Stephen. *The Beverly Hillbillies: A Fortieth Anniversary Wing Ding.* Nashville, TN: Cumberland House, 2003.

———. *The Hooterville Handbook, A Viewer's Guide to* Green Acres. New York: St. Martin's Griffin Press, 1993.

Cross, Malcolm, and Michael Keith, eds. *Racism, the City, and the State.* London: Routledge, 1993.

Cull, Nicholas. *Selling War: The British Propaganda Campaign against American Neutrality in World War II.* New York: Oxford University Press, 1995.

Dalton, Kathleen. *Theodore Roosevelt: A Strenuous Life.* New York: Vintage Press, 2004.

Davies, Gareth. *From Opportunity to Entitlement: The Transformation and Decline of Great Society Liberalism.* Lawrence: University of Kansas Press, 1996.

Davis, Angela. "Masked Racism: Reflections on the Prison Industrial Complex." *Colorlines: News for Action,* September 10, 1998.

Davis, Janet M. *The Circus Age: Culture and Society under the American Big Top.* Chapel Hill: University of North Carolina Press, 2002.

Davis, Mike. *City of Quartz: Excavating the Future in Los Angeles.* New York: Verso, 1992.

Deutsch, Nathaniel. *Inventing America's "Worst" Family: Eugenics, Islam, and the Fall and Rise of the Tribe of Ishmael.* Berkeley: University of California Press, 2009.

Di Silvestro, Roger L. *Theodore Roosevelt in the Badlands: A Young Politician's Quest for Recovery in the American West.* New York: Bloomsbury, 2011.

Docker, John, and Gerhard Fischer, eds. *Race, Colour, and Identity in Australia and New Zealand.* Sydney, Australia: University of New South Whales Press, 2000.

Domhoff, G. William. *Who Rules America? Challenges to Corporate and Class Dominance.* 6th edition. New York: McGraw Humanities, 2009.

Domanick, Joe. *To Protect and Serve: The LAPD's Century of War in the City of Dreams.* New York: Pocket Books, 2003.

Donaldson, Gary A. *The First Modern Campaign: Kennedy, Nixon, and the Election of 1960.* Lanham, MD: Rowman and Littlefield, 2007.

Douglas, Susan J. *Where the Girls Are: Growing Up Female with the Mass Media.* New York: Three Rivers, 1995.

Doyle, William. *An American Insurrection: The Battle of Oxford, Mississippi, 1962.* New York: Doubleday, 2001.

Drake, Richard. *A History of Appalachia.* Lexington: University Press of Kentucky, 2001.

Drinnon, Richard. *Facing West: The Metaphysics of Indian Hating and Empire Building.* Norman: University of Oklahoma Press, 1990.

Dorr, Gregory Michael. "Defective or Disabled? Race, Medicine, and Eugenics in Progressive Era Alabama and Virginia." *Journal of the Gilded Age and Progressive Era* 5, no. 4 (2006): 359–92.

———. *Segregation's Science: Eugenics and Society in Virginia.* Charlottesville: University of Virginia Press, 2008.

Dudziak, Mary L. *Cold War Civil Rights: Race and the Image of American Democracy.* Princeton, NJ: Princeton University Press, 2000.

Duffy-Burnett, Christina, and Burke Marshall, eds. *Foreign in a Domestic Sense: Puerto Rico, American Expansion, and the Constitution.* Durham, NC: Duke University Press, 2001.

Dunaway, Wilma. *The First American Frontier: The Transition to Capitalism in Southern Appalachia.* Chapel Hill: University of North Carolina Press, 1996.

Duranti, Alessandro, and Charles Goodwin, eds. *Rethinking Context: Language as an Interactive Phenomenon.* Cambridge, UK: Cambridge University Press, 1992.

Duster, Troy. *Backdoor to Eugenics.* New York: Routledge, 2003.

Dyer, Thomas G. *Theodore Roosevelt and the Idea of Race*. Baton Rouge: Louisiana State University Press, 1992.

Eagles, Charles W. *The Price of Defiance: James Meredith and the Integration of Ole Miss*. Chapel Hill: University of North Carolina Press, 2009.

Eberstadt, Nicholas. "Prosperous Paupers and Affluent Savages." *Society* 33, no. 2 (1998): 17–25.

Ehrenreich, Eric. *The Nazi Ancestral Proof: Genealogy, Racial Science, and the Final Solution*. Bloomington: Indiana University Press, 2007.

Eller, Ronald D. *Miners, Millhands, and Mountaineers: Industrialization of the Appalachian South, 1880–1930*. Knoxville: University of Tennessee Press, 1982.

———. *Uneven Ground: Appalachia since 1945*. Lexington: University Press of Kentucky, 2008.

Eskridge, Sara K. "Rube Tube: CBS, Rural Sitcoms, and the Image of the South, 1957–1971." PhD dissertation, Louisiana State University, 2013.

Fanon, Frantz. *The Wretched of the Earth*. 1961. Reprint, New York: Penguin, 2001.

Fernandez, Ashley K. "The Power of Dissent: Pierce Butler and *Buck v. Bell*." *Journal for Peace and Justice Studies* 12, no. 1 (2002): 115–34.

Finnegan, Cara A. *Picturing Poverty: Print Culture and FSA Photographs*. Washington, DC: Smithsonian Institution Scholarly Press, 2003.

Fitzgerald, John. *The Effects of the Marriage Market on AFDC Benefits on Exit Rates from AFDC*. Madison: University of Wisconsin Institute of Research on Poverty, 1989.

Flamm, Michael W. *Law and Order: Street Crime, Civil Unrest, and the Crisis of Liberalism in the 1960s*. New York: Columbia University Press, 2007.

Flynt, J. Wayne. *Dixie's Forgotten People: The South's Poor Whites*. New edition. Bloomington: Indiana University Press, 2004.

Fones-Wolf, Kenneth, and Ronald L. Lewis, eds. *Transnational West Virginia: Ethnic Communities and Economic Change*. Morgantown: West Virginia University Press, 2003.

Forret, Jeff. *Race Relations at the Margins: Slaves and Poor Whites in the Antebellum Countryside*. Baton Rouge: Louisiana State University Press, 2006.

Fraser, Steven, ed. *The Bell Curve Wars: Race, Intelligence, and the Future of America*. New York: Basic Books, 1995.

Galbraith, John Kenneth. *The Great Crash of 1929*. New York: Houghton Mifflin, 1954.

Gans, Herbert. *The War against the Poor: The Underclass and Antipoverty Policy*. New York: Basic Books, 1995.

Garaway, Colin. *The Scratch of a Pen: 1763 and the Transformation of North America*. New York: Oxford University Press, 2006.

Garland, David. *The Culture of Control: Crime and Social Order in Contemporary Society*. Chicago: University of Chicago Press, 2002.

Germany, Kent. "Historians and the Many Lyndon Johnsons: A Review Essay." *Journal of Southern History* 75, no. 4 (2009): 1001–28.

———. *New Orleans after the Promise: Poverty, Citizenship, and the Search for a Great Society.* Athens: University of Georgia Press, 2007.

Gerstle, Gary. *American Crucible: Race and Nation in the Twentieth Century.* Princeton, NJ: Princeton University Press, 2002.

Gibs, Joe. *Punishment and Prisons: Power and the Carceral State.* London: Sage Publishers, 2009.

Gilens, Martin. *Why Americans Hate Welfare: Race, Media, and the Politics of Antipoverty Policy.* Chicago: University of Chicago Press, 1999.

Gillon, Steven M. *The Kennedy Assassination 24 Hours After: Lyndon B. Johnson's Pivotal First Day as President.* New York: Basic Books, 2009.

Gilmore, Glenda Elizabeth. *Gender and Jim Crow: The Politics of White Supremacy in North Carolina, 1896–1920.* Chapel Hill: University of North Carolina Press, 1996.

Gilmore, Ruth Wilson. *Golden Gulag: Prisons, Surplus, Crisis, and Opposition in Globalizing California.* Berkeley: University of California Press, 2007.

Gitlin, Todd, and Nanci Hollander. *Uptown: Poor Whites in Chicago.* New York: Harper and Row, 1970.

Goad, Jim. *The Redneck Manifesto: How Hillbillies, Hicks, and White Trash Became America's Scapegoats.* New York: Simon and Schuster, 1998.

Gordon, Linda. *Dorothea Lange: A Life Beyond Limits.* New York: W. W. Norton, 2010.

Gosset, Thomas F. *Race: The History of an Idea in America.* 1967. Reprint, New York: Oxford University Press, 1997.

Gottschalk, Marie. *The Prison and the Gallows: Mass Incarceration in the United States.* Cambridge, UK: Cambridge University Press, 2006.

Gould, Stephen Jay. *The Mismeasure of Man.* Revised and expanded. New York: W. W. Norton, 1996.

Gordon, Linda. *Pitied but Not Entitled: Single Mothers and the History of Welfare, 1880–1935.* Cambridge, MA: Harvard University Press, 1998.

Greene, Christina. *Our Separate Ways: Women and the Black Freedom Movement in Durham, North Carolina.* Chapel Hill: University of North Carolina Press, 2005.

Greenberg, Polly. *The Devil Has Slippery Shoes: A Biased Account of the Child Development Group of Mississippi.* New York: Macmillan, 1969.

Gregory, James N. *The Southern Diaspora: How the Great Migrations of Black and White Southerners Transformed America.* Chapel Hill: University of North Carolina, 2005.

Griffin, Larry J. "Whiteness and Southern Identity in the Mountain and Lowland South." *Journal of Appalachian Studies* 10, nos. 1–2, (2004): 7–37.

Gross, Ariela. *What Blood Won't Tell: A History of Race on Trial.* Cambridge, MA: Harvard University Press, 2010.

Gugliotta, Angela. "'Dr. Sharp with His Little Knife': Therapeutic and Punitive Origins of Eugenic Vasectomy—Indiana, 1892–1921," *Journal of the History of Medicine* 53 (October 1998): 371–406.

Hackworth, Jason. *The Neoliberal City: Governance, Ideology and Development in American Urbanism.* Ithaca, NY: Cornell University Press, 2006.

Hale, Grace Elizabeth. *Making Whiteness: The Culture of Segregation in the South, 1890–1940.* New York: Vintage, 1999.

Hall, Stephen Ray. "Oscar McCulloch and Indiana Eugenics." PhD dissertation, Virginia Commonwealth University, 1993.

Hamamoto, Darrel Y. *Nervous Laughter: Television Situation Comedy and Liberal Democratic Ideology.* New York: Praeger, 1991.

Hammonds, Evelynn M. *The Nature of Difference: Sciences of Race in the United States from Jefferson to Genomics.* Cambridge, MA: MIT Press, 2009.

Harkins, Anthony. *Hillbilly: A Cultural History of an American Icon.* New York: Oxford University Press, 2004.

Harris, Cheryl I. "Whiteness as Property," *Harvard Law Review* 106, no. 8 (1993): 1707–91.

Harris, J. William. *Plain Folk and Gentry in a Slave Society: White Liberty and Black Slavery in Augusta's Hinterlands.* Baton Rouge: Louisiana State University Press, 1998.

Hartigan, John, Jr. *Odd Tribes: Toward a Cultural Analysis of White People.* Durham, NC: Duke University Press, 2005.

Hartman, Ian C. "Appalachian Anxiety: Race, Gender, and the Paradox of 'Purity' in the Age of Empire, 1873–1901." *American Nineteenth Century History* 13, no. 2 (2012): 229–55.

———. "West Virginia Mountaineers and Kentucky Frontiersmen: Race, Manliness, and the Rhetoric of Liberalism in the Early 1960s." *Journal of Southern History* 80, no. 3 (2014): 651–78.

Harvey, David. *A Brief History of Neoliberalism.* New York: Oxford University Press, 2007.

———. *Justice, Nature, and the Geography of Difference.* New York: Blackwell, 1996.

Hays, Sharon. *Flat Broke with Children: Women in the Age of Welfare Reform.* New York: Oxford University Press, 2004.

Helsing, Jeffrey. *Johnson's War/Johnson's Great Society: The Guns vs. Butter Trap.* Westport, CT: Praeger, 2000.

Henderson, Errol Anthony. "Military Spending and Poverty." *Journal of Politics* 60, no. 2 (1998).

Henry, C. Michael, ed. *Race, Poverty, and Domestic Policy.* New Haven, CT: Yale University Press, 2004.

Herrnstein, Richard, and Charles Murray. *The Bell Curve: Intelligence and Class Structure in American Life.* New York: Free Press, 1994.

Higham, John. *Strangers in the Land: Patterns of American Nativism.* 1955. Reprint, New Brunswick, NJ: Rutgers University Press, 2002.

Hofstadter, Richard. *The Age of Reform.* New York: Vintage, 1960.

Hoganson, Kristin L. *Fighting for American Manhood: How Gender Politics Provoked the Spanish-American and Philippine-American Wars.* New Haven, CT: Yale University Press, 2000.

Hohn, Maria, and Seungsook Moon, eds. *Over There: Living with the U.S. Empire from World War Two to the Present.* Durham, NC: Duke University Press, 2010.

Holland, Max, Robert David Johnson, David Shreve, and Kent B. Germany, eds. *The Kennedy Assassination and the Transfer of Power, November 1963–January 1964.* New York: W. W. Norton, 2005.

Hollis, Tim. *Ain't That a Knee Slapper: Rural Comedy in the Twentieth Century.* Jackson: University Press of Mississippi, 2008.

Holloway, Pippa. *Sexuality, Politics and Social Control in Virginia, 1920–1945.* Chapel Hill: University of North Carolina Press, 2006.

Holquist, Michael. *Dialogism: Bakhtin and His World.* New York: Routledge, 1992.

Horne, Gerald. *Fire This Time: The Watts Uprising and the 1960s.* Charlottesville: University of Virginia Press, 1995.

Horsman, Reginald. *Race and Manifest Destiny: Origins of American Racial Anglo-Saxonism.* Cambridge, MA: Harvard University Press, 1981.

Horton, Carol A. *Race and the Making of American Liberalism.* New York: Oxford University Press, 2005.

Hsiung, David C. *Two Worlds in the Tennessee Mountains: Exploring the Origins of Appalachian Stereotypes.* Lexington: University Press of Kentucky, 1997.

Huber, Patrick. *Linthead Stomp: The Creation of Country Music in the Piedmont South.* Chapel Hill: University of North Carolina Press, 2008.

Hutton, T. R. C. *Bloody Breathitt: Politics and Violence in the Appalachian South.* Lexington: University Press of Kentucky, 2013.

Inscoe, John C. *The Heart of Confederate Appalachia: Western North Carolina and the Civil War.* Chapel Hill: University of North Carolina Press, 2003.

———. *Mountain Masters: Slavery and the Sectional Crisis in Western North Carolina.* Knoxville: University of Tennessee Press, 1989.

———, ed. *Appalachia and Race: The Mountain South from Slavery to Segregation.* Lexington: University Press of Kentucky, 2001.

Isserman, Maurice. *America Divided: The Civil War of the 1960s.* New York: Oxford University Press, 2011.

———. *The Other American: The Life of Michael Harrington.* New York: Public Affairs, 2000.

Jackson, Kenneth T. *Crabgrass Frontier: The Suburbanization of the United States.* New York: Oxford University Press, 1987.

Jacobson, Matthew. *Barbarian Virtues: The United States Encounters Foreign Peoples at Home and Abroad, 1876–1917.* New York: Hill and Wang, 2001.

———. *Whiteness of a Different Color: European Immigrants and the Alchemy of Race.* Cambridge, MA: Harvard University Press, 1999.

Jeffries, Hasan. *Bloody Lowndes: Civil Rights and Black Power in Alabama's Black Belt.* New York: New York University Press, 2009.

Jeffries, Judson L. *On the Ground: The Black Panther Party in Communities across America.* Jackson: University Press of Mississippi, 2008.

Jenkins Cook, Sylvia. *Erskine Caldwell and the Fiction of Poverty: The Flesh and the Spirit.* Baton Rouge: Louisiana State University Press, 1991.

Jennings, La Vinia, ed. *At Home and Abroad: Historicizing Twentieth-Century Whiteness in Literature and Performance.* Knoxville: University of Tennessee Press, 2009.

Johnson, Chalmers. *The Sorrows of Empire: Militarism, Secrecy, and the End of the Republic.* New York: Metropolitan Books, 2004.

Johnson, Robert David. *Ernest Gruening and the American Dissenting Tradition.* Cambridge, MA: Harvard University Press, 1998.

Johnson, Robert David, Kent B. Germany, David Shreve, and Guian A. McKee, eds. *The Presidential Recordings: Lyndon B. Johnson.* Volumes 4–6, *Toward the Great Society, February 1, 1964–May 31, 1964.* New York: W. W. Norton, 2007.

Jones, Gerard. *Honey, I'm Home! Sitcoms: Selling the American Dream.* New York: St. Martin's Press, 1992.

Haney Lopez, Ian. *Dog Whistle Politics: How Coded Racial Appeals Have Reinvented Racism and Wrecked the Middle Class.* New York: Oxford University Press, 2014.

Hannah-Jones, Nikole. "Living Apart: How Government Betrayed a Landmark Civil Rights Law." *ProPublica*, October 29, 2012.

Hartnett, Stephen John, ed. *Challenging the Prison Industrial Complex: Activism, Arts, and Educational Alternatives.* Urbana: University of Illinois Press, 2010.

Hobbes, Thomas. *The Leviathan; or the Matter, Form, and Power of a Commonwealth Ecclesiastical and Civil.* Edited by Ian Shapiro. New Haven, CT: Yale University Press, 2010.

Kaiser, Charles. *1968 in America: Music, Politics, Chaos, Counterculture, and the Shaping of a Generation.* New York: Grove Press, 1988.

Kallina, Edmund F., Jr. *Kennedy v. Nixon: The Presidential Election of 1960.* Gainesville: University of Florida Press, 2010.

Kaplan, Amy. *The Anarchy of Empire in the Making of U.S. Culture.* Cambridge, MA: Harvard University Press, 2002.

Kaplan, Amy, and Donald Pease, eds. *Cultures of United States Imperialism.* Durham, NC: Duke University Press, 1994.

Karch, Andrew. *Early Start: Preschool Politics in the United States.* Ann Arbor: University of Michigan Press, 2013.

Katz, Michael B. *In the Shadow of the Poorhouse: A Social History of Welfare in America.* New York: Basic Books, 1996.

———. *The Undeserving Poor: America's Enduring Confrontation with Poverty.* 2nd edition, fully updated and revised. New York: Oxford University Press, 2013.

———. *The Undeserving Poor: From the War on Poverty to the War on Welfare.* New York: Pantheon Books, 1989.

Katznelson, Ira. *When Affirmative Action Was White: An Untold Story of Racial Inequality in Twentieth-Century America.* New York: W. W. Norton, 2006.

Kelly, Richard. *The Andy Griffith Show.* Winston-Salem, NC: John F. Blair, 1981.

Kelso, William. *Poverty and the Underclass: Changing Perceptions of the Poor in America.* New York: New York University Press, 1994.

Kennedy, N. Brent, and Robyn Vaughan Kennedy. *The Melungeons: The Resurrection of a Proud People.* Macon, GA: Mercer University Press, 1996.

Kevles, Daniel J. *In the Name of Eugenics: Genetics and the Uses of Human Heredity.* New York: Alfred A. Knopf, 1985.

Kim, Jodi. *Ends of Empire: Asian American Critique and the Cold War.* Minneapolis: University of Minnesota Press, 2010.

Kirk, John A. *Redefining the Color Line: Black Activism in Little Rock, Arkansas, 1940–1970.* Gainesville: University of Florida Press, 2002.

Klarman, Michael J. *From Jim Crow to Civil Rights: The Supreme Court and the Struggle for Racial Equality.* New York: Oxford University Press, 2004.

———. "How *Brown* Changed Race: The Backlash Thesis." *Journal of American History* 81, no. 1 (1994): 81–118.

Klein, Christina. *Cold War Orientalism: Asia in the Middlebrow Imagination, 1945–1961.* Berkeley: University of California Press, 2003.

Klotter, James C. "The Black South and White Appalachia." *Journal of American History* 66, no. 4 (1980): 832–49.

———. *Kentucky: Portrait in Paradox, 1900–1950.* Frankfort: Kentucky Historical Society, 1996.

Kluegel, James R., and Eliot Smith. *Beliefs about Inequality: America's Views about What Is and What Ought to Be.* New York: Aldine Transaction, 1986.

Kohler-Hausmann, Julilly. "'The Crime of Survival': Fraud Prosecutions, Community Surveillance, and the Original 'Welfare Queen.'" *Journal of Social History* 41, no. 2 (2007): 329–54.

Kohlke, Marie-Luise, and Luisa Orza, eds. *Negotiating Sexual Idioms: Image, Text, Performance.* New York: Rodopi, 2008.

Korstad, Robert, and James Leloudis. *To Right These Wrongs: The North Carolina Fund and the Battle to End Poverty and Inequality in 1960s America.* Chapel Hill: University of North Carolina Press, 2010.

Kotz, Nick. *Judgment Days: Lyndon Baines Johnson, Martin Luther King, Jr., and the Laws That Changed America.* Boston: Houghton Mifflin, 2005.

Kramer, Elsa. "Recasting the Tribe of Ishmael." *Indiana Magazine of History* 104, no. 1 (2008): 36–64.

Kuhl, Stefen. *The Nazi Connection: Eugenics, American Racism, and German National Socialism.* New York: Oxford University Press, 1994.

Kurlansky, Mark. *1968: The Year That Rocked the World.* New York: Random House, 2005.

Kushner, David Z. "John Powell: His Racial and Cultural Ideologies," *Min-Ad: The Online Journal of the Israel Musicology Society* 5, no. 1 (2006). Available online at http://www.biu.ac.il/hu/mu/min-ad/06/John_Powell.pdf (accessed November 17, 2014).

Lake, Marilyn, and Henry Reynolds. *Drawing the Global Colour Line: White Men's Countries and the International Challenge of Racial Equality.* Cambridge, UK: Cambridge University Press, 2008.

Largent, Mark. *Breeding Contempt: The History of Coerced Sterilization in the United States.* New Brunswick, NJ: Rutgers University Press, 2007.

Lears, Jackson. *Rebirth of a Nation: The Making of Modern America, 1877–1920.* New York: Harper Press, 2009.

LaFeber, Walter. *The Deadly Bet: LBJ, Vietnam, and the 1968 Election.* New York: Rowman and Littlefield, 2005.

———. *The New Empire: An Interpretation of American Expansion, 1860–1898.* Ithaca, NY: Cornell University Press, 1998.

Leftkowitz, Bernie. *Community Health Centers and the People Who Made It Happen.* New Brunswick, NJ: Rutgers University Press, 2007.

Leiter, Andrew. *In the Shadow of the Black Beast: African American Masculinities in the Southern and Harlem Renaissances.* Baton Rouge: Louisiana State University Press, 2010.

Leonardo, Zeus. *Race, Whiteness, and Education.* New York: Routledge, 2009.

Lerman, Amy E. and Vesla M. Weaver. *Arresting Citizenship: The Democratic Consequences of American Crime Control.* Chicago: University of Chicago Press, 2014.

Levine, Phillipa. *Prostitution, Race, and Politics: Policing Venereal Disease in the British Empire.* New York: Routledge, 2003.

Lewis, Ronald L. *Transforming the Appalachian Countryside: Railroads, Deforestation, and Social Change in West Virginia.* Chapel Hill: University of North Carolina Press, 1998.

Lichtenstein, Nelson. *The Retail Revolution: How Wal-Mart Created A Brave New World of Business.* New York: Metropolitan Books, 2009.

Lind, Michael. *Up from Conservatism: Why the Right Is Wrong for America.* New York: Free Press, 1996.

Linn, Karen. *That Half-Barbaric Twang: The Banjo in American Culture.* Urbana: University of Illinois Press, 1994.

Lippy, Charles. *Do Real Men Pray? Images of the Christian Man and Male Spirituality in Protestant America.* Knoxville: University of Tennessee Press, 2005.

Lombardo, Paul. *Three Generations, No Imbeciles: Eugenics, the Supreme Court and Buck v. Bell.* Baltimore: Johns Hopkins University Press, 2008.

Lombardo, Paul, ed. *A Century of Eugenics in America: From the Indiana Experiment to the Human Genome Era.* Bloomington: University of Indiana Press, 2011.

Loury, Glenn. *Race, Incarceration, and American Values.* Cambridge, MA: MIT Press, 2008.

Lovett, Laura L. *Conceiving the Future: Pronatalism, Reproduction, and the Family in the United States, 1890–1938.* Chapel Hill: University of North Carolina Press, 2007.

Lowenberg, Anton, and William H. Kaempfer, eds. *The Origins and Demise of South African Apartheid: A Public Choice Analysis.* Ann Arbor: University of Michigan Press, 1998.

Lowndes, Joseph. *From the New Deal to the New Right: The Southern Origins of Modern Conservatism.* New Haven, CT: Yale University Press, 2008.

Love, Eric T. *Race over Empire: Racism and U.S. Imperialism, 1865–1900.* Chapel Hill: University of North Carolina Press, 2004.

Lubetkin, John M. *Jay Cooke's Gamble: The Northern Pacific Railroad, the Sioux, and the Panic of 1873.* Norman: University of Oklahoma Press, 2006.

Mackenzie, C. Calvin, and Robert Weisbrot. *The Liberal Hour: Washington and the Politics of Change in the 1960s.* New York: Penguin Press, 2008.

Malone, Bill C., and David Strickland. *Southern Music/American Music.* 2nd edition. Lexington: University Press of Kentucky, 2003.

Marc, David, and Robert J. Thompson. *Prime Time, Prime Movers: From I Love Lucy to L.A. Law—America's Greatest TV Shows and the People Who Created Them.* 1992. Reprint, Syracuse, NY: Syracuse University Press, 1992.

Markusen, Anne R., Peter Hall, Scott Campbell, and Sabrina Dietrick, eds. *The Rise of the Gunbelt: The Remapping of Industrial America.* New York: Oxford University Press, 1991.

Massey, Douglas S., and Nancy A. Denton. *American Apartheid: Segregation and the Making of the Underclass.* Cambridge, MA: Harvard University Press, 1994.

Matusow, Allen J. *The Unraveling of America: A History of Liberalism in the 1960s.* New York: Harper and Row, 1984.

Mauer, Marc. *Race to Incarcerate.* New York: New Press, 1999.

McAdam, Doug. *Freedom Summer.* New York: Oxford University Press, 1988.

McCann, Carole R. *Birth Control Politics in the United States, 1916–1945.* Ithaca, NY: Cornell University Press, 1994.

McCarthy, Anna. *The Citizen Machine: Governing Television in 1950s America.* New York: New Press, 2010.

McCauley, Deborah Vansau. *Appalachian Mountain Religion: A History.* Urbana: University of Illinois Press, 1995.

McCormick, Thomas C. *America's Half Century: United States Foreign Policy in the Cold War.* Baltimore: Johns Hopkins University Press, 1995.

McCoy, Alfred, and Francisco Scarano, eds., *Colonial Crucible.* Madison: University of Wisconsin Press, 2009.

McDonald, Jason. "Making the World Safe for Eugenics: The Eugenicist Harry H. Laughlin's Encounters with American Internationalism." *Journal of the Gilded Age and Progressive Era* 12, no. 3 (2013): 379–411.

McElvaine, Robert S. *The Great Depression: America, 1929–1941.* New York: Random House, 1984.

McGerr, Michael. *A Fierce Discontent: The Rise and Fall of the Progressive Movement in America, 1870–1920.* New York: Oxford University Press, 2005.

McGirr, Lisa. *Suburban Warriors: The Origins of the New American Right.* Princeton, NJ: Princeton University Press, 2001.

McMahon, Kevin J. *Reconsidering Roosevelt on Race: How the Presidency Paved the Road to* Brown. Chicago: University of Chicago Press, 2003.

McMaster, H. R. *Dereliction of Duty: Lyndon Johnson, Robert McNamara, the Joint Chiefs of Staff, and the Lies That Led to Vietnam.* New York: HarperCollins, 1997.

McNeil, W. K., ed. *Appalachian Images in Folk and Popular Culture.* Ann Arbor, MI: UMI Research Press, 1989.

McWhiney, Grady. *Cracker Culture: Celtic Ways in the Old South.* Tuscaloosa: University of Alabama Press, 1988.

McWhorter, Diane. *Carry Me Home: Birmingham, Alabama, and the Climactic Battle Civil Rights Revolution.* New York: Simon and Schuster, 2001.

Melman, Seymour. *The Permanent War Economy: American Capitalism in Decline.* New York: Simon and Schuster, 1976.

Milkis, Stanley M., and Jerome M. Mileur, *The Great Society: The High Tide of Liberalism.* Amherst: University of Massachusetts Press, 2005.

Miles, Tiya. *The House on Diamond Hill: A Cherokee Plantation Story.* Chapel Hill: University of North Carolina Press, 2010.

———. *Ties That Bind: The Story of an Afro-Cherokee Family in Slavery and Freedom.* Berkeley: University of California Press, 2006.

Mishel, Lawrence, Jared Bernstein, and Heidi Shierholtz. *The State of Working America, 2008/2009.* Ithaca, NY: Cornell University Press, 2009.

Mitchell, Don. *The Right to the City: Social Justice and the Fight for Public Space.* New York: Guilford Press, 2003.

Mjagkij, Nina, ed. *Organizing Black America: An Encyclopedia of African American Associations.* New York: Garland Publishing, 2010.

Montgomery, Michael. *From Ulster to America: The Scotch-Irish Heritage of American English.* Belfast, Northern Ireland: Belfast Historical Foundation, 2006.

Montell, William Lynwood. *Killings: Folk Justice in the Upland South.* Lexington: University Press of Kentucky, 1986.

Moore, Leonard N. *Carl B. Stokes and the Rise of Black Political Leadership.* Urbana: University of Illinois Press, 2002.

Morrell, Robert. *From Boys to Gentlemen: Settler Masculinity in Colonial Natal.* Pretoria, South Africa: UNISA, 2001.

Morris, Edmund. *The Rise of Theodore Roosevelt.* New York: Modern Library, 2001.

———. *Theodore Rex.* New York: Modern Library, 2002.

Morrison, Toni. *Playing in the Dark: Whiteness and the Literary Imagination.* New York: Vintage, 1992.

Moye, J. Todd. *Let the People Decide: The Black Freedom Movement in Sunflower County, Mississippi, 1956–1986.* Chapel Hill: University of North Carolina Press, 2004.

Moore, Leonard N. *Carl B. Stokes and the Rise of Black Political Power.* Urbana: University of Illinois Press, 2002.

Nadasen, Premilla. *Welfare Warriors: The Welfare Rights Movement in the United States.* New York: Routledge, 2005.

Nagel, Joane. *Race, Ethnicity, and Sexuality: Intimate Intersections, Forbidden Frontiers.* New York: Oxford University Press, 2003.

Nai, Mae N. *Impossible Subjects: Illegal Aliens and the Making of Modern America.* Princeton, NJ: Princeton University Press, 2004.

Naylor, Celia. *African Cherokees in Indian Territory: From Chattel to Citizens.* Chapel Hill: University of North Carolina Press, 2008.

Negri, Antonio, and Michael Hardt. *Empire.* Cambridge, MA: Harvard University Press, 2001.

Neubeck, Kenneth J., and Noel A. Cazenave. *Welfare Racism: Playing the Race Card against America's Poor.* New York: Routledge, 2001.

Newcomb, Horace. "Appalachia on Television: Region as Symbol in American Popular Culture." *Appalachian Journal* 7, nos. 1–2 (Fall/Winter 1979): 155–64.

———. *Television: The Critical View.* New York: Oxford University Press, 1976.

Newitz, Annalee, and Matt Wray, eds. *White Trash: Race and Class in America.* New York: Routledge, 1997.

Ngai, Mae. *Impossible Subjects: Illegal Aliens and the Making of Modern America.* Princeton, NJ: Princeton University Press, 2003.

Noe, Kenneth W. *Southwest Virginia's Railroad: Modernization and the Sectional Crisis in the Civil War Era.* 1994. Reprint, Tuscaloosa: University of Alabama Press, 2003.

Noll, Steven. *Feeble-Minded in Our Midst: Institutions for the Mentally Retarded in the South, 1900–1940.* Chapel Hill: University of North Carolina Press, 1995.

Nunnelley, William A. *Bull Connor.* Tuscaloosa: University of Alabama Press, 1991.

Obermiller, Phillip J., Thomas E. Wagner, and E. Bruce Tucker, eds. *Appalachian Odyssey: Historical Perspectives on the Great Migration.* Westport, CT: Praeger, 2000.

O'Brien, Michael. *John F. Kennedy: A Biography.* New York: Thomas Dunne Books, 2005.

O'Connor, Alice. *Poverty Knowledge: Social Science, Social Policy, and the Poor in Twentieth-Century U.S. History.* Princeton, NJ: Princeton University Press, 2001.

Ordover, Nancy. *American Eugenics: Race, Queer Anatomy, and the Science of Nationalism.* Minneapolis: University of Minnesota Press, 2003.

Orleck, Annelise. *Storming Caesar's Palace: How Black Mothers Fought Their Own War on Poverty.* Boston: Beacon Press, 2006.

Orleck, Annelise, and Lisa Gayle Hazirjian, eds., *The War on Poverty: A New Grassroots History.* Athens: University of Georgia Press, 2011.

Painter, Nell Irvin. *Creating Black Americans: African-American History and Its Meanings, 1619 to the Present.* New York: Oxford University Press, 2005.

———. *A History of White People.* New York: W. W. Norton, 2010.

———. *Standing at Armageddon: The United States, 1877–1917.* New York: W. W. Norton, 1987.

Parenti, Christian. *Lockdown America: Police and Prisons in the Age of Crisis.* New York: Verso Press, 1999.

Payne, Charles M. *I've Got the Light of Freedom: The Organizing Tradition and the Mississippi Freedom Struggle.* Berkeley: University of California Press, 1996.

Patterson, James T. *America's Struggle against Poverty, 1900–2000.* Cambridge, MA: Harvard University Press, 2000.

———. *Grand Expectations: The United States, 1945–1974.* New York: Oxford University Press, 1996.

Paul, Diane P. *Controlling Human Heredity, 1865–Present.* New York: Humanity Press, 1995.

Perkinson, Robert. *Texas Tough: The Rise of America's Prison Empire.* New York: Picador, 2010.

Perlstein, Rick. *Before the Storm: Barry Goldwater and the Unmaking of the American Consensus.* New York: Nation Books, 2009.

———. *Nixonland: The Rise of a President and the Fracturing of America.* New York: Scribner, 2008.

Phillips, Kevin P. *The Emerging Republican Majority*. New York: Arlington House, 1969.

Piven, Francis Fox, and Richard Cloward. *Breaking of the American Social Compact*. New York: Free Press, 1998.

———. *Poor People's Movement: Why They Succeed, How They Fail*. New York: Vintage, 1977.

———. *Regulating the Poor: The Functions of Public Welfare*. New York: Vintage Press, 1971.

Prashad, Vijay. *The Darker Nations: A Peoples' History of the Third World*. New York: New Press, 2008.

Pudup, Mary Beth, Dwight B. Billings, and Altina Waller, eds. *Appalachia in the Making: The Mountain South in the Nineteenth Century*. Chapel Hill: University of North Carolina Press, 1995.

Quadagno, Jill. *The Color of Welfare: How Racism Undermined the War on Poverty*. New York: Oxford University Press, 1994.

Rafter, Nicole Hahn. *White Trash: The Eugenic Family Studies, 1877–1919*. Boston: Northeastern University Press, 1988.

Rasmussen, Birgit Brander, Eric Klinenberg, Irene J. Nexica, and Matt Wray, eds. *The Making and Unmaking of Whiteness*. Durham, NC: Duke University Press, 2001.

Reed, John Shelton. *Southern Folk, Plain and Fancy*. Athens: University of Georgia Press, 1986.

Reichly, James. *Conservatives in an Age of Change: The Nixon and Ford Administrations*. Washington, DC: Brookings Institution Press, 1982.

Renda, Mary. *Taking Haiti: Military Occupation and the Culture of U.S. Imperialism*. Chapel Hill: University of North Carolina Press, 2000.

Rhodes-Pitts, Sharifa. *Harlem Is Nowhere: A Journey to the Mecca of Black America*. New York: Little, Brown, 2011.

Richardson, Riche. *Black Masculinity and the U.S. South: From Uncle Tom to Gangsta*. Athens: University of Georgia Press, 2007.

Ripsman, Norrin, and T. V. Paul. *Globalization and the National-Security State*. New York: Oxford University Press, 2010.

Roberts, J. Timmons, and Amy Bellone Hite, eds. *The Globalization and Development Reader: Perspectives on Development and Social Change*. Malden, MA: Blackwell, 2007.

Robertson, Jennifer. "Blood Talks: Eugenic Modernity and the Creation of New Japanese." *History and Anthropology* 13, no. 3 (2002): 191–216.

Roediger, David. *Working towards Whiteness: How America's Immigrants Became White; The Strange Journey from Ellis Island to the Suburbs*. New York: Basic Books, 2006.

———. *How Race Survived U.S. History: From Settlement and Slavery to the Obama Phenomenon*. New York: Verso, 2008.

Rodgers, Daniel. *Atlantic Crossings: Social Politics in a Progressive Age.* Cambridge, MA: Harvard University Press, 2000.

———. *Coming to America: A History of Immigration and Ethnicity in American Life.* 2nd edition. New York: HarperCollins, 2002.

Rogin, Michael. "Wallace and the Middle Class: Backlash in Wisconsin." *Public Opinion Quarterly* 30, no. 1 (1966): 98–108.

Roman, James. *From Daytime to Primetime: The History of American Television Programs.* Westport, CT: Greenwood Press, 2008.

Rorabaugh, W. J. *The Real Making of the President: Kennedy, Nixon, and the 1960 Election.* Lawrence: University of Kansas Press, 2009.

Ruswick, Brent. *Almost Worthy: The Poor, Paupers, and the Science of Charity in America, 1877–1917.* Bloomington: Indiana University Press, 2013.

———. "The Measure of Worthiness: The Rev. Oscar McCulloch and the Pauper Problem, 1877–1891." *Indiana Magazine of History* 104, no. 1 (2007): 3–35.

Sabato, Larry A. *The Kennedy Half-Century: The Presidency, Assassination, and Lasting Legacy of John F. Kennedy.* New York: Bloomsbury, 2013.

Salvatore, Nick. *Eugene V. Debs: Citizen and Socialist.* Urbana: University of Illinois Press, 1984.

Satterwhite, Emily. *Dear Appalachia: Readers, Identity, and Popular Fiction since 1878.* Lexington: University Press of Kentucky, 2011.

Saxton, Alexander. *The Rise and Fall of the White Republic: Class Politics and Mass Culture in Nineteenth-Century America.* New York: Verso, 1991.

Schaller, Michael. *Right Turn: American Life in the Reagan-Bush Era, 1980–1992.* New York: Oxford University Press, 2006.

Schaller, Michael, and George Rising. *The Republican Ascendency: American Politics, 1968–2001.* Wheeling, IL: Harlan Davidson, 2002.

Schenkkan, Robert. *Kentucky Cycle.* New York: Dramatist Play Services, 1993.

Schrift, Melissa. *Becoming Melungeon: Making an Ethnic Identity in the Appalachian South.* Lincoln: University Nebraska Press, 2013.

Schulman, Bruce, and Julian E. Zelizer, eds. *Rightward Bound: Making America Conservative in the 1970s.* Cambridge, MA: Harvard University Press, 2008.

Schumacher, Michael, and Denis Kitchen. *Al Capp: A Life to the Contrary.* New York: Bloomsbury, 2013.

Schwartz, Joel. *Fighting Poverty with Virtue: Moral Reform and America's Urban Poor, 1825–2000.* Bloomington: Indiana University Press, 2000.

Scott, Joan Wallach. *Gender and the Politics of History.* Revised edition. New York: Columbia University Press, 1999.

Sears, Richard. *A Utopian Experiment in Kentucky: Integration and Social Equality at Berea, 1866–1904.* Westport, CT: Greenwood Publishing, 1996.

Seawell, Stephanie. "The Black Freedom Movement and Community Planning in Urban Parks in Cleveland, Ohio, 1945–1977." PhD dissertation, University of Illinois at Urbana-Champaign, 2014.

Self, Robert O. *All in the Family: The Realignment of American Democracy since the 1960s.* New York: Hill and Wang, 2012.

———. *American Babylon: Race and the Struggle for Postwar Oakland.* Princeton, NJ: Princeton University Press, 2005.

Seltzer, Curtis. *Fire in the Hole: Miners and Managers in the American Coal Industry.* Lexington: University Press of Kentucky, 1985.

Severo, Richard. "Homer Bigart, Acclaimed Reporter, Dies." *New York Times.* April 17, 1991.

Shahidullah, Shahid M. *Crime Policy in America: Laws, Institutions, and Programs.* Lanham, MD: University Press of America, 2008.

Shapiro, Henry D. *Appalachia on Our Mind: The Southern Mountains and Mountaineers in the American Consciousness, 1870–1920.* Chapel Hill: University of North Carolina Press, 1978.

Shigematsu, Setsu, and Keith Camacho, eds. *Militarized Currents: Toward a Decolonized Future in Asia and the Pacific.* Minneapolis: University of Minnesota Press, 2010.

Simon, Jonathan. *Governing through Crime: How the War on Crime Transformed American Democracy and Created a Culture of Fear.* New York: Oxford University Press, 2009.

Skocpol, Theda. *Social Policy in the United States: Future Possibilities in Historical Perspective.* Princeton, NJ: Princeton University Press, 1995.

Slap, Andrew, ed. *Reconstructing Appalachia: The Civil War's Aftermath.* Lexington: University Press of Kentucky, 2010.

Slotkin, Richard. *Gunfighter Nation: The Myth of the Frontier in Twentieth Century America.* New York: Harper Perennial, 1992.

———. *Regeneration through Violence: The Mythology of the American Frontier, 1600–1860.* Norman: University of Oklahoma Press, 1973.

Smethurst, James Edward. *The Black Arts Movement: Literary Nationalism in the 1960s and 1970s.* Chapel Hill: University of North Carolina Press, 2005.

Smith, Barbara Ellen. "De-gradations of Whiteness: Appalachia and the Complexities of Race." *Journal of Appalachian Studies* 10, nos. 1–2 (2004): 38–57.

Smith, Eliot. *Beliefs about Inequality: America's Views about What Is and What Ought to Be.* New York: Aldine Transaction, 1986.

Smith, J. Douglas. "The Campaign for Racial Purity and the Erosion of Paternalism in Virginia, 1922–1930: 'Nominally White, Biologically Mixed and Legally Negro.'" *Journal of Southern History* 68, no. 1 (2002): 65–106.

———. *Managing White Supremacy: Race, Politics, and Citizenship in Jim Crow Virginia.* Chapel Hill: University of North Carolina Press, 2003.

Smith, Joan, Jane Collins, Terrence Hopkins, and Akbar Muhammad, eds. *Racism, Sexism, and the World System.* New York: Greenwood, 1988.

Smith, Stephen A. *Myth, Media, and the Southern Mind.* Fayetteville: University of Arkansas Press, 1985.

Soja, Edward. *Postmodern Geographies: The Reassertion of Space in Critical Social Theory*. London: Verso, 1989.

———. *Seeking Spatial Justice*. Minneapolis: University of Minnesota Press, 2010.

Sowell, Thomas. *Ethnic America: A History*. New York: Basic Books, 1981.

Spigel, Lynn. *Make Room for TV: Television and the Family Ideal in Postwar America*. Chicago: University of Chicago Press, 1992.

Spigel, Lynn, and Michael Curtin. *The Revolution Wasn't Televised: Sixties Television and Social Conflict*. New York: Routledge, 1997.

Spiro, Jonathan Peter. *Defending the Master Race: Conservation, Eugenics, and the Legacy of Madison Grant*. Burlington: University of Vermont Press, 2008.

Stanton, Mary. *Freedom Walk: Mississippi or Bust*. Jackson: University Press of Mississippi, 2003.

Staples, Robert. "White Racism, Black Crime, and American Justice: An Application of the Colonial Model to Explain Crime and Race." *Phylon* 36, no. 1 (1975): 14–22.

Stern, Alexandra Minna. *Eugenics Nation: Faults and Frontiers of Better Breeding in Modern America*. Berkeley: University of California Press, 2005.

———. "'We Cannot Make a Silk Purse out of a Sow's Ear': Eugenics in the Hoosier Heartland." *Indiana Magazine of History* 103, no 1 (2007): 3–38.

Stewart, Bruce E., ed. *Blood in the Hills: A History of Violence in Appalachia*. Lexington: The University Press of Kentucky, 2012.

Stoler, Ann Laura, ed. *Haunted by Empire: Geographies of Intimacy in North American History*. Durham, NC: Duke University Press, 2006.

Stowell, David O. *Streets, Railroads, and the Great Strike of 1877*. Chicago: University of Chicago Press, 1999.

Straw, Richard, and H. Tyler Blethan, eds. *High Mountains Rising: Appalachia in Time and Place*. Urbana: University of Illinois Press, 2004.

Stricker, Frank. *Why America Lost the War on Poverty—And How to Win It*. Chapel Hill: University of North Carolina Press, 2007.

Sudbury, Julia, ed. *Global Lockdown: Race, Gender, and the Prison-Industrial Complex*. New York: Routledge, 2005.

Sugrue, Thomas. *The Origins of the Urban Crisis: Race and Inequality in Postwar Detroit*. Princeton, NJ: Princeton University Press, 1996.

———. *Sweet Land of Liberty: The Forgotten Struggle for Civil Rights in the North*. New York: Random House Trade Paperbacks, 2009.

Suri, Jeremi. *Power and Protest: Global Revolution and the Rise of Détente*. Cambridge, MA: Harvard University Press, 2005.

Taul, Glen Edward. "Poverty, Development, and Government in Appalachia: Origins of the Appalachian Commission." PhD diss., University of Kentucky, 2001.

Thernstrom, Stephan and Abigail Thernstrom. *America in Black and White: One Nation, Indivisible*. 2nd edition. New York: Touchstone, 1999.

Thomas, Evan. *The War Lovers: Roosevelt, Lodge, Hearst, and the Rush to Empire.* New York: Little, Brown, 2010.

Thomas, John L. *Alternative America: Henry George, Edward Bellamy, Henry Demarest Lloyd, and the Adversary Tradition.* Cambridge, MA: Harvard University Press, 1983.

Thompson, Heather Ann. *Whose Detroit? Politics, Labor, and Race in a Modern American City.* Ithaca, NY: Cornell University Press, 2004.

———. "Why Mass Incarceration Matters: Rethinking Crisis, Decline, and Transformation in Postwar American History." *Journal of American History* 97, no. 3 (2010): 703–58.

Thomsen, Brian M. *The Man in the Arena: Selected Writings of Theodore Roosevelt; A Reader.* New York: Forge Books, 2003.

Thornbrough, Emma Lou. *Indiana in the Civil War Era, 1850–1880.* Indianapolis: Indiana Historical Bureau and Indiana Historical Society, 1965.

Timburg, Craig. "At Virginia's Toughest Prison, Tight Controls," *Washington Post,* April 18, 1999.

Tonry, Michael. *Punishing Race: A Continuing American Dilemma.* New York: Oxford University Press, 2012.

Trachtenberg, Alan. *The Incorporation of America: Culture and Society in the Gilded Age.* 1982. Reprint, New York: Hill and Wang, 2007.

Trattner, Walter I. *From Poor Law to Welfare State: A History of Social Welfare in the United States.* New York: Free Press, 1998.

Trotter, Joe William, Jr. *Coal, Class, and Color: Blacks in Southern West Virginia, 1915–1932.* Urbana: University of Illinois Press, 1990.

Ture, Kwame, and Charles Hamilton. *Black Power: The Politics of Liberation.* New York: Vintage, 1967.

Turner, William, and Edward Cabbell, eds. *Blacks in Appalachia.* Lexington: University Press of Kentucky, 1985.

Tyson, Timothy B. *Radio Free Dixie: Robert Williams and the Roots of Black Power.* Chapel Hill: University of North Carolina Press, 1999.

Unger, Irwin. *The Best of Intentions: The Triumph and Failure of the Great Society under Kennedy, Johnson, and Nixon.* New York: Doubleday Books, 1996.

Vande Brake, Katherine. *How They Shine: Melungeon Characters in the Fiction of Appalachia.* Macon, GA: Mercer University Press, 2001.

Vaughan, Don Rodney. "Why *The Andy Griffith Show* Is Important to Popular Cultural Studies." *Journal of Popular Culture* 38, no. 2 (2004): 397–423.

Veracini, Lorenzo. *Settler Colonialism: A Theoretical Overview.* New York: Palgrave Macmillan, 2010.

Voloshinov, Valentin [Mikhail Bakhtin]. *Marxism and the Philosophy of Language.* Cambridge, MA: Harvard University Press, 1986.

Waller, Altina. *Feud: Hatfields, McCoys, and Social Change in Appalachia, 1860–1900.* Chapel Hill: University of North Carolina Press, 1988.

Wacquant, Loïc. *Prisons of Poverty*. Minneapolis: University of Minnesota Press, 2009.

———. *Punishing the Poor: The Neoliberal Government of Social Security*. Durham, NC: Duke University Press, 2009.

Ward, Geoffrey C. *Unforgivable Blackness: The Rise and Fall of Jack Johnson*. New York: Vintage, 2006.

Ward, Ronald David. "The Life and Works of John Powell (1882–1963)." PhD dissertation, Catholic University of America, 1970.

Watson, Bruce. *Freedom Summer: The Savage Season That Made Mississippi Burn and Made America a Democracy*. New York: Viking, 2010.

Watts, Sarah. *Rough Rider in the White House: Theodore Roosevelt and the Politics of Desire*. Chicago: University of Chicago Press, 2003.

Weaver, Vesla. "Frontlash: Race and the Development of Punitive Crime Policy." *Studies in American Political Development* 21 (September 2007): 230–67.

Weeks, Genevieve C. *Oscar Carleton McCulloch, 1843–1891: Preacher and Practitioner of Applied Christianity*. Indianapolis: Indianapolis Historical Society, 1976.

Weibe, Robert L. *The Search for Order, 1877–1920*. New York: Hill and Wang, 1966.

Weinstein, Cindy, ed. *The Cambridge Companion to Harriet Beecher Stowe*. Cambridge, UK: Cambridge University Press, 2004.

Weir, Margaret. *Politics and Jobs: The Boundaries of Employment in the United States*. Princeton, NJ: Princeton University Press, 1993.

Westad, Odd Arne. *The Global Cold War: Third World Interventions and the Making of Our Times*. Cambridge, UK: Cambridge University Press, 2007.

Wexler, Laura. *Tender Violence: Domestic Visions in an Age of U.S. Imperialism*. Chapel Hill: University of North Carolina Press, 2000.

Whisnant, David E. *All That Is Native and Fine: The Politics of Culture in an American Region*. Chapel Hill: University of North Carolina Press, 1983.

———. "Ethnicity and the Recovery of Regional Identity in Appalachia." *Soundings* 56 (Spring 1973): 124–38.

———. *Modernizing the Mountaineer: People, Power, and Planning in Appalachia*. Revised edition. Knoxville: University of Tennessee Press, 1994.

White, Richard. *Railroaded: The Transcontinentals and the Making of Modern America*. New York: W. W. Norton, 2011.

White, Theodore H. *The Making of the President, 1960*. New York: Harper Perennial, 1961.

Wilentz, Sean. *The Age of Reagan: A History, 1974–2008*. New York: Harper Books, 2007.

Williams, Eric J. *The Big House in the Small Town: Prisons, Communities, and Economics in Rural America*. Santa Barbara, CA: Greenwood, 2011.

Williams, John Alexander. *Appalachia: A History*. Chapel Hill: University of North Carolina Press, 2001.

Williams, Rhonda. *The Politics of Public Housing: Black Women's Struggles against Urban Inequality.* New York: Oxford University Press, 2004.

Williamson, J. W. *Hillbillyland: What the Movies Did to the Mountains and What the Mountains Did to the Movies.* Chapel Hill: University of North Carolina Press, 1995.

Wilson, Darlene. "The Felicitous Convergence of Mythmaking and Capital Accumulation: John Fox Jr. and the Formation of An(Other) Almost-White American Underclass." *Journal of Appalachian Studies* 1, no. 1 (1995): 5–44.

Wilson, Gregory S. *Communities Left Behind: The Area Redevelopment Administration, 1945–1965.* Knoxville: University of Tennessee Press, 2009.

Winant, Howard A. *Stalemate: Political Origins of Supply-Side Policy.* Westport, CT: Praeger, 1988.

Winkler, Wayne. *Walking toward the Sunset: The Melungeons of Appalachia.* Macon, GA: Mercer University Press, 2004.

Woodard, Kamozi. *Groundwork: Local Black Freedom Movements in America.* New York: New York University Press, 2005.

Woodruff, Nan. *American Congo: The African American Freedom Struggle in the Delta.* Cambridge, MA: Harvard University Press, 2003.

Woods, Randall B. *LBJ: Architect of American Ambition.* Cambridge, MA: Harvard University Press, 2007.

Woodward, C. Vann. *The Strange Career of Jim Crow.* Commemorative edition with a new afterword from William S. McFeely. 1955. Reprint, New York: Oxford University Press, 2002.

Wray, Matt. *Not Quite White: White Trash and the Boundaries of Whiteness.* Durham, NC: Duke University Press, 2006.

Wright, Kai. "Boxed In: How a Criminal Record Keeps You Unemployed for Life," *Nation,* November 25, 2013.

Wyndham, Diana. *Eugenics in Australia: Striving for National Fitness.* London: Galton Institute, 2003.

Yates, Donald N., and Elizabeth C. Hirschman. "Toward a Genetic Profile of Melungeons in Southern Appalachia." *Appalachian Journal* 38, no. 1 (2010): 92–111.

Zahniser, Keith A. *Steel City Protestant Laity and Reform in the Progressive Era.* New York: Routledge, 2013.

Zannes, Estelle. *Checkmate in Cleveland: The Rhetoric of Confrontation during the Stokes Years.* Cleveland: Press of Case Western Reserve University, 1972.

Zolberg, Aristide. *A Nation by Design: Immigration Policy in the Fashioning of America.* Cambridge, MA: Harvard University Press, 2006.

INDEX